"David Bell has the enviable talent of making obscure subjects not only interesting but fascinating. He ferrets out detail and anecdote to bring what we might otherwise think of as staid characters or situations to startling life, in all their living, breathing contradictions. In *Handmaid of the Lord* he excavates for us the place of Mary in the Cistercian tradition, touching on not only the well-known in Bernard of Clairvaux, but also the neglected, such as Stephen of Sawley and Ogier of Locedio, leading us finally to the surprising reverence given to Mary at la Trappe under the putatively stern Abbot Rancé. Bell's wit, sometimes caustic, and his erudition shine out of every page. This book will be indispensable for anyone interested in Mary's role among the Cistercians, but also in the church at large. A thoroughly enjoyable read."

— Fr. Lawrence Morey, OCSO

"In this book, David Bell offers his characteristic erudition in an accessible and engaging way, leading us from the life of Mary of Nazareth to her enshrinement as model of humility and monastic life in the thought of Armand-Jean de Rancé, leader of the monastic reform at la Trappe. This journey takes an extended sojourn among the Cistercians of the 12th and 13th centuries, correcting misperceptions and putting fine detail on the common generalizations about the flourishing devotion to Mary in these centuries. And like a suspense story, the conflicts about the Immaculate Conception and other Marian controversies are recounted with verve. Concluding with his new translations of Rancé's conferences on Marian feasts, David Bell provides a magisterial work that can serve as a reference point for any of the many subjects covered here."

— Anne L. Clark, Professor of Religion, University of Vermont

"Another delightful book from David Bell's prolific pen, permeated by his seemingly effortless erudition and comprehensive knowledge of Cistercians authors—both the figureheads and those who are more obscure."

— Mette Birkedal Bruun, Professor of C[illegible] History, University of Copenhagen

CISTERCIAN STUDIES SERIES:
NUMBER TWO HUNDRED NINETY-THREE

Handmaid of the Lord

Mary, the Cistercians, and Armand-Jean de Rancé

David N. Bell

Cistercian Publications
www.cistercianpublications.org

LITURGICAL PRESS
Collegeville, Minnesota
www.litpress.org

A Cistercian Publications title published by Liturgical Press

Cistercian Publications
Editorial Offices
161 Grosvenor Street
Athens, Ohio 45701
www.cistercianpublications.org

Cover design by Ann Blattner. The *Theotokos Hodegetria* (the God-Bearer Pointing the Way). Icon owned by the author.

Scripture passages in this book are translated by its author.

1 2 3 4 5 6 7 8 9

Library of Congress Cataloging-in-Publication Data

Names: Bell, David N., 1943– author.
Title: Handmaid of the Lord : Mary, the Cistercians, and Armand-Jean de Rancé / David N. Bell.
Description: Collegeville, Minnesota : Liturgical Press, [2021] | Series: Cistercian studies ; number 293 | Includes bibliographical references and index. | Summary: "An exploration of what Cistercian writers and preachers have said about Mary from the time of the founding fathers of the Order to Armand-Jean de Rancé"— Provided by publisher.
Identifiers: LCCN 2021019736 (print) | LCCN 2021019737 (ebook) | ISBN 9780879071882 (paperback) | ISBN 9780879075880 (epub) | ISBN 9780879075880 (pdf)
Subjects: LCSH: Mary, Blessed Virgin, Saint. | Cistercians.
Classification: LCC BT610 .B45 2021 (print) | LCC BT610 (ebook) | DDC 232.91—dc23
LC record available at https://lccn.loc.gov/2021019736
LC ebook record available at https://lccn.loc.gov/2021019737

Contents

Abbreviations

CCCM	Corpus Christianorum, Continuatio Mediaevalis. Turnhout: Brepols.
CF	Cistercian Fathers Series. Collegeville, MN: Cistercian Publications.
CS	Cistercian Studies Series. Collegeville, MN: Cistercian Publications.
PG	Patrologia Cursus Completus, Series Græca. Ed. J.-P. Migne.
PL	Patrologia Cursus Completus, Series Latina. Ed. J.-P. Migne.
RSB	Rule of Saint Benedict / *Regula sancti Benedicti.*
SBOp	Sancti Bernardi Opera. Ed. Jean Leclercq, C. Hugh Talbot, Henri M. Rochais. Rome: Editiones Cistercienses, 1957–1977.
SCh	Sources chrétiennes. Paris: Cerf.

Introduction

What This Book Is, and What It Is Not

This is not a history of Mary, of the ways in which she has been portrayed, described, idealized, idolized, represented, misrepresented, and so on. There are already too many books on these subjects, some of which are excellent and certainly worthy of attention, and many of which are not. My concern here is much more limited. It is to examine what Cistercian writers and preachers have said about Mary from the time of the founding fathers of the Order to Armand-Jean de Rancé, the great Reformer, who died in 1700. What has happened after that I must leave to those more qualified than I to discuss.

As to Mary, the academic study of her place in Christian theology and devotion really began more than half a century ago in 1963 when Hilda Graef published the first part of her *Mary: A History of Doctrine and Devotion*, "From the Beginnings to the Eve of the Reformation." The second part, "From the Reformation to the Present Day," followed in 1965.[1] There are obviously places in which the book now needs updating, and many of the primary sources used by Graef are now available in better editions, but the book retains its value. It covers an astonishingly wide range, and if you want brief, accurate, and

[1] Hilda Graef, *Mary: A History of Doctrine and Devotion*, 2 vols. (London: Sheed & Ward, 1963–1965). A combined edition, containing both parts, was published in 1985.

lucid accounts of the Marian theology of, say, the later Byzantine writers or the continental Reformers, you will find them here. The book remains an essential tool.

About a decade later there appeared another important study by Marina Warner, *Alone of All Her Sex: The Myth and the Cult of the Virgin Mary*.[2] This could not be more different from Graef's volumes and is divided into five sections: Mary as virgin, queen, bride, mother, and intercessor. Warner's approach is wide-ranging and contains some valuable insights. It is also a most enjoyable read.

Then, from 1998 onwards, a number of studies appeared, some dealing with Mary in general, others dealing more specifically with Mary in the patristic period and the Middle Ages. Jaroslav Pelikan's *Mary Through the Centuries: Her Place in the History of Culture* was published in a revised edition in 1998,[3] and Miri Rubin's excellent *Mother of God: A History of the Virgin Mary* appeared in 2010.[4] In 2007 Sarah Jane Boss edited *Mary: The Complete Resource*, and although it is not quite as complete as all that, it contains some very useful studies, some of which are of the greatest interest and not to be found elsewhere.[5]

For the patristic and medieval periods, we now have the two volumes by Luigi Gambero, *Mary and the Fathers of the Church* and *Mary in the Middle Ages*,[6] both similar in structure to Graef's earlier study, but not so comprehensive, and two very sound accounts by Stephen Shoemaker and Brian Reynolds.

[2] Marina Warner, *Alone of All Her Sex: The Myth and the Cult of the Virgin Mary* (London: Weidenfeld and Nicolson Ltd., 1976), and reprinted many times thereafter.

[3] Jaroslav Pelikan, *Mary Through the Centuries: Her Place in the History of Culture*, rev. ed. (New Haven: Yale University Press, 1998).

[4] Miri Rubin, *Mother of God: A History of the Virgin Mary* (New Haven: Yale University Press, 2010).

[5] *Mary: The Complete Resource*, ed. Sarah Jane Boss (London and New York: Continuum, 2007).

[6] Luigi Gambero, *Mary and the Fathers of the Church: The Blessed Virgin Mary in Patristic Thought*, and *Mary in the Middle Ages: The Blessed Virgin Mary in the Thought of Medieval Latin Theologians*, trans. Thomas Buffer (San Francisco: Ignatius Press, 1999, 2005).

Shoemaker's *Mary in Early Christian Faith and Devotion*[7] ends with the early fifth century; the first volume of Reynolds's *Gateway to Heaven*[8] extends into the medieval period. Two volumes were intended, but although the first was published in 2012, at the time of writing the second has not appeared. Both studies may be recommended.

I have profited from all these volumes, some more than others, and the fact that not all of them appear in footnotes does not mean I have not read them. I shall return to the matter of footnotes in a moment.

When I first began work on this book, in a fairly desultory fashion, I was not sure that it would be needed. The Cistercians, after all, were well known for contributing greatly to the veneration of the Virgin—the name of Bernard occurs again and again—but on reading more carefully what had been written, I found that much of it was repetitious, and that many of the writers had not read the relevant materials in sufficient detail. In some cases, too, they had not had access to volumes published after their own contributions (this is especially the case with Aelred of Rievaulx[9]), or they were unable to lay their hands on an exceedingly rare edition (this is especially the case with Ogier of Locedio[10]).

There was also a volume published in 1999 with the title *La Vierge dans la tradition cistercienne*, "The Virgin in the Cistercian Tradition,"[11] that would seem to cover the subject. It does not. The papers included in the volume examine the ideas of just

[7] Stephen J. Shoemaker, *Mary in Early Christian Faith and Devotion* (New Haven: Yale University Press, 2016).

[8] Brian K. Reynolds, *Gateway to Heaven: Marian Doctrine and Devotion, Image and Typology in the Patristic and Medieval Periods*. Volume 1: *Doctrine and Devotion* (Hyde Park, NY: New City Press, 2012).

[9] See chap. 9.

[10] See chap. 10.

[11] *La Vierge dans la tradition cistercienne, communications présentées à la 54e session de la Société française d'études mariales, Abbaye Notre-Dame d'Orval [15–17 septembre] 1998*, ed. Paul Longère, Études Mariales: Bulletin de la Société Française d'Études Mariales (Paris: Éditions Médiaspaul, 1999).

a few Cistercians, primarily French, and say nothing at all about the extremely important contributions of the English Cistercians.[12] In short, the more I read, the more I was impressed with what had been omitted, and I decided that there was indeed a need for a more comprehensive study of Mary and the Cistercians. It also gave me an opportunity to present translations of all five of Armand-Jean de Rancé's conferences for the feasts of Mary's Nativity, Annunciation, and Assumption, since none of them had been translated into English before, and one of my missions is to make the abbot of la Trappe, if not better liked, at least better known. Those who know the Cistercians will also be aware that this study is not comprehensive and that some names do not appear, Adam of Perseigne or Hélinand of Froidmont, for example. It is not that they have nothing to say about Mary, but what they do have to say is said elsewhere by the other writers who appear in these pages.

In presenting this account of the Virgin and the Cistercians, I wanted to avoid making it look like a doctoral dissertation with every second word footnoted. The great majority of the footnotes, though by no means all, are therefore limited to primary sources. I cannot say that I have read all the secondary sources—some of them are just not worth reading—though I have certainly read most of them, but when, for example, I have presented brief biographies of the writers that appear in these pages, I have not documented every statement. I have, however, used the most up-to-date studies available in a variety of languages. The chapter on Mary and the visionaries, for example—chapter twelve—might have been twice as long had I included all the extraneous material I was so strongly tempted to include. But what I wanted to write was a book about Mary in the Cistercian tradition, not about the Cistercian tradition in general, and not a Cistercian bibliography on Mary. Thus, readers who wish to find a detailed account, heavily documented, of the life and theological ideas of, say, Aelred of

[12] For a more detailed consideration of this volume, see the beginning of chap. 5.

Rievaulx, will not find them here. What they will find is a summary of Aelred's Marian ideas in all the sermons—more than forty of them—that he wrote for the great Marian feasts. I say this because I would prefer not to be accused of not doing something I had no intention of doing in the first place. In short, apart from references to primary sources, I have tried to reduce footnotes to an absolute minimum, and to restrict them, as far as possible, to sources in English.[13]

The book is divided, like Caesar's Gaul, into three parts. The first part, the first four chapters, presents some selective background material on Mary that is necessary for understanding where the Cistercian writers are coming from, and the sources and ideas they are using. There were two major areas of controversy, one lesser and one greater. The lesser of the two concerned the Dormition or Assumption of the Virgin, and the question of whether, at the end of her life, Mary died and was buried, and was then resurrected and her body taken up to heaven, or whether her body and soul were assumed into heaven together at the very moment of her death. The greater controversy concerned the doctrine of the Immaculate Conception, which, as one writer has rightly said, "occasioned what was perhaps the most prolonged and passionate debate that has ever been carried on in Catholic theology."[14]

The next eight chapters, the second part of the book, examine the Marian ideas of Cistercian writers from Bernard of Clairvaux to a number of visionaries, both male and female, who take us to the very end of the thirteenth century. There is then a gap of more than three centuries—the reasons are given at the end of chapter twelve—before we arrive at the birth of Armand-Jean de Rancé in 1626. The final chapters—part three of the book—summarize the life of Rancé, examine the place of Mary at la Trappe, and, as we said above, present annotated

[13] The major exception to this will be found in chap. 7, dealing with Geoffrey of Auxerre. Almost all the secondary sources are in Italian or Spanish; there is very little in English.

[14] See chap. 3, n. 13.

translations of Rancé's five conferences for three Marian feasts. An earlier version of chapters thirteen and fourteen appeared in 2013 in *Cistercian Studies Quarterly*,[15] but the versions that appear here have been considerably amended and corrected. I am grateful to the Editorial Board of *Cistercian Studies Quarterly* for permission to reproduce this material.

As to the translations that appear in these pages, from whatever language, they are all my own. I must be honest here. Many of the great and not so great Cistercian writers have appeared in English translation in the Cistercian Fathers Series (CF) published originally by Cistercian Publications, Kalamazoo, Michigan, and now by Cistercian Publications, Collegeville, Minnesota. Some of these are very sound, but many—to my eyes at least—are too free and, in some cases, not quite accurate. I admit that it is sometimes better to have a defective English translation than no translation at all, but in translating medieval texts from whatever language, accuracy is everything. I have not, therefore, added to the footnotes references to the CF translations of the various passages I have translated myself. It need hardly be mentioned that the Psalms are cited according to their enumeration in the Vulgate.

As to the editions used, if the version that appears in the old and invaluable Migne Patrologia Latina (PL) is not different from a more modern critical edition, I have cited the PL edition on the grounds that all the volumes, both Greek and Latin, are readily available free on the Internet. If a modern edition is not available in the PL, or if it is demonstrably more accurate, I have, naturally, cited that, though modern editions can be extremely expensive and generally require access to a good university library. Many earlier editions, many of them excellent and some of them indispensable, can now be found free on the Internet, thanks to the wonderful work of Mister Google.

[15] "Armand-Jean de Rancé (1626–1700) and the Mother of God: A Re-evaluation of His Position, with a Translation of His Conference for the Feast of the Nativity of the Virgin," *Cistercian Studies Quarterly* 48, no. 1 (2013): 39–78.

If I may be permitted a personal note, I thoroughly enjoyed my exploration of Mary and the Cistercians, and, at the same time, came to a deeper and richer appreciation of some writers whom earlier I had, quite wrongly, tended to overlook. I had not realized, for example, just how fine a theologian was Guerric of Igny, and reading all the sermons of Aelred of Rievaulx, not just those for the Marian feasts, so splendidly edited by Gaetano Raciti,[16] opened my eyes to Aelred's true depths as a theologian of the first importance. Isaac of Stella, whose works I have always enjoyed reading, is now well served by having the second and final volume of his sermons made available in a very sound English translation that appeared in October 2019.[17] What this means is that for those who are interested, the works of almost all the Cistercian writers mentioned in these pages are now, or will shortly be, available in English. The exceptions, at the time of writing, are the last of the sermons of Aelred of Rievaulx (the translation is now well in progress), most of the writings of Geoffrey of Auxerre, the verses of Roger of Forde on Our Lady, and, of course, the works of Armand-Jean de Rancé, whose ideas I have, from time to time, tried to make a little more accessible to Anglophone readers. You will find his conferences for the feasts of Mary's Nativity, the Annunciation, and the Assumption in the third and final part of this volume.

[16] In CCCM 2A (1989) sermons 1–46; 2B (2001) sermons 47–84; 2C (2012) sermons 85–182.

[17] *Isaac of Stella: Sermons on the Christian Year*, vol. 2, trans. Lewis White, intro. Elias Dietz, CF 66 (Collegeville, MN: Cistercian Publications, 2019).

Part One

Mary

Chapter One

Birth and Death

If this were a book about Mary herself, it would be a very short book. From a factual, historical point of view, we know hardly anything about her, and much of what we do "know," primarily from the gospels of Matthew and Luke, may well have been invented. Whoever she was, her name was not, of course, Mary, which is English. Her native language would have been Galilean Aramaic, and the spelling of her name in Aramaic would have been MRYM. Aramaic, like Hebrew and other Semitic languages, does not generally indicate short vowels, though if you really have to indicate them, you can add a series of small signs beneath the consonants. On the whole, however, TH CT ST N TH MT is clear enough. In Hebrew, the first short vowel in the name is an I: Miryam or Miriam. In Aramaic, it was an A: Maryam or Mariam. The nineteenth surah of the Qur'an, which tells, among other things, of Mary and the conception and birth of Jesus, is entitled Maryam. In Greek and Latin the final M tended to get dropped, and the name ended up as Maria. The modern English spelling, Mary, dates from the sixteenth century. The name of her son, by the way, was Yeshu. "Jesus" comes straight from the Latin, which was Jesus or Iesus (J and I were the same letter in Latin), and was pronounced, without exception, as "Yay-sus," not "Jee-sus."

So given that there is no more misleading an expression than *gospel truth*, and given that all the gospels, canonical and otherwise, are theological constructions, not biographical narratives, we shall not preface this chapter by asking what we know of Mary. We shall, instead, ask the far more relevant question of what the canonical gospels tell us of Mary, and, of what they do tell us, which parts were of greater or lesser importance to the writers who will appear in the pages of this book. All of them, without exception, accepted the New Testament as God's own word, and although they would frequently translate or interpret a text to suit their own interests, they never questioned whether the text was true. So when Matthew tells us that Herod massacred the innocents,[1] then Herod massacred the innocents, despite the fact that there is no other contemporary evidence for this grisly episode. And when Mary said "My soul magnifies the Lord," that is what she said. It was not a case of the evangelist taking the Song of Hannah from the Old Testament[2] and adapting it to suit his own purposes. Armand-Jean de Rancé died in 1700, and biblical criticism, especially that part of it that came to be known as the quest for the historical Jesus, began only after his death.

In the canonical gospels Mary is mentioned twenty-three times, of which seventeen appear in the infancy narratives in Luke and Matthew. Only the gospel of John has her standing at the foot of the cross on which her son is dying.[3] She makes her last appearance in the book of Acts, where she, Jesus' brothers, and "the women" are closeted in an upper room shortly after the Ascension.[4] The identification of Mary with "the woman clothed with the sun" of Revelation 12:1 has an ancient history, reaching back at least as far as the second / third century theologian, Hippolytus of Rome. We might note here that the Mary of the Gnostic gospel of Mary[5] is almost certainly

[1] Matt 2:16.

[2] 1 Sam 2:1-10. Hannah was Samuel's mother.

[3] John 19:25.

[4] Acts 1:13-14.

[5] For the text and a useful introduction, see http://gnosis.org/library/marygosp.htm.

Mary Magdalene, despite the attempts of some scholars, few in number, to identify her with the mother of Jesus.

For our present purposes, there are just three events in the canonical gospels that are of major significance, and all three of them appear in the gospel of Luke. The first is the Annunciation, when the archangel Gabriel appears to Mary and tells her she is about to conceive.[6] The second is the Visitation, when Mary, now pregnant, visits her cousin Elizabeth, who is also pregnant, in this case with John the Baptist.[7] And the third is the Purification or Presentation, when, forty days after the birth of Jesus, Mary and Joseph bring their newborn to Jerusalem to be presented to the Lord and there, in accordance with Leviticus 12:2-4, offer sacrifice for the ritual purification of Mary.[8] Medieval and later preachers certainly expound on the other episodes recounted in the gospels—Simeon's prophecy to Mary that "a sword shall pierce your own soul,"[9] for example, or the wedding feast at Cana of Galilee,[10] or the wonderful story of Mary and John at the foot of the cross[11]—but these three are the major ones.

What, then, of the conception of Mary, her birth, and her death? All three events are celebrated in Orthodox, Roman Catholic, and many Anglican churches, but there is no mention of any of them in the canonical gospels. The first we hear of Mary is when she is about to conceive, and in first-century Galilee she would probably have been betrothed to Joseph at the age of twelve or thirteen. Jewish law strictly forbade parents from giving a daughter in marriage before puberty and the onset of menstruation. The last we hear of her, as we saw

[6] Luke 1:26-38.
[7] Luke 1:39-45.
[8] Luke 2:22-24.
[9] Luke 2:35.
[10] John 2:1-11.
[11] John 19:25-27.

above, is in the book of Acts. After that, Mary vanishes from the scene, and all that follows is a matter of myth and legend.

To deal with Mary's conception, birth, and death, we must leave the pages of the New Testament and venture into the world of the New Testament apocrypha. In the early years of the growing faith, devout Christian writers were always happy to invent what they did not know, and to supply answers to intriguing questions on which the canonical Scriptures were silent. The most obvious of these was what Jesus was doing before he began his ministry, and what he was like as a child. The result was a series of so-called Infancy Gospels, pious novelettes that enjoyed great popularity and whose impact may still be seen on Christmas cards. The ox and the ass who regularly accompany the baby Jesus in the stable are not mentioned anywhere in the canonical gospels: they come from an apocryphal writing generally known as the gospel of pseudo-Matthew.[12]

My own favorite story concerns Joseph, who, as a carpenter, would go here and there in the town to offer his services. But he was always careful to take Jesus with him. Why? Because all too often Joseph made a mess of his work, and would cut a piece of wood too short or too long. He would then call for his son, who would stretch out his hand to the offending piece, and—pow!—it miraculously became just the right size. Joseph, therefore, never needed to finish anything himself, because (as we are told in the text), "he was not a very good carpenter."[13]

The story of Jesus and the clay birds was widely known, for it appears in three of the so-called Infancy Gospels and also in the Qur'an.[14] It seems that one Sabbath, when the five-year-old

[12] Gospel of pseudo-Matthew, §14; James K. Elliott, *The Apocryphal New Testament: A Collection of Apocryphal Christian Literature in an English Translation* (Oxford: Oxford University Press, 2005), 94.

[13] Arabic Infancy Gospel, §38.1–2; Aurelio de Santos Otero, *Los Evangelios Apocrifos* (Madrid: Editorial Católica, 1963), 330–31.

[14] See Elliott, *Apocryphal New Testament*, 75–76 (Infancy Gospel of Thomas, §2); 89 (Infancy Gospel of pseudo-Matthew, §27); 103 (Arabic Infancy Gospel, §36); Qur'an surah 5.110.

Jesus was playing by a stream, he took some clay and fashioned from it twelve little sparrows. But a Jew who was passing by saw this and reported what had happened to Joseph, Mary's husband. The boy Jesus had broken the commandment that forbids any work on the Sabbath. But when Joseph went to rebuke Jesus, Jesus clapped his hands and all the little birds flew off into the air, chirping. And not only that. Jesus blessed them and promised them that they would not meet death by any man's hands.

But to return to Mary. We do, in fact, have apocryphal writings that describe in detail the miraculous events of her conception, birth, and death; the first and earliest of these was an extremely popular work that circulated under the title of the book of the *Birth of Mary*, or the Revelation of James. It is more commonly referred to as the *Protevangelium of James*,[15] where "Protevangelium" means, literally, "the earliest form of the Gospel." It was a word invented by the French linguist, diplomat, and qabbalist Guillaume Postel (1510–1581) and appears in his Latin translation of the Greek text of the *Protevangelium* first published in 1552. The James to whom the book is attributed was James the brother of Jesus, who became a leader of the Jerusalem church and was martyred sometime in the 60s of the first century. It is quite impossible that he actually wrote it, and all the evidence seems to indicate that the earliest version of the work dates to the second half of the second century.

Up to now, more than 140 Greek manuscripts of the text have been identified, most of them late, and at various times the work was translated into Arabic, Armenian, Coptic, Ethiopic, Georgian, Latin, Slavonic, and Syriac.[16] There are numerous modern translations, and English versions are readily available on the Internet. The earliest surviving Greek version

[15] For a useful, brief, and balanced account, see Paul Foster, "The Protevangelium of James," *The Expository Times* 118 (2007): 573–82. See also Stephen J. Shoemaker, *Mary in Early Christian Faith and Devotion* (New Haven: Yale University Press, 2016), 47–61.

[16] See Elliott, *Apocryphal New Testament*, 53–55.

is to be found in what is technically known as Papyrus Bodmer V. This is one of a collection of twenty-two papyrus manuscripts discovered in Egypt in 1952 and then smuggled to Switzerland, where they were bought by the Swiss bibliophile and collector Martin Bodmer, after whom they are named. The date of the papyrus is uncertain—it may have been written in the late third century or the first half of the fourth—but that is almost certainly more than a hundred years after the work was originally composed.

The book purports to tell the story of the conception and birth of Mary and the conception and birth of Jesus, and those interested can read the whole thing in a very short time. The English translation I have before me is no more than ten pages in length.[17] For our present purposes, we need draw attention to no more than three points. The first concerns the names of the parents of the Virgin; the second, the miracle of her conception; and the third, what came to be known as the doctrine of Mary's *postpartum* or perpetual virginity, namely, that she conceived as a virgin and retained her virginity throughout the birth of her son.

The book is our only source to identify Mary's parents as Joachim and Anna, and the names have become part of the tradition of most of the mainline churches. Whether the tradition is true is another matter. As James Elliott has said, both names may be entirely fictitious:

> The name of Mary's mother, Anna, may have come from Luke's birth story, but the figures of Hannah, Samuel's mother, Susanna in the additions to Daniel, and Manoah's wife in Judges 13 have been models for Anna. The name Joachim may have been suggested by Susanna's husband in the additions to Daniel, but Manoah and Elkanah in 1 Samuel have also been models.[18]

[17] Elliott, *Apocryphal New Testament*, 57–67. Foster provides an excellent summary.

[18] Elliott, *Apocryphal New Testament*, 51. See also Foster, "The Protevangelium," 576.

Unhappily, Anna and Joachim (we will call them that for convenience) had no children, for Anna, we are told, was barren, something regarded as a curse and a punishment in the Judaism of the time. One day, when she was walking in her garden (for according to the *Protevangelium*, she and her husband were very wealthy), she saw a nest of newly hatched sparrows that brought back to her all the sorrow of her own condition. She gives way to a lament for her barrenness, pouring out her grief before the Lord, and lo! an angel appears to her telling her that God has had pity on her and that she will conceive and bear a child.

Meanwhile, Joachim is wandering in the desert, for he had tried to bring a sacrificial offering to the Jerusalem Temple but had been told it could not be accepted because he had not fathered a child in Israel. In despair, he leaves his wife and home, retires to the desert for forty days and forty nights, and vows to eat or drink nothing until God visits him. Now we come to the interesting part.

Anna is now visited by two more angels, who tell her that God has indeed heard the prayer of Joachim, that he too has been visited by an angel of the Lord, and that the angel has told him to leave his desert retreat and go home. And why? Well, we're not quite sure why, because there is a vital textual variant here that has major theological implications. The angel either says to Joachim, "Go home, for behold! your wife Anna has conceived in her womb," which is the past tense, or "Go home, for behold! your wife Anna will conceive in her womb," which is the future tense.[19] In the first case, the event has already happened while Joachim was away in the desert; in the second case, it is something that will happen once he's back home. The difference is clearly significant, since the first variant implies a miraculous virginal conception and the second does not. So which was the original?

[19] For the Greek text, see Foster, "The Protevangelium," 576.

The answer, probably but not certainly, is the past tense: Anna is already pregnant when Joachim returns. Such a reading has the support of the earliest Greek manuscripts, and, as Paul Foster has said, it "would be in line with the piety of this document that goes to extraordinary lengths to affirm Mary's purity. It would be strange if its author had allowed the heroine of his story to be tainted with carnal concupiscence."[20] If this is indeed so, it clearly lays the foundation for the later doctrine of the Immaculate Conception, for if Mary, like her son, was conceived by the direct action of God the Holy Spirit, there is no room here for any taint of Original Sin. We have not quite got there yet, but the seeds seem to have been sown in the second half of the second century.

The third thing we must note is the writer's insistence on Mary's perpetual virginity. The gospels of Matthew and Luke state clearly that Mary conceived as a virgin[21]—Mark, John, and Paul say nothing at all on the matter—but they do not state that she remained a virgin throughout the birth of her son and for the whole of her life thereafter. Indeed, the fact that the canonical gospels specifically mention Jesus' brothers and sisters—the four brothers were James, Joses, Jude, and Simon; the sisters are not named—would seem to imply that she did not. In the *Protevangelium*, the problem of these brothers and sisters is solved by identifying them as Joseph's children by a previous marriage.[22] This is why, in much Western religious art, Joseph is portrayed as being much older than Mary.

So when it comes time for the birth of Jesus, the wondrous event is witnessed by a Jewish midwife, who then tells her

[20] Foster, "The Protevangelium," 576. See also Shoemaker, *Mary in Early Christian Faith*, 56–57.

[21] Matt 1:18; Luke 1:34-35.

[22] The other explanation, popularized by Jerome, is that the brothers and sisters were actually Jesus' cousins or adopted siblings: see David N. Bell, *Many Mansions: An Introduction to the Development and Diversity of Medieval Theology West and East*, CS 146 (Kalamazoo, MI: Cistercian Publications, 1996), 244–47.

friend, Salome, that she has just seen a virgin give birth. Salome, reasonably, does not believe this for a moment, and demands that she be allowed to examine Mary physically to see whether her hymen remains unbroken. This she does, but at what cost! Mary is indeed *virgo intacta*, but Salome's hand with which she made the examination is consumed by fire. Fortunately for her, a convenient angel appears and tells her to reach out and touch the child who has just been born. This she does and is, of course, immediately healed. Mary was, is, and will remain ever virgin, and the Greek title *aeiparthenos*, "Ever-Virgin," is attested from the early fourth century. It was formally stated to be part of the faith by the fifth Ecumenical Council, the Second Council of Constantinople, in 553. In the West, the earliest explicit reference to the idea of Mary's perpetual virginity appears to be in the work of Zeno of Verona, who died in 371 or 380,[23] and it rapidly became the official teaching of the Western church. The standard proof text was Ezekiel 44:2: "This gate shall be shut. It shall not be opened and none shall pass through it, for the Lord, the God of Israel has entered by it. It shall therefore remain shut."

The book of the *Birth of Mary* was, as we have said, extremely popular and widely read, but the scholarly consensus is that it has no historical value whatever. It is an entirely theological document with a theological agenda. But the obvious rejoinder to this is that what we may have here is oral tradition, and that the names of Mary's parents, for example, had been reliably handed down for more than a century. Unfortunately, it has been shown clearly that oral tradition or folk memory is both unreliable and deceptive. This fact was clearly demonstrated in an important article by Professor Ronald Hutton, of the University of Bristol, published in 2003,[24] in which Hutton

[23] See Brian K. Reynolds, *Gateway to Heaven: Marian Doctrine and Devotion, Image and Typology in the Patristic and Medieval Periods.* Volume 1: *Doctrine and Devotion* (Hyde Park, NY: New City Press, 2012), 80, n. 113.

[24] Ronald Hutton, "How Myths Are Made," in his *Witches, Druids and King Arthur* (London/New York: Hambledon Continuum, 2003), 1–37.

presents case after case to show how little oral tradition can be trusted. To take but one example, it is said in Yorkshire that after the battle of Marston Moor in 1644, Sir Richard Graham, Master of the Horse to Charles I and a fervent Royalist, fled the field with more than twenty wounds on his body and rode back to his manor house at Norton Conyers. He was hotly pursued by Oliver Cromwell and his troopers and, if we may quote Joseph Smith Fletcher,

> It is further said that the pursuers caught up the old knight as he reached his house, and that Cromwell, forcing his horse to ascend the staircase, shook the last breath out of his enemy's body in Sir Richard's own chamber. In proof of this, the plain mark of a horse's hoof is shown on the staircase, but unfortunately for romance, the real facts are that Cromwell was not near Norton Conyers on the night of Marston Moor, and Sir Richard Graham did not die until ten years had elapsed since that decisive victory.[25]

Hutton also shows that a spurious oral tradition can arise in a surprisingly short time. He gives the example of the Russian soldiers who, late in 1914, were seen making their way through England, the snow still on their boots, to reinforce the allies on the Western Front in the early months of the First World War. They were reported as crowding railway carriages, calling out for vodka, and trying to force Russian rubles into English vending machines. "Thousands of them were reported, by hundreds of witnesses; but not a single one was actually there."[26]

In short, from an honest and critical point of view, we cannot put our trust in any of the information provided in the book of the *Birth of Mary*, though that will not, of course, stop those

[25] Joseph S. Fletcher, *A Picturesque History of Yorkshire*, 3 vols. (London: J. M. Dent & Co., 1900), 2:322.

[26] Hutton, "How Myths Are Made," 29.

who wish to believe it from doing so. On the other hand, the book does have a real importance in that it testifies to an early and, as Stephen Shoemaker has said, "a surprisingly developed interest in the Virgin as a significant figure in her own right as well as early devotion to her unique holiness."[27]

A feast celebrating the birth of Mary is first recorded in the sixth century, and it may well have begun in Syria or Palestine. By the seventh century it had spread to most of the Orthodox East, but its acceptance in the West was more hesitant, primarily because it was based entirely on apocryphal material. Eastern monks brought the feast to Rome towards the end of the seventh century, but it was another three hundred years before it was widely accepted and celebrated in the Latin West.

What, then, of Mary's death? Here, too, we must turn to the apocryphal literature, in this case a variety of texts recounting what in the Orthodox East was and is referred to as the Dormition of the Virgin and in the Latin West as the Assumption. The Dormition refers to Mary's physical dying; the Assumption refers to her being taken up to heaven in both body and soul.

We are fortunate here in having available a comprehensive study of the genre by Stephen Shoemaker, Professor of Religious Studies at the University of Oregon, who discusses a number of different traditions preserved in nine ancient languages.[28] His excellent study also includes seven appendixes with translations of early Dormition / Assumption narratives from sources in Ethiopic, Georgian, Greek, Coptic, and Syriac. The earliest of these appears to be the *Liber reliquiei Mariae*, the *Book of the Mary's Repose* which is preserved in its entirety only in an Ethiopic translation. The original Greek work probably

[27] See Shoemaker, *Mary in Early Christian Faith*, 5. For a very sound survey of the doctrine, see Reynolds, *Gateway to Heaven*, 293–329.

[28] Stephen J. Shoemaker, *The Ancient Traditions of the Virgin Mary's Dormition and Assumption*, Oxford Early Christian Studies (Oxford: Oxford University Press, 2006).

dates from the fourth century, though the late third is not impossible.[29] What does it say?[30]

It is really a very odd work, and it contains a considerable number of passages that are obscure, which is a polite way of saying that we have no idea what the writer is talking about. They reflect esoteric Christian traditions that have obvious affinities to the various Gnostic streams of the day, and they bear witness to some of the oddities of those alternative Christianities that caused such grave concern to the early Fathers of the Church. It is fairly clear that the early Ethiopic translator could not understand them either.

The book is fairly long and opens with "a great angel" appearing to Mary and telling her of her impending death. It will take place in three days' time, and the angel will send the apostles to Mary to prepare her body for burial. There then follows a section, very much in the Gnostic tradition, dealing with the power and importance of sacred names, that ends when Mary realizes that the "great angel" is actually her son, Jesus. The Jesus-Angel then involves Mary in a long conversation, some of which is intelligible and some of which is, as Stephen Shoemaker says, "utterly cryptic,"[31] culminating in Jesus' promise that four days after Mary's death he will come to take her body to Paradise. Further conversations ensue—some more, some less intelligible—after which Mary returns home.

Next day the apostles begin to arrive, John being the first, and after they have all come, Mary takes to her bed. A sweet and pleasant odor fills the room, and then Christ himself appears on a cloud, accompanied by hosts of angels. While the angels wait outside, Christ enters Mary's chamber, receives

[29] See Shoemaker, *Mary in Early Christian Faith*, 103.

[30] For a complete translation of the Ethiopic text, together with the Georgian and Syriac fragments, see Shoemaker, *Ancient Traditions*, 290–350, and for a comprehensive summary, the same author's *Mary in Early Christian Faith*, 104–28.

[31] Shoemaker, *Mary in Early Christian Faith*, 107.

her soul into his hands, passes it over to the archangel Michael, and tells the apostles to bury his mother's body in a tomb outside the city. This they proceed to do, but not without difficulty, for all the way they are hassled and harassed by the Jewish high priests and their followers. Fortunately for the apostles, the angels who were accompanying Mary's bier come to their aid and strike the Jews with blindness. Eventually, however, they reach the tomb, lay Mary's body to rest inside, and await the day when Christ will come to raise her, as he himself had promised.

Come he does, four days later, and issues a command that his mother's body be taken on a cloud to Paradise, accompanied by all the apostles and myriads of angels. This is the beginning of a celestial journey in which Mary and the apostles are given a lengthy guided tour of hell and heaven. The tour of hell is fairly detailed—it is always easier to describe innovative tortures than unending bliss—and here we see Mary interceding with her son for the souls in torment (this is important). The tour of heaven is considerably shorter, and when they enter Paradise the apostles are greeted by Elizabeth, John the Baptist's mother, and a number of Old Testament patriarchs. Finally, they are led up to the seventh heaven, the highest of all, where God himself is seated. They wish to go to him and embrace him, but this is impossible. Indeed, they cannot even see his face "for God is entirely fire."[32]

Christ now commands a seraph to bring in a throne for him, and a throne is immediately brought, pure and adorned, with no end to its glory, and surrounded by hosts of enthroned angels. The apostles are then instructed to return to earth and proclaim everything they have seen, but before they do so a second throne is brought in. For whom? For Mary! "And there were ten thousand angels and three thousand virgins surrounding it, and Mary sat on it and entered Paradise."[33] This, too, is

[32] Shoemaker, *Ancient Traditions,* 348 (§132).

[33] Shoemaker, *Ancient Traditions,* 350 (§135) (my translation).

a most important passage. The apostles then descend back to earth, and the *Book of the Mary's Repose* comes to an end.

The numerous Dormition / Assumption narratives that followed the *Book of Mary's Repose* all have their own variants, though four basic threads remain constant. First, Mary is warned, either by Christ or an angel (the same being in the *Book of Mary's Repose*), of her forthcoming death. Second, she is joined by the apostles, and the group makes its way to Jerusalem, where Mary takes to her bed and dies. Third, the apostles perform the burial rites and lay her body in a rock-cut tomb. And fourth, three days later, the tomb is found to be empty, and Mary, body and soul, has been received into heaven by her son.

The main differences lie in the question of whether or not Mary died a natural death before being assumed into heaven, and in the details of how that assumption took place. The overall consensus of the Greek East was (and is) that Mary died a natural death before being buried, and that on the third day her body was resurrected by Christ and taken to up to heaven, usually on a cloud. The Latin West was more ambivalent. Most of the narratives are clearly in line with the Eastern view, but some seem to imply that Mary was assumed into heaven at the very moment of her physical death. When on November 1, 1950, Pope Pius XII infallibly declared the doctrine of the Corporeal Assumption to be an Article of Faith that all Roman Catholics must accept, he deliberately left open the question of exactly when her body was taken up to heaven.

In the Greek East, the feast of the Dormition, or "Falling Asleep," of the Virgin was celebrated from about the year 600, and from the eighth century the doctrine was unquestioned. It received full approval from Saint John of Damascus (676–749), whose influence was profound both in the East and (in Latin translation) in the West, and who might be regarded as the voice of medieval Orthodoxy,[34] but its progress in the West

[34] See Reynolds, *Gateway to Heaven*, 306–8.

was more hesitant. It is a curious story in which a letter attributed to Saint Augustine, but not written by him, triumphed over a letter attributed to Saint Jerome, but not written by him, on the grounds that the authority of Augustine-who-was-not-Augustine was greater than the authority of Jerome-who-was-not-Jerome.

The letter attributed to Jerome was actually written by an eighth-century French Benedictine abbot named Paschasius Radbertus (785–865), who played an important role in certain eucharistic controversies that are not here our concern. Paschasius never actually denies the corporeal assumption of the Virgin, but simply says that since we do not know what really happened, we should not speculate on matters that God has preferred to keep secret. He rejects everything that appears in the apocryphal narratives except the empty tomb, but he lavishes the highest praise on the Virgin, the Queen of the World, *regina mundi*, herself. What he is saying, in effect, is that you don't have to accept a dubious doctrine to be wholly devoted to the Mother of God.[35]

This letter by Jerome-who-was-not-Jerome did not end Western speculation on the death of Mary, though it certainly diminished it, but at the end of the eleventh century or the beginning of the twelfth another letter appeared, this time, as we have said, attributed to no less an authority than Augustine, though the actual author remains unknown. As its theological basis, the writer turns to the unique intimacy of the relationship between Christ and his mother. Is it conceivable, he asks, that those who were so closely linked in their earthly lives and in the work of redemption should not also be united in death and glory? The flesh of Jesus was the flesh of Mary, and just as the flesh of Jesus did not suffer corruption but was taken into heaven at the ascension, neither did the flesh of his mother. It is unthinkable, he says, that the sinless body of the Mother

[35] For details, see Reynolds, *Gateway to Heaven*, 313–14. For an early example of Mary as *regina mundi*, see PL 30:126B.

of God should be delivered to the worms! No! "It is right that she should be with him whom she bore in her womb, that she should be in the presence of him to whom she gave birth and whom she suckled and cherished, Mary, who bore God, who nursed God, who ministered to God, and who followed God!"[36] In other words, wherever Jesus was, there too was his mother.[37]

The authority of the supposed Augustine, supported by popular piety, proved more persuasive than the hesitancy of the supposed Jerome, and from the twelfth century onwards, the doctrine of the corporeal assumption became ever more widely accepted in the West. After it had received approval from both Bonaventure and Thomas Aquinas, its acceptance was virtually universal, though there was still a question as to whether the assumption took place at the moment of Mary's death or a few days afterwards. In the following pages we shall see both points of view, and some writers who—pleading ignorance on the question—will quote Saint Paul's comment in 2 Corinthians 12:3: "whether in the body or apart from the body I do not know."

We might note, however, that even while the debate was going on, the feast of the Assumption was being celebrated, and had been celebrated in the West since the seventh century. In both East and West, the date was the same: August 15. As to the actual historicity of the assumption of Mary, there is obviously nothing to be said. You either believe it or you don't, and there is no doubt that all the writers we shall be discussing in the following pages accepted the doctrine as an unquestioned fact of the faith.

In summary, all that is known, or, more accurately, all that is believed of the events surrounding the birth and death of the Virgin comes from sources of very doubtful historical

[36] *ps.*-Augustine, *De assumptione beatae Mariae virginis*, 8; PL 40:1148: *Maria Dei genitrix, Dei nutrix, Dei ministratrix, et Dei secutrix.*

[37] See further Reynolds, *Gateway to Heaven*, 316–17.

value. Some would say from sources of no historical value whatever. This, however, will not stop those who wish to believe in them from believing in them, and the teachers and preachers we shall meet in these pages undoubtedly did so. But to appreciate the nature and content of their writings we need to provide a little more background and say something about three themes of major importance in Marian theology. The first is the parallelism between Eve, who sinned, and Mary, who did not. The second is that of the enthronement and coronation of the Virgin. The third is that of Mary as *mediatrix* and intercessor. The three are intertwined. We have already touched on some of these, but more needs to be said of them, and we also need to say a few words about the most important Marian hymns. These topics are the subjects of our next chapter.

Chapter Two

Themes and Titles

We will begin this chapter by referring to a statement at the very end of the *Book of Mary's Repose*, where Christ, who already has a glorious throne in Paradise, commands that a second throne be brought in for his mother.[1] The implication, obviously, is that son and mother are in some way co-rulers in heaven, but the story begins with Saint Paul and the development of what is known technically as the doctrine of recapitulation.

At its basis is the idea of Mary's perpetual virginity that we discussed in the last chapter. In this, Mary stood in marked contrast to Eve, who, having sinned together with Adam in the Garden of Eden, was expelled from the garden, had intercourse with Adam for the first time, and gave birth to Cain.[2] What Eve had lost, Mary retained, and as a consequence of Eve's transgression, she and all her female descendants (Mary alone excepted) would give birth to their children only with labor and severe pain.[3] But more than this, whereas the virgin Eve had been disobedient and fallen, the virgin Mary had been wholly obedient—"be it done with me according to your word"[4]—and

[1] See Stephen J. Shoemaker, *The Ancient Traditions of the Virgin Mary's Dormition and Assumption*, Oxford Early Christian Studies (Oxford: Oxford University Press, 2006), 349–50 (§135).

[2] See Gen 4:1.

[3] See Gen 3:16.

[4] Luke 1:38.

had not fallen. It was only logical, therefore, that the early church would see in Mary a second and perfect Eve just as it saw in Christ a second and perfect Adam.

The origin of this view lies, as we said, with Saint Paul, who, in his first letter to the Corinthians, tells us that "just as in Adam all die, so in Christ shall all be made alive" and goes on to contrast the first Adam, who was of the earth, earthy, with the second Adam, Christ, "a life-giving spirit."[5] The first Adam / second Adam parallelism is then taken up by the Greek theologian Justin, who was martyred in about 165 (hence his usual title of Justin Martyr), and perfected by Irenaeus, the second-century bishop of Lyon in what is now central France. The doctrine came to be known as the doctrine of recapitulation, which means "summing up all previous events" or "starting all over again." That is to say, whatever went wrong in the first Adam is put to rights in the second Adam, who is Christ. If the first Adam was disobedient, sinful, and imperfect, the second Adam was obedient, sinless, and perfect, and thus, in the incarnation, we see the beginning of a new and restored creation.

Now *Adam* in Hebrew means a human being in general. It does not mean a specifically male human being, a man, for which Hebrew has its own word, *'ish*. So what Irenaeus is saying is that whatever went wrong with the first human creation has been put right in Christ, and the first human creation includes all human brings, of whatever sex or gender. Theologically, therefore, since Christ is the second human being, not the second man, there is no need to have Mary as the second woman. When in the incarnation Christ became human, he took upon himself full humanity, not just masculinity, and when he canceled out the sinfulness and so on of Adam, he did not save only the male members of the human race. But it is easy to see how popular piety could overcome theology, and with

[5] See 1 Cor 15:22, 45-50.

an ever-increasing devotion to the Virgin, it was a simple matter to parallel Eve with Mary and Adam with Christ. We can see this as early as the second half of the second century in a writing by Justin Martyr, whom we just met, who tells us that

> when Eve was a virgin and undefiled, she conceived by the word of the serpent, and gave birth to disobedience and death. But Mary the Virgin received faith and joy when the angel Gabriel announced to her the good news that the Spirit of the Lord would come upon her and the power of the All-Highest would overshadow her, and that as a result the holy being to which she would give birth would be the Son of God.[6]

Following Justin, both Eastern and Western writers regularly cited the Eve-Mary parallel, and devised a number of neat phrases to express it. One of the neatest of these appeared in the West, and follows from the fact that in Latin, Eve is Eva. And how does the archangel Gabriel greet Mary in the first chapter of the Latin version of Luke's gospel? "*Ave, gratia plena*," he says, "Hail! Full of grace!"[7] And what is *Ave* but *Eva* reversed? Here is how it was expressed by the Jesuit martyr Robert Southwell, who was hanged, drawn, and quartered at Tyburn on February 21, 1595:

> Spell *Eva* back and *Ave* you shall find,
> The first began the last reversed our harms;
> An angel's witching words did *Eva* blind,
> An angel's *Ave* disenchants the charms:
> Death first by woman's weakness entered in,
> In woman's virtue life doth now begin.[8]

[6] Justin, *Dialogue with Trypho*, §100, quoting Luke 1:35; PG 6:712A. The *Dialogue* was written sometime between 155 and 165.

[7] Luke 1:28.

[8] *The Complete Poems of Robert Southwell, S.J.*, ed. Alexander B. Grosart (Privately Printed, 1872), 120 (the first verse of "Our Ladie's Salutation"). I have modernized the spelling.

In other words, the angel's salutation implies that Mary has reversed the woeful work of Eve, and that through her perfect obedience is cooperating with her Son in the work of redemption. The official Marian title that reflects this cooperation is, in Latin, *Co-Redemptrix*, or "Co-Redeemer" in the feminine gender, and it is fraught with theological problems that are not here our concern.[9] Suffice it to say that the idea that Christ needs the help of someone else in order to redeem the world conflicts with the idea clearly stated in the letter to the Hebrews that Christ offered himself as a single sacrifice for sins for all time.[10] But once again, we are in the realm of popular piety and the rapidly growing development of the veneration of the Mother of God.

As early as the second century, Irenaeus of Lyon had contrasted the disobedience and loss of virginity on the part of Eve with the obedience and virginity on the part of Mary, and for this reason, he says, she became "the cause of salvation both for herself and the whole human race."[11] "For what the virgin Eve had bound fast through unbelief, this the virgin Mary unbound through faith."[12] It is this popular idea of Mary as Second Eve, cooperating with her son in redeeming the world, that leads to her being seated on that second glorious throne mentioned in the *Book of Mary's Repose* and being crowned as Queen of Heaven, *regina coeli* or *regina coelorum*.

The title *regina coeli* appears three times in the book of Jeremiah,[13] but the reference there is not to Mary. Quite the contrary. It is to one of the pagan Semitic mother-goddesses,

[9] See Brian K. Reynolds, *Gateway to Heaven: Marian Doctrine and Devotion, Image and Typology in the Patristic and Medieval Periods. Volume 1: Doctrine and Devotion* (Hyde Park, NY: New City Press, 2012), 107–51, 246–92 (chaps. 3 and 6).

[10] Heb 10:12.

[11] Irenaeus, *Adversus haereses*, III.xxii.4; PG 7:959A: *et sibi, et universo generi humano causa facta est salutis.*

[12] Irenaeus, *Adversus haereses*, III.xxii.4; PG 7:959C–60A.

[13] Jer 7:18; 44:18, 25.

perhaps Asherah, and so far as I can tell (but I will be happy to be corrected in this), the earliest securely datable use of the title to refer to the Mother of God appears in the writings of Ildefonso or Ildephonsus of Toledo. He was born about 607, elected bishop of Toledo in 657, and died on January 23, 667. He was a man with a profound devotion to the Mother of God, and his most famous work was *De virginitate perpetua sanctae Mariae contra tres infideles*, "On the Perpetual Virginity of Holy Mary against Three Unbelievers."[14]

The three unbelievers were Jovinian, Helvidius, and an anonymous Jew. Jovinian (d. ca. 405) had already aroused the wrath of Saint Jerome for maintaining that virginity had no greater merit than married love, and that abstinence in food had no greater merit than ordinary eating, provided it was done with the right disposition. It is also clear that he denied the perpetual virginity of Mary. Helvidius (d. ca. 390) held much the same views, maintaining that Mary and Joseph had led a normal married life, and that after the birth of Jesus, Mary had produced a number of other children, Jesus' brothers and sisters. He also saw no greater merit in celibacy than in marriage and roundly criticized female monasticism on the grounds that there was no warranty for it anywhere in Scripture. He too had aroused the anger of Jerome. As to the anonymous Jew, the Jewish tradition has never advocated celibacy or a monastic lifestyle, on the grounds that they conflict with God's explicit instruction in Genesis 1:28 to be fruitful and increase in numbers. Nor does Judaism accept the story of Mary's perpetual virginity, for the Hebrew text of Isaiah 7:14 does not say "Behold, a virgin shall conceive," but "Behold, an *almah* shall con-

[14] PL 96:53–110; complete English translation by Malcolm D. Donalson, *A Translation from Latin into English of De Virginitate Perpetua Sanctae Mariae / The Perpetual Virginity of Holy Mary by Ildefonsus of Toledo (c. 650 A.D.)* (Lewiston, NY: Edwin Mellen Press, 2016). For a brief and useful summary, see Hilda Graef, *Mary: A History of Doctrine and Devotion*, 2 vols. (London: Sheed & Ward, 1985), 1:141–42.

ceive," and an *almah*, in Hebrew, is simply a young woman of child-bearing age. Ildefonso takes the arguments of the three unbelievers and demolishes them utterly—at least to his own satisfaction and that of his Spanish Christian readers.

The title *regina coelorum* is also given to Mary in a responsory in the Antiphonary attributed to Gregory the Great,[15] but that responsory is certainly not from the pen of Gregory and undoubtedly postdates the work of Ildefonso. In the Iberian peninsula, the Marian impact of Ildefonso was enormous, but it took some time for the title to leave the borders of Spain and make its way into the rest of Europe. By the twelfth century, however, it had become standard, and the celebrated hymn "*Regina coeli, laetare, alleluia*," "Queen of Heaven, rejoice, alleluia," appears to date from just that century.[16]

But queens, like kings, are crowned, and Mary was no exception. From about the same time—the twelfth century—representations in art and sculpture of the coronation of the Virgin become ever more common. One of the earliest of these dates from about 1170 and appears on the tympanum of the west portal of Senlis cathedral, about thirty-six miles north of Paris. It represents Christ and his mother, both wearing crowns, seated on identical thrones. Below is a representation of the Dormition and the Assumption, in which Mary is carried to heaven by angels. In most of the portrayals, if Mary is not already crowned, she is being crowned by her son, but in some it is God the Father who crowns both Christ and his mother. There is obviously a danger here of Mary becoming a sort of fourth member of the Trinity, but popular piety can often lead into areas that are theologically suspect.

[15] See PL 78:798C.

[16] *Regina coeli laetare, Alleluia, Quia quem meruisti portare. Alleluia, Resurrexit sicut dixit, Alleluia. Ora pro nobis Deum. Alleluia.* "Queen of Heaven, rejoice, alleluia, For he whom you deserved to bear, alleluia, has risen, as he said, alleluia. Pray for us to God, alleluia."

The *Book of Mary's Repose* also refers to her being given a guided tour of hell and interceding for the souls in torment,[17] an idea that leads us to discuss the very important role of Mary as *mediatrix* or "mediatress."[18] Although the germ of the idea may be seen in its earliest stages in the *Book of Mary's Repose,* it was not until the seventh / eighth century in the East that the term "mediatress"—*mesitis* in Greek—was used freely and the doctrine taught clearly and explicitly. The two persons most responsible for this were Germanus I, patriarch of Constantinople from 715 to 730, and Andrew of Crete, archbishop of Gortyna, who lived from about 660 to 740.[19]

When Germanus is speaking of Mary's mediation, his language is somewhat intemperate. After drawing the usual Eve-Mary parallel, he tells us that no one is filled with the knowledge of God except through her, no one is saved except through her, and no one is redeemed except through her. And in a startling passage in his second homily for the Dormition, he states that Mary, "having motherly power with God," can obtain from him the highest degree of forgiveness for even the very greatest sinners. And why? Because God never fails to hear her and obey her (the Greek verb admits of no ambiguity) as his pure and immaculate Mother.[20] In other words, God does what Mary tells him.

Andrew of Crete is more restrained, though still undoubtedly exuberant. Mary is blessed in heaven and glorified on earth. She is the mother of all life, and through her all things have been sanctified. Through her, sin has been abolished and

[17] See Shoemaker, *Ancient Traditions,* 345–46 (§§99–100). We mentioned this in the last chapter.

[18] For a detailed account, see Reynolds, *Gateway to Heaven,* 152–245 (chaps. 4–5).

[19] For very sound brief accounts, see Graef, *Mary,* 1:145–50 (Germanus), 1:150–53 (Andrew).

[20] Germanus of Constantinople, *In Dormitionem beatae Mariae, hom.* II; PG 98:352A; Graef, *Mary,* 1:146–47.

all the woes we inherited from the disobedience of Adam and Eve have been transformed into joy. Not only was she, who was the immaculate mother of the Maker, the mediation between his sublime nature and corruptible flesh, but, in the fourth homily for the birth of Mary, Andrew also calls her "the mediatress [*mesitis*] of law and grace."[21]

After Germanus and Andrew, Mary's mediation became a standard theme in Eastern theology, and it may be said to have reached its culmination—or perhaps over-reached its culmination—in the fourteenth century in the writings of Theophanes, archbishop of Nicaea, who died about 1381. To examine his ideas in detail would take us too far off track,[22] but it is interesting to note that for Theophanes, Mary is the way to Christ, and no one who seeks to be deified—that is, to become like God, which is the goal of Orthodoxy—can achieve this without Mary. If Christ is the head of the church, Mary is the neck that leads to that head. This is a typically Western idea, and it seems clear that Theophanes (who was well versed in Western theology and one of the first Greeks, if not the first, to study Aquinas's *Summa contra gentiles* and *Summa theologica* in Greek translation) took the idea from some Western source,[23] which leads us to the West itself.

We cannot be certain as to when the title *mediatrix* was first used of Mary in the West, for some of the writings in which it appears are of uncertain authorship and uncertain date. It may go back to the sixth century, but its real development and importance dates only from the eleventh century, rather later than

[21] Andrew of Crete, *In nativitatem beatae Mariae, hom.* IV; PG 97:865A.

[22] For a brief summary, see David N. Bell, *Many Mansions: An Introduction to the Development and Diversity of Medieval Theology West and East*, CS 146 (Kalamazoo, MI: Cistercian Publications, 1996), 250–51, and Graef, *Mary*, 1:334–39. For a comprehensive account, see Ioannis D. Polemis, *Theophanes of Nicaea: His Life and Works* (Vienna: Verlag der Österreichischen Akademie der Wissenschaften, 1996). The key text is the "Discourse on the Theotokos."

[23] See Graef, *Mary*, 1:337–38.

in the East. A prose (*prosa*) for the feast of the Assumption dating from the early eleventh century ends *Mediatrix nostra, quae es post Deum spes sola, tuo filio nos repraesenta, ut in poli aula laeti iubilemus alleluia,* "O our mediatrix, you who, after God, are our only hope, present us to your Son that in the courts of heaven we may sing a joyful alleluia."[24]

The Benedictine reformer Peter Damian, cardinal bishop of Ostia and (since 1828) Doctor of the Church, who died in either 1072 or 1073, had a great devotion to Mary and much to say of her. He also wrote an *Officium beatae Virginis,* "Office of the blessed Virgin." As we might expect, he emphasizes the Eve-Mary parallel, but adds a further dimension by relating it to the Eucharist. "Eve ate up food," he says, "and thereby punished us with eternal fasting. Mary brought forth food that opened for us the door to the heavenly banquet."[25] He also links Mary with the church, the Body of Christ, an idea that goes back at least to Ambrose of Milan. "Great and happy mother and blessed virgin Mary," says Peter Damian, "from whose womb Christ assumed flesh, from which, in turn, by water and blood,[26] the church flowed forth. Thus, in this way we see that the church also comes forth from Mary."[27]

But Peter has still more to say. The body of Christ exists in three forms: physical, mystical, and sacramental. The first is the actual body of Jesus of Nazareth, the second is the church, and the third is the consecrated bread and wine of the Eucharist. Thus, since Mary gave birth to Christ's human body, and since it is through the eucharistic body as a preeminent channel of grace that the Body of Christ (the church) goes to Christ, we

[24] Ulysse Chevalier, *Poésie liturgique traditionelle de l'Église catholique en Occident* (Tournai: Desclée, Lefebvre et Cie, 1894), 219 (no. 279). See also PL 180:38A, where the first part is quoted by Hermann of Tournai, who died sometime after 1147.

[25] Peter Damian, *Sermo* 45; PL 144:743C. The contrast is between *comedo* and *edo,* "to take in" and "to give out."

[26] See John 19:34.

[27] Peter Damian, *Sermo* 63; PL 144:861B.

may say that the members of the Body of Christ go to Christ through Mary. "We beseech you, most clement mother of devotion and mercy," says Peter in his forty-sixth sermon,

> that as we rejoice in ever reciting your praise here on earth, we might deserve to have the help of your intercession in heaven; for just as the Son of God condescended to come down to us through you, so we, too, through you are able to attain fellowship with him.[28]

In other words, to Jesus through Mary, an idea that reached its apogee in the work of Louis-Marie Grignion de Montfort (1673–1716),[29] but whose seeds may be seen very much earlier: in the writings of Germanus of Constantinople in the East and in Ildefonso of Toledo in the West. We shall have cause to return to this theme in later chapters.

From the beginning of the twelfth century onwards, the idea of Mary as the *mediatrix* of grace and our intercessor in heaven, the very path to Christ, became ever more popular. The themes appear in a multitude of writers, but few express it with such eminent clarity and in such flowing Latin as Bernard of Clairvaux. We shall say more on Bernard in due course, but for the moment we shall simply remark that for him, since it was through her whom he calls "the *mediatrix* of salvation and restorer of the ages"[30] that Christ came down to us, so it is through her that we must ascend to him: "Let us therefore venerate this Mary from the bottom of our heart, with all our deepest affection and all our desires, for this is the will [of God], who wills that we should have everything through Mary."[31]

[28] Peter Damian, *Sermo* 46; PL 144:761B.

[29] See Graef, *Mary*, 2:57–62.

[30] Bernard, *Epistola* 174.2; SBOp 7:389.

[31] Bernard, *Sermo in nativitate beatae Mariae (De aqueductu)*, 7; SBOp 5:279: *totum nos habere voluit per Mariam.*

But then Bernard continues in a passage reminiscent of the somewhat hyperbolic statements of Germanus of Constantinople, though he puts it rather more delicately. Do you stand in awe of the divine majesty of Jesus, he asks? He may have become truly human, but he is still God! Do you need an advocate with him? You have one in Mary! If she intercedes for you, she will surely be heard:

> The Son will certainly listen to the mother, and the Father will listen to the Son! Little children, here is the sinners' ladder, here lies my greatest trust, here is the sole reason for my hope! What? Can the Son refuse his mother anything, or be refused anything by his Father? Is it possible for the Son to refuse her, or for him to be refused? Is it possible for the Son not to hear her, or for him not to be heard? Neither, obviously! "You have found grace with God," said the angel.[32] Fortunately! She will always find grace, and grace is the only thing we need, for it is surely by grace alone that we are saved.[33]

For us who are in danger on the tempestuous seas of this world, Mary is our guiding star. If the winds of temptation arise, says Bernard, or if you run upon the rocks of tribulation, look to the star and call on Mary. If the vessel of your soul is beaten about by the winds of the passions, look to Mary. If you find yourself foundering in the gulfs of melancholy or despair, think on Mary.[34] Her very name, says Bernard, means Star of the Sea, *maris stella,* "that glorious star that arose from Jacob and that casts its radiance over the whole world,"[35] and we need to say a few words about this very popular title.

It is a curious story, being based on a manuscript misreading. It will be remembered that Mary's name, in her native

[32] Luke 1:30.

[33] Bernard, *Sermo in nativitate beatae Mariae,* 7; SBOp 5:279.

[34] See Bernard, *In laudibus Virginis Matris, hom.* 2.17; SBOp 4:34–35.

[35] Bernard, *In laudibus Virginis Matris, hom.* 2.17; SBOp 4:34.

Galilean Aramaic, was Maryam, and Saint Jerome, basing himself on the *Onomasticon* of Eusebius of Caesarea, read this as two Hebrew words, MR, with a short A, and YM, also with a short A, i.e., *Mar* and *Yam*. *Yam* is common enough and means "sea," but there are two meanings for *Mar*, one when it is an adjective and one when it is a noun. As an adjective, *Mar* is not uncommon and means "bitter" or "bitterness," but *Mar* as a noun is very rare indeed. It occurs only once in the whole of the Hebrew Scriptures, in Isaiah 40:15, and means "a drop." The Latin word for "a drop" is *stilla*, and in his Latin version of Isaiah, Jerome correctly translates *mar* as *stilla*. In other words, MAR-YAM could mean either "bitter sea" or "drop of the sea," and that, it seems, is how Jerome translated it in his *Liber de nominibus Hebraicis*, "Book of Hebrew Names": *stilla maris, sive amarum mare*, "drop of the sea, or bitter sea."[36] But the scribe or scribes who copied his manuscript misread or misheard *stilla* as *stella* "star," an error that is not too surprising given that the Latin word for star is far more common than the Latin word for drop. Thus, Mary / Maryam becomes "the Star of the Sea," and one of her most charming titles has its birth in a scribal error. The celebrated hymn to the Virgin, *"Ave, maris stella,"* "Hail, Star of the Sea," dates from about the eighth century, and after that the title becomes ever more popular and ever more widespread.

Even more popular and even more widespread is, of course, the Hail Mary, the *Ave Maria*, with its prayer for Mary's intercession in its final section. Here it is in its entirety in Latin and English: *Ave Maria, gratia plena, Dominus tecum. Benedicta tu in mulieribus, et benedictus fructus ventris tui, Iesus. Sancta Maria, Mater Dei, ora pro nobis peccatoribus, nunc et in hora mortis nostrae. Amen*. "Hail Mary, full of grace, the Lord is with you. Blessed are you among women, and blessed is the fruit of your womb, Jesus. Holy Mary, Mother of God, pray for us sinners, now and

[36] See Jerome, *Liber de nominibus Hebraicis*; PL 23:841–42.

at the hour of our death. Amen." What is the history of this most famous of all Marian prayers?

There are three sections to the prayer, two of which are taken directly from the Latin text of the gospel of Saint Luke, and one that was added very much later. The first section—"Hail Mary, full of grace, the Lord is with you. Blessed are you among women"—is taken directly from the angel Gabriel's salutation to Mary in Luke 1:28. The only difference is the addition of the single word Mary, which had been added to the text from at least the sixth century. The second part—"Blessed are you among women,[37] and blessed is the fruit of your womb, Jesus"—is taken from Elizabeth's greeting to Mary in Luke 1:42, once again with the addition of a single word, this time Jesus. When that was added is unclear, but it was probably not until the thirteenth century. What, then, of the third and final section, which reflects the development of the doctrine of Mary as *mediatrix* and intercessor?

Its earliest appearance in print appears to have been in Girolamo Savonarola's commentary on the *Ave Maria*, published in about 1495. Savonarola quotes the Latin text exactly as we have quoted it above, except that he omits the final word *nostrae*.[38] Given Savonarola's unhappy end—he was excommunicated by Pope Alexander VI, and, together with two followers, hanged and burned on May 23, 1498—it might be thought that this was not exactly the best publicity for the addition, but it slowly gained ground until, in 1566, it appeared in the Catechism of the Council of Trent. Two years later, in 1568, Pope Pius V included it in his revision of the Roman Breviary, and the rest, as they say, is history. We might also note that there is no sound evidence for the first two parts of

[37] The standard Vulgate text has *inter mulieres* for *in mulieribus*, but it means the same thing.

[38] *Expositione del Reuerendissimo in Christo padre Frate Hieronymo da Ferrara dell'ordine de predicatori sopra la oratione della Vergine gloriosa* (Florence, ca. 1495), at the very beginning of the unpaginated text.

the *Ave Maria* being used in Marian devotion before about the middle of the eleventh century.

A third Marian hymn, much beloved by the Cistercians, is the *Salve Regina*, which also testifies to the doctrine of Mary's intercession and advocacy. It is actually one of four seasonal antiphons sung in honor of the Virgin, of which one—*Regina coeli, laetare, alleluia!*—has already been mentioned. All four ask for Mary's intercession before the throne of God and beg her to have pity on us poor sinners. The other two antiphons are *Alma Redemptoris Mater*, "Loving Mother of the Redeemer," and *Ave Regina coelorum*, "Hail, Queen of Heaven," and all four antiphons echo themes we have discussed in this chapter.

The *Salve Regina* is the most commonly used of these four antiphons. It probably dates from the eleventh century and has been attributed to a variety of authors, more by hopeful guesswork than by any sound evidence. Here is a strictly literal translation: "Hail, Queen, Mother of Mercy; our life, sweetness, hope, hail! To you we cry, exiled children of Eve. To you we sigh, mourning and weeping in this vale of tears. Turn upon us then, O advocate, those merciful eyes of yours, and after this exile show us Jesus, the blessed fruit of your womb, O clement, O loving, O sweet Virgin Mary."[39] Mary as Queen of Heaven is a matter we have already discussed, as also the echo of the Eve-Mary parallelism in the phrase "exiled children of Eve." The title Mother of Mercy has been used of Mary certainly from the ninth century, and quite possibly earlier.[40] Among the Cistercians, the hymn has been sung daily after Compline since the thirteenth century, and still is.

[39] *Salve, Regina, mater misericordiae; vita, dulcedo et spes nostra, salve. Ad te clamamus, exsules filii Hevae. Ad te suspiramus, gementes et flentes in hac lacrimarum valle. Eia ergo, advocata nostra, illos tuos misericordes oculos ad nos converte. Et Iesum, benedictum fructum ventris tui, nobis post hoc exsilium ostende. O clemens, o pia, o dulcis Virgo Maria.*

[40] It appears in the *De corona virginis*, xiii; PL 96:302A, which has been attributed uncertainly to Ildefonso of Toledo. My own view is that the *De corona* postdates Ildefonso.

Here now is a literal translation of *Alma Redemptoris Mater*: "Sweet Mother of the Redeemer, that Passageway to Heaven, Gate of the Morning and Star of the Sea, help your people who have fallen, yet who try to rise again, you who, to the wonderment of nature, bore your holy Creator, virgin both before and after, you who received from the mouth of Gabriel that 'Hail (*Ave*)!' have mercy on us sinners."[41] Here we see the popular title "Star of the Sea" and the doctrine of the Perpetual Virginity of Mary as well as a plea for her intercession. The other two titles, "Passageway to Heaven (*pervia coeli*)" and "Gate of the Morning (*porta manes*)," are both rare, and, if used at all, derive from this hymn. It almost certainly dates from the twelfth century, but who wrote it is unknown.

Here, finally, is a literal translation of *Ave Regina coelorum:* "Hail, Queen of Heaven! Hail, Mistress of Angels! Greetings, O root. Greetings, O gate, from whom a light was born to the world. Rejoice, glorious virgin, beautiful beyond all others. Farewell, O truly lovely one, and pray for us to Christ."[42] We have already discussed the title "Queen of Heaven," but it is difficult to say when Mary was first addressed as "Mistress of Angels (*Domina angelorum*)." The problem is that some of the earliest examples appear, once again, in texts of uncertain date by uncertain authors, but it was definitely in use by the twelfth century, which is also the date of the antiphon itself.

As we have said, all four antiphons bear witness to the idea of Mary as *mediatrix* and intercessor, and although this, and the other common themes of Eve-Mary parallelism, Mary as *co-redemptrix,* Mary as Queen of Heaven, and the coronation

[41] *Alma Redemptoris Mater, quae pervia caeli porta manes, et stella maris, succurre cadenti, surgere qui curat, populo: tu quae genuisti, natura mirante, tuum sanctum Genitorem, Virgo prius ac posterius, Gabrielis ab ore, sumens illud Ave, peccatorum miserere*. These are six Latin hexameters.

[42] *Ave, Regina coelorum, Ave, Domina Angelorum: Salve, radix, salve, porta Ex qua mundo lux est orta: Gaude, Virgo gloriosa, Super omnes speciosa, Vale, o valde decora, Et pro nobis Christum exora*. This is two rhyming stanzas, and there are slightly differing versions of the text.

of the Virgin, might be theologically suspect, all were readily accepted by the writers we shall be considering in these pages. The same cannot be said for the doctrine of Mary's Immaculate Conception, and to that matter we must now turn our attention.

Chapter Three

A Question of Sin

That Jesus never sinned was never in doubt. The New Testament is quite explicit on the matter,[1] and the principle was never questioned. But what of his mother? Did Mary ever sin? Not according to Augustine of Hippo, the North African bishop and theologian who died in 430, and who was the most important formative influence on the development of Western theology. In his treatise *On Nature and Grace,* Augustine is attacking the views of Pelagius, who maintained that human beings were born without any taint of original sin, and that it was possible—though very rare—for us to avoid sinning by the strength of our own free will. Were there any who achieved this? There were indeed, says Pelagius, and he enumerates twenty-two men, beginning with Abel and Enoch and ending with Joseph, Mary's husband, and John the Evangelist, and seven women, beginning with Deborah and ending with Mary.[2] Augustine will have none of this. "Of our own power," he says elsewhere, "we can only fall."[3] According to Augustine, there was only one among all these twenty-nine who never sinned, and that was "the Mother of Our Lord and Savior." Out of all these, says Augustine,

[1] See, for example, 2 Cor 5:21; Heb 4:15; 1 Pet 2:22; 1 John 3:5.

[2] Pelagius, quoted by Augustine, in the latter's *De natura et gratia*, xxxvi.42; PL 44:267.

[3] Augustine, *Enarratio in Ps.* 129.1; PL 37:1696.

> I exclude only the holy virgin Mary, for with regard to her I do not wish to raise any question on the subject of sinning out of honor to the Lord; for we know from him what a superabundance of grace for overcoming every trace of sin was bestowed on her who was worthy to conceive and bear him who unquestionably had no sin.[4]

This was the standard view of the West until the eighteenth century brought in all manner of questions, but it was not always the view in the East. The learned, saintly, and courageous patriarch of Constantinople, Saint John Chrysostom (ca. 349–407), thought otherwise, as we may see from his account of what happened at the wedding feast in Cana of Galilee when the mother of Jesus told her son that the company needed more wine.[5] Why did she do this, asks John? Partly, indeed, to accommodate the guests, which is wholly commendable, and partly to make herself, through her son, more conspicuous, which is the sin of vainglory. Indeed, she may even have had the same idea as Jesus' brothers, when they told him to go and show himself to the world,[6] hoping thereby to use his miracles to gain credit for themselves.[7]

Even worse, perhaps, is Chrysostom's explanation of the episode in Matthew's gospel when Jesus is teaching the people, and his mother and his brothers arrive and want to speak with him. Someone tells him they are outside looking for him, but what does Jesus say? "Who is my mother, and who are my brothers?"[8] And why does he say this? Not because he is ashamed of his mother, says Chrysostom, and he is certainly not denying that she gave him birth. Indeed, had he been ashamed of her, he would not have passed through her womb. What Jesus is saying is that Mary gains no advantage from

[4] Augustine, *De natura et gratia*, xxxvi.42; PL 44:267.

[5] John 2:3.

[6] John 7:4.

[7] John Chrysostom, *In Joannem, hom.* 21 [20].2; PG 59:130.

[8] Matt 12:46-50.

being his mother unless she (like everyone else) does all that needs to be done, which is doing the will of Jesus' Father in heaven. What Mary was really trying to do was to show the people that she had power and authority over her son, and had the right to interrupt him even when he was teaching. This is simply vanity—indeed superfluous vanity—and Mary was guilty of it.[9]

It will come as no surprise to learn that, despite his great authority, Chrysostom's view was very much that of the minority. A few Greek theologians agreed with him, but the vast majority did not, and in the West it is rare indeed to find any writer who would even countenance the possibility that Mary had sinned. One such, however, was Philip of Harvengt. He was born at Harvengt, now Harveng in present-day Belgium, a little village about six miles south of Mons, at an unknown date in the early twelfth century, and received a sound education, probably at the cathedral school in Cambrai. He then took the monastic habit and, in 1130, entered the Premonstratensian abbey of Bonne-Espérance, where he was appointed prior. The abbey lies about twelve miles southeast of Mons, and the church in which Philip worshiped still stands. After various vicissitudes, not least an unpleasant dispute with Bernard of Clairvaux over a monk of Bonne-Espérance who wished to leave the abbey and enter Clairvaux, he was elected abbot of Bonne-Espérance in 1158, and governed the house well and efficiently until his death in April 1183.

In his Marian commentary on the Song of Songs, Philip states that "the Virgin, like others, was by nature a daughter of wrath (*filia irae*),"[10] by which he means that she, like everyone else, was conceived with original sin. Furthermore, he adds, before she became a worthy vessel for the incarnation of Christ, she may well have committed some trifling sins, and

[9] John Chrysostom, *In Matthaeum, hom.* 44 [45].1; PG 57:465.

[10] Philip of Harvengt, *In Cantica Canticorum*, VI.13; PL 203:459A. *Filia irae* is taken from Eph 2:3.

needed to be purified and have these "internal stains" (*internae maculae*) removed. It was only after this had been accomplished by an outpouring of the oil of grace, and there was no rebellion or opposition left in her, that she could truly say "Behold the handmaid of the Lord, be it done with me according to your word."[11] In other words, according to Philip, God made Mary a pure and sinless vessel for Christ not at the moment of her conception or of her birth, but only in time for the incarnation. But as Hilda Graef points out, "Though Philip attributes slight sins to Mary, he cedes to none in his devotion to her as the great mediating power between Christ and the faithful."[12]

Philip's ideas were decidedly unusual for a Western writer, and by the Middle Ages, almost all theologians, Eastern and Western, Greek and Latin, regarded the Virgin as having lived a life totally free from sin. But if there was no dispute on this—or no dispute of any consequence—the same cannot be said for the far more troubling question of when she had been rendered sinless. Was it at the moment of her conception? Or was it at the moment of her birth? In theological terms, we need to consider the development of the doctrine of the Immaculate Conception, a doctrine that, as Edward O'Connor has said, "occasioned what was perhaps the most prolonged and passionate debate that has ever been carried on in Catholic theology."[13]

The story begins with the variant reading in the *Protevangelium of James* that we discussed in Chapter One. Does the angel say to Joachim, "Go home, for behold! your wife Anna has conceived in her womb," which is the past tense, or "Go home, for behold! your wife Anna will conceive in her womb," which is the future tense? In the first case, as we said earlier,

[11] See Philip, *In Cant.* I.17–18; PL 203:227B–28D.

[12] Hilda Graef, *Mary: A History of Doctrine and Devotion*, 2 vols. (London: Sheed & Ward, 1963–1965), 1:255.

[13] Edward D. O'Connor, *The Doctrine of the Immaculate Conception: History and Significance* (Notre Dame: University of Notre Dame Press, 1958), vi.

the event has already happened while Joachim was away in the desert; in the second case, it is something that will happen now that he's back home. The difference is obviously important, since the first variant implies a miraculous conception while the second does not. It is almost certain that the original reading was the past tense.

But if Anna has conceived miraculously without benefit of intercourse, and if the transmission of original sin is in some way associated with concupiscence and sexual intercourse (which was the view of Augustine and the prevailing view in the West), then, logically, Mary would have been conceived without original sin. The *Protevangelium* does not say that in so many words, but the past tense in the variant may certainly be seen to imply it. The early history of the doctrine is, however, unclear, and the matter is not helped by the fact that many of the passages adduced in its support or otherwise are unclear and ambiguous.

The Eastern theologians, on the whole, had grave doubts on the question, which, to a large extent, were a consequence of the difference between East and West on the nature of original sin. East and West agreed that, before the Fall, Adam and Eve were in a state of blessedness and perfection. They could talk freely with God, all their wants were satisfied in Eden, and had they not sinned, they would not have died. East and West also agreed that, unfortunately, Adam and Eve did sin—they both fell to the lure of the Tempter—and that as a consequence of eating the forbidden fruit, they became mortal, sinful, and liable to disease and corruption. Finally, East and West agreed that the consequences of this first sin were passed down from Adam and Eve to their descendants—i.e., us—and that ever since Adam and Eve were expelled from the Garden of Eden, the human race has been born mortal, sinful, and liable to disease and corruption. The early theologians might not have been quite sure exactly how this corruption, this taint, was inherited, but, as we have said, the great majority of them thought that it was in some way associated with the physical act of sexual intercourse.

However it was inherited, the results were the same: human beings found it easier to sin than to do good. But here's the difference. The Eastern theologians never thought that this corruption was absolute. That is to say, they never thought that, as a consequence of the Fall, human beings had entirely lost the ability to do good. They had certainly lost the ability to do enough good, by their own strength and will, to achieve salvation—for that, grace was essential—but they were still capable of good actions. If, then, they did a good action, God would respond to this by making his grace available to them, and then in cooperation with this grace they could do more good actions. Thus, in cooperation with grace, and only in cooperation with grace, they might achieve salvation. They certainly could not do it on their own.

On the whole, this was also the view of Western theologians up to the time of Augustine of Hippo, whom we met at the beginning of this chapter. For much of his life, he was involved in theological controversies, and one of the most significant of these involved Pelagius. Pelagius was British and may have been a monk, but was more probably some sort of lay ascetic. He moved to Rome in about 400 and acquired a reputation, apparently justified, for his asceticism and learning. His view of sin was simple and logical. Souls are created by God, and God is perfectly good. But if God is perfectly good, he would not create something that was inherently flawed. A newly created soul, therefore, fresh from the hand of God, is not in any way tainted or corrupted, and it is unaffected by original sin. That we are sinners is not in doubt, but we become sinners by imitating our parents who were sinners, and not by some inherited taint. In modern terms, one might say we are socialized into sinning, but it is not something inherent in our nature.

Augustine would have none of this and, as a result of a misreading of Romans 5:12, maintained not only that human beings were innately corrupted, but that that corruption was total. The verse in question reads, in Greek, "Through one man sin entered this world, and through sin, death, and thus death passed on to all people because all sinned." But in the Latin translation used by Augustine, the Greek for "because" was rendered into Latin as *in quo*, which, unfortunately, can have two meanings. The first is "in that," which is the same as "because," and is what the original Greek says. The second is "in whom," and that is how Augustine read it. In other words, since the whole human race was present in potentiality in Adam, whatever Adam did, we did, and when Adam was tempted and fell, we fell with him. Thus, since we all fell "in Adam," so we are what Adam was: fallen, damned, doomed, guilty, and condemned.

In other words, the newly created soul was not only stained, but 100% stained, and, as a consequence, human beings came into this world utterly incapable of performing a single good action, any more than a perfectly dark room could emit a beam of light. As we said earlier, "Of our own power, we can only fall."[14] This idea leads ineluctably to the doctrine of predestination and a variety of problems that are not here our concern.[15] And how is this corruption transmitted to human beings? Augustine is in no doubt: by "the evil of carnal concupiscence, by means of which a human being, who is born as a result of this, contracts original sin."[16]

Such was the authority of Augustine that despite some severe criticism from other Western writers, the Augustinian idea of the total depravity of human beings rapidly became the standard teaching of Western theology. The East never accepted it (it still doesn't), and although Pelagius was condemned at the Third Ecumenical Council, held at Ephesus in 431, this does not mean that the East approved of Augustine.

[14] See n. 3 above.

[15] For a discussion, see David N. Bell, *A Cloud of Witnesses: An Introduction to the Development of Christian Doctrine to AD 500*, 2nd ed., CS 218 (Kalamazoo, MI: Cistercian Publications, 2007), 158–65.

[16] Augustine, *De nuptiis et concupiscentia* I.1; PL 44:413–14: *carnalis concupiscentiae malum, propter quod homo, qui per illam nascitur, trahit originale peccatum.*

What the East was doing was condemning Pelagius's idea that human beings were born with no trace of original sin; it was not giving its approval to the Augustinian doctrine of total depravity.

It was quite possible, therefore, for Eastern theologians to suggest that Mary might have been conceived or even born with original sin. They were not suggesting that she could do no good actions, but only that she, like the rest of the human race, was in need of grace to achieve salvation and that, as Saint Paul said, "Christ died for all,"[17] including his mother. But if a post-Augustinian Westerner were to suggest this, he or she would be implying that Mary was conceived or even born in a state of total depravity, and that the Mother of God was incapable of performing a single good action. Such an idea was wholly at odds with the ever-growing veneration of Mary, and no Westerner was going to suggest it. No. If Mary was conceived with original sin, she was cleansed of it by God's grace before she was born, and she came into the world as an immaculate vessel, fit to bear the Son of God. Putting it another way, for Western theologians, there might not have been an immaculate conception, but there was certainly an immaculate birth.

Such was the view of Bernard of Clairvaux. In about 1140, the Chapter of Canons of the cathedral of Lyon introduced, as a new feast, that of Mary's conception—not, let us note, the immaculate conception, but simply her physical conception—and Bernard exploded. The church of Lyon, he wrote to them, is first in importance of all the churches of France in its dignity, its regulations, its learning, its religious life, its wisdom, its authority, and its antiquity. In addition, it had always been cautious in adopting novelties and innovations. Bernard is amazed, therefore, that this church should now introduce a new feast of which the church knows nothing, which reason

[17] 2 Cor 5:15.

cannot approve, and which is not supported by ancient tradition. The royal Virgin, he says,

> needs no false honor, for she is abundantly endowed with true titles of honor and badges of dignity. Honor her indeed for the purity of her flesh and the holiness of her life. Marvel at the fruitfulness of a virgin. Venerate her divine offspring. Extol her who knew neither concupiscence in conception nor pain in giving birth. Proclaim her as revered by the angels, desired by the nations, foreknown by patriarchs and prophets, chosen from among all women, placed before all. Glorify her who found grace, the *mediatrix* of salvation, the restorer of the ages. Finally, exalt her who was exalted above the choirs of angels to the heights of heaven.[18]

He then goes on to make four points. First, that with the whole church, he most firmly believes her birth to have been holy, because, like Jeremiah and John the Baptist, she had been sanctified in her mother's womb. But, he says, "I would not be so rash as to say to what extent this sanctification prevailed over original sin."[19]

Second, the sanctification that Mary received before she came into this world was greater than that of Jeremiah, John, or any other, for it not only sanctified her birth, but also kept her free from all sin for all the days of her life. Such was only fitting for the Queen of Virgins, who would give birth to him who destroyed both sin and death.

Third, the argument that since we honor her birth, which was undoubtedly holy, we should also honor her conception, on the grounds that had she not been conceived she would not have been born, is just absurd. By the same logic, we should also honor the conception of Mary's parents, grandparents, great-grandparents, and so on *ad infinitum*. In which case, we

[18] Bernard of Clairvaux, *Epistola* 174.2; SBOp 7:388–89.
[19] *Epistola* 174.4; SBOp 7:389–90.

would have feasts without number! And if anyone should say that they have had a divine revelation that we should honor the conception of Joachim and Anna on the basis of Exodus 20:12, "Honor your father and your mother,"[20] Bernard does not believe it. Such revelations, he says, are supported neither by sound reason nor good authority.

Fourth and finally, Mary's conception was the result of the same physical acts as everyone else's conception, "unless perhaps someone should say that she was conceived by the Holy Spirit, and not by a man: but that is something hitherto unheard of."[21] That was true only of her son, and Bernard gives no credence to the story in the *Protevangelium*. But if concupiscence was involved in her conception, which it was, then (following Augustine), she must inevitably have been conceived with original sin. With the sole exception of Jesus, "all the children of Adam are in the same situation as he [David] who humbly and truly admitted of himself, 'I was conceived in iniquities, and in sin did my mother conceive me.'"[22]

In short, there is no place in the church for a new festival, a presumptuous novelty, which is "the mother of rashness, the sister of superstition, the daughter of levity."[23] In any case, if such a feast seemed advisable, the authority of the Apostolic See should first have been consulted. Bernard is happy to hand over a final decision to that authority, and should there be any matter on which he thinks differently from that See, he is prepared to change his opinion.

In the twelfth century, Bernard was far from being alone in his view. Rupert, the Benedictine abbot of Deutz who died in 1129, put the matter succinctly:

[20] Bernard appears to be referring to Elsinus, abbot of Peterborough, who died in 1055: see *ps.*-Anselm of Canterbury, *Miraculum de conceptione sanctae Mariae*; PL 159:324D–25A.

[21] *Epistola* 174.7; SBOp 7:391.

[22] *Epistola* 174.8; SBOp 7:392, quoting Ps 50:7.

[23] *Epistola* 174.9; SBOp 7:392.

> Indeed, you [Mary] were truly able to say, "For behold, I was conceived in iniquities, and in sin did my mother conceive me." For since you were from that lump [*massa*] that was corrupted in Adam, you were not free from the original stain of hereditary sin.[24]

Rupert quotes the same verse from Psalm 50 as did Bernard, and in his reference to the "lump" that was corrupted in Adam, he is referring directly to Augustine's grim statement that, at birth, the whole human race is *una massa peccati*, "one lump of sin."[25]

But Rupert, like Bernard and so many others, had not the least doubt that Mary did not remain stained with sin, and after stating that she could not have avoided the necessary consequences of her human heredity, he states that by the grace of God, all this sin is burned up, like stubble in a fire, "so that she might be made a holy habitation in whom God would dwell for nine whole months, material altogether pure, from which the holy wisdom of God would build himself an eternal house."[26] Indeed, Rupert had a profound devotion to the Mother of God, and his commentary on the Song of Songs appears to have been the first to interpret the book entirely from a Marian point of view.

For the vast majority of the twelfth-century theologians, then, Mary was certainly born without sin, but not conceived without sin. They bowed before the immense weight of Augustine, and if Mary was conceived by the normal processes of human reproduction, there was no way she could have avoided the inevitable human taint. But if she was cleansed of sin before birth, when did that cleansing take place? To answer

[24] Rupert of Deutz, *In Cantica Canticorum*, 1; PL 168:841C.

[25] Augustine, *De diversis quaestionibus ad Simplicianum*, I, *quaestio* 2 *argumentum* and §16; PL 40:110, 121.

[26] Rupert, *In Cantica Canticorum*, 1; PL 168:841CD. The reference to wisdom building himself a house is drawn from Prov 9:1, save that wisdom is there feminine.

that question we must move from the twelfth to the thirteenth century and take account of the invasion of the West by the ideas of Aristotle.

According to Aristotle, there are three types of soul: the nutritive soul, the sensitive soul, and the rational soul. The nutritive or vegetative soul is that which provides no more than growth and reproduction, and all living entities must, of necessity, possess this type of soul. But there is only one group—plants—that possesses this type of soul alone. Next in order, and at a higher level, are those beings that not only reproduce and grow, but have sense perception, the result of possessing a sensitive soul. In other words, they can feel pleasure or pain, desire or aversion, and move towards or away from the thing desired or not desired. Here we are speaking of animals, and animals possess both a nutritive soul and a sensitive soul. Then, third and finally, we reach the human creation, and human beings possess not only the nutritive and sensitive souls, but also *nous* or mind—the rational soul—that provides them with the power of abstract reasoning and moral decisions. In Latin translation, the moment when the rational soul was placed in the human body was termed animation—*animatio* in Latin—and if we may quote Albert the Great,

> We say that the Blessed Virgin was not sanctified before animation, and saying otherwise is a heresy condemned by blessed Bernard in a letter to [the Canons of] Lyon and by all the Masters of the schools of Paris.[27]

This is only logical. Sin requires rationality, moral judgment, and ethical decisions. That is not possible for those who possess only nutritive and / or sensitive souls. A dandelion cannot

[27] Albert the Great, *In III Sententiarum, distinctio III A, articulus 4 solutio; B. Alberti Magni, Opera Omnia, Volumen XXVIII, Commentarii in III Sententiarum*, ed. Stephanus C. A. Borgnet (Paris: L.Vivès, 1894), 47. We discussed Bernard's letter to the Canons of Lyon above.

sin, and when unneutered tomcats do what unneutered tomcats do, and do it rather frequently, this (according to Aristotle and his followers) is not sin. The Mother of God, therefore, could not have been sanctified—that is, cleansed from all stain of sin—before she was a rational human being.

Thomas Aquinas now takes up the tale, and in his *Summa theologica* he deals at length with six questions.[28] The first is whether the Blessed Virgin was sanctified before her birth from the womb. The second is whether the Blessed Virgin was sanctified before animation. The third is whether the Blessed Virgin was cleansed from all concupiscent desires. The fourth was whether, by being sanctified in the womb, she was preserved from committing any actual sin. The fifth was whether, by being sanctified in the womb, she received the fullness of grace. And the sixth was whether, after Christ, it was proper for the Blessed Virgin to be sanctified in the womb.

Here are Thomas's answers. To the first, yes, like Jeremiah and John the Baptist, she was sanctified in the womb. To the second, no, she could only have been sanctified after animation. To the third, no, she was not wholly freed from concupiscent desires, but they remained fettered (*ligatus*) and did not affect her single-minded devotion to do God's will. To the fourth, yes, by God's grace, Mary committed no actual sin, either mortal or venial. To the fifth, yes, the Mother of God received a greater fullness of grace than any other. And to the sixth, yes, it was entirely proper for her to have been cleansed from all taint of original sin while in the womb.

Thomas's main argument that Mary must have been conceived with original sin is not the sexual argument that we have seen earlier, but the unequivocal scriptural statements that Christ died for all: "If the soul of the Blessed Virgin had never been defiled by the contagion of original sin, this would be derogatory to the dignity of Christ, inasmuch as he is the

[28] See Thomas Aquinas, *Summa theologica, Pars* III, *quaestio* 27.

universal savior of everyone."[29] But sanctified she was, Thomas is in no doubt about that, though the precise time at which that happened—the day and the hour—remains unknown.

We might note here that Thomas was well aware of John Chrysostom's view, based on the passages from the gospels of Matthew and John that we discussed above, that Mary was guilty of the sin of vainglory. How does he respond to this? "In these words," he says, "Chrysostom goes too far. They may, however, be explained as meaning that the Lord checked in her not the disordered movement of vainglory with regard to herself, but what others might be thinking."[30] Mary, therefore, remains sinless.

Thomas was a Dominican, a member of the Order of Preachers that had been founded by the Spanish priest Dominic de Guzmán and approved by Pope Honorius III on December 22, 1216. What, then, of the followers of Saint Francis, the Franciscans or Friars Minor, the order that had been founded a few years before the Dominicans in 1209? Just as Aquinas was the leading voice among the Dominicans in the thirteenth century, so Bonaventure was the leading voice among the Franciscans. What was his view of the sinlessness of Mary?

Bonaventure agreed with Aquinas, whom he knew and whose friendship he enjoyed. He may have been less rigorous in his arguments, but his conclusion was identical, and he supported it by quoting directly from Bernard's letter to the Canons of Lyon that we discussed above. He also uses the same argument as Aquinas, that if Mary had not contracted original sin, she would not have needed to be redeemed. Thus, not only would this be a contradiction of Scripture, but the honor of her son as the universal Redeemer would have been diminished. Furthermore, says Bonaventure, since Mary was born with original sin, but totally cleansed from it after animation, this places her between us human beings, who are certainly

[29] *Summa Theologica*, III, q. 27, a. 2, reply to ob. 2.

[30] *Summa Theologica*, III, q. 27, a. 4, reply to ob. 3.

corrupted by original sin, and her divine son, who was never corrupted at all. Mary, therefore, is the *mediatrix* between us and Christ, as Christ is the mediator between us and God.[31]

The view that Mary, like all other human beings, was conceived with original sin, but was entirely cleansed from it by God so as to be a pure vessel for the incarnation, was the view of virtually all theologians to the last quarter of the thirteenth century. The Franciscan Bonaventure was in complete agreement on the matter with the Dominican Aquinas, but this harmony was not to last. After the death of Bonaventure in 1274 the Franciscans began to take a different approach, an approach more in keeping with popular piety and the ever-increasing veneration of the Virgin, and the Franciscan scholastics took it upon themselves to demonstrate logically and theologically not only the truth of an immaculate birth, but also the truth of an immaculate conception. How they did this will be the subject of our next chapter.

[31] For a more detailed account of Bonaventure's views of Mary, see Graef, *Mary*, 1:281–88; and Luigi Gambero, trans. Thomas Buffer, *Mary in the Middle Ages: The Blessed Virgin Mary in the Thought of Medieval Latin Theologians* (San Francisco: Ignatius Press, 2005), 206–15.

Chapter Four

Conception and Misconception

This part of the story realty begins with an Englishman named William of Ware. As his name implies, he was born at Ware in the south of England, a village about seventeen miles east of St. Albans. The precise year is unknown, but it must have been round about 1255–1260. He became a Franciscan, and studied and taught at Oxford. He may also have taught at Paris, though that is disputed, and according to tradition, which may or may not be correct, he was the teacher of John Duns Scotus, whom we shall meet in a moment. He died at the beginning of the fourteenth century, but, as with his birth, the exact year of his death is not known.

William takes up a theme first suggested in the late eleventh century by Eadmer of Canterbury (ca. 1060–ca. 1126), namely, that if God can do something (and for God nothing is impossible[1]), and if it is fitting and appropriate that he should do it, then he does it.[2] In later centuries, this became standardized as *potuit, decuit, ergo fecit*: "He was able to do it, it was fitting, therefore he did it." The logic is, in fact, flawed, not to say dangerous, but this, in time, became the standard argument for the doctrine of the Immaculate Conception. William himself is not absolutely certain that Mary was conceived without

[1] See Luke 1:37.

[2] See Eadmer of Canterbury, *De quatuor virtutibus quae fuerunt in beata Maria*, 7; PL 159:584AB.

original sin, but he would rather give her the benefit of the doubt. "There is another opinion," he says,

> that I myself wish to hold, namely, that she did not contract original sin. For if I must err, since I am not certain about the opposite point of view, I would rather err through superabundance, ascribing to Mary a certain privilege, than through defection, diminishing or taking away from her a certain privilege that she possessed.[3]

What, then, of the need for the redeeming passion of Christ? Did he not die for everyone? Yes he did, says William, even for his mother, but in the case of his mother,

> she needed the passion of Christ not because of any sin that was in her, but [because of the sin] that would have been in her if her son himself had not preserved her from it by faith. Thus Augustine, in his sermon on the Magdalene, says that there are two kinds of debt: those that are contracted and paid off, and those that are not contracted, but might possibly have been contracted, "for there is no sin committed by one person that could not have been committed by another person, unless they had been preserved [from committing it] by God."[4]

I must admit that I do not find this sort of argument particularly persuasive. We are in a murky world of mights, and shoulds, and could have beens but weren't. Yet it remains true that, so far as we know, William was the first to attempt to give logical and theological support to an idea that that was rapidly becoming an ever more-important part of popular piety.

[3] *Fr. Gulielmi Guarrae, Fr. Ioannis Duns Scoti, Fr. Petri Aureoli: Quaestiones disputae de immaculate conceptione Beatae Mariae Virginis*, Bibliotheca Franciscana Scholastica Medii Aevi, 3 (Quaracchi: Collegium S. Bonaventurae, 1904), 4.

[4] *Fr. Gulielmi Guarrae*, 10, referring to Augustine, *Sermo* 99.vi.6: PL 36:598.

Far more important than William in establishing the doctrine of the Immaculate Conception was John Duns Scotus, John the Scot from Duns on the Scottish border, perhaps William's student, though that is not certain. He was born ca. 1264, entered the Franciscan Order as a youth, and, like William, taught at Oxford. After several years of teaching, he left the university in about 1301 to continue his studies in Paris, and six years later he was transferred to the Franciscan house of studies in Cologne, where he died suddenly from unknown causes, still in his forties, in 1308.

His essential task, like that of William, was to reconcile the original sinlessness of Mary with the universality of Christ's redemption, and this he does in three steps.

First, Christ is the most perfect mediator and redeemer. No one would argue or disagree with that.

Second, what is the true nature of mediation? It is to reconcile the relationship between God and human beings that went awry with the Fall. Since Christ was the most perfect mediator—*perfectissimus mediator*—it might be expected that in at least one instance he would effect the most perfect act of mediation possible to demonstrate what mediation was all about. Perfect mediation involves the removal of anything and everything that could detract from a perfect relationship with God, and the most difficult thing to remove is original sin. That, after all, is not something we ourselves commit, but something with which we are born. It is only reasonable, therefore, that the one person whom Christ would select to be the subject of his most perfect mediation would be his own mother, and he demonstrated this mediation by preserving her from sin not only throughout her life, but in her conception as well. Mary, therefore, was the living example of what perfect mediation should be, and far from being excluded from her son's mediatory work, she was actually the one to be most affected by it.[5]

[5] See *Fr. Gulielmi Guarrae*, 14–16.

Third, Christ was not only the most perfect mediator, but also the most perfect redeemer. So in what does the most perfect redemption consist? The forgiveness of sins is certainly part of redemption, but to preserve a person from all sin and from sinning at all is obviously much more perfect. As we said above, original sin is not something we commit, but something inherent in our human nature. Preservation from original sin is thus much more perfect than preservation for actual sin, and, as with the most perfect mediation, it would only be expected that Christ, the universal Redeemer, would demonstrate this most perfect redemption at least once. This he did, by preserving Mary from original sin in her conception as well as actual sin in her life.[6] To celebrate a feast of the Immaculate Conception, therefore, was not only to honor the absolute purity of the Mother of God, but also to celebrate the saving, redeeming, and mediating power of her son. Scotus referred to this as the "pre-redemption," for the cleansing of Mary from all sin anticipated the redemption that took place on Calvary. What Christ had done so perfectly for his mother, he would, in time, also do for us.

Duns Scotus was followed by Petrus Aureolus or Peter Auriol, another Franciscan, who was probably about fifteen years younger than Scotus. He taught in Franciscan convents in Bologna and Toulouse before moving to Paris, where he lectured on the Sentences of Peter Lombard. He may have been a pupil of Duns Scotus, though that is not certain, but he certainly knew his work and followed him in his ideas. His greatest work was a massive commentary on the Sentences—more than 1100 folio pages—but his most important work for our purposes is his brief treatise on the Immaculate Conception. This was the first scholastic treatise to be devoted entirely to the subject, and was written between 1314 and 1315.[7] Auriol himself died seven years later, at the beginning of 1322.

[6] See *Fr. Gulielmi Guarrae*, 19–20.

[7] See *Fr. Gulielmi Guarrae*, 23–94.

For the most part, Auriol follows Duns Scotus, but in the second of the six chapters that comprise his treatise, he introduced a distinction of considerable importance in the history of the doctrine of the Immaculate Conception. What he says is that, if God so wills, it is possible for a person who has been conceived by the normal processes of human reproduction to inherit the taint of original sin in theory—*de jure*—but, because they have received a special grace from God, they have not inherited it in actuality, *de facto*. In this, we may see a distant echo of the ideas of William of Ware. Thus, says Auriol,

> It is not impossible that someone should contract [original sin] *de jure*, but, being preserved from it by God, not incur the aforesaid injury *de facto*. So what I can say is that someone who contracts original sin by natural necessity, because this is how they were conceived, may nevertheless not contract it because of a special grace. We may put it this way: one is a *child of wrath*[8] by nature, but freed from this by grace.[9]

So why should this be the case with Mary? Here Auriol invokes the arguments of his master, Duns Scotus. First, it is inconceivable that Mary should ever be called a "daughter of wrath." That would be something "horrid to pious ears and devout souls."[10] Secondly, what God *could* do (and God can do anything), he *would* do, provided it be appropriate. This, too, we mentioned above. Could he preserve Mary's soul from all taint of original sin and make her an utterly pure vessel to conceive and give birth to Christ? Of course he could. Would it be appropriate? Of course it would. Therefore he did. Third, he invokes the idea of the pre-redemption, in which Christ demonstrates in his mother what he intends to do for the whole human race. And fourth, since, as Augustine said, the flesh of

[8] Eph 2:3. See also chap. 3, n. 10.

[9] *Fr. Gulielmi Guarrae*, 47–48.

[10] *Fr. Gulielmi Guarrae*, 48.

Christ is the flesh of Mary,[11] and since Christ's flesh was absolutely sinless, it is only right that the flesh from which he took his flesh should also be absolutely sinless.

The *de jure / de facto* distinction proved extraordinarily useful to the defenders of the doctrine of the Immaculate Conception. Mary was conceived with original sin *de jure*, but not *de facto*. Many found the arguments of Scotus and Auriol persuasive, buttressed as they were by popular piety, but they certainly did not end the controversy. Dominican writers still tended to follow Thomas Aquinas, while Franciscan writers tended to follow Duns Scotus and Auriol, and over the centuries hundreds of volumes were published either attacking or defending the doctrine.

In 1439, however, it appeared to receive the approval of an ecumenical council, the Council of Basel, a long-drawn-out council that was not only concerned with a major dispute within the church as to whether popes or ecumenical councils had greater authority, but also with the dispute over the Immaculate Conception that was becoming ever more polemical. In its thirty-sixth session, held on September 17, 1439, the council endorsed the doctrine, and described it as being "in accord with the Church's worship, the Catholic faith, right reason, and Holy Scripture."[12]

Unfortunately, for a variety of convoluted political reasons, the Council of Basel was transferred to Ferrara and then to Florence, and after the whole messy business came to a close, the church accepted only the first twenty-two sessions of the Council of Basel. In other words, its endorsement of the doctrine of the Immaculate Conception had no authority. The Dominicans had won, but only for a short time.

[11] Augustine, *Sermo* 362.xiii.13; PL 39:1619: *sicut vera caro Mariae, vera caro Christi*.

[12] Quoted in Thomas M. Izbicki, "The Immaculate Conception and Ecclesiastical Politics from the Council of Basel to the Council of Trent: The Dominicans and Their Foes," *Archiv für Reformationsgeschichte* 96 (2005): 153.

On August 9, 1471, Francesco della Rovere was elected to the papacy as Pope Sixtus IV. He was a Franciscan and a determined supporter of Mary's immaculate conception. Indeed, before he was elected pope he had composed a lengthy sermon that, as Thomas Izbicki has said, "employed every possible proof text, from *Tota pulchra es*[13] to the *Revelations* of Bridget of Sweden, in support of the doctrine."[14] Thus, on February 27, 1477, as pope, he issued a constitution inviting "all the Christian faithful, for the pardon and remission of their sins, to give thanks and praise to almighty God for the wondrous conception—*mira conceptione*—of this immaculate Virgin."[15] A few years later, he issued two versions of the decree *Grave nimis* in 1482 and 1483 that "threatened excommunication and eternal damnation for anyone who preached or wrote against the doctrine; he stopped just short of condemning the opposing party for heresy."[16] Despite this, Dominican theologians continued to oppose the doctrine, though it was clear that they were losing ground. So what happened then?

At the Fifth Lateran Council, which lasted from 1512 to 1517, Pope Leo X proposed raising the question of the Immaculate Conception and perhaps issuing a dogmatic definition, but was persuaded not to do so by the determined arguments of Cardinal Thomas Cajetan, who was not only a superb theologian and Dominican, but Master of the Order.[17] The next ecumenical council, the hugely important Council of Trent (1545–1563), which was the last ecumenical council to be held

[13] Song 4:7, "You are wholly beautiful, my beloved, and there is no stain (*macula*) in you." This is one of the standard proof-texts for the doctrine of the Immaculate Conception.

[14] Izbicki, "Immaculate Conception," 155.

[15] Heinrich Denzinger, ed., Peter Hünemann, *Enchiridion symbolorum definitionum et declarationum de rebus fidei et morum: Compendium of Creeds, Definitions and Declarations on Matters of Faith and Morals. Latin – English*, 43rd ed. (San Francisco: Ignatius Press, 2012), 354–55, no. 1400.

[16] Izbicki, "Immaculate Conception," 155.

[17] See Izbicki, "Immaculate Conception," 160–64.

before modern times (the First Vatican Council was convened in 1869), avoided issuing any decree on the question, though it is clear that its sympathies lay with those who upheld the doctrine. In its fifth session, held on June 17, 1546, the session that dealt with original sin, the learned fathers, after asserting the universality of original sin, continued thus:

> This same holy Synod doth nevertheless declare, that it is not in its intention to include in this decree, where original sin is treated of, the blessed and immaculate Virgin Mary, the Mother of God, but that the Constitutions of Pope Sixtus IV, of happy memory, are to be observed, under the pains contained in the said constitutions, which it renews.[18]

But the trend was now clear and inexorable. Like the tide in the apocryphal English story of King Canute, it could not be stopped. A Dominican pope like Pius V, who governed the church from 1566 to 1572, might have reduced the solemnity of the feast, but to try to ban it would have been a papal disaster. In 1693 Innocent XII, pope from 1691 to his death in 1700—the year that Rancé died—who was neither Dominican nor Franciscan but a doctor of civil and canon law, extended the feast to the whole church, together with an Office and an Octave. But it was not until a little later, on December 6, 1708, that Pope Clement IX promulgated the Constitution *Commissis nobis divinitus* that not only prescribed the feast for the universal church, but made it a holy day of obligation for all Christians.[19]

[18] Denzinger, *Enchiridion*, 374, no. 1516; Theodore A. Buckley, *Canons and Decrees of the Council of Trent . . . Literally Translated into English* (London: G. Routledge & Co., 1851), 24. We may compare Session VI, Canon 23; Denzinger, *Enchiridion*, 387, no. 1573; Buckley, *Canons and Decrees*, 45. For the 1477 Constitution of Sixtus IV, see n. 15 above.

[19] For the text of the Constitution, see *Bullarum diplomatum et privilegiorum sanctorum Romanorum pontificum: Taurinensis Editio* (Turin, 1871), 21:338, no. CXX: *Mandatur ut festum Conceptionis beatae Mariae Virginis Immaculatae de praecepto ubique observetur*.

The rest of the story may be briefly told, for it takes us beyond the period covered in this present study. The doctrine was defined as an article of faith for Roman Catholics by Pope Pius IX on December 8, 1854, more than five hundred years after the death of John Duns Scotus, and received huge support from two miraculous visionary experiences. One of these occurred before, one after, the papal definition.

The first took place in 1830 when Catherine Labouré (1806–1876), then a member of the nursing order of the Daughters of Charity and a woman given to visions and revelations, had a vision of the Virgin standing on a globe within an oval frame. Around the margin of the frame appeared, in French, the words *Ô Marie, conçue sans péché, priez pour nous qui avons recours à vous*, "O Mary, conceived without sin, pray for us who have recourse to you." Catherine was instructed to have a medal cast after this model and told that everyone who wore the medal would receive great graces. The Miraculous Medal proved to be a triumphant success (not least economically), it was soon associated with many miracles, and is still worn by millions of Catholics around the world.

The second series of visions, which had perhaps even greater impact on the popularity of the doctrine, were those experienced by Bernadette Soubirous (1844–1879) between February 11 and July 16, 1858. There were eighteen appearances of a young woman to whom Bernadette simply referred as *Aqueró*, "That one," in Gascon Occitan, the local patois of the Pyrenean region. But when, at the sixteenth appearance on March 25, 1858, Bernadette asked *Aqueró* several times to tell her her name, the lady eventually said, in Gascon Occitan, *Qué soï era immaculado councepcioũ*, "I am the Immaculate Conception." Bernadette's visions led to the establishment of the great Marian shrine at Lourdes, one of the most popular destinations of pilgrimage in modern times and a place associated with innumerable undisputed and miraculous cures.

It is obvious that we have now come far on our Marian journey. It began with a young Jewish girl from Galilee called

Maryam who, according to the culture and customs of first-century Judea, would have been no older than fourteen. It has ended with a Second Eve, a woman who was conceived without sin and who never sinned throughout her whole life, the ever-virgin Queen of Heaven who cooperates with her Son in the work of redemption and who is the mediatress, the *mediatrix*, of our salvation. It is obvious that after the Reformation, there would be numberless Protestants who would accept none of this, and certainly not the concepts of Mary as *mediatrix* and *co-redemptrix*. On the other hand, within the Catholic fold, it is not difficult to find those whose devotion went somewhat too far, whose language was decidedly intemperate, and whom, in some cases, the church itself found it necessary to restrain.

A good example is the seventeenth-century "French School," *L'École française*, that began with Pierre de Bérulle (1575–1629), though he cannot really be regarded as its founder. Bérulle was born in the Château de Cérilly near Troyes in 1575 and received his early education from the Jesuits. He then studied at the Sorbonne in Paris and was ordained to the priesthood in 1599. He was one of the most important leaders of the Counter Reformation in France, and in 1611 he founded the Congregation of the Oratory of Jesus and Mary Immaculate—the Oratorians—that produced a considerable number of celebrated spiritual directors and played a major role in the development of education in France. He went on to play a significant role in international politics, and was made a cardinal by Pope Urban VIII in 1627, two years before his death on October 2, 1629.

Bérulle and his followers had a profoundly pessimistic view of human nature, solidly rooted in the Augustinian doctrine of total human depravity. "The state to which we have been reduced by the sin of our first father," wrote Bérulle,

> is so deplorable that it has more need of tears than of words, more need of continual abasement of our soul before God than of any worldly speeches or thoughts that are too inconsequential to portray its reality. For in this condition, we possess the right only to nothingness and hell. We can do

> nothing but sin, and we are no more than a nothingness opposed to God, deserving of his anger and his everlasting wrath.[20]

What this means is that the incarnation, with all that it brought about, was absolutely essential. Without Christ, all that we can hope for is nothingness and hell. And what was essential for the incarnation? Mary! And when Mary said *Fiat mihi*, "Let it be done with me according to your word," that *fiat* saved the world. Indeed, says Bérulle, that *fiat* of Mary was more powerful in what it brought about than those first *fiats* uttered by God at the very beginning of creation! Those first *fiats* may have created the world, but Mary's *fiat* produced the creator of the world.[21] It can hardly be denied that we are moving into some dubious theology here.

In Bérulle's thought, Mary occupies a unique place above the highest angels and just below God, and he established a principle that becomes one of the hallmarks of the French School, that in their spiritual journey, human beings go through Mary to Christ, and through Christ to the Trinity. But Christ, the second person of the Trinity, became incarnate, emptying himself and taking the form of a servant.[22] This is fundamental to Bérulle's spirituality, and the word *servus*, in the Vulgate text that Bérulle used, may mean servant or slave. What this means is that the human nature of Jesus, stripped of his own personality, remains in a state of perfect and permanent servitude to his divine nature, and since the essence of the Christian life is the imitation of Christ, what this implies is that we must imitate Christ in his servitude. If we cannot imitate him in his divinity, we can certainly try to imitate him in his humanity.

[20] Pierre de Bérulle, *Opuscules divers de piété*, XXIX: *Œuvres complètes du cardinal de Bérulle*, ed. Jacques-Paul Migne (Paris: J.-P. Migne, 1856), 958.

[21] Bérulle, *Discours de l'état des grandeurs de Jésus*, XI.x; *Œuvres complètes*, 376.

[22] Phil 2:7.

We, therefore, must be servants—slaves—of the incarnate Christ, and Bérulle hastens to say that there is nothing abject or servile in this:

> We are born to serve the Son of God, and we are his children so that we might be his servants with greater perfection and dignity. There is nothing base, abject, or servile in the term and condition of servitude. It is, rather, the title of honor that Saint Paul puts at the head of his letters: *Paulus servus Iesu Christi* ["Paul, a servant of Jesus Christ"].[23] It is the first term used by the Christians and the apostles to express their state and their duty to the Son of God. It is a servitude that does not come from fear, but from love and an excess of love, and which rejoices in the greatness and privileges of the love and charity of Jesus. It is at one and the same time filiation and servitude: filiation in grace and dignity, servitude in subjection and humility. It is a servitude formed on the servitude of Jesus, who is its model.[24]

Bérulle therefore offers himself completely to Jesus as his servant. He bids him enter into him and take total possession of his spirit and his life. He, Bérulle, seeks to become an empty vessel, filled not with himself but with nothingness, so that, in him, Christ can be all in all. With this desire, he says,

> I make to you, O Jesus my Lord, and to your deified humanity, humanity truly yours in its deification, and truly mine in its humiliation, its sorrows, and its sufferings: to you and to it I make a total, absolute, and irrevocable offering and gift of all that I am through you in being and in the order of nature and grace. . . . My wish is that my life, and all my actions, whether of nature or grace, should belong to you, as the life and actions of a slave [*esclave*], yours forever. I therefore commit myself wholly to you, O Jesus, and to your sacred humanity by the most humble and binding con-

[23] Rom 1:1; Phil 1:1.

[24] Bérulle, *Vœux à Jésus et à Marie*, XXX; *Œuvres complètes*, 623.

> dition I know, which is the condition and relationship of servitude.[25]

Such extravagant statements did not sit well with many of Bérulle's contemporaries, who saw in this not only a denial of Scripture, but also a denial of the essential nature of human freedom. Did not Christ say, "I will not now call you servants (*servos*), because a servant does not know what his master is doing. But I have called you friends (*amicos*)"?[26] But Bérulle goes further. The redeeming power of the incarnate Word is indeed central to his thought, but who was responsible for incarnating that Word? The blessed Virgin! And her incomparable dignity as Mother of God allows Bérulle to make to her the same vow of total servitude that he makes to her divine Son:

> I offer and subject myself, I devote and dedicate myself to Jesus Christ, my Lord and Savior, in a state of perpetual servitude to his most holy Mother, the blessed Virgin Mary. To the perpetual honor of the Mother and the Son, my wish is to be in a state and quality of servitude with regard to her whose state and quality is to be the Mother of my God, so that I might honor this quality, so high and so divine, in a more humble and holy way. I therefore give myself to her in the quality of a slave (*esclave*) in honor of the gift that the eternal Word made of himself in the quality of Son, through the mystery of the incarnation that he wished to bring about in her and through her.[27]

We have now moved from servitude to slavery, and if there was opposition to the idea of the former, there was even greater opposition to the idea of the latter. Bérulle, in fact, had no difficulty in defending himself against any accusation of Mariolatry,

[25] Bérulle, *Grandeurs de Jésus*, II.xii; *Œuvres complètes*, 181, 182.

[26] John 15:15.

[27] Bérulle, *Élévation III à Dieu en l'honneur de la sainte Vierge*, 10; *Œuvres complètes*, 527.

but it is easy to see how such intemperate language could be misunderstood and misinterpreted. It would become even more intemperate with some of Bérulle's followers.

Jean-Jacques Olier (1608–1657), for example, the founder of the Society of Saint-Sulpice and of the renowned Seminary of Saint-Sulpice in Paris, uses expressions which, as Hilda Graef has said, are "far less sober."[28] The main source for Olier's ideas on Mary is a volume compiled by Étienne-Michel Faillon (1799–1870), a Sulpician priest and historian, and published at Rome in 1866 with the title *The Inner Life of the Most Holy Virgin, a Work drawn from the Writings of M. Olier*.[29] This was a very rare work—Hilda Graef was unable to find a copy—but has now been digitized by Google and is readily available on the Internet.

Olier has no hesitation in referring to Mary as the spouse (*épouse*) of God the Father, and if, as we saw in Chapter Two, Germanus of Constantinople was prepared to say that Christ, as Mary's son, did what his mother told him in the matter of mediation,[30] Olier goes even further. Before the world came into being, he says, God the Father predestined us to be members of the body of Christ, his Son:

> But in calling each one of us in this way, and in preparing from all eternity the measure of the inward and outward means of sanctification that he would give us in time, God consulted with his holy spouse, whom he kept present to his Spirit. He saw in essence what would have gratified her with regard to each one of us, what could have pleased her, if she had been in the world, and he acted in accordance with Mary's intentions, in keeping with the divine decrees, and in accordance with her desires that he had already foreseen.

[28] Hilda Graef, *Mary: A History of Doctrine and Devotion*, 2 vols. (London: Sheed & Ward, 1963–1965), 2:35.

[29] Étienne-Michel Faillon, *Vie intérieure de la Très-Sainte Vierge, ouvrage recueilli des écrits de M. Olier* (Rome: Salviucci, 1866).

[30] See chap. 2, n. 20.

> He did this to please and indulge her, always examining and seeking what was most in keeping with her inclinations.[31]

In other words, God the Father brings about our salvation in accordance with the desires of his spouse, Mary—an extraordinary view that can hardly be called orthodox.

Just as extraordinary is Olier's view of Mary's conception of Jesus. Olier wishes to keep her immaculate in every possible way, and pregnancy and childbirth are a messy business. So what he says is that although Mary conceives Jesus, she takes no active part in this conception:

> When the blood that was necessary for the formation of a child had been prepared by the Holy Spirit, but was still the blood of Mary and about to pass into a human being like her, this divine Spirit, who was concealed in the midst of the blood, offered it up to the eternal Father in the same way that he would later offer up the blood of Jesus Christ for the redemption of the human race. And this he did in such a way that the Most Blessed Virgin, in whom these things, wonderful and incomprehensible to us, now came to pass, was purely passive (*purement passive*) in this operation, all of which was taking place only in her presence and in her person.[32]

And what is it that Mary conceives?

> Mary does not conceive a child, but a perfect human being. When God the Father begat the incarnate Word, he made him a perfect human being at that very moment. That is to say, as perfect in the light of his reason and as advanced in his wisdom (in which, properly speaking, lie the essential features of human life) as he would be at the age of thirty-three, which was how old he was at his death. Then, too, he poured into him "the fullness of the treasures of his wisdom

[31] Faillon, *Vie intérieure*, 63.

[32] Faillon, *Vie intérieure*, 205.

> and his knowledge."[33] "The woman encompasses the man,"[34] as it says in Scripture: this is the perfect man *par excellence*, of whom Adam, created perfect, was no more than a trifling figure that indicated what would be the wisdom of Jesus Christ at his birth, his perfection and his perfect likeness to God. For the second man does not simply resemble God, as did Adam, but is his essential image and his very essence.[35]

These are undoubtedly dangerous ideas. Apart from contradicting Luke 2:52, which states that Jesus "advanced in wisdom and age," it may also throw some doubt on the true nature of Mary's motherhood, and, indeed, on the true humanity of her son. Some early Fathers might have seen a trace of docetism here.

This is obviously not the place for an extended discussion of Olier's Marian views, tempting though it may be, and enough has been said to show how very easily devotion to the Mother of God could get out of hand. One final example will suffice, that of Henri-Marie Boudon (1624–1702), archdeacon of Évreux and follower of Olier. In 1662 he published a substantial volume of more than five hundred pages with the title *Dieu seul: Le saint esclavage de l'admirable Mère de Dieu*, "God Alone: The Holy Slavery of the Admirable Mother of God," in which he took the ideas of Pierre de Bérulle to their logical and sometimes startling conclusions. The slavery of which he speaks is not just the slavery of Mary to God, but of Boudon (and us) to Mary. And what is a slave? A slave, he says, is someone who owns nothing, not even himself, for all that he has and all that he is belongs to his Lord and Master.[36] Thus, to be a slave to the Mother of God means that

[33] Col 2:3.

[34] Jer 31:22.

[35] Faillon, *Vie intérieure*, 210.

[36] Henri-Marie Boudon, *Dieu seul: Le saint esclavage de l'admirable Mère de Dieu. Nouvelle edition* (Paris: Claude Hérissant, 1769), 6.

> We make a holy contract with the Queen of Heaven and Earth by which we consecrate our freedom to her so as to become one of her slaves, letting her be the absolute mistress of our heart, giving up to her whatever rights we have from all our good actions, dedicating ourselves entirely to the service of her greatness, and professing this in the strongest terms. Thus, whatever goods are possessed by those who are true slaves of the glorious Virgin—wealth or property, good qualities of body and mind—are no longer theirs, but belong to their good mistress, in such a way that they can dispose of them only in accordance with her holy will.[37]

As with Bérulle, there were many—not just Jansenists and Protestants—who thought this devotion went too far, and complaints were made to Rome. The result was that the Holy See prohibited the devotion of "slavery" since it could too easily give rise to abuses.[38] Boudon himself was well aware of this, and despite some of his more extravagant statements he was no Mariolater. His watchword was *Dieu seul*, "Only God."[39] Indeed, in 1678 he published another book with the title *Avis catholiques touchant la véritable dévotion de la bienheureuse Vierge*, "Catholic Opinions with regard to True Devotion to the Blessed Virgin," and in his preface "To the Reader" he explains why the book was necessary. It is his interest in proclaiming God alone, God alone, God alone, he says, and nothing more

> that prompts me to put before the public this little treatise on true devotion to his wholly pure and ever-immaculate Virgin Mother, since it is my opinion, which is not only mine but also that of the saints and doctors of the church, that God draws the greatest glory from the true veneration of the most Blessed Virgin. It all began when I was obliged to instruct

[37] Boudon, *Dieu seul*, 6–7.

[38] See Pierre Pourrat, trans. Donald Attwater, *Christian Spirituality: Later Developments. Part II: from Jansenism to Modern Times* (Westminster, MD: Newman Press, 1955), 118, 121–22.

[39] See Pourrat, *Christian Spirituality*, 115–17.

> the country people about this veneration, and I knew from my own experience how necessary it was. For I can truthfully say that when I was questioning these people on this subject, they often told me that the holy Virgin was on the same level as God himself, or even higher![40]

But let us now leave aside these baroque excesses, return to the Middle Ages, and see what the Cistercian writers have to say about Mary. After that we shall return to the seventeenth century, but to a world very different from that of Bérulle, Olier, or Henri-Marie Boudon.

[40] Henri-Marie Boudon, *Avis catholiques touchant la véritable dévotion de la bienheureuse Vierge*, "Au lecteur"; *Œuvres complètes de Boudon, Grand Archidiacre d'Évreux*, ed. Jacques-Paul Migne (Paris: J.–P. Migne, 1856), 2:325–26, *autant ou plus que Dieu même*.

Part Two

The Cistercians

Chapter Five

Cistercian Beginnings and Bernard of Clairvaux

Let us begin by recapitulating the major themes discussed in the last four chapters. For the supposed details of much of Mary's birth, life, and death, we are dependent upon the apocryphal *Protevangelium of James* and a variety of later Dormition / Assumption narratives. Following these, Mary is associated with six important titles: Ever Virgin, Second Eve, *Mediatrix, Co-Redemptrix*, the crowned Queen of Heaven, and Star of the Sea. She was a woman who, by God's grace, never sinned, and who was either conceived or born immaculate, cleansed from original sin, *Mater intemerata*. All these themes will reappear in the course of the following pages.

We might note here that, should anyone wish for more detail on the life of the Virgin, they will find it in the six volumes of Maria of Ágreda's *Mystical City of God: The Divine History and Life of the Virgin Mother of God*, first published in Spanish in 1670. The author was a Spanish nun, Maria de Jesús, who lived from 1602 to 1665, and was abbess of the monastery of the Immaculate Conception in her hometown of Ágreda. Throughout her life, she was associated with visions and paramystical phenomena, and it was in visions that the Mother of God herself revealed to Maria the story of her entire life, from immaculate conception to death and corporeal assumption, in the minutest detail. The whole book, as Hilda Graef has said, is "a hodgepodge of apocryphal stories and her own fertile imagination,"[1] and contains descriptions and imprudent statements far more extreme than anything written by Bérulle or Olier or Boudon. It is not surprising to learn that in 1681 Pope Innocent XI forbade its reading by Roman Catholics, and in 1698, three years after it had been translated into French, it was condemned by the Sorbonne on the grounds that its rash assertions and apocryphal revelations would expose the Catholic religion to ridicule and contempt. It remains, however, remarkably popular, and English translations, both abridged and unabridged, are readily available from a variety of online bookstores.

It is therefore something of a relief to return to the sobriety of the earliest statutes of the Cistercian General Chapter, the *Capitula*, that probably date from the abbacy of Stephen Harding, who administered the abbey of Cîteaux from 1108 to his resignation in 1133.[2] The ninth *capitulum* states simply, "It has been decreed that all our monasteries should be founded in honor of the Queen of Heaven and Earth."[3] Somewhat later, probably in about 1147, this was expanded to read:

> That all monasteries are to be dedicated in honor of blessed Mary. Because our predecessors and fathers first came from the church of Molesme, [dedicated] to the honor of blessed Mary, to the place [called] Cîteaux, we therefore decree that all our churches and those of our successors shall be founded and dedicated in memory of the same Queen of Heaven and Earth, Saint Mary.[4]

[1] Hilda Graef, *Mary: A History of Doctrine and Devotion*, 2 vols. (London: Sheed & Ward, 1963–1965), 2:53.

[2] See Chrysogonus Waddell, *Narrative and Legislative Texts from Early Cîteaux: Latin Text in Dual Edition with English Translation and Notes*, Studia et Documenta, IX (Brecht: *Cîteaux – Commentarii cistercienses*, 1999), 167–75, 398.

[3] Waddell, *Narrative and Legislative Texts*, 408. The term for monasteries is *coenobia*, and the text says that they *should* be founded (*fundari debere*) in honor of Mary, not that they *must* be founded in her honor. The title "Queen of Heaven and Earth" was discussed in chap. 2.

[4] Waddell, *Narrative and Legislative Texts*, 463 (*Instituta Generalis Capituli*, XVIII). We have now moved from "should be" to "must."

The churches may be dedicated to other saints as well, but first and foremost they are to be dedicated to Mary.

Now some may think that all that is said from here on is irrelevant. After all, in 1999 there was published a volume of collected papers with the title *La Vierge dans la tradition cistercienne*, "The Virgin in the Cistercian Tradition"[5]—the papers are the printed versions of communications delivered at a conference on Mary in the Cistercian tradition held at the abbey of Orval in September 1998—so why reinvent the wheel? The problem is that the book is mistitled. It should really be "The Virgin in the Cistercian Tradition in France and Belgium," for apart from one paper on Thomas Merton, all the others are limited to authors or developments associated with continental Europe. The principal authors are Bernard, William of Saint-Thierry, Guerric of Igny, and Dom Jean-Baptiste Chautard, abbot of Sept-Fons (1858–1935). The other papers discuss Mary at Port-Royal, Marian devotion and piety, primarily in the Low Countries, the place of Mary in Cistercian liturgy, and Mary in Cistercian art. Armand-Jean de Rancé makes no appearance, but for a sad reason. Father Lucien Aubry, chaplain to the Cistercian nuns of Échourgnac and a respected writer on Rancé, was scheduled to speak on Rancé at the conference but died suddenly in June 1998 with his presentation unfinished. Since it was impossible, in the short time available, to find another person to take Father Aubry's place, another paper was substituted on Mary in contemporary Cistercian hymnody.

More significant is the lack of any discussion in this volume of the contributions of the English Cistercians, especially Aelred of Rievaulx, Stephen of Sawley, and Baldwin and John of Forde, all of whom are of first importance in the development of Cistercian attitudes to the Mother of God.

[5] *La Vierge dans la tradition cistercienne, communications présentées à la 54e session de la Société française d'études mariales, Abbaye Notre-Dame d'Orval [15–17 septembre] 1998*, ed. Paul Longère, Études Mariales, Bulletin de la Société Française d'Études Mariales (Paris: Éditions Médiaspaul, 1999).

The first paper in the volume, however, is extremely useful. It was compiled by the editor, Jean Longère, a Sulpician priest and *directeur de recherche honoraire* of the Centre National de la Recherche Scientifique, and is entitled "Elements for a Marian Cistercian Bibliography in the Middle Ages."[6] It contains bibliographical references to twenty-four authors of the twelfth and thirteenth centuries whose work contains extensive material on Mary. In the following pages, we shall deal with the contributions of the English Cistercians, introduce a number of continental writers who are absent or almost absent from the 1999 collection, and, in the third and final part, deal at some length with Armand-Jean de Rancé.[7]

There is only one place to begin, and that is with Saint Bernard, and the most obvious place to begin in Bernard is with his four homilies *in laudibus Virginis Matris*, "in praise of the Virgin Mother."[8] But first of all, who was Bernard of Clairvaux?

He was born in 1090 to a noble Burgundian family, the third of seven children, and, in due course, underwent much the usual education for his time and place. Even reading through the stained glass of hagiography, it seems clear that he was a boy of unusual devotion, especially to the Virgin Mary, and after his mother's death in 1107, he determined to enter the religious life. This he did in 1112 when he, together with thirty companions (Bernard never did anything by halves), entered

[6] *La Vierge dans la tradition cistercienne*, 13–38.

[7] We may also mention the study by E. Rozanne Elder, "Shadows on the Marian Wall: The Cistercians and the Development of Marian Doctrine," in *Truth As Gift: Studies in Honor of John R. Sommerfeldt*, ed. Marsha L. Dutton, Daniel M. La Corte, and Paul Lockey, CS 204 (Kalamazoo, MI: Cistercian Publications, 2004), 537–74, but this, too, is not what it might be. The author has much to say about Bernard and Anselm of Canterbury, who was not a Cistercian, but not a great deal about other important Cistercians. The English Cistercians merit only half a dozen pages.

[8] The most recent English translation is found in *Magnificat: Homilies in Praise of the Blessed Virgin Mary by Bernard of Clairvaux and Amadeus of Lausanne*, trans. Marie-Bernard Saïd and Grace Perigo, intro. Chrysogonus Waddell, CF 18 (Kalamazoo, MI: Cistercian Publications, 1979), 3–58.

the newly established abbey of Cîteaux. Three years later, in 1115, he was sent with twelve monks to found the new abbey of Clairvaux, and as abbot of Clairvaux he would remain until his death on August 20, 1153.

His life was nothing if not eventful. He was deeply involved in church councils, church politics, politics in general, the support of the Knights Templar, the papal schism, the second crusade, and legal procedures against those he considered heretics and/or schismatics, especially Henry of Lausanne, Gilbert de La Porrée, and Peter Abelard. He traveled constantly and was often away from Clairvaux, and he had the ear of popes and princes. The details of his life must be read elsewhere,[9] for our concern here lies not with Bernard's exploits outside the cloister, but with what he has to say about the Virgin Mary, to whom he unquestionably had the deepest devotion.

His four homilies in praise of the Virgin Mother represent his exegesis of Luke 1:26-27, *Missus est angelus Gabrihel*, "The angel Gabriel was sent from God," and so on. As Chrysogonus Waddell has said, these were written "not for any practical purpose or to answer to a precise pastoral need, but simply to satisfy the exigencies of their author's personal devotion."[10] The homilies are an early work, being preceded only by the *Steps of Humility and Pride*, and date from about 1120 when Bernard was thirty. What do they say?

The essential theme of the first homily—a theme, in fact, that runs through all of them—is the virtue of humility, and we must remember that in the Latin text used by Bernard, Mary says to Elizabeth, "My spirit has rejoiced in God my

[9] There is no recent biography of Bernard in English that is wholly satisfactory, and for those interested I would strongly recommend two old but valuable studies: the brief and incisive account by Bruno Scott James, *Saint Bernard of Clairvaux: An Essay in Biography* (London: Hodder & Stoughton, 1957), and, for those who wish to examine Bernard's life in somewhat overwhelming detail, Watkin Williams, *Saint Bernard of Clairvaux* (Manchester, UK: Manchester University Press, 1935; repr. 1953). Williams's work remains indispensable, though the source references, naturally, now need to be updated.

[10] Waddell, intro., *Magnificat*, xiii.

Savior because he has regarded the humility—*humilitatem*—of his handmaid."[11]

Bernard begins by taking the proper names Gabriel, Nazareth, and Galilee, and explaining their meaning (here he is following Jerome) in order to show where and by whom the annunciation took place. When he arrives at the section "to a Virgin espoused," he introduces the theme of the association of virginity with humility, and he continues with this to the end of the homily. "Virginity," he says, "is a commendable virtue, but humility is far more necessary. The former is a counsel, the latter a requirement."[12] Virginity is not for all, but for a few. So if you cannot imitate Mary in her virginity, imitate her in her humility! The young Jesus, who was God the Son himself, obeyed Mary and Joseph as his parents. Is not this the perfection of humility? Yet, on the other hand, she who gave birth to the God-man is exalted above all the choirs of angels. Is she proud of this? Not at all. It was her humility that rendered her virginity pleasing to God.

The second homily is rather richer in content. Here we see the doctrines of the perpetual virginity of Mary, her sinlessness, the old Eve-Mary parallelism, and, most important, her mediation. Once again, Bernard speaks of the essential place of humility, but enters upon dangerous ground when, like Jean-Jacques Olier (who is following him in this), he maintains that Jesus possessed the fullness of wisdom—indeed, he *was* Wisdom—at the very moment of his conception. "He was perfect from the beginning,"

> from the beginning, I say, he was filled with spirit of wisdom and understanding, the spirit of counsel and might, the spirit of knowledge and piety, and the spirit of the fear of the Lord.[13]

[11] Luke 1:47–48.

[12] Bernard, *In laudibus Virginis Matris, hom.* 1.5; SBOp 4:17.

[13] *In laudibus Virginis Matris, hom.* 2.9; SBOp 4:27, quoting Isa 11:2-3.

So what are we to do about Luke 2:52, the verse that tells us that "Jesus increased in wisdom"? Don't worry about that, says Bernard. This is said not of things as they were, but of things as they appeared to be, "for he never acquired anything new that he did not previously possess, but only appeared to acquire it when he himself wished it to appear."[14] In other words, although always omniscient and always full of all grace, he accommodated to the needs of those listening to him. This is a dangerous idea that casts doubt on the true nature of the incarnation, and is certainly contrary to the statement in the Dogmatic Definition issued by the Fourth Ecumenical Council, the Council of Chalcedon (451), that Christ is consubstantial with the Father as regards his divinity, and consubstantial with us as regards his humanity, "like us in all respects, except for sin."

Bernard then goes on to praise Joseph at some length—it is pleasant to see the poor man get a decent hearing—and then begins his exegesis of "and the virgin's name was Mary": "We will say a little about this name, which, being interpreted, means Star of the Sea."[15] We discussed the history of this title in Chapter Two. The idea of a star implies not only the doctrine of Mary's perpetual virginity (stars emit their light without any harm or injury to themselves), but, much more important, Mary as our helper, guide, intercessor, and *mediatrix*. The passage that follows is justly celebrated and very lovely, and we summarized it in an earlier chapter. For us who are in danger on the tempestuous seas of this world, Mary is our guiding star. If the winds of temptation arise, or if you run upon the rocks of tribulation, look to the star and call on Mary. If the vessel of your soul is beaten about by the winds of the passions, look to Mary. If you find yourself foundering in the gulfs of melancholy or despair, think on Mary:[16]

[14] *In laudibus Virginis Matris, hom.* 2.10; SBOp 4:28.
[15] *In laudibus Virginis Matris, hom.* 2.17; SBOp 4:34.
[16] Chap. 2, n. 34.

> Do not let her leave your mouth, do not let her leave your heart, and to obtain the favor of her prayer, do not forsake the example of her way of life. Following her you will not go astray, calling on her you will not despair, thinking on her you will not err. With her bearing you up, you will not fall, with her protecting you, you will not be afraid, with her leading you, you will not grow weary, with her looking favorably upon you, you will reach your goal.[17]

The third and fourth homilies are not quite so dramatic. The third is primarily concerned with explaining what is meant by being "full of grace," and what is meant by being "blessed among women." We too shall be blessed, he adds, if we obey the Lord's commands: "Do what Jesus says, and he will count you among his people."[18] But this obedience is threefold. We must obey what he commands in the gospels, what he commands in the Law and the Prophets, and what he commands "through his ministers who are in the church," and in this last case, we are to be subject to them not only if they are good and restrained, but also if they are *dyscolus*, which means overbearing, harsh, irritable, peevish, or (if I may be permitted to use the modern slang term) just plain PITAs.[19] Bernard ends with yet another paean in praise of humility, and this leads him to his fourth homily, in which Mary's humility is revealed in her perfect obedience.

The homily opens by making it clear that praise given to the mother touches the son, and praise for the son touches the mother. When we honor the one, we honor the other. But the most dramatic part of this homily is surely the splendid build-up to the moment that Mary says *Fiat mihi*, "Be it done with me according to your word." She has been told that she will conceive and bear a son, that it will be the work of the Holy Spirit, not a man. Will she agree? Will she accept? "The angel

[17] *In laudibus Virginis Matris, hom.* 2.17; SBOp 4:35.
[18] *In laudibus Virginis Matris, hom.* 3.11; SBOp 4:44.
[19] *In laudibus Virginis Matris, hom.* 3.11; SBOp 4:44.

is waiting for a reply, for it is time for him to return to the One who sent him. We, too, O Lady, are waiting for this merciful word, we who are wretchedly weighed down by a sentence of condemnation."[20] And so it goes on. Bernard keeps us on tenterhooks. Will she not say the word for which earth and hell and heaven are waiting? Is she the one promised, or must we look for another? Will she not consent? Will she not agree? And then finally, at last! we hear her reply: "Behold the handmaid of the Lord. Be it done with me according to your word." It really is a magnificent piece of writing.

But do we not see the quintessence of humility in those three words *Ecce ancilla Domini*, "Behold the handmaid of the Lord"? Indeed we do, for humility and divine grace always go hand in hand, says Bernard, and Mary has put the whole of herself, soul and body, at the disposal of her Creator. He then concludes by saying that he is quite sure that what he has written will not please everyone, and that some will say that what he has set down is unnecessary since everything he says has been said earlier by the Fathers of the Church. But so what? "If what has been said after the Fathers is not contrary to the Fathers, I do not see why it should displease either the Fathers or anybody else."[21]

Such, in essence, is Bernard's Marian teaching in the homilies in praise of the Virgin Mother. Is there anything new here? There is not. If I may quote Chrysogonus Waddell once again, the four homilies are "hopelessly unoriginal, at least as regards content. Search though you may, you will be hard pressed to discover a single idea, a single new interpretation of a biblical text. At the level of content, nothing can be found that cannot be traced to an earlier source—and inevitably a source of unimpeachable orthodoxy."[22] Bernard is the "witness to tradition."[23]

[20] *In laudibus Virginis Matris, hom.* 4.8; SBOp 4:53.

[21] *In laudibus Virginis Matris, hom.* 4.11; SBOp 4:58.

[22] Waddell, intro., *Magnificat*, xvi.

[23] See Waddell, intro., *Magnificat*, xvi–xviii.

What, then, of Bernard's other Marian works? Once again, we recognize familiar themes. In the brief notes on the annunciation that form sermon 47 of the *Sermones diversi*, for example, Bernard tells us that Mary was indeed "full of grace (*gratia*), because she is pleasing (*grata*) to God, to angels, and to human beings. To human beings by her fruitfulness, to angels by her virginity, to God by her humility. She bears witness that it is in her humility alone that she was looked upon by the Lord."[24] And Bernard then goes on to deal with the dangers of pride, the opposite of humility.

In sermon 51 of the *Sermones diversi*, Bernard deals with Mary's purification and Christ's circumcision. Did Mary need purifying? Obviously she did not. Did Christ need to be circumcised? Obviously he did not. So why was it done? It was done for us! And thereby he offers an example to the penitent, so that, "by abstaining from vices, we are first circumcised by that very abstinence, and then purified from committing them by penitence."[25] We will see the same theme of Mary's purification, not for herself but for us, in later writers who follow in these pages.

The fifty-second sermon, "On holy Mary," in the same series is more interesting. Bernard's text here is Proverbs 9:1, "Wisdom has built herself a home," a text commonly associated with the Virgin. What sort of wisdom? asks Bernard. Obviously not the wisdom of the flesh or the wisdom of this world, but the wisdom that descends from above, Wisdom itself, the Wisdom that was of God and was God—Bernard is quoting the first verse of the gospel of John—who made himself a home in the womb of the Virgin Mary.

But the Proverbs text continues: "she has carved out its seven pillars." What does this signify? The number seven equals three plus four, and the three refers to faith, because of the holy Trinity, while the four refers to morals, because of the

[24] Bernard, *De diversis, sermo* 47.1; SBOp 6/1:266.
[25] *De diversis, sermo* 51; SBOp 6/1:273.

four cardinal virtues, fortitude, prudence, temperance, and justice. Both were to be seen in the soul of Mary. The Trinity was there because the Son cannot be separated from the Father and the Holy Spirit, and the four cardinal virtues were there because, as Bernard goes on to demonstrate, "she was strong in purpose, temperate in silence, prudent in questioning, and just in bearing witness."[26] If we, then, also wish to become a home for the same Wisdom, we too must establish a house within ourselves set on the same seven columns of faith and morals, and in this we may take the Mother of God as our model.

More important than any of these brief accounts, however, is the long sermon for the birth of Mary, usually cited as the sermon on the aqueduct.[27] This is really a sermon on Mary's mediation, though most of the old themes appear again: Mary's humility, her obedience, the Eve-Mary parallel, Mary as surpassing the angels, and so on. The essential point of the sermon may be simply put: if Christ, her Son, is the Fountain of Grace, Mary is the aqueduct that brings that grace to us. The aqueduct "does not exhibit all the fullness of the Fountain, but infuses drops of grace into our parched hearts, more to some, less to others. The aqueduct itself is always full, so that others may receive from its fullness,[28] but not the fullness itself."[29] Hence the later title given to Mary: Aqueduct of Grace. As Bernard says, "Let us seek grace, and let us seek it through Mary,"[30] and again, "Let us therefore venerate this Mary from the bottom of our heart, with all our deepest affection and all our desires, for this is the will [of God], who wills that we should

[26] *De diversis, sermo* 52.4; SBOp 6/1:276.

[27] The most recent English translation is found in *Bernard of Clairvaux: Sermons for the Autumn Season*, trans. Irene Edmonds, revised by Mark Scott, intro. Wim Verbaal, CF 54 (Collegeville, MN: Cistercian Publications, 2016), 70–84.

[28] See John 1:14, 16.

[29] Bernard, *In nativitate beatae Mariae, sermo* 3; SBOp 5:277.

[30] *In nativitate beatae Mariae, sermo* 8; SBOp 5:280.

have everything through Mary."[31] According to Fr. Chrysogonus, the image of Mary as the aqueduct "seems to be Bernard's one claim to originality in the forging of marian imagery,"[32] but the story may actually be a little more complicated.

The second-century Gnostic Valentinus appears to have said that there are some who believe that Christ "passed through Mary as water through a pipe"[33]—an idea, we might add, not dissimilar from that expressed by Jean-Jacques Olier five hundred years later.[34] But when Thomas Aquinas refers to this view in the section "On the errors of Valentinus" in the *Summa contra Gentiles*, he translates it thus: "Valentinus said that Christ did not have an earthly body, but brought one down from heaven, and that he received nothing from the Virgin Mother, but passed through her as through an aqueduct."[35] It is possible, then, that the word *aquaeductus* may have been used of Mary before Bernard, but it is also possible that Thomas is simply echoing Bernard. What remains true, however, is that Bernard's own interpretation of the aqueduct as a symbol is, as Fr. Chrysogonus says, quite new, and is a rather lovely interpretation at that.

But if the imagery of the aqueduct is new, there is, as we have seen, nothing new in the theology behind it. Nor is there anything new in Bernard's other writings on Mary.[36] The same standard themes occur again and again, though the question of whether Bernard accepted the doctrine of the corporeal assumption remains open to question. That Mary is in heaven

[31] *In nativitate beatae Mariae, sermo* 7; SBOp 5:279, quoted in chap. 2, n. 31.

[32] Waddell, intro., *Magnificat*, xvii.

[33] Irenaeus of Lyon, *Contra haereses*, I.7.2; PG 7:513A. A pipe, in Greek, is σωλήν.

[34] See chap. 4, n. 32.

[35] Thomas Aquinas, *Summa contra Gentiles*, IV.30.1: *per eam quasi aquaeductum transivit*.

[36] See Waddell, intro., *Magnificat*, xiv, Graef, *Mary*, 1:235, or Luigi Gambero, trans. Thomas Buffer, *Mary in the Middle Ages: The Blessed Virgin Mary in the Thought of Medieval Latin Theologians* (San Francisco: Ignatius Press, 2005), 132–33.

as our intercessor and *mediatrix* is not in doubt, but nowhere does Bernard state explicitly that she was carried there body and soul either by angels or by her divine Son. As to his refusal to accept the doctrine of an immaculate conception as distinct from an immaculate birth, we have said enough on that matter in Chapter Three.

By far the most important role of the Virgin—apart, of course, from her giving birth to the Savior—lies in her intercessory and mediatory powers. There are few places in which this is clearer than in the sermon on the aqueduct that we have just discussed, and, in my own view, even more so in the sermon for the Sunday within the Octave of the Assumption.[37] Indeed, as Wim Verbaal says in his excellent introduction to Bernard's *Sermons for the Autumn Season*, in the entire Marian cycle of the final liturgical collection, this sermon "is the first truly Marian sermon, taking up the most central Marian themes."[38]

In this sermon, in an unusual passage, Bernard describes Mary's greatness in mystical terms. His exegesis is of Revelation 12:1, "And a great sign appeared in heaven: a woman clothed with the sun, and the moon under her feet, and on her head a crown of twelve stars," and this is what he says:

> The moon is usually taken as a symbol not only of the defect of [human] corruption, but also of human folly, and it sometimes designates the church on earth: the former because of its changeability; the latter because it receives its splendor from another source. Both of these moons, if I may put it thus, are rightly placed under the feet of Mary, one in one sense, and one in another. For if "the fool changes like the moon, the wise person continues [in wisdom] like the sun."[39] In the sun, indeed, is heat and unchanging splendor, but in the moon only splendor, and that so changeable and uncertain

[37] For the most recent English translation, see Bernard of Clairvaux, *Sermons for the Autumn Season*, 55–69.

[38] *Sermons for the Autumn Season*, xxvi.

[39] Sir 27:12.

> that it never continues in the same state.[40] Justly, therefore, is Mary represented as being clothed with the sun,[41] for she has penetrated, beyond anything we can conceive, the most profound depths of divine wisdom, so much so that she is seen to be immersed in that inaccessible light, as far as is possible for any created being without being personally united with it. [That light] is the fire that purified the prophet's lips,[42] the fire that inflames the seraphim.[43] But Mary deserves far more [than prophet or seraphim], not as one lightly touched by that fire, but as one wholly clothed with it, surrounded and enveloped by it.[44]

In other words, Mary does not become the inaccessible light—there is no "personal union"—but she is entirely clothed with it and enveloped by it. Bernard then moves on to discuss the symbolism of each of the twelve stars in Mary's crown, but we do not need to deal with all that material here.

In short, from a doctrinal point of view, there is hardly anything new in anything that Bernard has to say about Mary. He was, as we have seen, a witness to tradition, and that is what he intended to be. He and the vast majority of his contemporaries looked askance at new ideas and novelties and, in general, regarded them as both perilous and pernicious. They based themselves on the advice given to Timothy in 1 Timothy 6:20: "O Timothy, guard what has been committed to you (*depositum custodi*), avoiding the profane novelties of words (*profanes vocum novitates*) and the oppositions of knowledge falsely so-called." The contrast is between the *depositum*, which is the

[40] See Job 14:2.

[41] Rev 12:1.

[42] See Isa 6:6-7.

[43] In Hebrew, the *seraphim* are "the burning / flaming ones."

[44] Bernard, *Domina infra Octavam Assumptionis, sermo* 3; SBOp 5:264. The key passage reads *Iure ergo Maria sole perhibetur amicta, quae profundissimam divinae sapientiae, ultra quam credi valeat, penetravit abyssum: ut quantum sine personali unione creaturae condictio patitur, luci illi inaccessibili videatur immersa*. For *lux inaccessibilis*, see 1 Tim 6:16.

traditional teaching of the church, handed down from Christ to his apostles, and from the apostles to the members of the post-Apostolic College, who are the bishops of the church, and the new and profane ideas put forth by heretics such as Peter Abelard or Gilbert de La Porrée or Henry of Toulouse.

It has been calculated that, of all Bernard's authentic writings, only 3.5% are devoted to the Virgin,[45] so how does he come to be regarded as "the Marian Doctor *par excellence*"?[46] Three reasons are commonly cited. The first is because of the intensity of his devotion, though there were many others just as intensely devoted. The second is because of the beauty of his language, though not all that he wrote on the Mother of God is especially beautiful. Sometimes, as was common at the time, we have little more than a catena of biblical texts with some minor exegesis. For Bernard and his monastic contemporaries, the Latin text of the Bible was not just part of their thinking and speaking, but part of their very being. Fr. Chrysogonus has said that "Bernard was at his best when ambling through the paradise of Scriptures,"[47] but Fr. Chrysogonus was a Cistercian monk, and the Scriptures were the Paradise in which he himself loved to amble. Not being a monk myself, I would not say that Bernard was at his best here, but he was certainly at his most typical.

The third reason is the impact of a number of popular Marian writings that circulated under name of Bernard but were not written by him. The immensely popular *Planctus Mariae*, "Mary's Lament," for example, was attributed to Bernard for centuries, and it was not until 1952 that Henri Barré identified it as an extract from the "Tractates in Praise of God's Holy Mother" written by Ogier of Locedio, a far more obscure and unjustly neglected figure whom we shall consider in due

[45] Graef, *Mary*, 1:235.

[46] Henri Barré, "Saint Bernard, docteur marial," *Analecta Sacri Ordinis Cisterciensis* 9 (1953): 113.

[47] Waddell, intro., *Magnificat*, xv.

course. Indeed, it is my own view that Bernard's fame as a "Marian doctor" stems to a large extent from Bernard's fame in general. His name was well known and his writings, genuine and otherwise, circulated very widely, unlike some of those of other Cistercians. Any politician knows the importance of name recognition, and Bernard's name was recognized throughout Europe. He may not have added anything new to the development of Marian devotion, but he certainly popularized it.

And who inspired him to write what he wrote? Henri-Marie Boudon, grand archdeacon of Évreux, whom we met in Chapter Four, was in no doubt. It was Mary herself. Given that Boudon was the author of *Le saint esclavage de l'admirable Mère de Dieu*, "The Holy Slavery of the Admirable Mother of God," we will not be too surprised to find her portrayed as the force and power behind everything Bernard did. In his panegyric on Bernard, preached to an unknown congregation in an unknown year, this is what he says:

> It is the divine Mary who illumines this wholly divine man. If Bernard is indeed a man full of grace, there is nothing surprising about that, for he calls himself a nursling of the Mother of Grace.[48] If his thoughts are wholly angelic, it is because he is the favorite of the adorable Princess of the Angels. If his sermons are more pleasant to the taste than honey itself—*mel et lac sub lingua tua* ["honey and milk are under your tongue"[49]]—it is because he is suckled by her virginal milk.[50] If his actions are wholly heavenly, it is be-

[48] See Bernard, *In labore messis, sermo* 3.3; SBOp 5:223 (lines 25–27).

[49] Cant 5:11.

[50] This is a specific reference to the legend of the Lactation of Saint Bernard, when the saint was nourished by milk from the Virgin's own breast: see Léon Dewez and Albert van Iterson, "La Lactation de saint Bernard: légende et iconographie," *Cîteaux in der Nederlanden* 7 (1956): 165–89; and Patrick Arabeyre, "La Lactation de saint Bernard à Châtillon-sur-Seine: données et problèmes," in *Vies et légendes de saint Bernard de Clairvaux: Création, diffusion, réception (XII–XXe siècles). Actes des Rencontres de Dijon, 7–8 juin 1991*, ed. Patrick Ara-

> cause they are carried out under the guidance of the august and most worthy Queen of Paradise. If Bernard is a great marvel, if he is a patriarch filled with miracles, if he is the Thaumaturge of the West,[51] it is because Jesus has entrusted him to the care of her whom he uses to work his greatest wonders.[52]

At this point there are some who would say that we must now leave Bernard and move on to the "other Cistercians," but this is to impute too great a role to Bernard and to diminish the importance of those who followed him. True, they trod in Bernard's footsteps and regarded him as their master, but their own contributions were sometimes strikingly original—more so than anything that came from Bernard's pen—and they cannot be relegated to a secondary position. They deserve their own voice and their own hearing. Let us begin with William of Saint-Thierry and Guerric of Igny.

---

beyre, Jacques Berlioz, and Philippe Poirrier (Brecht and Saint-Nicolas-lès-Cîteaux: "Présence cistercienne"; *Cîteaux – Commentarii cistercienses*, 1993), 173–97.

[51] *Le Thaumaturge de l'Occident*. The title has almost certainly been taken from the penultimate page of the unpaginated preface "to the Reader" of Antoine Le Maistre's *La vie de S. Bernard, premier abbé de Clairvaux* (Paris: A. Vitré and la veuve M. Durand, 1648): "quelques Auteurs Catholiques ont eu raison de l'appeller *le Thaumaturgue de l'Occident*." The Thaumaturge of the East was Saint Gregory Thaumaturgus (ca. 213–ca. 270).

[52] David N. Bell, *A Saint in the Sun: Praising Saint Bernard in the France of Louis XIV*, CS 271 (Collegeville, MN: Cistercian Publications, 2017), 367.

Chapter Six

Two Disciples of Bernard: William of Saint-Thierry and Guerric of Igny

In this chapter we shall look at the Marian views of two of Bernard's devoted followers, one of whom spent many years at Clairvaux itself. The first is William of Saint-Thierry, Bernard's biographer and one of his closest friends, who said very little about Mary. The second is Guerric of Igny, who said a very great deal.

William was born at Liège at an uncertain date, sometime between 1075 and 1085. He was almost certainly educated at the cathedral school of Reims, and, sometime after 1111, he and his brother Simon entered the Benedictine abbey of Saint-Nicaise in Reims. Simon would go on to become abbot of Saint-Nicolas-aux-Bois, and in 1119 William was elected abbot of Saint-Thierry. His life changed when he met Bernard of Clairvaux, and the two became close friends, especially after 1125 when Bernard was convalescing at Clairvaux after a serious illness. William wished to transfer his stability to Clairvaux and adopt the Cistercian habit, but Bernard would have none of this. He required William to remain at Saint-Thierry to govern the monastery. This he did until 1135, when his desire for the contemplative life together with his physical frailty led him to resign the abbacy and seek entry into the newly founded Cistercian abbey of Signy. There he devoted himself to the liturgy, prayer, study, and writing—his poor health prevented him from doing much in the way of manual labor—and it was there that he died, probably on September 8, 1148.

William says hardly anything about Mary, and in what little he does say there is nothing new at all. But what is the reason for this? Why does this man, who at one time was actually comforted by a vision of the very Mother of God herself, say so little about her? This is what we read in the early biography of William:

> Not long after his election [to the abbacy of Saint-Thierry], William had reason to visit the city of Soissons, there to discuss certain matters with some close friends. There is a village on the way that the local inhabitants call Bazoches,[1] and while the man of God was passing nearby, he was consumed by an insurmountable desire for sleep. Therefore, being overcome with drowsiness, he settled himself down under a tree that had grown up by the roadside and fell asleep. And then he saw, standing nearby, a woman of most venerable appearance who gently took his head in her hands and laid it on her breast. And although the blessed man realized that this had occurred in his sleep, he nevertheless sensed such a holy and spiritual joy that he could not recall ever having experienced the like before. And as a result of this, when he arose from his sleep, he was so strengthened in the Lord that he required no further human comfort, and so left his journey but half completed and returned to the place from which he had started out.[2]

[1] The village of Bazoches, in the valley of the Vesle, lies about nineteen miles west of Saint-Thierry, a little over halfway to Soissons. It is now called Bazoches-sur-Vesles and must not be confused with the more famous Bazoches in central France, dominated by the huge bulk of the Château de Bazoches.

[2] David N. Bell, "The *Vita Antiqua* of William of Saint-Thierry," *Cistercian Studies [Quarterly]* 11 (1976): 248, slightly amended. This was not the only time the Virgin intervened in William's life: see Jean-Marie Déchanet, trans. Richard Strachan, *William of St Thierry. The Man and his Work*, CS 10 (Spencer, MA: Cistercian Publications, 1972), 45–46.

This is not an experience you forget in a hurry, not something easily dismissed. The Mother of God clearly played a vitally important role in William's life; so why does he say so little about her? Apart from a few incidental references, all that we have is a brief passage in the *Speculum fidei* when William is discussing faith and doubt. A faithful soul, he says, should not be concerned about fleeting moments of trepidation with regard to what it believes, for sometimes it just believes, while at other times it wants to know. Consider the Lord's Mother, "that special sign of faith."[3] Once she had received the good news of our salvation and that she would conceive by the Holy Spirit, she believed without any doubt—*certissime*—that all this would come to pass, yet she still had a question. There was something she still needed to know, namely, how this was to happen since she was a virgin: "She was accepting the fact of it by faith; she wanted to know the manner [in which it would occur]."[4]

Already, says William, she could sense the Holy Spirit at work in her in a unique way, but as to all the wonderful things he had promised, she did not know "how he could bring them about in her flesh without the help of the flesh."[5] That is when the angel tells her that the Holy Spirit will come upon her, and the power of the Most High will overshadow her.[6] And that is all. William then turns to the importance of the Spirit in our spiritual understanding of baptism and the transformation of bread and wine into the body and blood of Christ in the Eucharist. There is nothing new in this brief discussion, and we must once again raise the question of why William says so little about the Virgin.

Dom Jean-Marie Déchanet's explanation is that "we may take it that William chose to leave to St. Bernard all the glory

[3] William of Saint-Thierry, *Speculum fidei*, §59; *Guillaume de Saint-Thierry, Le Miroir de la foi*, ed./trans. Jean Déchanet, SCh 301 (Paris: Cerf, 1982), 124.

[4] *Speculum fidei*, §59; SCh 301:126.

[5] *Speculum fidei*, §59; SCh 301:126.

[6] Luke 1:35.

of worthily praising God's peerless Mother,"[7] but I cannot say that I find this suggestion persuasive. Jacques Delesalle's explanation is rather better. He points out that the sources for the Marian views of most twelfth-century writers is to be found in their sermons for the great Marian feasts: the Nativity of Mary, the Annunciation, the Purification, and so on. And how many such sermons do we have from William's pen? None at all.[8] In other words, rather than simply stating that William says hardly anything about the Virgin, we should say that he says hardly anything about her in his surviving works, and that those works in which he might have said a great deal—the Marian homilies he must have preached as abbot of Saint-Thierry—are entirely lacking.

There is also another point to be considered. Putting it crudely, William was more interested in the divinity of Christ than in his humanity, and Mary, obviously, is most closely associated with his humanity. This is what William himself says:

> If we sometimes clasp the feet of Jesus[9] in our prayer, and develop a certain quasi-corporeal affection for the form of his humanity, on the grounds that it is one person with the [divine] son of God, we do not err, but we do, nevertheless, retard and hinder spiritual prayer.[10]

[7] Déchanet, *William of St Thierry*, 46, n. 6.

[8] Jacques Delesalle, "La Vierge Marie dans les œuvres de Guillaume de Saint-Thierry," in *La Vierge dans la tradition cistercienne, communications présentées à la 54e session de la Société française d'études mariales, Abbaye Notre-Dame d'Orval [15–17 septembre] 1998*, ed. Paul Longère, Études Mariales, Bulletin de la Société Française d'Études Mariales (Paris: Éditions Médiaspaul, 1999), 107.

[9] See Matt 28:9.

[10] *Oratio domni Willelmi*, 7; CCCM 88:170; David N. Bell, "The Prayer of Dom William: A Study and New Translation," in *Unity of Spirit: Studies on William of Saint-Thierry in Honor of E. Rozanne Elder*, ed. F. Tyler Sergent, Aage Rydstrøm-Poulsen, and Marsha L. Dutton, CS 268 (Collegeville, MN: Cistercian Publications, 2015), 35.

And for William, spiritual prayer is prayer without any images: "for as long as someone praying thinks of anything corporeal in him to whom he prays, he prays devoutly (*pie*), but not wholly spiritually (*non omnino spiritualiter*)."[11] The contemplation of the humanity and passion of Christ is only a stepping-stone to something more exalted, for when we think on all the good things that Christ has done for us, we may suddenly be led to the contemplation of the Highest Good, which is beyond all images and sensory imagination.[12] For William, then, Mary's role in his theology, though not necessarily in his life, can only be secondary, for she belongs to the world of images and sensory imagination, the world that William longs to transcend and soar into that unknown, imageless, and indescribable region "where neither ground is for the feet, nor any path to follow."[13] Nevertheless, it is important that we remember Jacques Delesalle's caution: we simply do not have all the material we need to make a final and definitive judgment.

In the case of William's contemporary, Guerric of Igny, we are on much safer ground, for we have no fewer than fourteen Marian sermons: five for the feast of the Purification, three for the Annunciation, four for the Assumption, and two for the Nativity of Mary. All are available in English translation.[14] But first of all, who was Guerric of Igny?

Of his early life we know very little, and some of that is speculation, though speculation that is fairly well founded. He was born in Tournai at an unknown date—probably sometime between 1070 and 1080—and almost certainly studied at the cathedral school in that city. Whether he was taught by the celebrated Odo of Tournai, master of the school between 1087

[11] William, *In Cantica canticorum*, 17; SCh 223:90. For a more detailed discussion, see Bell, "Prayer," 25–28.

[12] See Bell, "Prayer," 27.

[13] Walt Whitman, "Darest Thou Now, O Soul," in *Leaves of Grass*.

[14] *Guerric of Igny: Liturgical Sermons*, trans. Monks of Mount Saint Bernard Abbey, 2 vols., CF 8, 32 (Spencer, MA: Cistercian Publications, 1970, 1971), 1:99–32, 2:32–54, 167–203.

and 1092, is uncertain. Equally uncertain is whether he was a canon of the Chapter of Tournai and, in due course, master of the School, though both are possible. What is certain is that while still a young man, he decided to commit himself to the solitary life and retired to a small house near the cathedral.

Sometime later, he heard about Bernard of Clairvaux, was clearly impressed with what he heard, and resolved to make his way to Clairvaux to meet its celebrated abbot. He had not intended to stay, but only to pay his respects, but Bernard appears to have recognized Guerric's potential and urged him to remain. Guerric, too, was clearly swept away by Bernard's charisma. He therefore entered Clairvaux as a Cistercian novice, probably around 1125, and would stay there for about thirteen or fourteen years.

Meanwhile, in 1128, Bernard had founded the abbey of Our Lady of Igny and had appointed Humbert, a monk of Clairvaux, to be its first abbot. Humbert did well, rather too well, in fact, and after about eight years thought that he had done quite enough to put the abbey on a secure footing, and expressed his desire to return to Clairvaux. Bernard did not agree. But Humbert, taking advantage of Bernard's absence in Italy, went back to Clairvaux anyway. Bernard, like Queen Victoria, was not amused, and wrote to Humbert threatening him with hell and damnation. Humbert, however, held fast (Bernard and he were eventually reconciled), and Igny had to elect a new abbot. Their choice fell on Guerric, who did not want the job, but since Bernard had given his approval, he had little choice in the matter. Thus, in 1138, Guerric became the second abbot of Igny. The abbey appears to have flourished under his administration, and he would govern the house for just under twenty years, dying in 1157, probably on August 19. After the vicissitudes of the French Revolution and its destruction by the Germans at the end of the First World War, the abbey church was rebuilt in 1927, and Guerric's remains are now interred there in a side chapel. His literary heritage is the series of fifty-four liturgical sermons preached to his community during his time as abbot of Igny.

Guerric, as we have said, was a monk at Clairvaux for many years and was deeply influenced by Bernard and his writings. He calls him "our master, that interpreter of the Holy Spirit."[15] We may see his influence in a multitude of places, not least in Guerric's approach to the annunciation and the assumption. Not for him the doctrine of the Immaculate Conception, but rather, echoing Bernard, "[Mary's] cleansing from original sin is placed just at the moment in which, by her free consent, the Holy Spirit comes upon her so that she conceives the Son of God."[16] Similarly, in his four sermons for the Assumption, Guerric, again like Bernard, makes it clear that Mary is with her Son in glory, and that she is enthroned as the crowned Queen of Heaven, but he gives no indication as to how she got there. It was Jesus, says Guerric, who instructed his disciples to follow the commandment to honor their fathers and their mothers,[17] and he himself does the same. To honor his Father, he descended to earth, and to honor his Mother, "I re-ascended to heaven. I ascended and prepared a place for her, a throne of glory, so that the crowned queen might sit on the right hand of the king, in gold-woven garments."[18]

But Guerric goes further, and seems to imply a sort of mystical union between mother and son. Mary's throne, says the glorified Christ, will not be a throne set apart from mine,

> but rather she will be my throne. Come, then, my chosen one, and in you I will set up my throne.[19] In you I shall establish for myself the seat of my kingdom, from you I shall decree judgments, through you I shall give heed to prayers.

[15] Guerric d'Igny, *Sermons*, ed. John Morson and Hilary Costello, trans. Placide Deseille, 2 vols., SCh 166, 202 (Paris: Cerf, 1970, 1973), 2:396.

[16] John Morson, *Christ the Way. The Christology of Guerric of Igny*, CS 25 (Kalamazoo, MI: Cistercian Publications, 1978), 62, with further discussion on pages 62–65.

[17] Matt 19:19; Mark 10:19, quoting Exod 20:12.

[18] Sermon 48.6 (second sermon for the Assumption); SCh 202:440, quoting Ps 44:10.

[19] The antiphon *in officio Sanctarum mulierum*.

> No one ministered to me more in my humility; there is no one to whom I wish to minister more abundantly in my glory. Among other things, you shared with me what made me man; I shall share with you what makes me God. You used to demand the kiss of my mouth, [but now], more than that, I shall kiss all of you with all of me. I shall not press lips to lips, but spirit to spirit in an everlasting and indissoluble kiss. Because I have longed for your beauty[20] even more than you have desired mine, I shall not see myself as being sufficiently glorified until you are glorified with me.[21]

And Guerric ends his sermon by saying, "May the glorification of your mother redound to your glory and, for us, to our forgiveness."[22]

So far as I am aware, this interpretation of Mary's enthronement and glorification is unique to Guerric, and demonstrates clearly that he was not simply a slavish imitator of his master Bernard. We may see the same thing in other areas, not least in the idea that lies at the very heart of Guerric's spirituality: the formation of Christ in us. Bernard, Guerric, and everyone else recognized, of course, that Christ had two forms, the form of his humanity, which is the form of the flesh, born of Mary, and the form of his divinity, which is the form of the Word, eternally begotten by God, the two forms being united in the mystery of the hypostatic union. But he now introduces a third form, midway between these two, that we might refer to as Christ-in-action, and he explains what he means in his second sermon for the feast of Mary's Nativity:

> Therefore, between the form of the flesh and the form of the Word, like a sort of intermediate stage [leading] from one to the other, there is another form of Christ, the spiritual form, but showing itself openly in the flesh. This is the form of the

[20] Ps 44:12.

[21] Sermon 48.6; SCh 202:440. The final verb is *conglorificeris,* "until you are co-glorified."

[22] Sermon 48.6; SCh 202:440.

> life he led in the body for the formation of those who were to believe in him.[23] For if Christ shall have been formed in us[24] by our following the example of the life and conduct he showed forth in himself, then indeed we shall be able to see not only the form that was formed for our benefit, but the very form that formed us.[25]

In this way, says Guerric, Christ has taken one form in the flesh, a second in the way he lived his life, and a third in his eternal generation. In the first form he is our brother, in the second our teacher (*magister*), and in the third our God. He took on the first form for our salvation, the second to be our example, and he will reveal himself to us in his third form as our reward. But in order for Christ to be formed in us, Mary plays a vital role. Why?

> Because she desires to form her Only-begotten in all her adopted children,[26] to whom, even though they have been begotten by the word of truth,[27] she nevertheless gives birth every day by her desire and devoted care, until they attain to the stature of a perfect human being, in the measure of the age of the fullness of her Son,[28] to whom she gave birth and brought forth once and for all.[29]

Guerric explains the matter further in his first sermon for the Assumption, where he is discussing the standard Eve-Mary parallelism.[30] The old Eve, he says, was a stepmother (*noverca*) rather than a mother, for what she handed down to her chil-

[23] 1 Tim 1:16.
[24] See Gal 4:19.
[25] Sermon 52.1 (second sermon for the Nativity of Mary); SCh 202:486–88.
[26] See Gal 4:5; Eph 1:5.
[27] Jas 1:18.
[28] Eph 4:13.
[29] Sermon 52.3; SCh 202:492.
[30] Fr. Bernard-Joseph Samain refers to paragraphs 3–5 of this sermon as Guerric's "short treatise on Mary's spiritual motherhood": see his "Guerric

dren was certain death. She may be called the mother of the living in Scripture,[31] but a more accurate title would be mother of the dying, since all she brought forth was death. It is Mary who deserves to be called the mother of the living, "for she herself, like the church of which she is the type (*forma*), is the mother of all who are reborn to life."[32]

> She is the mother of the Life by which all live, and when she brought it forth from herself, then, in a certain way, she also brought to rebirth all those who would live by that Life. One was being born, but we were all being reborn.[33] How? Because if we think of the seed that brings about that rebirth, at that very moment we were all present in him. For just as we were all in Adam from the beginning by the seed of physical birth, so, much more, [were we] in Christ before the beginning by the seed of spiritual rebirth.[34]

This is a dense passage and perhaps requires some explanation. There are three points. First, Mary gives birth to Christ, in whom, according to Saint John, was life, and who himself was the life.[35] For the second point, we need to go back to Saint Augustine's explanation of how we inherited the sin and guilt of Adam's fall. As we saw in chapter three, Augustine takes the Latin text of Romans 5:12 and reads it thus: "Through one man sin entered this world, and through sin, death, and thus death passed on to all people, for *in him* all sinned." The original Greek simply says "and thus death passed on to all people *because* all sinned." But for Augustine (and Guerric), since the whole human race was potentially present in Adam,

---

d'Igny: Court traité sur la maternité spirituelle de Marie," in *La Vierge dans la tradition cistercienne*, 109–21.

[31] Gen 3:20.

[32] Sermon 47.2 (first sermon for the Assumption); SCh 202:416–18.

[33] Both verbs are in the imperfect tense.

[34] Sermon 47.2; SCh 202:418.

[35] John 1:4; 14:6.

whatever Adam did, we did. Thus, when Adam fell and was condemned, we, too, fell and were condemned. We now come to the third point.

If the whole human race was potentially present in Adam by the seed of physical birth, then the whole human race was also potentially present in Christ by the seed of spiritual rebirth. But since Christ is eternally begotten of the Father, the human race was in Christ *ante initium*, "before the beginning," which brings us to Mary. The principle behind all this is 1 Corinthians 15:22, "And as in Adam all die, so also in Christ shall all be made alive."

Mary, obviously, is not the mother of the third form of Christ, his divine nature, but she is certainly the mother of his first form, his human nature, and it was in his first form that Jesus of Nazareth walked and talked with people, showing them by his life and example how he, Christ, could be formed in us. This, as we saw above, is Christ's second form, and if Mary had not given birth to Christ's first form, the second form would not have been possible. So just as Mary formed the first form of Christ within her womb, we form the second form of Christ within our souls, and become, as it were, little Marys. As Mary was the mother of the first form of Christ, so we are the mothers of the second form of Christ, and Guerric says so in two remarkable passages.

The first is to be found in his second sermon for Christmas, when he has been speaking of the need for the prelates of the Church to exercise motherly care over their flocks. But he then goes on to remind his monks that they, too, are mothers:

> Brothers, this name of mother is not restricted to prelates, even though they are charged in a special way with maternal care and devotion: it is also shared by you who do God's will.[36] Indeed, you too are mothers of the child who has been born for you and in you, from the moment, that is, when you conceived through the fear of the Lord and gave birth

[36] See Matt 12:50.

> to the spirit of salvation. Take care, then, oh holy mother (*o mater sancta*), take great care of this newly-born until Christ, who was born for you, be formed in you.[37] For the younger he is, the more easily can he perish for you, he who never perishes for himself. If the spirit who is in you should be extinguished in you, he returns to the God who gave him.[38]

The second passage, which is even more remarkable, is to be found at the end of Guerric's second sermon for the Annunciation, and this is what he says:

> Thanks be to you, Spirit, who breathe where you will.[39] By your gift I see not one but innumerable souls of the faithful pregnant with that noble embryo. Take care what you do, lest any of these be aborted and the divinely conceived offspring be expelled, shapeless and dead. You too, O blessed mothers (*o matres beatae*) of such a glorious offspring, watch over yourselves until Christ be formed in you.[40] Take care that no violent blow from outside should injure this delicate fetus, that you do not introduce into your womb—that is, your soul—anything that might extinguish the spirit you have conceived. If you do not spare yourselves, be sure to spare the Son of God in you. Spare him, I say, not only from evil deeds and words, but also from harmful thoughts and deadly pleasures that must clearly stifle the seed of God.[41] Take great care to guard your heart, for from it life will come forth,[42] that is to say, when everything has come to term, the childbirth will take place, and the life of Christ that is now hidden in your hearts[43] will be shown forth in your mortal flesh. You have conceived the spirit of salvation, but you are

[37] Gal 4:19.

[38] Sermon 8.5 (third sermon for Christmas); SCh 166:198. For the last few words, see Eccl 12:7.

[39] John 3:8.

[40] Gal 4:19.

[41] See Matt 22:16.

[42] Prov 4:23.

[43] Col 3:3.

> still in labor and have not yet given birth. If there is travail in giving birth, there is great comfort in the hope of an offspring. A woman in labor is in distress, but when she has brought forth her child she will no longer remember the anguish in her joy that a man, Christ, will be born in the outer world of our body,[44] which we commonly call a microcosm (*minor mundus*).[45] For he who is now conceived, God in our spirits, conforming them to the Spirit of his charity, will then be born as man in our bodies, conforming them to the body of his glory[46] in which he lives and is glorified, God, for ever and ever.[47]

In other words, it is through Mary, the mother of the first, physical form of Christ, that we become mothers of the second, spiritual form of Christ. Thus, in introducing the spiritual form of Christ, Guerric gives Mary a far more significant role in the process of salvation than she has in Bernard and so many others, where her role is essentially one of intercession and mediation. For Guerric, the heart of the spiritual life lies in the birth of Christ in us according to his spiritual form, and that spiritual form—Christ's birth in our souls—is achieved by imitating him and his mother in their life and conduct or, putting it another way, by pursuing a life of Christian virtue. But is there any one virtue more important than any other? There is indeed. It is that virtue so lauded by Bernard and everyone else: humility. But Guerric emphasises the need for humility with even greater vehemence than his master.

"Upon whom shall I rest," asks God, "if not with the humble and the quiet?" Guerric is quoting the Old Latin version of Isaiah 66:2, which he could have found in a multitude of au-

[44] See John 16:21.

[45] The term was common and goes back to the time of Plato. It appears in Jerome, *In Ezechielem*, I, on Ezek 1:7; PL 25:22C, and very many times thereafter. See also p. 143, n. 2, of the second volume of the Morson / Costello edition of Guerric's *Sermons*.

[46] The expression is borrowed from Vigils for the first Sunday of Advent.

[47] Sermon 27.5 (second sermon for the Annunciation); SCh 202:140–44.

thors from Cyprian of Carthage to Bernard himself. "In all I sought rest," God continues, "but I found it with a humble handmaid."[48] In Mary was found the fullness of humility, which is why the fullness of the Godhead was pleased to dwell within her. But then Guerric brings us back again to Christ. Mary might have been humble, but Christ was far more humble. Mary showed her humility by laying aside all vestiges of self-will and saying to the angel, "Be it done with me according to your word." Christ showed his humility in a way incomparably greater by emptying himself and taking the form of a servant.[49] What was the purpose of the incarnation? The answer, as John Morson rightly says, is that "God has become a citizen of earth that man may be a citizen of heaven,"[50] which is an old patristic idea admirably expressed in the words of Athanasius the Great in the fourth century: "God became human that in him we might become God."[51] It is the essence of what the Orthodox Church calls *theiosis* or deification.

If, like Naaman the leper,[52] we wish to be perfectly cleansed, we must imitate Christ in his humility, and that involves imitating him in no less than seven different ways. First, from being rich Christ became poor. Second, he took poverty to the extreme and was laid in a manger. Third, he was subject to his mother. Fourth, he bowed his head before one of God's servants, John the Baptist. Fifth, he put up with a disciple who he knew was both thief and traitor. Sixth, he was meek before an unjust judge. And seventh, he was so forgiving that he interceded with his Father for those who were putting him to death.[53] How are we to imitate all this? Guerric tells us, but we must remember that it is an abbot speaking to his monks:

[48] Sermon 49.4 (third sermon for the Assumption); SCh 202:452.

[49] Phil 2:7.

[50] Morson, *Christ the Way*, 51.

[51] Athanasius of Alexandria, *Ad Adelphium*, 4; PG 26:1077A.

[52] See 2 Kgs 5:1-14.

[53] Sermon 14.7 (fourth sermon for the Epiphany); SCh 166:302.

> You will follow in this giant's footsteps, even if from a long way off, if you love poverty, if you choose to be in the last place among the poor, if you subject yourselves to the discipline of the monastery, if you place yourselves under the orders of a superior who is younger than you, if you put up with false brethren patiently,[54] if you conquer by meekness when you are judged, if you repay with charity those who make you suffer unjustly.[55]

This is the humility that opens for us the doors of heaven and that forms Christ in our souls. But without Mary, we would have no one to imitate. For both Bernard and Guerric, she is the *Mater misericordiae*, the Mother of Mercy, a title that does not mean just "merciful mother," but, as John Morson puts it, "the Mother of the One who is not only God's supreme expression of mercy, but is himself the 'Mercy of God.' "[56] But Mary is, of course, merciful in herself, and when we fall, as fall we surely shall, she will be our intercessor and our *mediatrix*.[57] It is through Mary that the divine Christ will give heed to our prayers.[58]

Guerric's thought on the role of Mary breaks new ground, as also does his concept of the second, spiritual form of the body of Christ. Indeed, in this last we may see the hesitant beginnings of ideas that would come to full fruition in the teachings of Meister Eckhart and the Rhineland mystics. My own view of the matter—and I am aware that in stating this I shall be led out and stoned in some public place—is that in what he says of the spiritual motherhood of Mary and her

[54] See RSB 7.43.

[55] Sermon 14.7; SCh 166:302.

[56] Morson, *Christ the Way*, 69. For more detail, see 69–71. So far as I can ascertain, the earliest securely datable use of this title appears in Rabanus Maurus, *De passione Domini*, vi; PL 112:1428B, dating from the first half of the ninth century.

[57] See Morson, *Christ the Way*, 107–13.

[58] See Sermon 48.6; SCh 202:440, quoted at n. 21 above.

desire that we too, all of us, should become mothers, it is Guerric rather than Bernard who deserves the title of the Marian doctor.

When William died in 1148, Bernard was still alive. He would live for another five years before going to meet his Maker at Clairvaux on August 20, 1153. Guerric would survive him by exactly four years, and it is most probable—though it has also been disputed—that on his death in 1157 he was succeeded as abbot of Igny by another of Bernard's biographers, his former secretary and companion on his travels, Geoffrey of Auxerre. But apart from his significant contributions to the *Vita prima* of Saint Bernard, Geoffrey (if we are to believe the late Professor Ferruccio Gastaldelli) had some quite remarkable things to say about Mary, not least on the question of her Immaculate Conception, a doctrine, it will be remembered, for which Bernard himself had no time at all. This is important, and we must examine the matter with some care in our next chapter.

Chapter Seven

Bernard's Secretary and Biographer: Geoffrey of Auxerre

Ferruccio Gastaldelli was born in 1927 and ordained in June 1954. He was a diocesan priest of the diocese of Macerata in central Italy, and for many decades a professor in the Facoltà di Lettere e Filosofia, Faculty of Letters and Philosophy, at the University of Macerata. He was immensely learned, a superb Latinist, and a meticulous editor, and he died at Macerata in 2011 in his mid-eighties. He spent much of his scholarly life in presenting Geoffrey of Auxerre and his writings in a new light, and it was he who was responsible for the publication, in 1974, of the two volumes of Geoffrey's idiosyncratic but extremely interesting commentary on the Song of Songs.[1]

If Professor Gastaldelli is right, Geoffrey goes considerably beyond Bernard in what he has to say about the corporeal assumption of the Mother of God, and directly contradicts him in what he has to say about the doctrine of the Immaculate Conception. It will be understood, therefore, that it is with some trepidation that I must present the argument that in his presentation of Geoffrey's views on the Immaculate Conception, Professor Gastaldelli is, in fact, quite wrong. But first of all, who was Geoffrey of Auxerre?

[1] *Goffredo di Auxerre, Expositio in Cantica Canticorum*, ed. Ferruccio Gastaldelli, Temi e Testi 20 (Rome: Edizioni di Storia e Letteratura, 1974), cited below as *Expositio*.

The exact date of his birth in Auxerre is unknown, but it must have been somewhere around 1120, perhaps a year or two earlier. In due course he was ordained and moved to Paris, where he attended the lectures of Peter Abelard. These had a deep impact on his way of thinking and his exegesis, and rather than seeing in Geoffrey's writings the old reliance on accepted patristic authorities, we see a more individualistic mode of biblical interpretation based on theology and philosophy. Scripture, of course, remains as its basis, but Geoffrey's approach to Scripture is decidedly his own.

He was certainly in Paris when Bernard came there in 1140 and preached his celebrated sermon on conversion—*De conversione ad clericos*—and the impact of this sermon was to lead Geoffrey, together with a number of companions, to leave the Schools of Paris and make their way to the gates of Clairvaux. This was early in 1141 and is the first precise date we have in the life of Geoffrey. He was probably in his early twenties.

After taking the Cistercian habit at Clairvaux, Geoffrey was appointed secretary or *notarius* to Bernard and, between 1145 and 1148, accompanied him on a number of his journeys. He was with him in Languedoc in 1145, and again in 1146–1147 when Bernard was preaching the Second Crusade in various cities in France and the Rhineland. He was also present at the Council of Reims in 1148 and took an active part in the discussions relating to the supposed errors of Gilbert de la Porrée / Gilbert of Poitiers.

According to the abbé Paul-Louis Péchenard, whose nineteenth-century history of the abbey of Igny remains indispensable, Geoffrey was then elected abbot of Igny in 1157 and governed the house until 1161.[2] In this, Péchenard was following a number of ancient authorities,[3] and an abbot Gaufridus

[2] Paul-Louis Péchenard, *Histoire de l'abbaye d'Igny de l'Ordre de Cîteaux, au Diocèse de Reims, avec pièces justificatives inédites* (Reims: Imprimerie coopérative de Reims, 1883), 89–110.

[3] See Watkin Williams, *Saint Bernard of Clairvaux* (Manchester: Manchester University Press, 1935; repr. 1953), 376–82.

certainly appears in the cartulary of Igny for the years 1157, 1158, 1159, and 1161 (Old Style).[4] More recently this has been challenged, primarily on the grounds that Geoffrey was a common name, and we cannot be certain that the Geoffrey mentioned was Geoffrey of Auxerre. Personally, I see no reason not to follow the thirteenth-century *Chronicon Clarevallense*, the Chronicle of Clairvaux, that tells us that in 1162 Geoffrey, the former abbot of Igny, was elected fourth abbot of Clairvaux for a period of about four years,[5] but was forced to resign the position for reasons that are not entirely clear.[6] According to the Chronicle, he had aroused antagonism in certain quarters, but the Chronicle adds that this may have been just or unjust, *juste sive unjuste*.[7]

Whatever the facts of the matter, Geoffrey resigned the abbacy and, again according to the Chronicle of Clairvaux, spent some time in contemplation before being appointed abbot of Fossanova near Rome in 1170, and then abbot of Hautecombe near Aix-les-Bains in Savoy in 1176.[8] According to Péchenard, it was "in this charming solitude, situated on the lovely waters of Lake Bourget," that Geoffrey ended his days in about 1188,[9] but the more recent researches of Gastaldelli have shown clearly that he must actually have survived until the first years of the 1200s.[10]

Of Geoffrey's numerous writings (some of which still remain in manuscript), the best known, obviously, is his contri-

[4] See Péchenard, *Histoire*, 90, n. 2.

[5] *Chronicon Clarevallense*; PL 185:1247C. The text adds that Geoffrey was a most learned man who wrote a commentary on the Song of Songs and many other books and sermons. There can be no doubt of whom we are speaking here.

[6] See Adriaan H. Bredero, "Thomas Becket et la canonisation de saint Bernard," in *Thomas Becket: Actes du Colloque International de Sédières, 19–24 août 1973*, ed. Raymonde Foreville (Paris: Beauchesne, 1975), 59–60.

[7] PL 185:1248A.

[8] PL 185:1249A.

[9] Péchenard, *Histoire*, 107.

[10] See Ferruccio Gastaldelli, "The Marian Reflections of Geoffrey of Auxerre," *Cistercian Studies Quarterly* 52 (2017): 182.

bution to the *Vita prima* of Saint Bernard, but that is not our concern here. We are concerned with certain sermons edited by Gastaldelli, as he thought for the first time, and with a few passages in Geoffrey's commentary on the Song of Songs.

The sermons were not, in fact, edited for the first time by Professor Gastaldelli, but had been edited more than thirty years earlier by the Spanish Claretian José María Canal, who published not a critical but a diplomatic edition, with useful notes, of all the relevant sermons, together with certain others.[11] His edition, based on Troyes, *Bib. mun.*, MS 503 (from Clairvaux), contains six sermons for the Assumption and six sermons for the Nativity of Mary, and there is only one sermon in which Gastaldelli's edition is significantly different. That is the sermon on the woman clothed with the sun, for which Canal's edition,[12] based only on the Troyes manuscript, is incomplete. The sermon on Mary's Nativity that appears in Geoffrey's commentary on the Song of Songs was also edited by Canal.[13] Gastaldelli appears to have been unaware of this earlier edition. There are no sermons on Mary's conception, since that feast was introduced into the Cistercian calendar only in 1356.[14]

Gastaldelli's own critical editions of the sermons, with an extensive commentary, were published in two articles, both in Italian, that appeared in 2004 and 2006. The first bore the title "A Twelfth-Century Avant-Garde Mariology: The Immaculate Conception and Corporeal Assumption of Mary according to Geoffrey of Auxerre,"[15] and the second, "The Sermon 'On the

[11] José María Canal, "El Marial inédito de Gaufredo de Auxerre (m. c. 1178)," *Ephemerides Mariologicae* 19 (1969): 217–77.

[12] Canal, "Marial," 247–48.

[13] Canal, "Marial," 266–70.

[14] See Gastaldelli, "Marian Reflections," 176.

[15] Ferruccio Gastaldelli, "Une mariologia d'avanguardia nel secolo XII: Immacolata concezione e Assunzione corporea di Maria secondo Goffredo d'Auxerre," in *Figure poetiche e figure teologiche nella mariologia dei secoli XI e XII*, ed. Clelia M. Piastra and Francesco Santi (Florence: Galluzzo, 2004), 71–107.

Woman Clothed with the Sun' by Geoffrey of Auxerre and a Comparison with Saint Bernard."[16]

Then, in 2009, Professor Gastaldelli published a third article, "The Marian Reflections of Geoffrey of Auxerre: With an Unedited Sermon,"[17] that summarized his earlier work while adding a few further insights. Before his death in 2011, the professor submitted this article to *Cistercian Studies Quarterly* in the hope that it might be translated into English and that his reflections might reach as wide an audience as possible. The article was excellently translated by Fr. Elias Dietz of the abbey of Gethsemani and published in 2017.[18] But more than that, the same issue of the journal also contains very sound English translations by Sr. Grace Remington of Mississippi Abbey of four of the essential sermons edited by Gastaldelli: the sermon on Proverbs 11:16 for the Assumption, the sermon on "the woman clothed with the sun" from Revelation 12:1, the sermon on the calling of the bride in the Song of Songs, and the sermon on Sirach 24:11-12 for Vespers for the feast of the Assumption.[19] There is as yet no English translation of the important sermons that appear in Geoffrey's commentary on the Song of Songs, but there is a good French translation,[20] though now out of print.

We shall begin our examination of Gastaldelli's suggestions with what he has to say about the doctrine of the Immaculate

[16] Ferruccio Gastaldelli, "Il sermone 'De muliere amicta sole' di Goffredo d'Auxerre e un confronto con san Bernardo," in *Maria, l'Apocalisse e il Medioevo: Atti del III Convegno Mariologico della Fondazione Ezio Franceschini, Parma 10–11 maggio 2002*, ed. Clelia M. Piastra and Francesco Santi (Florence: Galluzzo, 2006), 59–79.

[17] Ferruccio Gastaldelli, "La riflessione mariana di Goffredo d'Auxerre: Con un sermone inedito," *Theotokos* 17 (2009): 479–99. The sermon was not actually unedited; it had been edited by Canal in 1969.

[18] Gastaldelli, "Marian Reflections," 161–86.

[19] Pages 187–97, 199–203, 205–12, and 213–20.

[20] *Geoffroy d'Auxerre: Exposé sur le Cantique des Cantiques*, 2 vols., trans. Pierre-Yves Emery, Pain de Cîteaux 27–28 (Oka: Abbaye cistercienne Notre-Dame-du-Lac, 2008–2009).

Conception, for if he is right in what he says, Geoffrey not only directly contradicts Bernard, whose polemical letter to the canons of Lyon leave us in no doubt on the matter,[21] but is the earliest Cistercian to defend the doctrine.

The first passage he considers appears in the homily on the calling of the bride, which is an exegesis of Song of Songs 4:7-8, "You are wholly beautiful, my love, and there is no stain in you. Come from Lebanon, my bride," and so on.[22] Mary is beautiful, says Geoffrey, in her birth, in her conceiving and giving birth to the Son of God, and in being assumed and raised up to him at her death. And when it says in the Song of Songs 4:7 that "there is no stain in you" (*macula non est in te*), this obviously means that Mary was free from original sin. That, as we have seen, is standard teaching, but the question here is not whether she was cleansed or freed from original sin, but whether she was conceived without it. Gastaldelli's key text states that Satan, "who is lying in wait for you, did not prevail over any part of you, the least or the most, for you forcefully crushed his whole head,"[23] and this, he says, "is a clear declaration that Mary was never touched by sin either in conception or at the end of her life."[24] Gastaldelli's statement is incorrect. The sentence certainly declares that Mary was *sine macula*, "without stain," but not that she was conceived without original sin. Indeed, had she been conceived without original sin, there would have been no satanic head for her to crush.

Further to this, let us consider two passages from two other sermons of Geoffrey, one from that on the woman clothed with the sun, the other from that on Sirach 24:11-12. In the first of

[21] See chap. 3.

[22] Gastaldelli, "Une mariologia d'avanguardia," 99–102; Canal, "Marial," 237–42.

[23] Gastaldelli, "Une mariologia d'avanguardia," 100, lines 37–38; Canal, "Marial," 238, lines 48–50: *Ille tibi insidians, nec in minima vel extrema qualibet parte praevaluit, quia tu omne caput eius viriliter contrivisti*, referring to Gen 3:15.

[24] Gastaldelli, "Marian Reflections," 177.

these Geoffrey, following Revelation 12:1, tells us that the woman—Mary—is not only clothed with the sun, but is also crowned with twelve stars, four of which pertain to her body, four to her soul, and four to both body and soul. The four that pertain to the body are that she conceived Jesus virginally, gave birth to him while preserving her virginity, suckled him in purity, and, being freed from death, ascended to heaven without delay (*sine dilatione*).[25]

The four stars that pertain to the soul are, first, the greatness of her faith, second, the way she kept everything that the shepherds had been told in her heart and pondered on it, third, the sword that pieced her soul at her son's passion, and, fourth, her compassion and intercession for those in misery that are so prompt, loving, and effective.

But of the four stars that pertain to both body and soul the most important is the first: Mary's prevenient sanctification (*sanctificatio praeventa*) in her mother's womb, "either from all time or, if we entertain the notion put forward by certain sciolists, from [the time of] the angelic salutation."[26] The other three are the fact that she was not bound by any ignorance or offence, that she was not only free from guilt but full of grace and perfect in every virtue, and that she was assumed into heaven in body and soul to a place higher than the angels. But why do I use the somewhat obscure English word *sciolist*? The answer is important.

It reflects Geoffrey's own use of the term in the sermon when he speaks of the opinion or notion put forward by *quibusdam sciolis*, but the translation that appears in *Cistercian Studies Quarterly*—"by certain knowledgeable people"—is misleading.[27] *Sciolus*, just like *sciolist* in English, was a pejorative term,

[25] Gastaldelli, "Il sermone 'De muliere amicta sole'," 78, line 44.

[26] Gastaldelli, "Il sermone 'De muliere amicta sole'," 78, lines 67–69: *quod in utero matris sanctificatione praeventa; quod vel omni tempore vel, si quibusdam sciolis morem gerimus, ab angelica salutatione sine ulla quamlibet levissima vixit ignorantia vel offense.*

[27] "The Sunday within the Octave of the Assumption of Mary, on the Words 'The woman clothed with the sun,'" *Cistercian Studies Quarterly* 52 (2017): 202.

and referred to someone with a smattering of knowledge, a pretender to learning, a pseudo-scholar, and the unquestionable implication of Geoffrey's comment is that he himself does not believe for a moment that Mary's prevenient sanctification dated from the time of Gabriel's visit. She was cleansed at the very moment of her conception.

To the matter of Mary's bodily assumption we shall return in due course, but the idea of her prevenient sanctification in her mother's womb is precisely in accord with Bernard's own teaching: there was an immaculate birth, but not an immaculate conception. Indeed, if Mary had been conceived without original sin, what need would there have been for any prevenient sanctification?

Turning now to the second sermon, that on Sirach 24:11-12, Geoffrey is here explaining what it means when Mary, taking to herself the words of Wisdom, says, "In all these things I sought rest." We are not speaking here of any temporal rest, says Geoffrey, but rest in the Lord's inheritance. "For more than all mortals except the Son, she alone sought rest in all things, who, having been sanctified from original sin before she was born, committed no actual [sin] whatever."[28] As José María Canal points out, this is a direct reference to Bernard's letter to the canons of Lyon, and an outright rejection of the doctrine of the Immaculate Conception.[29] This is the prevenient sanctification mentioned in the sermon on the woman clothed with the sun, and is also echoed in the homily on the calling of the bride in the Song of Songs, when Geoffrey asks, "How special was the sanctification that came upon that flesh that, when the Holy Spirit came upon it, conceived from its very self the true flesh of Christ?"[30]

[28] Gastaldelli, "Une mariologia d'avanguardia," 103, lines 13–15; Canal, "Marial," 242, lines 17–19: *Nam et prae cunctis mortalibus, excepto Filio, haec sola in omnibus requiem quaesivit, quae a peccato originali sanctificata antequam nata, actuale omnino non habuit.*

[29] See Canal, "Marial," 242, n. 122.

[30] Gastaldelli, "Une mariologia d'avanguardia," 102, lines 125–26; Canal, "Marial," 241, lines 151–53: *Quam specialis enim in carne illam sanctificatio*

Gastaldelli's second passage in defense of his hypothesis that Geoffrey accepted the doctrine of the Immaculate Conception comes from his exegesis of Song of Songs 6:8, "One is my dove, my perfect one." Geoffrey offers three interpretations of the dove, ecclesiastical, monastic, and mariological, and tells us that Mary was chosen by God in advance in a unique way, and that there was no one like her, either before or after. But why a dove? "Because the Spirit came upon her, a dove with no poison of sin, for in contrast to all others the power of the Most High completely overshadowed her."[31] And Geoffrey continues: "Greater grace was given [to her] to overcome every kind of sin, because she was deemed worthy to conceive and bring forth him who was certainly without sin."[32] These two passages, says Gastaldelli, clearly state that Mary was exempt from both original and actual sin,[33] but this, again, is not the case. What they say is that by the overshadowing power of God and the influence of the Holy Spirit, she was able to overcome or vanquish—the verb is *vinco*—every kind of sin. If she had been conceived without original sin, there would have been nothing to be overcome.

Furthermore, let us glance at the context in which these passages appear. Immediately after stating that Mary lacked the poison of sin (*fel peccati*) because the power of the Most High completely overshadowed her, Geoffrey continues thus: "as blessed Augustine says in his book *On Nature and Grace*: 'I exclude only the holy virgin Mary, for with regard to her I do not wish to raise any question on the subject of sinning out of honor to the Lord.'"[34] This is a text to which we have referred

---

supervenit, quae veram perinde ex se ipsa carnem Christi superveniente Spiritu Sancto concepit?

[31] Geoffrey, *Expositio*, 2:418, citing Luke 1:35: *Columba quia in ea Spiritus supervenit, columba sine felle peccati quia omnino ei prae ceteris omnibus virtus obumbravit Altissimi.*

[32] *Expositio*, 2:418: *Inde enim scimus, quod ei plus gratiae sit collatum ad vincendum ex omni parte peccatum.*

[33] Gastaldelli, "Une mariologia d'avanguardia," 87.

[34] *Expositio*, 2:418, quoting Augustine, *De natura et gratia*, xxxvi.42; PL 44:267.

in an earlier chapter,[35] and it is part of Augustine's refutation of the ideas of Pelagius. Pelagius had maintained that human beings were born without any taint of original sin, and that it was possible—though very rare—for us to avoid sinning by the strength of our own free will. Were there any who achieved this? There were indeed, says Pelagius, and he enumerates twenty-two men and seven women of whom (he maintains) this was true. Augustine wholly rejects Pelagius's arguments and, as we saw earlier, says that of all the twenty-nine, there was only one who was able to overcome every trace of sin:

> I exclude only the holy virgin Mary, for with regard to her I do not wish to raise any question on the subject of sinning out of honor to the Lord; for we know from him what a superabundance of grace for overcoming every trace of sin was bestowed on her who was worthy to conceive and bear him who unquestionably had no sin.[36]

This is clearly Geoffrey's view. By a superabundance of God's grace Mary was cleansed from all sin and able to overcome any temptation to sin. Geoffrey does not say that she was conceived without original sin, and we do not have here a statement of the doctrine of the Immaculate Conception.

Gastaldelli's next proof text comes from Geoffrey's sermon on the Nativity of the Virgin that appears both in his commentary on the Song of Songs and in the collection of sermons in Troyes MS 503.[37] Gastaldelli calls it "an exaltation of the immaculateness[38] of the Virgin,"[39] and so it is. But it not an exaltation of her Immaculate Conception. She is blessed, says Geoffrey, "who, in contrast to all others, came forth as a new dawn and who, from the first moment of her birth, never at

[35] Chap. 3, n. 4.

[36] Augustine, *De natura et gratia*, xxxvi.42; PL 44:267.

[37] *Expositio*, 2:422–27; Canal, "Marial," 266–70.

[38] Or immaculacy (*immacolatezza*), a cumbersome word in both English and Italian.

[39] Gastaldelli, "Une mariologia d'avanguardia," 87.

any time strayed into any vice or sin."[40] This is an eminently clear statement that Mary never sinned, but it has nothing to do with her conception. And when we read, just four lines further on, of "Mary, sanctified before her birth,"—*Maria sanctificata antequam nata*—we are left in no doubt. This phrase is the same, word for word, as that which appears in Geoffrey's homily on Sirach 24:11-1, a homily we have already considered,[41] and is a direct allusion to Bernard's letter to the canons of Lyon, explicitly denying any idea of an immaculate conception.

What, then, of Geoffrey's statement in his sermon for the Purification of the Virgin, that Mary was *expers reatus originalis*, "without, or freed from, original guilt"? Is not this, as Gastaldelli suggests, a clear statement of the doctrine of the Immaculate Conception?[42] It is not. Once again, let us look at the context. Geoffrey's text for the sermon is Song of Songs 6:3, "I am my beloved's and my beloved is mine," and he goes on to explain how this is so:

> She is her beloved's, she who, alone of all of us, was chosen by the Son before she was pregnant with the Son or before the Son would be born; and he is hers who, alone of all of us, was beholden to no [human] father in his humanity, but only to a mother alone. She is her beloved's, she who gave birth to a man without ever knowing a man. He is hers, who, being made a sharer in her birth, [was] without original guilt."[43]

What this passage says is what we have seen before and will see many times again: Christ is born without original sin since he was not conceived by the normal processes of human

[40] *Expositio*, 423, lines 6–9; Canal, "Marial," 267, lines 28–31: *non declinans aliquando in vitium aliquod vel peccatum.*

[41] See n. 28 above.

[42] See Gastaldelli, "Une mariologia d'avanguardia," 87.

[43] *Expositio*, 2:393, lines 1–6: *ipse ei, particeps factus originis, expers reatus originalis.*

reproduction, and the flesh he took from Mary was sinless flesh because she had been cleansed or freed from original sin *antequam nata*, "before she was born." When did this cleansing take place? Geoffrey is quite certain that it was at the very moment of her conception, not before, and he is not prepared to countenance the views of those pseudo-scholars who maintained that it took place at the moment of the Annunciation.[44] But the overwhelming weight of the evidence is that in the matter of Mary's conception, he entirely supported the views of his master, Bernard, and that Professor Gastaldelli was quite wrong in suggesting that he was an avant-garde representative of the doctrine of the Immaculate Conception.

When it comes to the bodily assumption, however, Professor Gastaldelli is quite right. Geoffrey does not contradict Bernard, but he certainly goes beyond him. Bernard never actually denies the corporeal assumption of the Virgin, but neither does he ever actually affirm it. "He seems deliberately to have left it in the dark," says Hilda Graef.[45] Geoffrey, on the other hand, had no doubts at all on the question. His six sermons on the Assumption, edited by José Maria Canal, are paeans of praise to Mary's glory in Paradise, for when she ascended into heaven, was she not greeted by all the prophets, patriarchs, and angels? And when she saw Christ enthroned at the right hand of the Father, "should we not believe that her Son went out to meet her?"[46]

But the glory that surrounds Mary in Paradise, Geoffrey continues, is not her own. It is the glory of the Father himself, who once, by an indescribable grace, permitted her to be the mother of his Son, and now, in heaven, shares the glory of the divine majesty with both his Son and his Son's mother. The gate of glory, the portal of Paradise, closed by Eve, has now

[44] See n. 26 above.

[45] Hilda Graef, *Mary: A History of Doctrine and Devotion*, 2 vols. (London: Sheed & Ward, 1963–1965), 1:236.

[46] Canal, "Marial," 232, line 83.

been re-opened by Mary, and just as she was supremely humble in her life on earth, so is she now wholly glorious in heaven.[47]

But is it only her sinless soul that is in heaven, or is her body there as well? Geoffrey is in no doubt whatever. We saw above that the woman who was clothed with the sun was also crowned with twelve stars, and of these, two are of immediate relevance. The fourth of the four stars that pertain to her body was that she ascended to heaven without delay (*sine dilatione*)—we shall deal with the *sine dilatione* in a moment—and the fourth of the stars that pertain to both body and soul was that she was assumed into heaven in both body and soul—*in utroque*—to a place higher than the angels.[48]

But Geoffrey is aware that there are some who will question this on the grounds that it is nowhere mentioned in the canonical Scriptures, and he offers four reasons as to why we should believe it. First of all, if Mary's body was not taken up to heaven, it must have been buried somewhere. "But in no country whatsoever is there any rumor of the presence of her most holy body."[49] Second, how could he who wrote the commandment to honor one's father and one's mother[50] allow the body of such a mother to be hidden in the ground? Third, can we imagine that the very flesh from which Christ himself took flesh, the belly that he filled, the breasts that he sucked, has been taken away and hidden somewhere *sine gloria*, "without glory"? And fourth, from a logical point of view, those who don't believe in Mary's assumption because it is not mentioned in Scripture ought not to believe in her death, because that isn't mentioned in Scripture either![51]

Consider, too, Geoffrey's sermon on the calling of the bride in the Song of Songs. What does the text say? It says that the

[47] Canal, "Marial," 233–34, lines 127–49.

[48] Gastaldelli, "Il sermone 'De muliere amicta sole'," 79, lines 71–72.

[49] Gastaldelli, "Il sermone 'De muliere amicta sole'," 78, lines 48–50.

[50] Exod 20:12; Deut 5:16.

[51] Gastaldelli, "Il sermone 'De muliere amicta sole'," 78, lines 47–58.

Bride is *tota pulchra*, "wholly beautiful," which, we may assume, refers to her beauty in both sinless body and sinless soul. Thus, says Geoffrey,

> Since she has been declared most truthfully to be wholly beautiful, why should we not believe that she has been wholly assumed? How could he not summon the whole of her equally, he who commended the whole of her in this way? Or, if I may put it more plainly, how can we believe that he abandoned that maternal body to the earth, he who from the beginning gave the commandment to honor one's mother?[52]

Furthermore, says Geoffrey, if all human flesh has hope in the future resurrection because of its kinship with the Lord's flesh, "will the flesh of Mary, from which [the Lord's flesh] was specifically taken, have nothing unique to itself?"[53] Mary's flesh, in fact, was like the flesh of Eve before the Fall, wholly lacking concupiscence, and as we saw in chapter three, it was a direct consequence of eating the forbidden fruit that Adam and Eve became mortal, sinful, and liable to disease and corruption. Thus, says Geoffrey, "who could believe that that body saw corruption, which, by the over-shadowing power of the Most High, had no knowledge of concupiscence?"[54] It follows, then, that "since she was so hidden on earth that her deeds were not even written down, she went wholly (*tota*) to heaven."[55]

[52] Gastaldelli, "Une mariologia d'avanguardia," 102, lines 119–22; Canal, "Marial," 241, lines 144–48.

[53] Gastaldelli, "Une mariologia d'avanguardia," 102, lines 129–30; Canal, "Marial," 241, lines 157–58: *Et Mariae caro, unde proprie sumpta est, proprium nil habebit?*

[54] Gastaldelli, "Une mariologia d'avanguardia," 104, lines 35–36; Canal, "Marial," 243, lines 45–47, with a useful note.

[55] Gastaldelli, "Une mariologia d'avanguardia," 104, lines 56–58; Canal, "Marial," 244, lines 72–73.

There can be no doubt, then, that as far as Geoffrey is concerned, Mary was assumed into heaven in both body and soul, but when? Did the bodily assumption take place at the moment of her death or shortly afterwards? What is the meaning of the *sine dilatione*, "without delay," that we mentioned above, the fourth star that pertains to Mary's body? Geoffrey explains in the very next sentence. It is a *resurrectio sine mora*, "a resurrection without a lapse of time."[56] In other words, as Geoffrey makes clear in his homily on the woman clothed with the sun, the "delay" or the "lapse of time" refers to the period between our normal physical death and the general resurrection, a period during which bodies are subject to the usual processes of decay and corruption. That did not happen to the body of Mary—no concupiscence, no corruption—but the implication of the word *resurrectio* is that Mary died, that her sinless body was laid to rest in a tomb, and then, a short time later—I don't think that Geoffrey anywhere says three days, though I may be wrong on that—her body was raised and assumed into heaven, there to be enthroned in glory by the side of her divine Son.

In short, there is no doubt that Professor Gastaldelli is right when he tells us that in his insistence on the corporeal assumption of the Virgin, Geoffrey goes further than Bernard, but nor do I think there is any doubt that the professor is wrong when he suggests that Geoffrey was an advocate of the doctrine of the Immaculate Conception. He was not, and his Mariology, in fact, is far less avant-garde than Gastaldelli has suggested.

Geoffrey, like Bernard and, indeed, everyone else, emphasizes the supreme importance of Mary's humility. In the eyes of God, he says, she was the most humble of all women, and her humility here below finds its recompense in her glory when she was assumed into heaven.[57] Indeed, it was because of her

[56] Gastaldelli, "Il sermone 'De muliere amicta sole'," 78, line 47.

[57] See, for example, Canal, "Marial," 230–31, lines 1–61, and Gastaldelli, "Il sermone 'De muliere amicta sole'," 77–78, lines 3–36.

supreme humility that God filled her with grace, she who was greeted by the angel as *gratia plena*, "full of grace," but not only is she herself filled with grace, but she acts as a channel for God's grace to sinful men and women. "For where sin will abound, through you, in truth, grace will superabound."[58] It was to intercede for us sinners that Mary was taken from this world, and, since she is "God's friend"—*amica Dei*[59]—God will listen to her plea. Her compassion and intercession for those in misery is so prompt, loving, and effective, that anyone who appeals to her in faith will be happily rewarded.[60]

So does this mean that we can casually sin away and rely on Mary's intercession to save us? Indeed it does not. As José Maria Canal points out in his "Synthesis of Geoffrey's Marian Doctrine,"[61] two of the most important features of this error are "Mary as Mirror and Model of All the Virtues," and "Mary as "the Heavenly Mediatrix and Advocate," which means "our living the Christian life in company with Mary and with her help."[62] In this, Geoffrey is again following Saint Bernard. Mary is certainly our mother, for "if you belong to Christ, then you are more the offspring of Mary than of Abraham."[63] Thus, as our mother, she will care for her children, but, like any mother, she expects those children to behave. Mary's intercession is not for those who treat sin lightly, but for those who strive to follow the way of Christian virtue—to imitate her and her divine Son—but who of necessity will sometimes fall away and be in urgent need of her help, advocacy, and mediation.

[58] Gastaldelli, "Une mariologia d'avanguardia," 101, lines 93–94; Canal, "Marial," 240, lines 113–14, echoing Rom 5:20: *Ubi enim abundabit peccatum, per te quidem superabundabit et gratia.*

[59] Gastaldelli, "Une mariologia d'avanguardia," 102, line 140; Canal, "Marial," 241, line 171.

[60] Gastaldelli, "Il sermone 'De muliere amicta sole'," 78, lines 62–63.

[61] Canal, "Marial," 273–77.

[62] Canal, "Marial," 275.

[63] Gastaldelli, "Une mariologia d'avanguardia," 104, lines 43–44; Canal, "Marial," 243, lines 56–57, echoing Gal 3:29.

In all this, the Mariology of Geoffrey of Auxerre is not avant-garde, but the Mariology of his times.

Indeed, in my own view, if we are seeking new light on Marian doctrine, we will find more of it in the writings of the two travelers whose ideas we shall examine in the next chapter—Isaac of Stella and Amadeus of Lausanne—than in the works of Geoffrey of Auxerre. To Professor Gastaldelli we can only be eternally grateful for his excellent critical editions of Geoffrey's commentaries on the Apocalypse and the Song of Songs, but I think we may say without hesitation that he was wrong in seeing in Geoffrey an advocate of the doctrine of the Immaculate Conception. As Horace said in his *Ars poetica,* "Even Homer nods."

Chapter Eight

Two Travelers: Isaac of Stella and Amadeus of Lausanne

Isaac and Amadeus were contemporaries. Amadeus was born around 1110 and died in 1158; Isaac must have been born about the same time, perhaps a little earlier, and died a decade later in 1169. Both began their life in one country and ended it in another. Isaac moved from England to France, and Amadeus from France to Switzerland. They were both abbots, but not at the same time, and there is no evidence that they ever met.

Compared with other Cistercians of the twelfth century, Isaac has been unjustly neglected, but in recent years more and more studies have been devoted to him. There are translations of his works in all the major European languages, though the English translation of his sermons took forty years to complete. The first volume appeared in 1979, the second, which is very much better, in 2019.[1] Given what I have called Bell's Law,

[1] *Isaac of Stella: Sermons on the Christian Year, Volume One*, trans. Hugh McCaffery, intro. Bernard McGinn, CF 11 (Kalamazoo, MI: Cistercian Publications, 1979); and *Isaac of Stella: Sermons on the Christian Year, Volume Two*, trans. Lewis White, intro. Elias Dietz, CF 66 (Collegeville, MN: Cistercian Publications, 2019). The second volume contains an up-to-date Select Bibliography of works in English, French, German, Italian, and Spanish on pages xxvii–xxviii. For those who can read German, the 2016 study by Wolfgang Buchmüller is excellent.

namely, that the number of studies of a given person varies directly with the availability of that person's work in English, we may look for further studies in the future. In 1955 Louis Bouyer could state that Isaac was "the great mystery among the Cistercians" and that there were practically no studies of him,[2] but that is certainly not the case now. The only mystery is the mystery of his life, the details of which are both obscure and elusive.[3] The following paragraphs summarize what we actually know, which is singularly little, and what might confidently be suggested.

That Isaac was English is certain. He says so himself.[4] But where he was born and when he was born we do not know. The usual date suggested is about 1100, but it may have been a few years after that. At a later date, again unknown, he made his way to France to study in the Schools. Which Schools? We do not know, though Paris and / or Chartres both seem likely. But study he did, of that there is no doubt, and then decided to embrace the monastic life in the Order of Cîteaux. When? We have no idea. Where? We do not know, though Pontigny and its daughter house of Stella have both been suggested. What we do know, and know for a fact, is that in 1147 he was consecrated as abbot of Stella. That is our first solid date.

Stella—the abbey of Notre-Dame de l'Étoile—lies about twenty miles east of Poitiers and was not originally Cistercian. It was actually founded in 1117 by a hermit, Isembaud de l'Étoile, and became Cistercian in the line of Pontigny in 1145. About a decade later, Isaac, together with the abbot of neighboring Trizay, made a request for a Cistercian foundation on the island of Ré, just off the coast of La Rochelle, and after some

[2] Louis Bouyer, *La spiritualité de Cîteaux* (Paris: Flammarion, 1955), 195.

[3] For an up-to-date and comprehensive survey of the relevant literature and conflicting opinions, see Travis D. Stolz, "Isaac of Stella, the Cistercians and the Thomas Becket Controversy: A Bibliographical and Contextual Study," Marquette University, Ph.D. dissertation, 2010, readily available online at http://epublications.marquette.edu/dissertations_mu/87.

[4] See Isaac of Stella, *De officio missae*; PL 194:1896A.

fairly complex negotiations, the abbey of Notre-Dame des Châteliers was founded there, probably, but not certainly, in 1156. Isaac himself was there for some months in 1166, but the standard reason given for this—that he was exiled there as a result of his support for Thomas Becket in the Becket controversy—appears to be without foundation.[5] It has also been suggested that Isaac was abbot of Les Châteliers, but there is no sound evidence for this. He was certainly still abbot of Stella in 1167, but not in 1169, when we find the name of a new abbot. Since there is no evidence to suggest that Isaac resigned his abbacy, we may therefore place his death with some confidence shortly before 1169.

Three works have survived from his pen. The most popular was the *De officio missae*, an allegorical commentary on the canon of the Mass addressed to John of Canterbury, bishop of Poitiers. The second was the letter to Alcher on the soul—the *Epistola ad Alcherum de anima*—and the third his series of sermons for the Christian year. Of these last, four are specifically Marian: one for the feast of the Nativity of Mary, and three for the feast of the Assumption. What, then, does the abbot of Stella have to say about the Mother of God?

What he has to say about Mary is an integral part of his theology of the restoration of the image of God in us and the recovery of the lost likeness. There is, of course, nothing new in this—the theme is standard and ubiquitous—though the way in which Isaac explains it is very much his own. The broad themes of his thought are not, in fact, difficult to understand and are solidly rooted in the patristic tradition, but they are couched in a language that makes them appear more difficult than they are. To appreciate Isaac's writing demands a knowledge of the terminology of the Schools and an understanding of the principles of later Platonic philosophy. But if I were

[5] See the study by Travis Stolz cited in n. 3 above, and the acute paper by Elias Dietz, "When Exile Is Home: The Biography of Isaac of Stella," *Cistercian Studies Quarterly* 41 (2006): 141–65.

forced into a corner and asked, on the spur of the moment, to name the three most important influences on Isaac, I would say, without hesitation and in chronological order, pseudo-Dionysius, Augustine, and Bernard of Clairvaux.

The pervasive atmosphere of Bernard is unmistakable in Isaac, and in his second sermon on the Assumption, he praises Bernard by name and lauds all his works, especially his commentary on the Song of Songs. "We have seen a man," he says, "who undoubtedly possessed something of the superman."[6] Like Bernard, Isaac is uncertain as to the details of the Assumption, and is not prepared to go beyond what the Fathers have said:

> Limiting myself by the bounds set by the Fathers, which we are forbidden to pass, we dare not state anything other than this: that on this day she was taken up, whether with the body or without the body I do not know, God knows, to the everlasting and blessed dwelling, to the highest heaven of heavens.[7]

Yet Isaac is no slavish follower of Bernard, as may be seen in his comments on the Knights Templar. Bernard, as we know, played a pivotal role in planning, promoting, and praising the Templars in his *De laude novae militiae*, "In Praise of the New Knighthood," but what does Isaac say of them?

> There has sprung up a new knighthood, a new monster, that someone has wittily called "the Order of the Fifth Gospel," since it was founded to force unbelievers into the [Christian] faith by means of lances and cudgels, and may freely pillage those who do not bear the name of Christian and butcher them in the name of religion. But if any of them are killed in this marauding, they are called martyrs of Christ.[8]

[6] Sermon 52.15 (second sermon for the Assumption); SCh 339:232–34.

[7] Sermon 51.1 (first sermon for the Assumption); SCh 339:198–200, quoting Prov 22:28 and 2 Cor 12:2.

[8] Sermon 48.8 (third sermon for the nativity of John the Baptist); SCh 339:158–60.

Isaac clearly has no time for the Templars, though his final word on the subject is more balanced and charitable than we might expect. He links the new Order with the new doctrines that were being propounded in his time—those "astonishing novelties"[9] his own monks found so fascinating—and, he says, "we do not condemn them, but neither do we praise them, not because everything they do may be evil, but because it can lead to future evils."[10]

Isaac's theology is grounded in a well-known theme. It is simply that human beings, created to the image and likeness of God, have retained the image but lost the likeness. The phrase in Latin is *ad imaginem et similitudinem Dei*,[11] and the *ad* is important. It is not *in*. *In* could imply a stable situation already achieved; *ad* indicates a process, a progression. There is a difference between being in a particular room, and advancing towards a particular room. In the one case, we have arrived at our destination; in the other, we have not. In Adam before the Fall, both image and likeness were perfect, or at least as perfect as was possible in a created nature, but as a result of the first sin the likeness was lost, though the image remained. We, therefore, having fallen in Adam (Isaac is here solidly Augustinian), and being tarnished with both his sin and our own, have fallen into the *regio dissimilitudinis*, the "region of unlikeness," a well-known phrase used by a multitude of writers, including Isaac.[12]

It follows from this that our salvation consists, in essence, in restoring the lost likeness, and this was made possible only by the incarnation of the Son of God. It was he who restored the flow of grace between the perfect Creator and his imperfect human creation, and enabled us, by grace and only by grace, to live a life of asceticism by which, virtue by virtue, we might restore what we lost in Adam's Fall.

[9] Sermon 48.5; SCh 339:156.

[10] Sermon 48.9; SCh 339:160.

[11] Gen 1:26.

[12] See Sermon 2.13 (second sermon for All Saints); SCh 130:106.

In other words, what we lost in Adam is restored in Christ, and as we descended in Adam into the region of unlikeness, so we must ascend with Christ and be re-conformed to his divine nature. "Outwardly," says Isaac, "you are a beast, [conformed] to the image of the world, for which reason a human being is called a microcosm; inwardly, a human being is [made] to the image of God, and for this reason you can be deified."[13]

Is there anything new in this? There is not. We might substitute for the name of Isaac that of virtually any other patristic or medieval writer, Greek or Latin, and hear the same thing. What is new, and what is quite remarkably new, is Isaac's interpretation of the image and likeness, and his conception that in being conformed to Christ, we are conformed to the *whole* Christ, which, as we shall see in a moment, brings in the essential role of Christ's human mother.

On the first point—the nature of the image and likeness—we will be brief, tempting though it is to write several chapters on the subject. That, however, would take us far off course, and we will confine ourselves to quoting Isaac himself in a passage from his first sermon for Septuagesima Sunday:

> To turn away from God, whether it be from truth by our sense of reason or from charity by our way of life, is night, when it is impossible to work. But to turn towards God by investigation and imitation is day, when men and women go forth to their work,[14] which is to know and love God, and to delight in this knowledge and love. This is why human beings were made to the image and likeness of God,[15] and through these they are restored and re-conformed to both:

[13] Sermon 2.13 (second sermon for All Saints); SCh 130:106: *Foris pecus es ad imaginem mundi, unde et minor mundus dicitur homo; intus homo ad imaginem Dei, unde potes deificari*. On the human being as a microcosm, a common theme, see chap. 6, n. 45. The verb *deificari*, in any of its various forms, appears only three times in Isaac's sermons: here, and in Sermons 25.13 and 26.6.

[14] Ps 103:23.

[15] Gen 1:26.

> by the sense [of reason] to the image and by their way of life to the likeness. Yet being made to the image and the likeness, they are restored to the likeness and the image [in that order] by the reformation of their lives, that must be re-conformed so as to participate in [the divine] nature. To know the true God is eternal life, but to love him with one's whole heart is the eternal way. Charity, therefore, is the way, the truth, and the life.[16] Charity is the likeness; truth is the image. Charity is service; truth, the reward. We are led by charity; we are settled in our place by truth.[17]

To appreciate this passage, we must remember that, in Latin, there are three words for love: *amor*, *dilectio*, and *caritas*. *Amor* is the general term and may be used for any kind of love, selfless or selfish, good or bad. *Dilectio* is usually used for love that is directed toward a virtuous end, though one can find exceptions to this. But *caritas* or charity always and without exception refers to the highest and most perfect form of love, a love that comes from God and is directed towards God. When we read in the Latin version of 1 John 4:8 that "God is love," the word for "love" is *caritas*.

Love / *caritas*, then, is the motive power that brings about our re-conformation to Christ, but, as we said above, it is a re-conformation to the whole Christ. What does Isaac mean by this? The basic principle could not be simpler, though its ramifications are astonishingly rich. To be a live human being, we need both a body and a head. A body without a head or a head without a body are both ugly sights, and both are decidedly dead. That is the simple and unobjectionable basis of Isaac's thought. So let us now turn to the second Person of the Trinity and follow, briefly, Isaac's ideas as he presents them at length in his sermon for the Ascension.[18]

[16] John 14:6.

[17] Sermon 16.15–16 (first sermon for Septuagesima); SCh 130:322–24.

[18] See CF 66:104–11 for a good English translation.

If Christ had descended from heaven only to take back up to heaven the human nature he had assumed in the womb of the Virgin, we human beings would have profited nothing. But that was not Christ's intention. His intention was to unite the Bridegroom—himself—with his bride, the church, to unite the head with the body so as to make one man, whole and complete (*totus et integer*). Christ, therefore, is, at one and the same time, "one body with all its members, which, with its head, is the one Son of Man."[19] But since the Son of Man is also the Son of God, and since the Son of God is also God, what this means is that "the whole body with its head is the Son of Man, the Son of God, and God himself."[20] And Isaac proves his point by resorting to Christ's own words: "Father, as I and you are one, so I wish that they may be one with us."[21]

Thus, when Christ, the Son of Man, descended from heaven in the incarnation, he was alone (*solus*) in his divinity, but not complete (*totus*) in his humanity. Why not? Because he was a head without a body. But when he ascended to heaven after his resurrection, he ascended alone and complete—*solus et totus*—because the head was now joined to the body:

> Suppose my foot could speak like my tongue, what it would say is what my tongue says: "I'm Isaac." In just the same way, the faithful and rational members of Christ can truly call themselves what he himself is, namely, the Son of God and God. But what he is by nature, we are by association (*consortio*) with him. What he is in its fullness, we are by participation in him. And what the Son of God is by generation, we are by adoption, as it is written: "You have received the spirit of adoption as children, whereby we cry 'Abba, Father.'"[22]

[19] Sermon 42.11 (for the Ascension); SCh 339:44.
[20] Sermon 42.11; SCh 339:44.
[21] John 17:21.
[22] Sermon 42.14–15; SCh 339:48, quoting Rom 8:15.

It follows from this, Isaac continues, that we can regard Christ's birth from three points of view. First, there is his eternal generation from the unbegotten Father, a birth without a mother. Second, there is his birth from his human mother, Mary, a birth without an earthly father. And third, there is his sacramental birth "from God the Father through the Holy Spirit, and from his virgin mother, the church."[23] For just as it was by the power of the Holy Spirit that the womb of the Virgin gave birth to the Son of Man—our head—so, too, it is by the power of the Holy Spirit that from the font of baptism we are re-born as children of God and his body. Only then is Christ *totus et integer*, whole and complete, head and body united.

Does this mean, then, that the whole Christ, head and body, must have two virgin mothers, Mary and the church? Indeed it does, and Isaac says so:

> For Christ, sole and complete, head and body, is one. And this one, from the one God in heaven and the one mother on earth, is both many sons[24] and one son. And just as the head and its members are both one son and many sons, so Mary and the church are one mother and many, one virgin and many. Each is mother and each is virgin. Each conceives without lust through the same Spirit, and each, without sin, brings forth an offspring for God the Father. The former, in the absence of all sin, gave birth to a head for the body; the latter, by the remission of all sins,[25] brought forth a body for the head. Each is a mother of Christ, but neither one, without the other, gives birth to the whole [Christ]. Thus, whatever is said in the divinely inspired Scriptures of the virgin mother church universally applies to the virgin mother Mary individually, and [what is said] of the virgin mother Mary in particular is rightly to be understood of the virgin mother

[23] Sermon 42.16; SCh 339:50.

[24] I would normally translate this as "children," but the contrast here is between one son and many sons, *unus filius* and *plures filii.*

[25] Acts 2:38.

> church in general. And when a passage speaks of either one or the other, what it says can be applied to both, almost without difference or distinction. Each and every faithful soul may be understood, in a certain way, to be a bride of the Word of God, a mother and daughter and sister of Christ,[26] virgin yet fruitful.[27]

Thus, in a universal sense, says Isaac, the Lord's inheritance[28] is the church; in a special sense, it is Mary; and in a particular sense, it is every faithful soul: "In the tabernacle of Mary's womb, Christ dwelt for nine months; in the tabernacle of the faith of the church, until the end of the world;[29] and in the knowledge and love[30] of the faithful soul he will dwell for ever and ever."[31]

It can hardly be denied that this is a rich and profound theology. Isaac merges Christology, Mariology, Ecclesiology, and sacramental theology and makes it clear that the only way in which we human beings can be re-conformed to the whole Christ—*totus et integer*—is through Mary and the church. By being united to the whole Christ we are, by definition, united to his head and body, and therefore to his sinless mother and to the church that, by grace, has the power to remit all sins. Putting it another way, if God is our Father, Mary and the church are our mothers, the mothers of all Christians, and (says Isaac) what is said of the one may generally—the Latin *fere*[32] is a gentle caution—be said of the other.

[26] Matt 12:50.

[27] Sermon 51.7–8 (first sermon for the Assumption); SCh 339:202–4.

[28] Isaac is commenting on Sirach 24:11: "I shall abide in the inheritance of the Lord."

[29] See Matt 28:20.

[30] Here Isaac uses the word *dilectio*.

[31] Sermon 51.24; SCh 339:214–16.

[32] In the text at n. 27 above, what Isaac says is, in Latin, *fere permixtim et indifferenter*, which I rendered above by "almost without difference or distinction." *Fere* means "nearly, generally, almost, approximately, roughly, usually," or "commonly." But its implication is positive rather than negative.

In short, Mary plays an essential and pivotal role in the process of our salvation, which begins with the distorted and disfigured likeness to the whole Christ, and ends in union with that indescribable Oneness that is number beyond number, measure beyond measure, weight beyond weight, that can only be described as super-wisdom, super-righteousness, and, indeed, super-substantial—the terms are drawn straight from the *Mystical Theology* of pseudo-Dionysius—and that, effectively, leaves us speechless: "We are not saying what God is, but neither are we altogether silent; for if he is none of these things, all these things may be put aside, and, of him, the negative statements are more true."[33]

Let us now turn from these exalted apophatic realms to the other traveler in these Marian regions, Amadeus of Lausanne, in whom we will find a theology of Mary and her role in the redemptive process that could not be expressed in a style more different from that of the abbot of Stella.

Amadeus, of noble stock, was born on January 21, 1110, in the Château de Chatte in the Dauphiné in southeastern France. His father, also named Amadeus, was lord of Clermont-Hautrive, an ancient house of high lineage, but he was also a man of deep religious sensibilities and came to prefer monastic anonymity to aristocratic eminence. Thus, in about 1119, he took himself, his son, and seventeen knight-companions to the newly founded Cistercian abbey of Bonnevaux and there sought entry. Understandably, he was welcomed, but he did not stay there long. He demanded a good, solid education for his son, and, since that was not provided at Bonnevaux, Amadeus Senior took the boy, left the monastery, and transferred both of them to the great abbey of Cluny. The move was not a success. Amadeus Junior did not receive the education his father expected, and Amadeus Senior was so unhappy and disillusioned with Cluniac life that, after a time, he left the

[33] Sermon 22.8 (fifth sermon in Sexagesima); SCh 207:68.

abbey and returned to Bonnevaux. Amadeus Junior, meanwhile, had been sent to the court of Conrad von Hohenstaufen, the future Conrad III of Germany.

Amadeus spent three years at Conrad's court, but his heart remained set on monastic life, and in 1125 he sought entry into Clairvaux, where Bernard had been abbot for a decade. He was accepted, became a Cistercian novice, and would spend the next fourteen years at the abbey under the tutelage and guidance of Bernard, or, more accurately, for those years when Bernard was actually at Clairvaux. This period came to an end in 1139 when Bernard, recognizing his talents, appointed him abbot of Hautecombe, near Aix-les-Bains in Savoy. The abbey flourished under his administration, but he was not there long. In 1144 the bishop of Lausanne, Guy de Maligny, resigned, and Amadeus was chosen to succeed him. He had no desire to do so, and it was only at the insistence of Pope Lucius II that he agreed to accept the position. His years as bishop were not easy—Lausanne was a troubled diocese—and he needed to call on all his skills as organizer, administrator, and peacemaker. He died on August 27, 1158, at Lausanne, where in 1911 his tomb was discovered in the old cathedral; his relics were then taken to Fribourg. Apart from two letters and a few episcopal *acta*, the eight homilies on the praises of blessed Mary are all that has been preserved from his pen.[34]

In the homilies, all the usual Marian themes make their appearance, but all expressed in flowing and flowery Latin that

[34] The standard biography of Amadeus remains the old but comprehensive study by Anselme Dimier, *Amédée de Lausanne: Disciple de saint Bernard* (Abbaye S. Wandrille: Éditions de la Fontenelle, 1949). The text of the homilies in PL 188:1303–46 has now been entirely superseded by the Sources chrétiennes edition: *Amadée de Lausanne: Huit homélies mariales*, ed. Jean Deshusses, trans. Antoine Dumas, intro. and notes by Georges Bavaud, SCh 72 (Paris: Cerf, 1960). For a complete English translation, see *Magnificat: Homilies in Praise of the Blessed Virgin Mary by Bernard of Clairvaux and Amadeus of Lausanne*, trans. Marie-Bernard Saïd and Grace Perigo, intro. by Chrysogonus Waddell, CF 18 (Kalamazoo, MI: Cistercian Publications, 1979), 61–135.

is far more emotive and sensual than that which appears in the four homilies of Bernard, and radically different from the language of Isaac of Stella. Indeed, some of the expressions are quite startling and of such a physical nature as to leave some readers a little uncomfortable. To a certain extent, this must surely be due to Amadeus's exposure to the language, literature, and culture of the court of Conrad von Hohenstaufen. But Amadeus also has what Chrysogonus Waddell describes as a "compulsive recourse to series based on the mystic number three,"[35] and this is something that is not always to our modern taste. His thought "seems to move in triplets. We might wish at times that he had been a bit more subtle, that he had given free rein less often to his obsession with ternary patters."[36] In Amadeus's defense, however, it must be said that this was fairly typical of his time, and it appears even more clearly (and tediously) in the long commentary on the Song of Songs compiled by Thomas of Perseigne sometime between 1170 and 1189.[37] It would continue down the centuries, and may still be seen in the 1600s in the writings of the royal counselor and *prédicateur du roi*, Jacques Biroat (d. ca. 1666), who was roundly criticized for doing it.[38]

The first homily is essentially an introduction. Amadeus places Mary between two golden baskets, filled with fruits and decorated with flowers, baskets that represent the two Testaments, the Old and the New. The one represents the law of death, *lex mortis*, that produces sinners; the other represents the law of life, *lex vitae*, that takes sin away. But the two baskets may also represent the glory of Christ and the child-bearing of the Virgin, and both Testaments, taken together, have the

[35] Waddell, intro., *Magnificat*, xxvii.

[36] Waddell, intro., *Magnificat*, xxix.

[37] See David N. Bell, "Le Commentaire du Cantique des Cantiques de Thomas de Perseigne revisité," *Annales de Bretagne et de Pays de l'Ouest* 120 (2013): 127–28.

[38] See David N. Bell, *A Saint in the Sun: Praising Saint Bernard in the France of Louis XIV*, CS 271 (Collegeville, MN: Cistercian Publications, 2017), 74.

same goal and the same end: to proclaim Christ, to show forth Christ, to announce Christ and the Virgin Mary. The Old Testament foretells these things; the New Testament reveals them. Mary, therefore, links the two Testaments, since the Messiah and Savior of the world foretold in the one reveals himself in the other, and that revelation is possible only because Mary, in her humility, became the immaculate vessel for the incarnate Lord. Thus "the praise of the son enriches the mother, and the divine birth heaps honors on her who was in labor."[39] In other words, as we have said before and shall say again, since mother and son are inseparable, honoring Mary is in no way detrimental to her son, and in praising her son, we must also be praising the mother.

In the second homily, Amadeus sets out his scheme for praising the Mother of God. She progresses from virtue to virtue, from glory to glory, in seven stages, each one of which, in order, will be the subject of the next seven homilies:

> First, she deserves to be adorned with the beauty of all the virtues. Second, she was joined to the Holy Spirit by a contract of marriage (*foedere maritali*). Third, she became the mother of the Savior. Fourth, a sword pierced her soul,[40] and, by the flesh assumed from her flesh, the ruin of the lost world is repaired. Fifth, she rejoices in her Son's rising and ascending above the heaven of heavens to the right hand of the Father. Sixth, she is carried off from this world, and, with the Lord hurrying to meet her, she is placed above all the inhabitants of heaven. Seventh, she will finally be perfected when the fullness of the Gentiles shall come and all Israel be saved.[41]

Furthermore, each of these stages will be associated with the seven gifts of the Holy Spirit as we find them enumerated in Isaiah 11:2, though not in the same order. Her adornment

[39] *Huit homélies*, 64.

[40] Luke 2:35.

[41] *Huit homélies*, 68–70. The last sentence is a quotation from Rom 11:25-26.

with all the virtues is associated with the spirit of the Lord, her virginal conception with godliness (*pietas*), the birth of the Savior with knowledge, her agony at the foot of the Cross with fortitude, her joy at witnessing her son's resurrection with counsel, her assumption into heaven—Amadeus is in no doubt whatever about that—with understanding, and her glorification in heaven with wisdom. It can hardly be denied that this is a formidable agenda, though Amadeus achieves his goal by means of a great deal of fairly florid exegesis.

Much of what he says is, as we would expect, standard material—perpetual virginity, perfect humility, divine motherhood, second Eve, holiness, queenship, mediation, and so on—though couched in Amadeus's own unmistakeable style. So is there anything new in Amadeus's homilies? The answer is, very little, though a few things deserve mention. First, there is the odd exegesis at the beginning of the fourth homily, that concerned with the virgin birth of Jesus, in which Amadeus invokes the classical legend of Orpheus and his lyre to explain the hypostatic union of God and man in the one person of Jesus of Nazareth. He was consubstantial with his Father in his divinity and consubstantial with his mother in his humanity, "a giant of twofold substance," who used the lyre (*cithara*) of his body to make such music as could raise up stones, move trees, draw wild beasts, and lead us to salvation. But this excursus does not last long, and Amadeus is soon back on safer ground with a more appropriate singer, David the Psalmist.[42]

In the same homily, Amadeus is also unusual in introducing a passage directed against the Muslims, the "Gentiles" as he calls them, and their "pseudo-prophet," whom he does not name. His argument is simple: (1) Muslims do not believe that Christ is God. (2) But the Muslim Prophet states that Jesus was born of a virgin and that he lived a life free from sin and falsehood. (3) If, then, the Prophet admits that Jesus never lied, and if Jesus stated in the gospels that he was God and the Son of

[42] See *Magnificat*, 87–88.

God, how can Muslims not believe this? (4) The conclusion is inevitable: it is the Prophet who is lying. Here is what Amadeus actually says:

> And what shall I say about you gentiles? You are our flesh and our bone,[43] something that gives us greater concern for your salvation. But why do you not believe that Christ is God? You believe that he was born, and born of a virgin, and that he lived without sin. But because you do not believe that he is God, you make a disastrous error and commit a most ruinous wrong. But you say, "That is what we have been taught to believe by our prophet." If you want to know that your prophet was false, we condemn him by his own words and reject his foolishness from his own lips. He says that Christ was truly born of a virgin, and that he lived his life with no falsehood and no sin. But Christ, who, according to this testimony, was always truthful (such being attested by prophets and apostles), stated openly in the gospel that he was God and the Son of God. Thus, he who claimed that Christ was not God was a liar.[44]

Amadeus's source for this is Peter the Venerable's *Tractatus adversus nefandam sectam Saracenorum*, "Treatise against the Odious Sect of the Saracens,"[45] and what Peter and Amadeus say is more or less correct. The Qur'an states explicitly that Jesus was born of a virgin,[46] but it does not state explicitly that he was wholly free from sin and falsehood. In later Muslim tradition, however, Mary and all the prophets were regarded as sinless, and there is a saying, a *hadith*, attributed to Muhammad, in which the Prophet says that no child is born without

[43] See Gen 2:23.

[44] *Huit homélies*, 122–24.

[45] PL 189:659–720.

[46] The texts are conveniently presented in Geoffrey Parrinder, *Jesus in the Qur'an* (London: Faber and Faber, 1965), 60–74. The key verse is surah 19:20, "How shall I have a boy, seeing that no man has touched me, and I have not been unchaste?"

being touched by a demon at the moment of his birth. There were only ever two exceptions to this: Mary and Jesus.[47] The Muslims, then, are proved wrong by their own logic, and Amadeus begs them to seek refuge in the catholic and apostolic church, for just as in the days of Noah the one and only refuge was the ark, so now the one and only refuge is the *ecclesia Christi*, the church of Christ.

The church of Christ, in fact, and Mary are intimately linked in the thought of Amadeus, especially in what he has to say in his seventh homily, that on the assumption. Again, the logic is simple and straightforward. In giving birth to Jesus, Mary gave birth to the body of Christ. But the body of Christ is also the church. In a certain way, therefore, Mary is the mother of the church as well as the mother of God. We may note here both the similarities and differences between the exegesis of Amadeus and that of Isaac of Stella. But Amadeus opens his homily by posing the question as to why, after his ascension, Christ let Mary remain on earth. Why did he not take her up to heaven with him straightaway? She certainly deserved it. Why the delay?

It was to console the disciples and offer to the world the *remedia salutis*, the medicines of salvation. True, the disciples had been taught by the Holy Spirit, but they could be taught still more by the one who brought forth, in and from all purity, the very fount of wisdom itself: "In short, with wonderful godliness, provision was made for the primitive church, so that since it now no longer saw God present in the flesh, it might see his mother and be revived by that most delightful of sights."[48] She also shared with that church all her gifts of grace, one of which was a flowing river of fire that poured forth from her. It set fire to her foes, warmed her friends, helped her neighbors, and consumed her enemies.

[47] See Parrinder, *Jesus in the Qur'an*, 62.

[48] *Huit homélies*, 184.

Then, finally, Mary is assumed into heaven, body and soul. Unlike some of the early assumption narratives, Amadeus, like Isaac, gives no details as to how this occurred, save that it did. She hastened to her Lord and Son accompanied by choirs of angels, and, seeing the Son of God, born from her, sitting at the right hand of the Father, she said to him, in an adaptation of Psalm 15, "My heart has been glad and my tongue has rejoiced. My flesh, too, shall rest in hope, for you did not leave me in the world; neither did you let the body of your mother see corruption."[49] Mary is then seated on a throne—the one left vacant by the fall of Lucifer—and is crowned as Queen of Heaven. All this is narrated at considerable length—Amadeus seldom uses two words when ten will do—but he leaves us in no doubt as to the reality of Mary's corporeal assumption. It is not surprising, then, to find him being quoted by Pope Pius XII on November 1, 1950, when, in the Apostolic Constitution, *Munificentissimus Deus*, the pope infallibly declared the doctrine of the Corporeal Assumption to be an article of faith.

It is from this exalted position that Mary comes into her own as our intercessor and *mediatrix*, lifting up her prayers for all the clergy, for all men and women, for the living and the dead. She gathers up the sinner's prayers and pleads with her Son on behalf of all those who are penitent. She is the Star of the Sea—we have now come to the eighth and last homily—who guards all those who sail upon the dangerous seas of the world, who would have foundered had it not been for Mary's aid. They would have been engulfed by the abyss of Scylla or lured to their death by the Sirens—Amadeus is now borrowing from Virgil[50]—if Mary had not protected them. But protect them she does, and all penitent sinners who look to her can be sure that she will hear them: "Through the Mother they are reconciled to the Son and through the Virgin to God, wholly snatched

[49] Ps 15:9-10, adapted; *Huit homélies*, 200–202.
[50] Virgil, *Aeneid*, III.432 and V.864.

back from death and given over to life."[51] Amadeus's explanation of the title Star of the Sea is very much his own. He may have been under Bernard's guidance for fourteen years, but, like Isaac, he is no slavish imitator of his master, and according to Hilda Graef, his homilies had considerable influence, since they were read at Matins on Saturday in Amadeus's own cathedral in Lausanne.[52]

It is time now to return to Isaac's homeland and introduce an Englishman who, save for a short sojourn in Rome, remained tied to his native country, who was born there and died there, and who made significant contributions to the development of Marian theology. He is Aelred, the celebrated abbot of Rievaulx, and since he left so many sermons on Mary—no fewer than forty-four—and made a significant contribution to the early development of the Rosary meditations, he deserves a chapter to himself.

[51] *Huit homélies*, 214.

[52] Hilda Graef, *Mary: A History of Doctrine and Devotion*, 2 vols. (London: Sheed & Ward, 1963–1965), 1:247.

Chapter Nine

An English Abbot: Aelred of Rievaulx

There is today an immense bibliography on Aelred of Rievaulx, some of it excellent, and some of it simply not worth reading.[1] The facts of his life are fairly clear, and we are fortunate in having a valuable biography of the man written shortly after his death by Walter Daniel, a member of the Rievaulx community.[2] Given that Walter had spent seventeen years at Rievaulx during Aelred's abbacy, that he had acted as his secretary, and that he had attended him as his physician in his later years, he was well qualified to write his life.

Aelred was born in Hexham, not far from the Scottish border, in 1110, and he may have received his early education at the cathedral school at Durham. In about 1124 he was sent off to the court of David I, King of Scots, at Roxburgh in order

[1] See Anselme Hoste, *Bibliotheca Aelrediana: A Survey of the Old Manuscripts, Old Catalogues, Editions and Studies concerning St. Aelred of Rievaulx* (Steenbrugge: In Abbatia Sancti Petri, 1962); Pierre-André Burton, *Bibliotheca Aelrediana Secunda: Une bibliographie cumulative (1962–1996)* (Louvain-la-Neuve: FIDEM, 1997), and Pierre-André Burton, "Bibliotheca aelrediana secunda: Supplementa," in *A Companion to Aelred of Rievaulx (1110–1167)*, ed. Marsha L. Dutton (Leiden: Brill, 2017), 294–324.

[2] *The Life of Ailred of Rievaulx by Walter Daniel*, ed. Frederick M. Powicke (Oxford: Clarendon Press, 1978; repr. Kalamazoo, MI: Cistercian Publications, 1994).

to learn how to become a gentleman, and there he remained for a decade. He was clearly a young man of considerable talent, and during his ten years at court, he rose to the rank of *echonomus*—seneschal or steward or Master of the Household—and, as such, he was acquainted with many of the nobles of northern England, including Walter Espec, who would found the abbey of Rievaulx in 1132.

Aelred, however, had the soul of a monk, not that of a worldly diplomat, and in 1134 he left the court of King David to enter Rievaulx, founded just two years earlier. Here he found his true home, though he was obviously not your average novice. William, abbot of Rievaulx, had no hesitation in making use of his education, diplomatic abilities, and contacts, and Aelred found himself involved in important diplomatic negotiations on the Scottish border and, in 1142, was representing his abbot in Rome. On his return to Rievaulx he was appointed novice master, though he did not hold the position for long. In 1143 he was sent off to the newly founded abbey of Revesby in Lincolnshire as its first abbot, and governed the house with manifest efficiency and obvious competence.

His time at Revesby came to an end in 1147. William, abbot of Rievaulx, had died in 1145, and his successor, Maurice, had found the burdens of office too great and resigned towards the end of 1147. By November of that year, Aelred had been recalled to Rievaulx and installed as its third abbot—the choice was hardly surprising—and would govern the house for twenty years until his death on January 12, 1167, at the age of fifty-seven. He appears to have brought to Rievaulx all the abbatial skills he had demonstrated at Revesby, and the abbey flourished under his administration.[3]

Aelred was a prolific writer and a fine Latinist. He was also an acute theologian, whose talents and contributions in this

[3] See further the entry "Ailred [Ælred, Æthelred] of Rievaulx (1110–1167)," by David N. Bell in the *Oxford Dictionary of National Biography* (2004). The old study (1981) by Aelred Squire, *Aelred of Rievaulx: A Study*, retains its value.

area have not always been recognized. But our concern here is more limited. What does Aelred have to say about Mary the Virgin? Our sources for what he has to say are now considerably greater in number than they once were. When Hilda Graef was writing her pages on Aelred in 1963,[4] she was effectively limited to the works printed in volume 195 of the Migne Patrology and the twenty-four *Sermones inediti* published by C. H. Talbot in 1952 from what is now referred to as the Durham Collection.

The number of sermons has now been wonderfully expanded to no fewer than 182 by the labors of Gaetano Raciti,[5] and of this large number we have eight sermons for the feast of the Purification, eleven for the Annunciation, twelve each for the feasts of Mary's Assumption and Nativity, and a single sermon for her Conception.[6] These forty-four sermons appear in five collections known today as the First and Second Clairvaux Collections, the Durham and Lincoln Collections, and the Reading-Cluny Collection, but an occasional sermon appears in more than one collection. It cannot be denied, how-

[4] Hilda Graef, *Mary: A History of Doctrine and Devotion*, 2 vols. (London: Sheed & Ward, 1963–1965), 1:249–50.

[5] CCCM 2A (1989) Sermons 1–46; 2B (2001) Sermons 47–84; 2C (2012) Sermons 85–182.

[6] For a listing of all the sermons, see Domenico Pezzini, "The Sermons of Aelred of Rievaulx," in *A Companion to Aelred*, 73–76. To the English translations of the First and Second Clairvaux Collections cited on p. 74, n. 8, of Pezzini's study, may now be added *Aelred of Rievaulx, The Liturgical Sermons. The Durham and Lincoln Collections. Sermons 47–84*, trans. Kathryn Krug, Lewis White, and the *Catena Scholarium*, CF 80 (Collegeville, MN: Cistercian Publications, 2018). An English translation appears in Aelred of Rievaulx, *The Liturgical Sermons: The Reading-Cluny Collection*, trans. Daniel Griggs, 2 vols., CF 81, 87 (Collegeville, MN: Cistercian Publications, 2021, 2022). An English translation by Athanasius Sulavik of eleven sermons from the first Clairvaux Collection also appeared as "Sermons on the Feasts of Saint Mary by Aelred of Rievaulx," *Cistercian Studies Quarterly* 32 (1997): 37–125. A French translation of the Reading-Cluny Collection is available in Aelred de Rievaulx, *Sermons. La collection de Reading (sermons 85–182)*, trans. Gaetano Raciti and Gaëtane de Briey, 2 vols., Corpus Christianorum in Translation (French edition) (Turnhout: Brepols, 2015).

ever, that this is a substantial number, and they contain almost everything that Aelred has to say about Mary. The only exceptions are a brief passage in his treatise *De Iesu puero duodenni*, "When Jesus was a Boy of Twelve" (1153–1157), and a very important section that we shall discuss in due course in *De institutione inclusarum*, "On the Institution of Recluses," a work that dates from 1160–1162 and that was addressed to Aelred's sister, herself a recluse. Some of the sermons, we might add, were by no means short. By my reckoning, the long Sermon seventy-four on the assumption cannot have been delivered in much less than an hour and a quarter.[7]

The most recent study (so far as I am aware) of the place of Mary in the writings of Aelred appeared in 2017, but the author—Marie Anne Mayeski—limited herself to the passages in the *De institutione inclusarum* and the eight sermons in the First Clairvaux Collection.[8] It appears that the prime reasons for this were a lack of time and resources, but it cannot be denied that the result is disappointing and does not do justice to all that Aelred has to say on Mary. The brief summary that follows here takes account of all forty-four sermons, though some, clearly, are of much greater significance than others.

Throughout all the sermons, all the usual Marian titles appear, as do all the usual doctrines. Mary is the Mother of God, our Lady (*domina nostra*), the Queen of Heaven, holy Mary, our *mediatrix* and advocate, and so on. Occasionally the title is a little more unusual, as when he is prepared to refer to Mary as "our sister":

> But do not think I'm being presumptuous in saying this. The Son of God himself is also the Son of Man and therefore our brother. But while his human nature comes only from his

[7] This is obviously not the place to enter into the difficult question of the relationship between the oral presentation of the sermons and their literary composition.

[8] Marie Anne Mayeski, "'At the Feet of His Dearest Mother': Aelred's Teaching on Mary in the Sermons of the First Clairvaux Collection," in *A Companion to Aelred*, 149–66.

> mother, hers is from both a father and a mother. See how daring we can be with her, given that she is our sister! Let us love her, for she certainly loves us. We ought to love this sister, whose holiness, whose benevolence, whose purity has been of such benefit not only to herself but also to all of us.[9]

Aelred was not averse to making startling statements and startling comparisons, and I must admit to smiling to myself when, in a sermon on the birth of Mary, he likens his Lord Jesus to an elephant.[10]

As to Mary herself, we see, as we would expect to see, the old Eve-Mary parallel—it occurs frequently—and Aelred draws just the same conclusion we have seen in other writers. What did Eve bring upon us but old age, disease, death, darkness, and corruption? But through blessed Mary we have been reborn in a different way, a much better way, "for since Christ was born of her, in place of old age we regain newness [of life], in place of corruption incorruption, in place of darkness light. She herself is our mother, the mother of our life, the mother of our incorruption, the mother of our light."[11] And in another sermon, explaining the "swift cloud" of Isaiah 19:1, Aelred tells us that the "swift cloud" may refer to "the immaculate Virgin (*intemerata Virgo*), namely, Jesus' mother, through whom the heavenly light has shone on us in the darkness of this world."[12]

We also see the usual emphasis on Mary's perpetual virginity, which goes hand in hand with her humility, chastity, and charity. She is, as the angel said, "full of grace," and if in Christ we may see the seven virtues of humility, obedience, righteousness, forbearance, mercy, purity, and charity, then, "as an outstanding example of all these virtues, we have the most blessed Virgin Mary."[13] She also received the seven gifts of the Holy

[9] Sermon 23.13; CCCM 2A:187.
[10] Sermon 75.20; CCCM 2B:274.
[11] Sermon 23.7; CCCM 2A:185.
[12] Sermon 60.26; CCCM 2B:136.
[13] Sermon 58.21; CCCM 2B:112.

Spirit,[14] and in her we may witness, at one and the same time, the virtues of both Martha and Mary, the active and the contemplative lives.[15]

Overall, however, the primary thrust of all Aelred's Marian sermons is to exhort all of us, but especially the monks to whom he was preaching, to imitate her virtues and purity, and take her as our model.[16] In 1995, when only the first volume of Raciti's edition was available, Daniel La Corte stated that Aelred's Marian sermons "reflect his responsibilities as abbot and focus, not surprisingly, on issues of monastic life."[17] This was true at the time, and it remains true of the sermons now available in the second and third volumes of Raciti's edition. An excellent example is the whole of his long seventy-fourth sermon for the feast of the Assumption.[18] Indeed, many of the Marian sermons say singularly little about Mary herself, but a great deal about her role as our exemplar and model.[19] This

[14] See Sermon 74.24; CCCM 2B:252–53. As we saw in the last chapter, Amadeus of Lausanne says the same thing.

[15] See especially the whole of sermon 21, but also sections of sermons 21 and 32. The first two are for the feast of the Assumption, the third for the Purification. For the liturgical connection of Mary and Martha with the feast of the Assumption, see the beginning of chapter 16 below.

[16] See, for example, Alf Härdelin, "St. Aelred of Rievaulx on the Imitation of Mary," in *Mary and the Churches: Papers of the Chichester Congress, 1986, of the Ecumenical Society of the Blessed Virgin Mary*, ed. Alberic Stacpoole (Dublin: Columba Press, 1987), 30–41. Härdelin's conclusions still hold true, though his paper was published before any of the Raciti editions. Many more illustrative examples could now be cited.

[17] Daniel M. La Corte, "The Abbatial Concerns of Aelred of Rievaulx Based on his Sermons on Mary," *Cistercian Studies Quarterly* 30 (1995): 267. See also the same author's "Aelred on Abbatial Responsibilities," in *A Companion to Aelred*, 48–69.

[18] CCCM 2B:246–68.

[19] As Shawn Madison Krahmer said in 2000: what strikes us about the Marian sermons (she was speaking of just the first volume of Raciti's edition) "is that a good number of them say so little about Mary that on the surface of it, they hardly deserve to be called 'Marian' at all, except that they are preached on a Marian feast and generally, though not always, grow out of the prescribed readings and liturgy of the day" (Shawn Madison Krahmer, "Aelred of Rievaulx and the Feminine in the Marian Sermons for the Feasts

is especially true of the sermons for the feast of the Purification, most of which say very little about Mary, but a great deal about our need to purify ourselves from sins and uncleanness, and the need for penance and, through grace, the forgiveness of sins.

On the other hand, Aelred can always surprise us, as he does with his introduction of the elephantine Christ. In one of his sermons for the feast of the Purification, he takes as his text the Jewish laws for ritual cleansing after childbirth as set out in the twelfth chapter of Leviticus, and begins by exhorting his audience to imitate Mary's wonderful humility. Nowhere is this more apparent than in her offering herself for ritual purification, she who had no need to be purified at all![20] She wished to appear as no more than an ordinary young Jewish woman, not the Mother of God. But later in the sermon, Aelred reminds us that the Jewish law states that an offering should be made *for the woman herself* so that she might be completely cleansed. But what does the gospel say? It says (and here Aelred is quoting a liturgical variant of Luke 2:24), "In accordance with the legal custom, they gave *for him* a pair of turtledoves and two young pigeons."

> What's this? Are we saying that the evangelist is lying? Certainly not! He may perhaps have wanted to show us by these words that the most blessed Mary had no need of any purification. But what then? Are we actually saying that her *son* needs it? He does indeed need it, but only if you understand the way in which he needs it![21]

Does Christ in heavenly glory need food or drink or clothes? Obviously not. But remember Matthew 25:40: if we give food and clothes and so on to the least of Christ's brothers and

---

of the Assumption and Purification," *Cistercian Studies Quarterly* 35 (2000): 460–61.

[20] See also chap. 5, n. 25 (Bernard).

[21] Sermon 33.40; CCCM 2A:276.

sisters, we give it to him. He is, after all, our Head as we are his Body. Thus, since *we* certainly stand in need of purification, so does he! "His mother did not need purification, because she had been purified. He was in need of it, because not all his members had yet been purified."[22] In other words, each one of us has a role to play in purifying Christ. It is an awesome responsibility, and although I can certainly see what Aelred is saying, I am not sure I would dare to preach it from the pulpit.

The feast of the Purification, otherwise known as the feast of the Presentation of Our Lord in the Temple and, since at least 1014, Candlemas,[23] was and is celebrated on February 2, and has since the fourth century been one of the oldest Marian feasts in the Christian calendar. There was never any doubt about what had happened, supported, as it was, by the unquestioned authority of Saint Luke the Evangelist. By the time of her purification, Mary was alive and well, and doing her duty as a young Jewish mother, but the question as to when and how she herself was conceived, and what happened to her after her death, were other questions entirely. What does Aelred have to say on these matters?

In his time, as we have seen in earlier chapters, there was dispute on what came to be known as the doctrine of the Immaculate Conception and uncertainty as to exactly what happened at the assumption. The two questions that were being asked were, first, when was Mary cleansed from original sin, and second, was she assumed into heaven in both body and soul at the same time, or did she first die in the body, was then resurrected by the power of her divine son, and then assumed into heaven to be in his presence in glory? Aelred has singularly little to say on the first question, but a considerable amount on the second, especially in the sermons published by Gaetano Raciti.

[22] Sermon 33.41; CCCM 2A:276.

[23] The earliest occurrence of the term, in late Old English (*candelmæsse*), appears in the *Anglo-Saxon Chronicle* for that year.

As to the first, Charles Dumont, writing from the limited resources available to him in 1958, suggested that Aelred favored the tradition that Mary was cleansed from all original sin at the moment of the annunciation,[24] but it must be admitted that Aelred is unclear on the matter and never actually says what he thinks. It is also possible to find hints that he simply followed Bernard,[25] and thought that Mary had been purified sometime before her birth. In Aelred's single brief sermon *in conceptione sanctae Mariae*, "for the Conception of holy Mary,"[26] he says nothing whatever about her conception. He takes as his main text the prophecy of Balaam, son of Beor, in Numbers 24:17, "a star shall rise out of Jacob, and a scepter shall spring up from Israel," and says a great deal about "blessed Mary, Queen of Heaven, Mistress of the World, Mother of Mercy, Gate of Life, Star of the Sea."[27] She is our guide, our model, and our advocate,

> so let us take refuge in our star, let us call on Mary, that she may commend us to her son, who, at the prayers of his mother, might cleanse us from all sin, and, once cleansed, might protect us in this world so that we may see and glorify him in heaven.[28]

But how and when Mary herself was cleansed from original sin, Aelred does not say, though we may state with confidence that he did not believe in her immaculate conception. As Hilda Graef has rightly said, "the influence of St. Bernard was too

[24] See Charles Dumont, "Aspects de la dévotion du bienheureux Aelred à Notre Dame," *Collectanea Cisterciensia* 20 (1958): 316.

[25] I find it interesting that, although there are a number of allusions to and clear echoes of Bernardine works in the Aelredian corpus, though far fewer than one might imagine, Aelred refers to Bernard by name only once in all his writings, in a wholly inconsequential context, in the second chapter of his account of the Battle of the Standard.

[26] Sermon 161; CCCM 2C:496–501.

[27] Sermon 161.4; CCCM 2C:497.

[28] Sermon 161.14; CCCM 2C:501.

strong in his order to allow for independent thought on this matter."[29]

On the question of the assumption, however, Aelred is more specific, and he becomes ever more specific as time goes by. In his twentieth sermon, the second for the feast of the Assumption, he tells us that although Mary, through death, had lost Jesus in the flesh, yet today—the day of the feast—she found him again, because

> although it may be, as some believe (*sicut quidam credunt*), that she was assumed into heaven with her body as well, yet that body had assuredly been made spiritual, so that all that love with which she loved her Lord, her son, is not according to the flesh, but according to the spirit.[30]

But a little later in the same sermon, Aelred is much more specific. What does it mean, he asks, when, in the Song of Songs 3:2, the bride says, "I will arise and go about the city"?

> If I dared (*si auderem*), I would say that Mary, the most blessed mother of God, first left the flesh, and then, in that same flesh, was resurrected to eternal life. But although I dare not state this as a fact, because I have no argument that could convince anyone who does not believe it, I still dare to give this opinion, and dare to state, unhesitatingly,[31] that on this very day the blessed Virgin, whether in the body or out of the body I do not know,[32] ascended to heaven and

[29] Graef, *Mary*, 1:249.

[30] Sermon 20.6; CCCM 2A:156–57.

[31] CCCM 2A:163, line 305, reads *dubitanter* "with hesitation." Bertrand Tissier amended this to *indubitanter* "unhesitatingly," which I believe to be correct. That Mary was assumed into heaven was never disputed. What was disputed was whether her body was taken there at the same time, and Aelred, just like Isaac of Stella, covers his bases by quoting Saint Paul.

[32] 2 Cor 12:3, which is exactly the same verse quoted by Isaac of Stella: see chap. 8, n. 7.

> went about the whole of that celestial city with the full acuity of her mind.[33]

Aelred says much the same thing in the long sermon 45, also composed for the feast of the Assumption. After the death and resurrection of her son, Mary was in misery since she longed to join him whom she loved. But today, on this feast, Jesus rescued her from this life, bore her up to heaven, and placed her on a throne in his kingdom, raised above the ranks of the angels and ready to intercede for us: "Today she passed over from this world and ascends to the heavenly kingdom, where she has begun to contemplate his glory, power, and divinity."[34] Christ has prepared a place for her, and today he receives her there, "and conforms the body of his most blessed mother to the glory of his own body."[35]

> And although I dare not state this as a fact, since we do not have sure testimony from Scripture to prove it if someone should wish to deny it and vigorously refute it, yet I find it sweet to hold this opinion: namely, that he who can do all things, because of his measureless love for his mother, did not only place her soul in heaven, but also raised up her body, so that she could be in his presence with both body and soul and may even now have received that bodily immortality for which everyone hopes on the day of Judgment.[36]

Why, after all, do normal human bodies putrefy after death? Because of original sin, concupiscence of the flesh, and unlawful desires. The corruption of the flesh is the penalty for sin. It follows logically, then, that if there is no original sin, no concupiscence, and no unlawful desires, there would be no corruption after death. We know, says Aelred, that there are

[33] Sermon 20.32; CCCM 2A:163.
[34] Sermon 45.9; CCCM 2A:354.
[35] Sermon 45.9; CCCM 2A:355.
[36] Sermon 45.10; CCCM 2A:355.

some who had so perfectly conquered the desires of the flesh and preserved their virginity that, by God's grace, their bodies are still whole and sound and preserved from all corruption (he is referring to King Edward the Confessor, whose body was found incorrupt when his tomb was opened in 1102). But if Our Lord can grant such a gift to his sinful servants, what manner of gift do we think he would have granted to his most blessed mother, to her who was utterly pure and sinless from her birth? "No Christian, therefore, should doubt the incorruption of her holy body."[37]

Aelred's argument from the incorrupt bodies of certain saints is interesting, though not entirely original. He had clearly read the very popular treatise on the assumption attributed (incorrectly) to Saint Augustine,[38] but his own view is eminently clear. Mary died a natural death, she was resurrected by her divine son, and then, after that resurrection, she was taken up to heaven, body and soul, to be reunited with the one to whom she had given birth and to contemplate him in glory, a matter that requires further discussion.[39]

In Sermon 9 for the feast of the Annunciation, it takes Aelred some considerable time even to mention Mary,[40] but then, commenting on Song of Songs 1:2, "While the king reclined on his couch," he speaks of the marriage between the bridegroom, God, and the bride, Mary. The bridegroom's messenger is, of course, Gabriel. But in these nuptials, the Virgin did not

[37] Sermon 45.12; CCCM 2A:355.

[38] See Brian K. Reynolds, *Gateway to Heaven: Marian Doctrine and Devotion, Image and Typology in the Patristic and Medieval Periods. Volume 1: Doctrine and Devotion* (Hyde Park, NY: New City Press, 2012), 316–17. The work, by an unknown author, dates from about the end of the eleventh century. See chap. 1, n. 36.

[39] There is a valuable examination of this question by Marsha L. Dutton, "Christ Our Mother: Aelred's Iconography for Contemplative Union," in *Goad and Nail: Studies in Medieval Cistercian History, X*, ed. E. Rozanne Elder, CS 84 (Kalamazoo, MI: Cistercian Publications, 1985), 22–45.

[40] She makes her first appearance in Sermon 9.10: CCCM 2A:73.

lose her virginity, the bridegroom did not lose his divinity, and the angel did not lose his dignity. But what is an even greater miracle, the bridegroom here is a son, and the bride is a mother! "He is the bridegroom," says Aelred, "because he conjoined (*coniunxit*) the soul of that holy Virgin with his divinity."[41] What does he mean by this? Let us turn to sermon 75 for the feast of Mary's Nativity.

Here Aelred is offering an exegesis of 1 Kings 10:18-20, a passage that describes the magnificent throne that Solomon made for himself. Its back, we are told, was rounded at the top, and "this throne is clearly that most holy woman who in some way comprehended the incomprehensible, enclosed the infinite, and contained within her womb the one who contains all things."[42] But this throne, Aelred continues, has two parts, a lower and an upper. The lower part symbolizes the senses; the upper part the intellect (*intellectus*), the highest part of the rational soul. And in Mary's case, her intellect "was illumined by divinity itself, whose dwelling-place it was, and, so to speak, deified (*deificata*) in God."[43] It thus came to participate in divine eternity, in truth, and in charity, and in this way, "in the highest point of this virginal soul—namely, in the mind or intellect—the image and likeness of God shines forth."[44] Mary's soul is strengthened by eternity, put in order by charity, and illumined by truth.

The verb *deificari*, in any of its grammatical forms, is rare in Aelred. It appears only seven times, and of these, two refer to Mary—in the sermon we have just mentioned and in a very similar passage in Sermon 162, a sermon composed for the same feast and using the same text from 1 Kings[45]—two refer

[41] Sermon 9.16; CCCM 2A:74. We are reminded here of John of Forde, who had almost certainly read certain of Aelred's works: see chap. 11, n. 36.

[42] Sermon 75.7; CCCM 2B:270.

[43] Sermon 75.9; CCCM 2B:271.

[44] Sermon 75.9; CCCM 2B:271.

[45] Sermon 162.11; CCCM 2C:505.

to the deification of the human soul in God in mystical union,[46] and three are not of any consequence.[47]

But Aelred has not finished, and a little later in Sermon 75 he explains in more detail just how the rational soul in general, and the rational soul of Mary in particular, experiences God. To do this he cites his own study of the soul, the *De anima*,[48] and Augustine's celebrated Trinitarian analogy of memory, understanding or reason, and will. The principle here is simple. In order to perform an action, such as picking up a book, we must remember what a book is, understand what is involved in picking it up, and have the will to do it. These are three distinct factors that act inseparably in performing a single action, and this may be regarded as a distant, a very distant, analogy of the Trinity, in which the three distinct persons always act as a unity.[49]

These three, says Aelred, are sometimes referred to as parts of the soul, but that is incorrect. They *are* the soul, for the nature of the soul is simple, "and it cannot be split up, scattered, extended, or divided, because it is everywhere whole at one and the same time."[50] It follows, then, that there is but one substance (*substantia*) of reason, memory, and will, but each of these has its own distinct function. Consideration (*consideratio*)

[46] Both in Sermon 51.19; CCCM 2B:47, referring to the spiritual kiss of bride and Bridegroom, "in which the created spirit and the uncreated are merged, so that they may be two in one, or, rather, two [who are] one, as justifying and justified, as sanctifying and sanctified, as deifying and deified (*deificans et deificatus*)."

[47] Sermon 122.8; CCCM 2A:223, is simply a quotation from RSB Prol. 9. The other two are from sermon 172.27 for the feast of the Nativity of Edward the Confessor and from chap. 18 of the life of Edward, referring to an altar consecrated to the deified Trinity.

[48] Aelred, *De anima* 1.63; CCCM 1:705.

[49] For a convenient discussion in English (there are better accounts in French and German), see John E. Sullivan, *The Image of God: The Doctrine of St. Augustine and its Influence* (Dubuque: Priory Press, 1963), especially chapter IV.

[50] Sermon 75.12; CCCM 2B:272.

belongs to reason, choice (*electio*) to the will, and remembrance (*recordatio*) to the memory. The soul, therefore,

> seeks, finds, or considers God with the reason, chooses or rejects, loves or disregards him with the will, and remembers, holds, and embraces him with the memory. Thus, the continual remembrance of God is, in a certain way, like the seat of Solomon's throne,[51] and this was something that most blessed Mary possessed more fully and more perfectly than any other created being, just as she loved [him] more abundantly.[52]

Could Mary achieve these remarkable heights on her own? Indeed not. "She could not have done anything without you," says Aelred, addressing the Lord Jesus, "she who was worthy to carry you in her very womb":

> It is your hands that uphold this seat [of Solomon's throne], for it is your hands that support the head of your most sweet mother—that is, her most holy soul (*mens*)—so that you never withdraw from her memory. On one side, as with your left hand, you pour into her the remembrance of your passion, and on the other, as with your right hand, you breathe into her the sweetness of your divinity.[53]

It is only reasonable, then, to suppose that she who was so intimately associated with her son in his humanity and divinity would act as a *mediatrix* between humanity and divinity, between us and God, and so she does, though Aelred seldom uses the actual term *mediatrix*. In fact, in all his works it appears in only four sermons.[54] After God, he says, she is especially (*specialiter*) our advocate, after her son she alone is our hope,

[51] I.e., the throne of 1 Kings 10:19, Aelred's text at this point.

[52] Sermon 75.13; CCCM 2B:272.

[53] Sermon 75.14; CCCM 2B:272.

[54] All are mentioned below.

> and just as her son, our Lord, is the mediator between us and the Father, so she herself becomes the *mediatrix* between him and us.[55] She demands with a sort of right the salvation of sinners, for which reason she herself deserves to become their mother. For if no sinner had existed, neither the God-man nor the mother of God herself would have existed."[56]

Let us note Aelred's vocabulary here. Mary not only desires the salvation of sinners, but *demands* it with a certain right (*iure quodammodo exigit*). "She herself is our mother and our *mediatrix*, and, after God, our only hope,"[57] and it is she, says Aelred, using a very rare word, who is the *liberatrix animarum nostrarum*, the one who frees our souls from the consequences of the Fall.[58] It must be observed, however, that although the actual term *mediatrix* is rare in Aelred, the principle appears unmistakably in many of his sermons for the great Marian feasts, and, as Luigi Gambero has said, "Aelred expresses himself extremely clearly and even boldly when speaking on this theme."[59]

Let us therefore take refuge in this mother who loves us and intercedes for us with her divine son. She is *maris stella*, the Star of the Sea,[60] and to her we should lift our eyes so that she may guide us, illumine us, help us to ascend the ladder of the virtues, and encourage us when we fall.[61] And in Sermon 159, in a lengthy passage obviously indebted to Bernard's second homily *in laudibus Virginis Matris*,[62] Aelred speaks of Mary as

[55] Aelred says much the same thing in Sermon 58.26; CCCM 2B:114.

[56] Sermon 45.3; CCCM 2A:352–53.

[57] Sermon 119.17; CCCM 2C:205.

[58] Sermon 153.4: CCCM 2C:440. This is the sole appearance of the word *liberatrix* in all of Aelred's writings.

[59] Luigi Gambero, trans. Thomas Buffer, *Mary in the Middle Ages: The Blessed Virgin Mary in the Thought of Medieval Latin Theologians* (San Francisco: Ignatius Press, 2005), 165.

[60] The title appears in six sermons: 24, 110, 159, 161, 162, and 163.

[61] See Sermon 24.20; CCCM 2A:195.

[62] See chap. 2, n. 34, and chap. 5, n. 16.

the shining star who can guide us through the storms and vicissitudes of this life, help us to overcome the trials, tribulations, and temptations that assail us, and offer us succor in times of need, difficulty, distress, dilemmas, or doubt. "With your eyes on this star, you will not be afraid, following this star you will not be led astray, following it to the end, you will rejoice in eternity."[63]

It is time now to leave Aelred's sermons and turn to an important passage in his *De institutione inclusarum*. This is the threefold meditation on the past, present, and future that constitutes the last section of the work, and which, Aelred trusts, will enable "the sweet love of Jesus" to grow in the affections of the contemplative.[64] The first meditation takes us from the annunciation through Jesus's life and death, and ends with his post-resurrection appearance to Mary Magdalen when she mistakes him for the gardener. The second is less a reflection on the life of Christ than Aelred bewailing his own utter sinfulness, his shameful desires, how he slid down the precipice of vice to be drowned in the whirlpool of debauchery, only to be rescued by the grace of God. Personally I doubt that he was ever as debauched as he maintains, but this sort of rather tedious lament is not uncommon in the writings of those who seek nothing but utter and complete perfection. In the third meditation, if I may quote Marsha Dutton,

> Jesus appears again, but this meditation concentrates less on Jesus than on the Judgment and the beatitude prepared for the blessed. It is the first meditation with its presentation of the life of Jesus and the contemplative's participation in that life that was so new in Christian spiritual writing.[65]

[63] Sermon 159.19; CCCM 2C:488. There is a close parallel to this in sermon 161.4–5; CCCM 2C:497, though it ends "following it, you will be safe from every danger."

[64] Aelred, *De institutione inclusarum* 29; CCCM 1:883–84.

[65] Marsha L. Dutton, "The Cistercian Source: Aelred, Bonaventure, and Ignatius," in *Goad and Nail*, 152. Dutton's entire article (151–78) is recom-

It is indeed the first meditation that is so significant for the way in which it plunges us into the events of the life, death, and resurrection of Christ. Enter Mary's very room! Be there with her at her side. Join her in reading the books that prophesy the virgin birth. Wait on tip-toe for the coming of the archangel, all glory and feathers. Listen to him utter his words of greeting, and so on, and so on. We are there, right there, with Mary, the angel, her new-born baby, the magi, and all else in that splendid story, and those who wish to embrace its vibrancy and effectiveness may read it for themselves.[66]

But there is more to it than this. The recluse, says Aelred, should follow Mary when she visits Elizabeth, she should be with her when she gives birth to Jesus, she should join her tears to those of Mary at the blood-drenched passion of her son, and in visualizing all these things in this way and in meditating upon them so deeply, "we see quite clearly," as Hilda Graef says, "the beginnings of the Rosary meditations."[67] This is true, and Aelred deserves his proper place in that, though we see them even more clearly in the writings of Stephen of Sawley. But an account of his "Meditations on the Joys of the Blessed and Glorious Virgin Mary" must be left until our next chapter.

mended reading for this important meditation. A complete English translation of the *De institutione* by Mary Paul Macpherson may be found in CF 2:79–102.

[66] There are many passages in the sermons where Aelred uses the same technique, bringing us fully and personally into the midst of the events he is narrating.

[67] Graef, *Mary*, 1:250.

Chapter Ten

Two Neglected Sources: Stephen of Sawley and Ogier of Locedio

Why neglected? Because in the usual surveys of the development of Marian literature and devotion, the meditations of Stephen of Sawley on the joys of the blessed and glorious Ever-Virgin Mary tend to be given short shrift, and Ogier of Locedio, despite having written one of the longest series of homilies of any in praise of God's Holy Mother, is often not mentioned at all. To take but two examples. Hilda Graef, while recognizing Stephen's work to be "a little gem of Marian literature,"[1] devotes less than a page to their author, and Luigo Gambero ignores him completely. In neither survey does Ogier make any appearance whatever.[2] We need to remedy this.

Stephen came from Eston in the North Riding of Yorkshire. We know neither the date of his birth nor when he took the Cistercian habit at Fountains. At some date, also unknown, he was appointed cellarer of Fountains, but he could not have held the post after about 1223, when he was elected abbot of

[1] Hilda Graef, *Mary: A History of Doctrine and Devotion*, 2 vols. (London: Sheed & Ward, 1963–1965), 1:264.

[2] Brian K. Reynolds, *Gateway to Heaven: Marian Doctrine and Devotion, Image and Typology in the Patristic and Medieval Periods. Volume 1: Doctrine and Devotion* (Hyde Park, NY: New City Press, 2012), 147, 149, 225, 283–84, does a little better, but it is still not enough.

Sawley or Sallay, about five miles northeast of Clitheroe in Lancashire. He governed the abbey for more than ten years, to at least October 1233, before being elected abbot of Newminster, the mother house of Sawley. There he remained until late in 1247 when he was transferred to Fountains, the mother house of Newminster and one of the most important Cistercian abbeys in England. It was a distinguished career. He was abbot of Fountains until his sudden and unexpected death on September 6, 1252, while he was on an abbatial visitation of the abbey of Vaudey in Lincolnshire, a daughter house of Fountains. He was buried in the Vaudey chapter house, but although there were reports of miracles at his tomb, there is no trace of any local cult.[3]

The two most important works attributed to Stephen are the *Meditationes de gaudiis beatae et gloriosae semper virginis Mariae*, which are here our concern, and a *Speculum novitii*, which is an introduction to the monastic life for a Cistercian novice. In 2014, however, serious doubts were cast on the authorship of the *Speculum novitii* by Dr. Tristan Sharp, and it is quite possible that the earlier attribution to Stephen cannot be sustained.[4] The *Meditationes*, on the other hand, are attributed in the manuscripts to "Dom Stephen, the venerable abbot of Sawley,"[5] so there can be no doubt that he did indeed compose them.

[3] See further the entry by David N. Bell, "Stephen [Stephen of Sawley]," in the *Oxford Dictionary of National Biography* (2004).

[4] See Tristan Sharp, "A Treatise with Too Many Authors? The *Speculum novitii* Attributed to Stephen of Sawley," *Cîteaux – Commentarii cistercienses* 65 (2014): 277–97.

[5] See André Wilmart, "Les méditations d'Étienne de Salley sur les Joies de la Vierge Marie," in André Wilmart, *Auteurs spirituels et textes dévots du Moyen Âge latin: Études d'histoire littéraire* (Paris: Études augustiniennes, 1971), 339. The whole of Wilmart's article, which contains the Latin text of the *Méditationes*, goes from page 317 to 360. For a rather too free English translation by Jeremiah F. O'Sullivan, see CF 36:27–62.

Stephen himself tells us what he intends to do. He will arrange the meditations in three groups of five, and the total of fifteen represents the fifteen steps at the entrance to the temple in Jerusalem that Mary, at the age of three, ascended with no help from her parents when she was presented there. The ultimate source for this tale is the fourth chapter of the apocryphal gospel of pseudo-Matthew.[6] Each meditation will concentrate on a particular joy, there will be a petition addressed to the Virgin by the person who is meditating, and each will end with the Angelic Salutation—the *Ave Maria*—"supplemented by a few words of devotion."[7] The first group of five will cover the period from the birth of the blessed Virgin to the birth of the Savior, the second from the birth of the Savior to his passion, and the third from the passion to the assumption of the blessed Virgin. "It is only right," says Stephen, "that we begin with the birth of the holy Mother of God, whose holy and singular birth announced joy to the whole world."[8]

The fifteen meditations then take the following order: the birth of Mary (I), the life of Mary (II), the annunciation (III), the conception of Jesus (IV), the visitation to Elizabeth (V), the birth of Jesus (VI), the coming of the magi (VII), the purification (VIII), Jesus at the age of twelve (IX), the beginning of Jesus' public life (X), the crucifixion (XI), the resurrection (XII), the ascension (XIII), Pentecost (XIV), and the death and assumption of the Mother of God (XV).

The meditations are not replete with Marian theology. Indeed, they are not replete with very much theology at all, although, as we shall see, theology is not absent. They are, however, of considerable significance in the development of medieval devotion to the Virgin. They are a sort of first cousin

[6] James K. Elliott, *The Apocryphal New Testament: A Collection of Apocryphal Christian Literature in an English Translation* (Oxford: Oxford University Press, 2005), 88 (Ps-Matthew §4).

[7] Wilmart, "Méditations," 339. See also page 358.

[8] Wilmart, "Méditations," 340.

to the threefold meditation at the end of Aelred's *De institutione inclusarum* and the numerous similar affective passages that appear in his sermons. Stephen, like Aelred, wants to bring us into the events he describes. He wants us to visualize, to imagine, to picture, to dwell upon, to participate in these events. We must be there, for example, and form in our soul a picture of Mary when, in her chamber, she is confronted by an angelic messenger who tells her she is to bear a child who will be the savior of the world. We must be there with the magi when they discover the child Jesus, "squalling in his little bed or resting on his mother's bosom or suckling at her breasts or stretched out in the virgin's arms, as if ready to be embraced and kissed."[9] And so on. There is a great deal of such intimate and physical language, and Stephen penetrates to the heart of the events he describes with remarkable psychological acuity.

Mary herself is described with all the usual titles—Mother of God, Ever-Virgin, Queen of Heaven, Mistress of the World, Mother of Mercy (and also, once, Queen of Mercy[10]), Star of the Sea, Empress of the Angels, and so on—and, as a theme that runs throughout all the meditations, Stephen quotes a line from the last part of the *Salve Regina*, the daily prayer that ended (and still ends) Compline in Cistercian monasteries:[11] *O clemens, o pia, o dulcis Maria*, "O clement, O loving, O sweet [Virgin] Mary."[12]

She is also our *mediatrix*, advocate, and intercessor—Stephen leaves us in no doubt about that—and it is therefore to her "that the souls in hell (*in inferno*) look to be delivered, those in heaven to be glorified, and those on earth to be saved."[13] Stephen quotes "blessed Bernard" as his authority here, and Bernard's influence is obvious throughout the whole work.

[9] Wilmart, "Méditations," 346.

[10] Wilmart, "Méditations," 357: *regina clemencie*.

[11] See chap. 2 for a translation and discussion.

[12] Wilmart, "Méditations," 341, and numerous times thereafter.

[13] Wilmart, "Méditations," 343. See also 341 the end of the First Joy.

Stephen cites him three times by name, though his quotations are paraphrases rather than quotations, and one of them may not be by Bernard at all.[14]

The overwhelming atmosphere of the meditations is one of joy, not just the obvious joy of Mary in the various events of her life, but a more deep-seated joy that permeates the whole work. Reading some of the hyper-pessimistic literature that was so popular in the Middle Ages—the pseudo-Bernardine *Meditationes piisimae* are a case in point[15]—can lead to a strong desire to throw oneself off the nearest cliff (not difficult in Newfoundland); reading Stephen's meditations can leave one with a smile on one's face and a desire for a glass of good wine. Even in the eleventh meditation, when Mary is at the foot of the cross, regarding the blood-stained body of her son, her own soul pierced by the sword of his suffering, there is joy. For in the midst of such anguish and sorrow, asks Stephen,

> did you not think of mercy, Lady, of that mercy, I say, that concerned both you and the redemption of the whole world? Did you not rejoice with unspeakable joy when, from the unshakeable certainty of faith, you knew beyond any doubt that, by the precious blood of your son, the whole world had been redeemed, hell had been despoiled, the devil, though strong, had been chained, and the gate of the Kingdom of Heaven laid open?[16]

But let us note that it is the precious blood of Jesus that achieves all this. Stephen is no Mariolater. Mary might inter-

[14] See Wilmart, "Méditations," 340 line 47, 341 line 89, and 343 line 150, with Wilmart's accompanying notes.

[15] *Meditationes piisimae de cognitione humanae conditionis*, "Most Devout Meditations for Understanding the Human Condition," PL 184:485A–508B. For English translations, see David N. Bell, "A Bibliography of English Translations of Works by and attributed to St Bernard of Clairvaux: 1496–1970," *Cîteaux* 48 (1997): 127. The work was immensely popular.

[16] Wilmart, "Méditations," 351.

cede for us, she might be our *mediatrix* and advocate, but whatever is brought about is brought about from the Father, through the Son, in the grace of the Holy Spirit. As Bede Lackner has said, Stephen strongly insists that all the prerogatives of Mary "were God-given and not the fruit of human efforts. Mary was singled out by the Holy Trinity; God himself had chosen to dwell in her and wished to save mankind through her."[17]

Mary is also, of course, our model. Like almost everyone else, Stephen lauds her profound humility, her dedicated virginity, and the power of her charity, three virtues that are not only presented to us for our imitation, but that also redound to Mary's own glory:

> From the first virtue she deserved to be called Queen of Heaven, from the second, the Immaculate Mother of the virgin-born Son of God, from the third, the Mother of Mercy.[18]

And in his petition to this second meditation, Stephen prays to the sweetest virgin that she might establish his life in these virtues of hers, so that when he dies she might recognize him, unworthy as he is, as one of her servants, *"o clemens, o pia, o dulcis Maria."*[19]

In the seventh meditation, when the magi find the child Jesus, what do they bring? They bring him gold, myrrh, and incense, and so proclaim him to be both the God-man and the threefold Trinity. Gold symbolizes the Father's power, myrrh symbolizes the Son's wisdom and his mortal humanity, incense symbolizes the sweetness and fragrance of the Holy Spirit. But the three gifts also apply to us, for Stephen begs his sweetest lady that, ever under her patronage, he may present to her son

[17] Bede K. Lackner, "Introduction," to the English translation of the Meditations, CF 36:14.

[18] Wilmart, "Méditations," 341.

[19] Wilmart, "Méditations," 342.

the mystical gift of myrrh, which is perfect mortification of the flesh, the incense of devout prayer, and the gold of true discernment (*discretio*).[20] And where does this lead? Where else but to the joys of Paradise and the vision of God? "Sweetest Lady," says Stephen,

> by your holy and sublime joys, I beg you to purify this wretched soul of mine, still journeying in this bodily abode, from all its desires, to have it yearn inwardly for your most beloved son, and, by way of faith, to be offered to God the Father in his holy temple, until, having departed in peace, it may be worthy to contemplate the Sun of Righteousness[21] himself, with God the Father and the Holy Spirit, the one and only light of the physical and spiritual creation, in the vision of the heavenly Jerusalem, o clement, o loving, o sweet Mary.[22]

And Stephen concludes his petition with a slightly expanded version of the *Ave Maria*.

What, then, of Mary's conception and assumption? Does Stephen express any opinion on these disputed matters? He does, and we will not be surprised to find him following in the footsteps of blessed Bernard, his master. In his fourth meditation on the conception of the Virgin, Stephen clearly implies, even if he does not explicitly state, that Mary was cleansed and wholly purified from all sin at the very moment she conceived God incarnate. It was only after "the whole divine wave had gently poured itself into her virginal womb and pervaded it"[23]—it is a striking image—that Mary was freed from all carnal thoughts and experienced nothing but the fullness of grace.

[20] Wilmart, "Méditations," 347.

[21] Mal 4:2.

[22] Wilmart, "Méditations," 348.

[23] Wilmart, "Méditations," 343. One is tempted to translate *tota divinita unda* as "the divine tsunami."

As to the assumption, however, it is not clear what Stephen believed. Jesus, he says, ascended to heaven to take his own place at the right hand of the Father and to prepare for his beloved mother "a place of immortality" (*locus immortalitatis*[24]), and that is where she is now, "seated in her body (*corporaliter*) on a throne of glory on the right hand of her son," and attending day and night to the concerns and laments of those who call upon her.[25] After the death of her son she had been left in this world "for our salvation and for the instruction and consolation of the apostles,"[26] but then her son had come "with an infinite multitude of the heavenly hosts,"[27] to visit his most holy mother, "glorifying her in both body and soul,"[28] and to take her away from the wretched pilgrimage of this world. He raises her above all the heights of heaven and seats her on a throne of glory on his right hand, "where, with him and the holy angels, she rules triumphantly forever, the Mistress of the World, the Queen of Heaven, the Empress of the Angels, the hope of the afflicted, and the appeasement of sinners."[29] But whether this occurred at the moment of her death or after she had died and had been resurrected, Stephen does not say. That his sweetest lady is in heaven *corporaliter* is not in question, but exactly when she got there remains a mystery.

In 1963 Hilda Graef observed that in its structure of fifteen meditations grouped into three sections of five each, "the similarity to the later Dominican Rosary is remarkable,"[30] and in

[24] Wilmart, "Méditations," 354 lines 549–50 and 557–58.

[25] Wilmart, "Méditations," 356.

[26] Wilmart, "Méditations," 356. Stephen may well have borrowed this from Amadeus of Lausanne: see chap. 8, n. 48. Jeremiah O'Sullivan considers Amadeus to have been one of Stephen's important sources (see CF 36:61), and includes numerous allusions to Amadeus in the notes to his English translation.

[27] Wilmart, "Méditations," 356. This is a common theme in the assumption literature.

[28] Wilmart, "Méditations," 357: *in corpore et anima glorificans.*

[29] Wilmart, "Méditations," 356.

[30] Graef, *Mary*, 1:264. Wilmart, "Méditations," 325, also remarks on the similarity.

an important article published in 2015 Matthew Mills expanded on this simple comment at much greater length.[31] Those interested in the details of Dr. Mills's arguments must read his paper for themselves, for in it he presents a brief history of the rosary, a comparison of its standard fifteen mysteries—joyful, sorrowful, and glorious—and the fifteen meditations of Stephen,[32] a brief account of Stephen's teaching on Mary, and an assessment of the importance of his work in the development of the rosary. His conclusion is that Stephen's *Meditations* are an important antecedent to the development of the rosary, and that

> the resonances between them are striking and extend beyond form . . . to include a deep catechetical purpose, to promote orthodox doctrine using an affective devotional method. The significance of this is to trace the history of the rosary (as well as, incidentally, the *Ave Maria*) back to the Cistercians in England for perhaps the first time.[33]

Let us now leave the climes of northern England and make our way to the abbey of Lucedio[34] in the topmost northwest corner of Italy, about twelve miles southwest of Vercelli. The abbey, one of the oldest Cistercian foundations in Italy, was founded in 1124 as a daughter house of La Ferté, and survived for more than six centuries before being closed and secularized in 1784. Problems appear to have developed in the late seventeenth century—there were rumors of devil worship, satanic rites, and all manner of perversions—and things became so bad that Pope Pius VI closed the abbey in 1784 and transferred the remaining monks to a Jesuit college in Castelnuovo Scrivia, about fifty miles south of Vercelli. How much of the rumor is

[31] Matthew J. Mills, "Stephen of Sawley's Meditations on Our Lady's Joys and the Medieval History of the Rosary," *Cistercian Studies Quarterly* 50 (2015): 423–39.

[32] See especially the table on page 427 of Mills's article.

[33] Mills, "Stephen of Sawley's Meditations," 439.

[34] The earlier spelling was Locedio, with an O.

true is unclear, but Lucedio still has an evil reputation and appears on various websites as "the most haunted place in Italy" or "the Satanic Lucedio Abbey" and other such lurid titles.[35] Today the abbey operates as an organic rice farm, but it cannot be denied that there is something disturbing about the place.

The satanic invasion, however, occurred long after Ogier of Locedio had gone to meet his Maker, for he died in 1214, and, so far as we know, neither he nor any of his monks had any dealings with the Prince of Darkness. Who, then, was Ogier or, in Latin, Ogerius?[36] He was born in Trino, just about four miles from the abbey, but when he entered the monastery is unknown. What we do know is that he was elected abbot in 1205 and governed the abbey until his death on September 10, 1214. If Dom Andreas Irico of Locedio was correct when, in the early eighteenth century, he stated that Ogier was seventy-eight at the time of his death, he must have been born in 1136.[37] A local cult developed almost immediately after his death, and he was accorded the title of *beatus*, but it was not until 1875 that this was given official recognition by Pope Pius IX. He is now Blessed Ogier of Locedio, with his feast day on September 10, the day of his death.

The homilies *in laudibus sancte Dei Genetricis* survive in a single manuscript, originally from the Cistercian abbey of Santa Maria di Staffarda, and are a substantial work of sixty-eight folios of the manuscript, ninety-eight pages of the 1873 edition by Giovanni-Battista Adriani (the only edition so far[38]),

[35] Just type "Lucedio abbey most haunted" into your search engine for a variety of websites.

[36] The form Oglerius, with the intervening L, appears to have developed after his death.

[37] See *Ogier of Locedio: Homilies: In Praise of God's Holy Mother. On Our Lord's Words to His Disciples at the Last Supper*, trans./annot. D. Martin Jenni, CF 70 (Kalamazoo, MI: Cistercian Publications, 2006), 4.

[38] *Beati Oglerii de Tridino, abbatis monasterii Locediensis ordinis Cisterciensium in diocesi Vercellensi, Opera quae supersunt . . .*, ed. Giovanni-Battista Adriani (Turin: Ex Officina Regia, 1873), cited below as Adriani.

and no fewer than 143 pages in Dr. Martin Jenni's English translation. This is no small composition, no insignificant opuscule, so why have the homilies been so neglected? Or, more precisely, why have about 92% of them been neglected?

The exception is the twelfth and penultimate homily, which, for centuries, circulated as the very popular *Planctus Mariae*, "Mary's Lament," or the *Quis dabit* (its *incipit*), and was attributed incorrectly to Bernard of Clairvaux. It was only in 1952 that Henri Barré identified it as a work of Ogier,[39] and a new critical edition was published by C. W. Marx in 1994.[40]

But why have the rest of the homilies been neglected? The reason, I suspect, is that Adriani's 1873 edition is an exceedingly rare volume, and it may well be that earlier writers were simply unable to find a copy. When Martin Jenni was about to undertake his translation of Ogier's homilies, he wrote to me saying that he could find no trace of the book anywhere in North America, and did I know where there might be one. As it happens, I did: I had a xeroxed copy on my shelf, and how it came to be there still brings a smile to my face.

More than thirty years ago, long before the internet or scanning, I put in a request for the book to the miracle workers in the Inter-Library Loans Department of my university in Newfoundland. I had very little hope of ever seeing a copy of this rarest of editions, but there was no harm in trying. But several weeks later—*mirabile dictu*—I was informed by Inter-Library Loans that they had located a copy in Turin, that it had been mailed to Newfoundland, and that it was sitting in the university library awaiting my attention. I went and collected it immediately—it was not even restricted to in-library use—and made a xeroxed copy. It was a copy of that copy that I sent to

[39] See Henri Barré, "Le *'Planctus Mariae'* attribué à saint Bernard," *Revue d'ascétique et de mystique* 28 (1952): 243–66.

[40] C. W. Marx, "The *Quis dabit* of Oglerius de Tridino, Monk and Abbot of Locedio," *Journal of Medieval Latin* 4 (1994): 118–29.

Martin Jenni so that he could begin work on his translation,[41] and it is that copy that I am now using to see what Ogier of Locedio has to say about God's holy mother. Let us therefore take the advice of the King of Hearts in *Alice in Wonderland* and begin at the beginning and go on until we come to the end.

The division into a prologue and thirteen homilies is due to Jenni.[42] Neither the Staffarda manuscript nor Adriani's edition divides the text thus, but it is clear from the doxologies and other indicators that what appears there as a continuous text was originally a series of sermons. Jenni's division is perfectly sound, and I have had no hesitation in following it. It is also fairly clear that the homilies were delivered before Ogier became abbot.[43]

He opens with the not unfamiliar *topos* of declaring how unfit he is to take on the task he has set himself, and then, in a very great deal of fulsome Latin, shows us that we cannot take his plea too seriously. In the first homily, Ogier asks the Mother of God to deign to speak with him and tell him about herself. And so she does, though what she says pertains as much to her divine son as to her. She begins with her father and mother—Joachim and Anna—and summarizes her life through the annunciation, the birth of Jesus, his miracles, the passion and her grief at that passion, to her son's resurrection and his ascension into heaven. Much more will be added in the ensuing homilies.

The second homily deals with Mary's birth and childhood. His sources here are primarily the apocryphal gospels, especially the *Protevangelium* of James, and Jenni is quite right when he states that "Ogier not only embraces the legendary with a credulity the Abbot of Clairvaux would have deemed rash, he

[41] Jenni's translation, as he himself points out, contains a number of paraphrases and some minor abridgements.

[42] See CF 70:12.

[43] See CF 70:7.

treats such material in much the same way as his biblical sources."[44] In this homily, however, Ogier says nothing about how Mary was conceived, save that she was a child of Joachim and Anna's old age. It is in the later *Expositio in Evangelium in Cena Domini*, "Commentary on the Gospel Passage concerning the Lord's Supper," that we find the key statement:

> There is not one among the children of men and women, whether great or small, who, possessed of such holiness or honored with such privileged devotion, was not conceived in sin (*in peccatis fuerit conceptus*) or, afterwards, did not live in sin, with the exception of the Mother of the Immaculate One, who never committed sin, but bore the sin of the world.[45]

It is difficult to see this as anything other than a statement of the doctrine of the Immaculate Conception, though Ogier does not dwell on it. If so, he is the first of the Cistercians we have encountered in these pages to take it upon himself to contradict the views of Bernard of Clairvaux, of whom, in almost everything else, he was a devoted follower.

The third homily tells us of Mary's early life in the Temple of Jerusalem and, once she had accepted the angel's words that she would bear the Savior of the World, of her longing for that event to transpire. Again Ogier is dependent on the apocryphal narratives, though some of the details may well have been his own. Mary, for example, is not brought to the Temple at the age of three, as we find in Stephen of Sawley and the gospel of pseudo-Matthew, but immediately after she was weaned, and Ogier has no hesitation in putting into her mouth prayers that can only have come from his own devout imagination. Yet his eyes remain fixed on his Savior, from whom alone comes salvation, and he follows Bernard in saying that since to praise God is also to praise his mother, and to praise the

[44] CF 70:9.

[45] Adriani, *Beati Oglerii de Tridino*, 226 = PL 184:941C.

mother is to praise "her most beloved Son, our God," Ogier will continue to sing the praises of her who shall be called blessed by all generations.[46]

In the fourth and fifth homilies Ogier deals with the Annunciation and Mary's response to it. He introduces Joseph and tells us that he was much older than Mary, and that their relationship was not in any way sexual. His business was to serve her and care for her, and, in the guise of a husband, "be a most faithful guardian of that absolute virginity."[47] This explanation for Jesus' brothers and sisters—that they were Joseph's children by a previous marriage—was commonplace and derives ultimately from the *Protevangelium* of James.

In the fifth homily, which is heavily indebted to Bernard's homilies *in laudibus Virginis Matris*, Ogier invites us to picture the scene when Gabriel appears to Mary and greets her as "full of grace." There is some nonsensical etymology here, some of it unquestionably Ogier's own,[48] but Ogier also invokes the old Eva-Ave inversion that shows how everything that went wrong with Eve was put right in Mary:

> Just as in our Mary Eva is transformed into Ave, and, through the grace of Mary, Eve's fault is destroyed, so are we delivered from the double and everlasting death of body and spirit, and enter that life that is blessed and more than blessed, that knows no end.[49]

The rest of this homily is essentially a paraphrase of Bernard, but there is an interesting passage towards the end when Ogier tells the story of a man he knew, who, "more than fourteen years ago," was seriously ill, with leprous flesh and skin covered with scabs. Since he dared not pray to Christ for healing

[46] Adriani, *Beati Oglerii de Tridino,* 10, and, for Bernard, see Jenni's note at CF 70:42, n. 28.

[47] Adriani, *Beati Oglerii de Tridino,* 13.

[48] See Jenni's note at CF 70:54–55, n. 46.

[49] Adriani, *Beati Oglerii de Tridino,* 19.

(so often had he offended him), he prayed instead to the Mother of Grace and Mercy, beseeching her help and intercession. In her compassion, she restored to him the hope of salvation, and after he had run to the church and confessed his sins, he was healed. From that time on the Blessed Virgin saw to his care, and "[says Ogier] I do not say that after this he did not sin, but after this he did not have the will to sin, except where human frailty could not wholly avoid it."[50]

The question, of course, is whether this was indeed a man whom Ogier knew, or Ogier himself, and I think it significant that he opens his description in words similar to those of Saint Paul in 2 Corinthians 12:2. *Novi hominem ante quatuordecim annos,* "I knew a man, more than fourteen years ago," says Ogier.[51] *Scio hominem in Christo ante anno quatuordecim*, "I know a man in Christ more than fourteen years ago," says Saint Paul. There is general agreement that in this passage Paul is speaking of himself, and my own suspicion is that the same is true of Ogier. I may well be wrong in this and I can think of other explanations, but here I stand.[52]

The sixth and seventh homilies are concerned primarily with the incarnation. The sixth, which is fairly short, describes the greatness of Christ and his virtues, and urges us to imitate him. We should wrestle with our vices and desires, and be crucified to the world as the world is crucified to us.[53] We should deny ourselves by means of vigils and penance and manual labor, and thus "follow the Lord Jesus Christ in this life through grace, and in the next through glory."[54] And on whom should we call to help us in this, for we certainly cannot achieve it on our own? Who else but the "glory of the world and my glory, my Lady, the Mother of Glory, the Mother of

[50] Adriani, *Beati Oglerii de Tridino*, 24.
[51] Adriani, *Beati Oglerii de Tridino*, 23.
[52] See also Adriani, *Beati Oglerii de Tridino*, 28–29.
[53] See Gal 6:14.
[54] Adriani, *Beati Oglerii de Tridino*, 27.

Everlasting Joy,"[55] Mary herself, who, by the grace of God, conceived and gave birth to the Word made flesh.

How this was possible is the subject of the much longer seventh homily. How could Mary conceive a child without violating that virginity she has offered to God? Ogier considers the matter at some length, and explains what it means for "the Holy Spirit to come upon her."[56] But in so doing, he implies a far more conventional approach to her own conception than that which appears, or which may appear, in the later commentary on the Lord's Supper. The Most High, says Ogier, will cause the shadow of his power to extinguish in Mary any trace of sin: "So chaste and holy will you be that now you cannot sin or will [to sin]. He who sanctified you in your mother's womb will illumine you with such grace that in you there is no sin, nor any possibility [of sin]."[57]

This is in accord with the views of Bernard and of all the other Cistercians we have considered so far: Mary is sanctified or purified in her mother's womb sometime before her birth, but she is not conceived immaculately. That, in Ogier, appears to be a later development. Indeed, this whole homily is permeated with the thought of Bernard, whom he met and whom he mentions by name,[58] though it is interrupted by a vigorous condemnation of false monasticism and the need for repentance and reformation. And how is this to be done? Through the great virtue of humility—we are back with Bernard's homilies in praise of the Virgin Mother—for though virginity is noble, nobler by far is humility.[59] And if we seek examples of perfect humility, we need look no further than Mary and her divine Son. Ogier will elaborate on this in the next two

[55] Adriani, *Beati Oglerii de Tridino*, 28.

[56] Luke 1:35.

[57] Adriani, *Beati Oglerii de Tridino*, 32.

[58] Adriani, *Beati Oglerii de Tridino*, 34, line 13.

[59] Adriani, *Beati Oglerii de Tridino*, 39. For the Bernardine source, see Jenni's note at CF 70:84, n. 85, and chap. 5 of this present volume.

homilies, when he discusses the meaning and implications of the *Magnificat*.

The eighth homily begins with Mary's visit to Elizabeth, and Elizabeth's greeting her as "blessed among women."[60] There is nothing here on which we need to dwell, nothing to catch our attention. It is when Ogier begins his exposition of the *Magnificat* that things become more interesting. Mary, as Saint Luke tells us, begins her song of praise by saying "My soul magnifies the Lord"—*Magnificat anima mea Dominum*—but how, exactly, is the Lord magnified? In two ways, says Ogier. First, he is not magnified by ordinary human speech,

> but when our soul, created in God's image, conforms itself by righteousness to Christ, who is the image of the Father. And when [the soul] magnifies Christ himself by imitating him, it is raised still higher by participating in a certain way in his greatness, so that by imitating his virtue in a certain way, it is seen to show forth that image [of Christ] in the glittering colors of blessed works.[61]

Mary, of course, did precisely this, and so, second, it is therefore in Mary herself that the Lord's magnificence is most perfectly proclaimed. "Truly," says Ogier, "the Lord is magnified by you, Mary, Star of the Morning, outshining all stars, holiest of all mortals, more glorious than the angels in the sight of the eternal splendor."[62]

But then Mary continues by saying that while her soul (*anima*) magnifies the Lord, her spirit (*spiritus*) rejoices in God her Savior. Is there then a difference between her soul and her spirit? There is not, says Ogier: "the human spirit and soul are

[60] Luke 1:42.

[61] Adriani, *Beati Oglerii de Tridino*, 49. We may compare the ideas of Isaac of Stella: see chap. 8, n. 17.

[62] Adriani, *Beati Oglerii de Tridino*, 49.

the same."[63] In this he has Augustine to support him,[64] and he does not dwell, as do some of his colleagues (William of Saint-Thierry, for example, or Aelred of Rievaulx) on the difference between the feminine noun *anima* and the masculine noun *spiritus*. As far as Ogier is concerned, "the soul and spirit of most blessed Mary are one and the same."[65] But then, for the first time, Ogier waxes philosophically theological, or theologically philosophical, and says that a few remarks with regard to the soul and its powers might be profitable.[66]

The soul, he says, has three powers: the sensory, the rational, and the appetitive. By means of the first, the body perceives everything external to itself through the bodily senses. By means of the second, it analyzes what it perceives by the senses but goes far beyond this in examining matters that wholly transcend the senses. It is this power of the soul that recognizes the virtues and that, when fully developed, contemplates God. By means of the third power, the appetitive, the soul desires what it may perceive through the senses and / or what it may consider or contemplate through the power of reason. Desire, therefore, may be bad or good. If we desire sinful things—anything associated with the vices, for example—desire is, by definition, bad. If we desire something good—to magnify the Lord by conforming ourselves to his image, for example—desire is, by definition, good. In Mary's case, says Ogier, she magnified the Lord with all three powers of her soul, indeed, with her whole being, "and ever rejoiced in him, as in her God, in her Creator, in her Savior."[67]

[63] Adriani, *Beati Oglerii de Tridino*, 51.

[64] Augustine, *In Evangelium Joannis, tract.* 26.13; PL 35:1613: *Spiritus dico, quae anima vocatur*.

[65] Adriani, *Beati Oglerii de Tridino*, 51.

[66] A little earlier in this same homily he has briefly echoed Aristotle with his mention of final causes and material causes: see Adriani, *Beati Oglerii de Tridino*, 51.

[67] Adriani, *Beati Oglerii de Tridino*, 55.

This threefold analysis of the powers of the soul has its origins in Plato, but Ogier has almost certainly borrowed it from the popular *De spiritu et anima*, formerly attributed to Augustine,[68] as is certainly incorrect, and, more recently, to Alcher of Clairvaux, as is almost certainly incorrect.[69] The true author of this influential text remains unknown.

But now Ogier leaves aside Platonic philosophy and returns to the *Magnificat*. Why does Mary magnify the Lord? Because he has regarded the humility of his handmaiden, and the text leads him into yet another paean of praise of humility. "O happy humility," he says, "so loved by the Most High King of all the Ages that he established his royal throne upon it!"[70] As we saw above, virginity is good, but humility is better. It was because of Mary's perfect humility that the Second Person of the Trinity deigned to be born of her, and it is only right, therefore, that henceforth all generations will call her blessed.

Ogier continues his exposition of the *Magnificat* in his ninth homily. "The Lord," says Mary, "has done great things for me."[71] What great things? The answer is obvious: she conceived not by any human agency, but virginally, by the Holy Spirit, and bore in her created womb the very creator of the universe. But there is more to it than that, for it is through these great things that we ourselves, every day, receive great things. And what are these? Ogier leaves us in no doubt:

> God descended into your womb and there took on flesh, and the Holy Spirit dwells in our heart who was given to us through you. In your womb he clothed himself in our humanity and so made us participants in his divinity. Clothed in your flesh, he clothed us in his divinity. From heaven he

[68] It appears among his works in PL 40:779–832.

[69] See Bernard McGinn's introduction to *Three Treatises on Man: A Cistercian Anthropology*, ed. Bernard McGinn, CF 24 (Kalamazoo, MI: Cistercian Publications, 1977), 63–68.

[70] Adriani, *Beati Oglerii de Tridino*, 55.

[71] Luke 1:49.

> descended into you, so that through you he might draw us to himself in heaven. God came to earth and there became human, so that humans might ascend to heaven, there to become God.[72]

This an eminently clear statement of the Eastern Christian doctrine of deification, of becoming like God, and we have seen another example already in the writings of Guerric of Igny.[73] But what is notable here is the role of Mary in this process, for in Ogier's thought, she plays an integral part in the process of redemption.

For all his Marian devotion, Ogier never loses sight of the fact that mercy, grace, and salvation come only from God, in and through his Son and the Holy Spirit. Yet it is through Mary that God's mercy comes to us—he is commenting on "his mercy is on those who fear him" at Luke 1:50—and he spends some time in explaining exactly what it means to fear the Lord. We then move on to the proud being scattered and the mighty put down, which leads Ogier into a brief excursus on the fall of Lucifer. And what was the real cause of that fall? Pride indeed, for "pride is doing anything contrary to the will of God."[74] And what is the opposite of pride? Humility, of course—we are back with that ever-recurring theme—and when the *Magnificat* goes on to extol the humble, the meek, the hungry, and the poor, it is poverty of spirit, not poverty in goods, of which we are speaking. Our business here below is to eradicate self-will and imitate the model of perfect humility by saying and meaning, "Be it done with me according to your word." It is to overcome sin and the vices, for it was sin that led to that dreadful Fall, when Adam and Eve were banished from Eden into "the valley of calamity and death,"[75] and doom fell upon the human race.

[72] Adriani, *Beati Oglerii de Tridino*, 60.

[73] See chap. 6, nn. 50–51.

[74] Adriani, *Beati Oglerii de Tridino*, 64.

[75] Adriani, *Beati Oglerii de Tridino*, 68.

But all was not lost, for God, the Lord of Mercy, remembered his mercy,[76] and "could not forget his compassion, nor persist in his wrath."[77] He therefore came to the aid of his servant Israel, but not just to any Israel, for there are four distinct sorts of Israel: a wicked Israel, a false Israel, a pure Israel, and an adopted Israel. Of these, the most important, obviously, are the last two, for the pure Israel consists of those who are born of the Holy Spirit and who, "from the first day of their creation, have burned with love for their Creator."[78] The adopted Israel comprises "all who are reconciled to God the Father through the blood of Jesus Christ,"[79] and who, from the fullness of their heart, wholly abandon the paths of error and tread instead the ways of truth. It is they who shall see God, the Lord of Everlasting Blessedness. And so Ogier ends his homily by beseeching Mary, through her merits, to bring us all to that blessedness.

In the next two homilies, both brief, we move from Mary's sojourn at the house of Elizabeth and Zechariah to the birth of Jesus, the purification, the flight into Egypt, the passion, and Mary's own assumption into heaven. Things are now moving very swiftly, and Ogier does not dwell long on any of these events. It is interesting, though, that he tells us that the reason that Joseph was so unwilling to wed Mary and divorce her secretly,[80] given that she was pregnant by some person unknown, was not so that she would not be exposed to public disgrace, but because the true nature of the child she was carrying had been revealed to him, and he felt totally unworthy to be near her. Happily, a convenient angel appears and puts his mind to rest but also makes it clear that in marrying Mary, he is to guard and serve both her and her child, and that the normal physical pleasures of marriage will have no place in this holy relationship.

[76] We are now at Luke 1:54.

[77] Adriani, *Beati Oglerii de Tridino*, 68.

[78] Adriani, *Beati Oglerii de Tridino*, 69.

[79] Adriani, *Beati Oglerii de Tridino*, 69.

[80] See Matt 1:19.

In describing the birth of Jesus—the eleventh homily—Ogier begins by launching into a plethora of those paradoxes so beloved by so many of his contemporaries: the infinite becomes finite, the incomprehensible becomes comprehensible, the Creator becomes a creature, God becomes human, and so on and so on. Those interested can read his peroration for themselves, but towards the end of this homily we find the beginning of that text that, as we saw above, circulated for so long under the name of Bernard, the *Planctus Mariae* or "Mary's Lament."[81] It is a dramatic and moving narrative, some of it in words that Ogier puts into the mouth of Mary, some of it in words he puts into the mouth of her son. It takes us from Pilate's condemnation of Jesus to his entombment, and it ends with John taking Mary into his own house, where "he loved her with his whole heart as his very own mother."[82]

There is now a fairly extensive literature on the *Planctus* and its relationship to medieval liturgical drama, the Passion Plays, and medieval music, though this is not the place to examine it, but the sorrow and grief of this outpouring of pain comes to an end with the glory of the Resurrection in the last of Ogier's homilies.

At the beginning of the homily, however, Mary is still grieving the loss of her son. But then we see the stone rolled away from the door of an empty tomb, and Ogier breaks forth into the Ambrosian hymn, *Claro paschali gaudio*, "That Easter was bright with joy," sung at Lauds on Easter Sunday.[83] Ogier follows Ambrose and a few others in saying that the resurrected Christ appeared first to his mother, and then to Mary Magdalene and all the other apostles,[84] and goes on to describe the universal joy that was heralded by this glorious event. But then the risen Lord ascends to heaven, and Mary is once again

[81] The text begins on page 80, line 5, of Adriani's edition, but for a critical edition, see Marx, "The *Quis dabit* of Oglerius de Tridino."

[82] Marx, "The *Quis dabit*," 129.

[83] Adriani, *Beati Oglerii de Tridino*, 92. See Jenni's note at CF 70:160, n. 139.

[84] See Jenni's note at CF 70:160, n. 140.

bereft of her son and, in her grief, longs to be reunited with him.

She will remain so for two years—Ogier has taken this from pseudo-Meito of Sardis[85]—but then her son comes to her once again, this time, at last, to take her soul to heaven. Unlike some we have seen, Ogier is in no doubt as to what happened. Mary died, and her soul, accompanied by choirs of angels, was taken up to heaven. Her body was prepared for burial, guarded by angels, and then buried by the apostles who had been with her at her death. It was three days later that she was resurrected—the gospel parallel is obvious—and, "rising from the dead, now, immortal, reigns with Christ her son in blessed eternity,"[86] enthroned at his side as Queen of Heaven. Ogier's prayer, then, as he draws his last homily to a close, is that, through the mercy of Christ, he might behold both of them, son and mother, in glory:

> This alone will satisfy me, I shall seek nothing more than this. May your Virgin Mother, my Lady, obtain this for me, to whom I commit myself, and [to whom I] commit all of myself, body and soul, and the whole of my life, death, and resurrection. May she be blessed for ever.[87]

And so ends Ogier's "little book in praise of Paradise, namely, the mother of the eternal king, the sacred Virgin."[88] It is not a theological treatise, and I would not call it a devotional masterpiece. There is no doubt that it came from the heart, but with all his love for the Mother of God, Ogier never loses sight of the fact that she is the Mother *of God*. *Kyrios Christos*, "Jesus is Lord,"[89] and it is he who, as we have said, is the sole fountain of grace and salvation. Ogier's sources are,

[85] See Elliott, *Apocryphal New Testament*, 709 (pseudo-Melito §III.1).
[86] Adriani, *Beati Oglerii de Tridino*, 96.
[87] Adriani, *Beati Oglerii de Tridino*, 98.
[88] Thus the colophon in Adriani, *Beati Oglerii de Tridino*, 98.
[89] Rom 10:9; 1 Cor 12:3.

for the most part, standard and unexceptional. The most important are Bernard, Ambrose, Augustine, and (as usual for the etymologies) Jerome, though in the later homilies on the Lord's Supper, we find brief quotations from Ovid, Persius, and Virgil.[90] I must say, if I might add a personal note, I enjoyed reading Ogier, though his Latin is sometimes difficult, and I can fully appreciate the remarkable popularity of the *Planctus Mariae*.

Ogier died at Locedio in 1214, and in that very same year, John, abbot of Forde, also died in far-away England. And it is to England now that we must return, and see what two abbots and one monk of Forde had to say about the blessed Virgin.

[90] See Jenni's list of "Extra-Biblical Sources" in CF 70:337–40.

Chapter Eleven

Mary at Forde: Baldwin, John, and Roger

The abbey of Forde, in the southwest of England, was initially founded in 1136 as a Cistercian priory at Brightley, about two miles north of Okehampton in Devon. But since the ground proved too infertile to sustain the priory, the monks moved to a new site on land that had been given to them close to the River Axe. The new priory, later to become an abbey, was named Ford because of its proximity to an ancient river crossing. In recent years, an E has been added to Ford, which has thus become Forde. Baldwin was its third abbot, John its fifth, and Roger—not to be confused with the Roger who was the sixth abbot of the house—was a monk of Forde, and, as we shall see, an unusual monk at that. Let us begin with Baldwin.

In the words of Gerald of Wales, who had a biting tongue, Baldwin was a better monk than abbot, a better abbot than bishop, and a better bishop than archbishop.[1] There is some truth in this, though it is not the whole truth, but this is not the place to present an *apologia* for Baldwin.[2] He was born in

[1] Gerald of Wales, *Itinerarium Kambrensis*, II.xiv, ed. James F. Dimock, Rolls Series 21/6 (London: H.M.S.O. [1868]), 149; and *Vita Sancti Remigii*, xxix, ed. James F. Dimock, Rolls Series 21/7 (London: H.M.S.O. [1877]), 71.

[2] For an account of Baldwin's life, see the very sound entry by Christopher Holdsworth in the *Oxford Dictionary of National Biography* (2004); and David N. Bell, *Baldwin of Ford: Spiritual Tractates, Volume One*, CF 39 (Kalamazoo, MI: Cistercian Publications, 1986), 9–18.

Exeter around 1125 and most probably began his studies at the cathedral school there. By 1150, however, he was in Italy and, having studied law at Bologna, was appointed tutor to the nephew of Pope Alexander III. By 1155 he was back in Exeter, and seven years later, in 1162, was appointed archdeacon of Totnes. He served in that position for some eight years when he relinquished secular life to enter Forde Abbey. Part of the reason for this decision was to escape involvement in the ever-growing factionalism resulting from the conflict between Henry II and Thomas Becket, but it is also true that Baldwin was a deeply spiritual man, of profound devotion, with the soul of a monk. Exactly when he entered the abbey is uncertain—it was about 1170—and by 1173 he had been elected abbot. Given his talents, training, and contacts, this is not particularly surprising.

As abbot, he was still much involved with the world beyond the abbey walls, and he acted as papal judge-delegate in a considerable number of cases. It was perhaps inevitable that a man of such ability should not be allowed to remain long in the cloister, and in August 1180, with the support of Henry II, Baldwin was consecrated bishop of Worcester. His four years there were not especially eventful—the best-known incident is that he saved a man from being hanged (he had already been strung up when Baldwin intervened)[3]—but he carried out his pastoral duties with care and diligence and continued to act as judge-delegate.

Unfortunately for Baldwin, Henry's respect for him continued to grow, and when the see of Canterbury became vacant in February 1184, Henry's eye turned towards Baldwin. He was translated to Canterbury at the end of 1184 and consecrated as archbishop on May 19, 1185, and he remained archbishop until his death. It was not a happy time, for Baldwin was continually in conflict with the Canterbury monks—a conflict that came to involve two kings and three popes—and this conflict

[3] For the story, see Bell, *Spiritual Tractates*, 1:12.

may well have played a role in his decision to leave Canterbury and England and join the Third Crusade.

It appears that the crusade was something close to his heart. He had taken the cross at Geddington in January 1188, and he spent much of that year preaching the crusade in Wales. He left England in March 1190, together with Hubert Walter, bishop of Salisbury, and an advance party, and never returned. By August of that year they had reached Marseille; by October 12 they had arrived at Acre. But Baldwin was now no longer young, and the heat and conditions of Palestine took their toll. It seems, too, that he was deeply distressed by the unChristian conduct of the crusading army, and, having contracted some sort of fever, died during the siege of Acre on November 19, 1190.

The great majority of Baldwin's extant theological and spiritual writings were composed during his years as abbot of Forde, but of the twenty-two sermons that survive,[4] only one is specifically devoted to Mary: the sermon on the annunciation.[5] Part of another sermon, that on the power and effectiveness of the word of God, contains a brief section dealing with Mary's suffering at the death of her son,[6] but it is the sermon on the annunciation that contains Baldwin's essential Marian teachings. So what does he have to say?

There is nothing new in Baldwin's sermon; the two main themes are the old Eve-Mary parallel, and, echoing Bernard, the essential importance of the virtue of humility. His text is brief—"Hail, full of grace, the Lord is with you; blessed are you among women"[7]—though towards the end of his sermon he adds the following as a sort of addendum: "Every day we

[4] Critical edition by David N. Bell in CCCM 99 (1991).

[5] Latin text in CCCM 99:193–207; English translation in Bell, *Spiritual Tractates*, 1:191–213.

[6] Latin text in CCCM 99:293–94; English translation in Bell, *Spiritual Tractates*, 1:164–66.

[7] Luke 1:28.

devoutly use this angelic salutation to greet the most blessed Virgin, just as it was given to us, but we normally add to it 'and blessed is the fruit of your womb,' "[8] and he goes on to explain why he added it and what it signifies.

He begins his sermon by distinguishing two sorts of greeting—those that are sincere and those that are false—and then swiftly moves on to consider the difference between those who were filled with grace (such as Stephen the first martyr or Elizabeth) and Mary, who was greeted by the angel as being full of grace. What does this mean? It means that the fullness of grace in Mary renders the first sin void and restores our nature. Mary, says Baldwin, "was full of grace so that through her the grace of God might abound in us."[9] But this grace was not just a single grace, it was a triple grace: the grace of beauty, favor, and honor, which made her beautiful, gracious, and glorious, and Baldwin then proceeds to examine Mary's beauty, favor, and honor in greater detail.

Baldwin defines beauty in Augustinian terms, the essential features being regularity and balance,[10] and in Mary this balance is best seen in the balance of her great humility as the handmaid of the Lord with her equally great dignity as the mother of God. Christ, of course, is the perfect example of humility, for he emptied himself, taking the form of a servant[11]—we have seen this before—and Baldwin never fails to make it clear that Mary's greatness is always secondary to that of her divine son. She is Mistress of the World and Queen of Heaven, she has been made "the agent and collaborator in the divine plan,"[12] she brought forth the Savior who is himself the world's salvation, but grace is given by God alone:

[8] Sermon 13.45; CCCM 99:206. The addition is Luke 1:42, part of Elizabeth's greeting to Mary.

[9] Sermon 13.7; CCCM 99:195.

[10] See Sermon 13.8; CCCM 99:195, referring to Augustine, *De Trinitate* VIII. iii.4; PL 42:949.

[11] Phil 2:7.

[12] Sermon 13.26; CCCM 99:200. The Latin terms are *ministra et cooperatrix*.

> In this work of our salvation, a work that begins from fullness of grace and is consummated in fullness of grace, fullness of grace is specifically mentioned [in the text of the sermon], and praise is ascribed to the author of grace, who, with the cooperation of the Virgin, is revealed as the author of this work.[13]

Baldwin then goes on to explain why Mary is blessed among women, and here he returns to the old Eve-Mary theme and, once again, to the importance of Mary's humility. There are two sorts of humility, he says, one that comes from a command and one that is the result of our own deliberation and decision. The former is an obligation; the latter comes from our own free will. And of the two, humility that is the result of our own decision is the greater good. Such, of course, was the humility of the Mother of God.

Similarly, Baldwin follows Bernard in distinguishing between things that are commanded in Scripture and things that are advised or recommended.[14] As was the case with Mary's humility, so too was the case with Mary's virginity. In Scripture, virginity or barrenness is generally seen as a curse, but Mary "fell in love with virginity, and the virginity she embraced she offered and dedicated to God in an odor of sweetness, and defied the shame of the curse."[15] Then, to that virginity that had hitherto been barren was added fertility, and the fruit that the Virgin brought forth was "a fruit more precious than any fruit of marriage."[16] It was, of course, the Savior of the World,

> who destroyed death[17] and turned away the condemnation due to us, and it is to Mary, therefore, after God, that we owe

[13] Sermon 13.27; CCCM 99:200. The key phrase is *qui Virgine cooperante*.

[14] See chap. 5, n. 12.

[15] Sermon 13.37; CCCM 99:203.

[16] Sermon 13.38; CCCM 99:204.

[17] 2 Tim 1:10.

> everything: that we are freed from the curse and blessed with all manner of spiritual blessings in the heavens.[18] Thus, as she is ever blessed before God, so too she should be ever blessed by us.[19]

There is, as we have said, nothing new here. There are no new insights such as we find, for example, in Guerric of Igny, and certainly no Plotinian flight of the alone to the alone such as we find in Isaac of Stella. Indeed, Baldwin's spirituality has much in common with that of Armand-Jean de Rancé: it is a down-to-earth practical spirituality, rooted in the Rule of Saint Benedict and the Cistercian life, and although Baldwin obviously recognized the possibility of a true mystical encounter with God, he has hardly anything to say on these exalted matters.[20]

When Baldwin was elevated to the see of Worcester in 1180, he was succeeded as abbot of Forde by Robert, who governed the house from 1180 to his death in 1190, and then by John, whose career was far less eventful than that of Baldwin, but who has left us a handful of sermons on the Mother of God. His early life is a series of probabilities. He was probably born around 1150, probably in the west of England, and probably entered Forde abbey in about 1170. He became prior of Forde, and then, probably around 1187, was appointed to the abbacy of Bindon in Dorset, Forde's first daughter house. He was there for about four years before being recalled to Forde to succeed Robert as abbot. He would remain there until his death on April 21, 1214. He was an effective abbot, and Forde flourished under his administration. His talents, especially in law and negotiations, were recognized both by the Cistercian General Chapter and the English church, but his last years were overshadowed by the problems of the six years of the Interdict

[18] Eph 1:3.

[19] Sermon 13.44; CCCM 99:205.

[20] See David N. Bell, "The Ascetic Spirituality of Baldwin of Ford," *Cîteaux* 31 (1980): 247–48.

imposed on England between 1208 and 1213 by Pope Innocent III, and continual financial difficulties resulting from high taxation.[21]

John was the author of a number of works, but apart from an isolated sermon for Palm Sunday, only two have survived: a charming life of Wulfric of Haselbury, a local hermit (Haselbury Plucknett is just about ten miles from Forde), and the long, rambling, ruminative commentary on the Song of Songs that was intended to complete the commentary by Bernard of Clairvaux. The life of Wulfric justly enjoyed considerable popularity, but the commentary on the Song of Songs exists today only in a single manuscript and was never widely circulated. The reason is simple: it was essentially out of date. Times had changed by the late twelfth century, and "by John's day, the scholastic *quaestio*—short, snappy, logical—was becoming the preferred mode of thought."[22] His long and prolix commentary was just too much out of fashion to succeed. It comprises 120 sermons, of which just 3—sermons 70, 73, and 75—are devoted entirely to Mary, though there are sections in sermons 4, 8, and 59 that are also of importance.[23]

[21] For John's life and times, see Christopher J. Holdsworth, "John of Forde 1191–1991," in *A Gathering of Friends: The Learning and Spirituality of John of Forde*, ed. Hilary Costello and Christopher Holdsworth, CS 161 (Kalamazoo, MI: Cistercian Publications, 1996), 17–42, and the same author's brief entry "Forde [Ford], John of," in the *Oxford Dictionary of National Biography* (2004).

[22] David N. Bell, "*Agrestis et infatua interpretatio*: The Background and Purpose of John of Forde's Condemnation of Jewish Exegesis," in *A Gathering of Friends*, 148.

[23] There is an account of "Our Lady, Mother of Jesus" in Hilary Costello, *Sky-Blue is the Sapphire, Crimson the Rose: Stillpoint of Desire in John of Forde*, CF 69 (Kalamazoo, MI: Cistercian Publications, 2006), 125–45, but it is of little use. Far better is the discussion in Matthew J. Mills, "Behold Your Mother: The Virgin Mary in English Monasticism, c. 1050–c. 1200," D.Phil. dissertation, Regent's Park College, Oxford, 2016, 156–70, freely available online at https://ora.ox.ac.uk/objects/uuid:c72df193-cdbe-4fc1-b59f-714015846599/download_file?file_format=pdf&safe_filename=Mills%2BDPhil%252C%2BDissemination%2BCopy.pdf&type_of_work=Thesis. The Latin text of the commentary is to be found in CCCM 17–18 (1970), and an English translation,

For the most part, John says all that we would expect him to say, and the influence of Bernard is obvious and apparent. His language is more physical and sensual than that of Bernard, but that is because he is dealing with the navels, bellies, breasts, necks, and eyes of Song of Songs 7:2-4. Above all, John praises Mary's humility, her "supereminent humility"[24]—there is nothing surprising about this—but he links it with the greatness of her charity, the highest form of love:[25]

> Just as among the whole body of the saints, the first place in humility, purity, and godliness (*pietas*) is held by the blessed Virgin, the mother of Jesus, so, too, she shines forth gloriously among all those who love God in the eminence of her charity.[26]

She is, in fact, "the highest and principal model of love,"[27] who brings forth into the world love itself. Humility and charity cannot be separated, and John spends much of his seventy-third sermon elaborating on the nature of Mary's humility. Humility, he says, is "the mother of all the virtues,"[28] and, following Bernard,[29] he tells us that Mary exhibited this virtue in three forms: first, humility with regard to herself, second, with regard to her neighbor, and third, with regard to God. What are these three forms? "The first lies in the truest knowledge of oneself; the second in compassion and respect for one's neighbor; the third in the most humble contemplation of God."[30]

---

which is not always quite what it should be, in CF 29, 39, 43–47 (seven volumes).

[24] John of Forde, Sermon 73.2; CCCM 18:507.

[25] We discussed the difference between *amor*, *dilectio*, and *caritas* in chap. 8.

[26] Sermon 70.1; CCCM 18:489.

[27] Sermon 70.2; CCCM 18:489. The word for love here is *amor*, love in general.

[28] Sermon 73.5; CCCM 18:509.

[29] Bernard, *De gradibus humilitatis et superbiae*, iii.6; SBOp 3:20.

[30] Sermon 73.5; CCCM 18:509.

John implies rather than explains what he means by "the most humble contemplation of God"—there is no passage comparable to that remarkable description we find in Guerric of Igny,[31] though John had certainly read Guerric—but at the very end of sermon 73, John has Mary, the pure bride of Christ, lost in the contemplation of her spouse, who is eternal Wisdom, and, like the psalmist, she too experiences an *excessus mentis*,[32] an ecstasy or rapture, that leads her to exclaim, "Your knowledge has become wonderful to me; it is high, and I cannot reach it."[33] "She may turn her eyes in every direction in that inaccessible Light,[34] and she returns to herself more humble."[35] And in sermon 75, in a concise passage based on 2 Corinthians 3:18, John tells us that after Mary had known Christ in the flesh, she then walked on (the verb is *ambulare*) from glory to glory. For it cannot be doubted, he says, that by continual contemplation she had achieved such a high degree of spiritual penetration that she would have seen Christ in glory and have been transformed into the same image.[36]

All this is possible because Mary, as we know from Saint Luke, is "full of grace," and John tells us that she had received the seven gifts of the Holy Spirit.[37] He does not elaborate on this, as, for example, do Amadeus of Lausanne and Aelred of

[31] See chap. 6, n. 21.

[32] See Dyan Elliott, "*Raptus* / Rapture," in *The Cambridge Companion to Christian Mysticism*, ed. Amy Hollywood and Patricia Z. Beckman (Cambridge: Cambridge University Press, 2012), 189–99. Much could be said on this subject, but this is not the place to say it.

[33] Sermon 73.10; CCCM 18:513, quoting Ps 138:6.

[34] See 1 Tim 6:16. The "inaccessible Light" appears in countless writers from Ambrose of Milan onwards.

[35] Sermon 73.10; CCCM 18:513. This is a commonplace of the Christian mystical tradition. The momentary experience of God's perfection reveals all too clearly our own manifest imperfection.

[36] Sermon 75.4; CCCM 18:521: *sed ambulasse eam non dubium est de claritate in claritatem iugique contemplatione in spiritualem evassisse aciem atque in eandem se transfundisse imaginem.*

[37] See Sermon 75.3; CCCM 18:521.

Rievaulx,[38] but he leaves us in no doubt that the grace of the Holy Spirit is fundamental to the incarnation, and, *ipso facto*, to our salvation. If Eve, who was the "mother of the living,"[39] left us all a legacy of death and became the "mother of wrath," *mater irae*—we are back with the old Eve-Mary parallel—"how much more truly can Mary be called the mother of the living, she who brought forth life for every generation of believers, she who became the mother of grace, *genetrix gratiae*?"[40]

But more than that, if Mary brought forth the life and light of the world in the person of her son, let us also remember that that son is also the Head of the church, and that the church is the Body of Christ. Thus, as we have seen in earlier chapters, the motherhood of Mary is not confined to being the mother of Jesus. Far from it:

> The mother of Jesus, I say, is not only the mother of our glorious head, Christ Jesus, the mediator between God and humanity, but also the mother of all those who love Jesus, of the whole of Jesus' sacred body.[41]

She is indeed our mother, "the restorer of her people, our *mediatrix* with God, the model of holiness, and the defender of piety."[42]

There is nothing here that we have not seen before, sometimes with much greater elaboration, but in one area John found himself treading on thin theological ice. Let us turn to his eighth sermon and his discussion of original sin, Mary's absolute freedom from it (he does not speculate as to when this occurred), and the transmission of this utter purity to her child, Jesus.[43]

[38] See chap. 8 and chap. 9, n. 14.
[39] See Gen 3:20.
[40] Sermon 70.5; CCCM 18:491.
[41] Sermon 70.5; CCCM 18:491.
[42] Sermon 59.5; CCCM 17:418.
[43] See Sermon 8.4; CCCM 17:82–83.

The contagion of original sin, he says, did not completely corrupt and spoil human nature. It left in the bodies of newborn infants the little flower of virginity, *flosculum virginitatis*, even though this was but weak and feeble. Everyone, therefore, is born a virgin, even though everyone (as the psalmist says) is conceived in iniquity.[44] But in Mary's case, we have a virginal conception followed by a virginal birth. In her, the heat of bodily concupiscence was not just overcome and put to sleep, but completely killed and buried. Thus, it follows logically that "the glory of virginal honor, which she received as a free gift, she transmitted as an inheritance to her offspring."[45] In other words, Mary made a positive contribution to the purity and innocence of Jesus.

But John is aware that some of his listeners are disturbed by what he has just said, that the Lord Jesus received innocence from his Virgin Mother by heredity, and they may well think that what he has suggested is a novelty—that dangerous word!—and therefore impious or blasphemous. He must therefore defend himself by citing his sources, and so he does. But whom does he cite? Anselm of Canterbury[46] and *Igniacensis vir catholicus et utique eruditissimus*, "that catholic and, to say the least, most learned man from Igny,"[47] in other words, Guerric. The importance of this lies not so much in what Guerric actually says, but in John's invoking him as an *auctoritas*, an authority, alongside the saintly Anselm. John was composing his commentary some forty or so years after the death of Guerric, and to cite him side by side with Anselm is surely to imply that, at least in Cistercian circles, he was considered to be of much greater importance than has hitherto been recognized.

[44] Ps 50:7.

[45] Sermon 8.4; CCCM 17:82.

[46] See Anselm of Canterbury, *Cur Deus homo*, ii.16; PL 158:416–19, and *De conceptu virginali* 20; PL 158:452. No one would argue with Anselm.

[47] Sermon 8.4; CCCM 17:83, referring to Guerric's Sermon 27.1 (the second sermon for the Annunciation); SCh 202:126–28.

Such, in summary, are John's views on the Virgin. More could be said, certainly, but it would not break any new ground, and we shall therefore turn our attention to our last representative from Forde, the elusive monk Roger.

That Roger was a monk of Forde is not in doubt, but when he entered the abbey is unknown. Earlier authorities tell us that he was a pupil of Baldwin, which was indeed the case, and that he flourished around 1182. He did not, however, stay at Forde. He left the abbey for Europe, perhaps for somewhere in the Rhineland, at an unknown date, and, so far as we know, never returned to England.[48] His best known work is a two-volume collection of the revelations of Saint Elisabeth of Schönau, whom we shall discuss in more detail in due course, but the work with which we are concerned here is his poem in praise of the Virgin, first edited, rather carelessly, by C. H. Talbot in 1939,[49] and then, fifty years later, in a far superior edition, by the late Arthur Rigg in 1989.[50]

As it stands, the poem contains 288 lines of rhyming elegiac couplets, but it is not complete. At the very end of his poem, Roger summarizes eight miracles of the Virgin, and in the last two lines, and also in his dedicatory letter to the poem, says that he is going to leave it to his confrère Maurinus or Marinus[51] to add more. Whether this was ever done, we do not know. The sense of the poem is clear and obvious, the rhyme is attractive, but the Latin itself is by no means easy. There are also

[48] The most recent account of Roger's life is the entry by Derek Baker in the *Oxford Dictionary of National Biography* (2004), but that account needs to be supplemented by Christopher J. Holdsworth, "John of Ford and English Cistercian Writing 1167–1214," *Transactions of the Royal Historical Society* 11 (1961): 125–26 (which obviously now needs updating).

[49] Charles H. Talbot, "The Verses of Roger of Ford on Our Lady," *Collectanea O.C.R.* 6 (1939): 44–54.

[50] Arthur G. Rigg, "Roger of Ford's Poem on the Virgin: A Critical Edition," *Cîteaux* 40 (1989): 200–14.

[51] On Maurinus or Marinus, see Rigg, "Roger of Ford's Poem," 213, note to lines 287–88.

a few allusions—not least the ants of lines 31–32 and the gladiatorial oxen on lines 205–6—for which I can offer no satisfactory explanation. Arthur Rigg's annotations are essential, but there are times when even he seems baffled. The poem must have been written after the murder of Becket at the very end of December 1170—lines 109–10 refer to his death—and before 1176 or 1178,[52] and it bears witness to the ever-increasing popularity of the veneration of the Virgin.

The main theme of the poem is to extol the various virtues of Mary and show how they reveal the deficiencies of his fellow-monks, heretics, Jews (if you Hebrews can accept the story of the burning bush, says Roger, that gave forth flame but was not consumed, why do you deny the man born of a virgin?[53]), and so-called Christians in general. By the second line, he has praised Mary's perpetual virginity, and by the fourth he has lauded her as Star of the Sea. By the fifteenth line we are with her when the angel greets her at the Annunciation, and, as we might expect, it is her humility that Roger praises first. Mary then meets Elizabeth, and as soon as Elizabeth hears her greeting, the baby in her womb—John the Baptist—leaps for joy. Roger then utters an impassioned plea that Mary's voice may sound in his own ears before going on to contrast Mary's humility, stability, silence, sobriety, perseverance, patience, austerity, asceticism, and sorrow with the way of life of his own contemporaries. There is no need to go into the details here, for there is nothing that we have not heard before, even though it is now couched in Latin verse. More interesting is the section in lines 211 to 218 dealing with the question of the bodily assumption of the Virgin.

We have seen in earlier chapters that there was considerable controversy about this, and that the Cistercians, following

[52] For the arguments, see Ruth J. Dean, "Elizabeth, Abbess of Schönau, and Roger of Ford," *Modern Philology* 41 (1944): 214.

[53] Lines 78–79 of Rigg's critical edition. The Burning Bush had long been interpreted in Marian terms.

Bernard, were cautious about expressing any definite opinion. Whether she ascended "with the body or without the body, I do not know: God knows," said Isaac of Stella and Aelred of Rievaulx.[54] But Roger was intimately familiar with the writings of Elisabeth of Schönau, and Elisabeth was in no doubt whatever as to exactly what had happened and, indeed, when it happened.

In about 1156, she tells us, she was in a trance, and Mary appeared to her "in her usual way."[55] Elisabeth asked her, very courteously, whether she had been assumed into heaven in spirit alone, or in the flesh as well, but was told that she could not know this at that time, but that it might be revealed to her in the future. Elisabeth persisted in her questioning, and after more than a year she was told by an angel of the Lord that Mary had indeed been assumed into heaven in body as well as in spirit. So when did this happen, asked Elisabeth? She died on August 15, replied the angel, but was resurrected in the body forty days later, on September 23. Elisabeth, however, was fearful of publishing this revelation, lest she be accused of inventing novelties—always a dangerous matter. We might also add that Mary herself told Elisabeth that she, Mary, was fifteen years old at the time of the annunciation, and that she had died just over a year after Christ's ascension.[56]

There can be no doubt that Roger had read this text, and in his poem he begins to speculate on the question of whether the assumption occurred with or without Mary's physical body, but then stops short. Why? Because Baldwin had advised him to be cautious in dealing with this controversial topic. It would be possible here, says Roger, to discuss these various

[54] See chap. 8, n. 7, and chap. 9, n. 33.

[55] *Elisabeth of Schönau: The Complete Works*, intro. / trans. Anne L. Clark, preface by Barbara Newman (New York/Mahwah: Paulist Press, 2000), 209.

[56] For all this, see the very sound translation of "The Resurrection of the Blessed Virgin" in *Elisabeth of Schönau: The Complete Works*, 200–11.

arguments, "but I fall silent, since that, dear teacher, is what you advise."[57]

The poem concludes, as we noted above, with brief allusions—just two lines each—to eight very common miracles of the Virgin, all of which are identified by Talbot and Rigg,[58] and the last two lines tell us that Roger's colleague Marinus will complete the poem by adding the rest of these "miracles of the holy Mother."

Roger was not the only monk at Forde to evince an interest in the miracles of the Virgin. Abbot John himself told a certain William of an abbot of Morimond who had been saved from eternal damnation by Mary's intercession. William had been a monk at Forde before being transferred to Forde's daughter house of Bindon as its abbot, and after he had resigned the abbacy he wrote down the story. John's own account, written in the first person—"You have asked me, my William, to tell you the wonderful story of the Lord Abbot of Morimond"[59]—appears in the huge and extremely important collection of Marian miracles, the largest collection extant, in Cambridge, Sidney Sussex College, MS 95.[60] Another miracle appears in the collection in MS 137 of the library of the university of Aberdeen, there attributed specifically to "Dom William, formerly abbot of Bindon."[61]

This is not to say that there was any greater interest in Marian miracles at Forde and Bindon than anywhere else—

[57] Lines 217–18: *Possunt hinc varie superinduci rationes / Sed sileo, quia sic, doctor amande, mones.*

[58] Talbot, "Verses of Roger of Ford," 46–48; Rigg, "Roger of Ford's Poem," 212–13.

[59] Cambridge, Sidney Sussex College, MS 95, fol. 138r (modern foliation).

[60] See now https://cudl.lib.cam.ac.uk/view/MS-SIDNEYSUSSEX-00095/1. This complements the description in M. R. James's 1895 catalogue and contains a superb digitalized reproduction of the entire manuscript.

[61] Aberdeen, University Library, MS 137, fol. 132r: see Montague R. James, *A Catalogue of the Medieval Manuscripts in the University Library, Aberdeen* (Cambridge: Cambridge University Press, 1932), 45: *Incipit miraculum sancte dei genitricis Marie editum a dom. Willelmo quondam abbate de bintona.*

they were one of the most widespread forms of medieval popular literature, both in Latin and various vernaculars—and I suspect that what we see at Forde may have been seen at many another Cistercian abbey in the Middle Ages and after. The numerous Marian miracle stories in the *exempla* literature and, above all, in the *Dialogus miraculorum*, the "Dialogue on Miracles," of Caesarius of Heisterbach, compiled between about 1219 and 1223, belong to the same genre.[62] All Cistercian abbots were required to deliver a homily on "all the solemnities of holy Mary,"[63] and it is to be regretted that not more of them have survived. Many of them, to be sure, would no doubt have been fairly pedestrian pieces—the number of Bernards, Guerrics, and Isaacs was obviously somewhat limited—but how many other abbots produced homilies comparable to or better than those of Baldwin or John, we do not know. They "lived faithfully a hidden life," if I may quote George Eliot, "and rest in unvisited tombs."[64]

We must now leave England and return to continental Europe, but before we do so, we should, perhaps, add a footnote. At this point the reader may say, "But what about Gilbert of Hoyland? Was he not English? Did he not compose forty-seven sermons on the Song of Songs, a series that was taken up and completed by John of Forde? Why have you not included his views on the Mother of God?" The answer is simple. Because when it comes to Mary, Gilbert is on a par with William of Saint-Thierry. He says virtually nothing about her.

Hoyland does not refer to the town of that name in the north of England, but to Hoyland or Holland, the fenland area around the Wash on the east coast of England. Gilbert was abbot of Swineshead in Lincolnshire from about 1147 to his

[62] We shall discuss these in the next chapter.

[63] *Les Ecclesiastica Officia cisterciens du XIIème siècle*, ed. Danièle Choisselet and Placide Vernet, La Documentation cistercienne 22 (Reiningue: Abbaye d'Œlenberg, 1989), 190 (67.3).

[64] George Eliot, *Middlemarch* (1871–72), the very last sentence.

death in 1172, and he did indeed write forty-seven sermons on the Song of Songs (the forty-seventh is incomplete). Mary appears in seven of them,[65] but then only in passing. In fact, we can summarize all that Gilbert says about the Virgin in a single sentence. She is the model of purity, chastity, and virginity, and although, being human, she could have sinned, by the grace of God she was prevented from doing so. When it comes to the question of the corruption of carnal provocation, says Gilbert, "in Jesus there is neither cause nor corruption. In his mother, although there is the cause, yet there is no corruption. In everyone else, there is both cause and corruption."[66] And that is all. So far as we know, Gilbert, unlike William, never had a vision of the Mother of God to comfort and console him, which was certainly not the case with those numerous men and women whom we shall meet in the next chapter.

[65] Gilbert of Hoyland, Sermons 15.3, 16.3, 17.5 and 6, 27.4, 37.5, 40.6, and 47.6.

[66] Sermon 40.6; PL 184:211B.

Chapter Twelve

Mary and the Visionaries

There are two basic problems in dealing with the visionaries, neither of which I shall attempt to answer. Most, though not all, of the most important Cistercian visionaries were women, and the question of whether a certain women's religious house was formally or officially Cistercian can be exceedingly tricky to determine. In some cases, there is little doubt on the matter, but in others, it is sometimes unclear whether a house was officially recognized by the General Chapter as being Cistercian, or whether it was simply following Cistercian usages—whether it was Cistercian *de jure* or *de facto*, one might say. There is now an extensive literature on this difficult and important problem, and it would take us far out of our way to discuss it here.[1] For my purposes I shall include here women visionaries who were certainly Cistercian as well as some who were sort-of-Cistercian, and even one—Elisabeth of Schönau—who was not Cistercian at all, but whose visions and revelations were recorded by a Cistercian whom we met in the last chapter, Roger of Forde, and whose visions had a deep impact on Cistercians and non-Cistercians alike.

The second problem, of course, is what to say about the authenticity of these visions. There can be no doubt that the

[1] Some of the best work on the subject has been done by Constance Berman of the University of Iowa, Anne Lester of Johns Hopkins University, and Elizabeth Freeman of the University of Tasmania.

men and women who experienced them recorded what they experienced in good faith—they were not lying in their teeth merely to bemuse their readers or listeners—but in our modern sceptical day and age, we might have problems with a Virgin who cites pseudo-Jerome and pseudo-Augustine, or who appears in association with Saint Ursula and the 11,000 virgins of Cologne, which is unquestionably a medieval legend and quite possibly the result of a scribal error. I have no intention whatever of venturing into this dangerous territory, and my only concern will be to report what the visionaries said they experienced, and leave it at that. Nor have I any intention of venturing into a discussion of the psychological or psychophysical stimuli for these visions. If someone says they saw the Virgin, then as far as I am concerned they saw the Virgin, and that is all there is to it.

As we said above, although the majority of the most important visionaries were women, they were certainly not alone. In chapter six we told the story of how William of Saint-Thierry, on the road to Soissons, had a vision of Our Lady of Bazoches, a vision in which "he sensed such a holy and spiritual joy that he could not recall ever having experienced the like before."[2] And there are few more dramatic visions than that experienced by Saint Bernard when the Virgin nourished him with milk from her own breast.[3] In neither case, however, did Mary speak to William or Bernard—there were no revelations or remarkable prophecies—but in the following pages the Virgin will not remain so silent.

This visionary literature, as we mentioned in the last chapter, is closely associated with the very popular and widely read accounts of the miracles of the Virgin. Caesarius of Heisterbach devotes the seventh book of his *Dialogue on Miracles* to tales of the Virgin, and the vast majority of those to whom she appears are male. Caesarius (ca. 1180–ca. 1240) was prior of Heisterbach,

[2] See chap. 6, n. 2.
[3] See chap. 5, n. 50.

and he compiled his collection of miracle stories between 1219 and 1223. The Virgin who appears therein comes to the aid of priests who are not too intelligent, supports the Cistercian Order, converts some from a life of vice to a life of virtue, blesses monks in their sleep, heals those who need it, delivers others from temptations and the attacks of the devil, joins the monks in choir, and comforts them at the hour of their death. The last of the fifty-nine visions is the famous one in which a Cistercian monk falls into a trance and is vouchsafed a vision of heaven. He looks around and sees representatives of the whole church triumphant as well as a variety of monks and canons regular. But where are the Cistercians? There is not one to be seen, not a single one in sight. And so,

> turning with a groan to the blessed Mother of God, he said, "Most holy Lady, why is it that I see here no one from the Cistercian Order? Why are your servants, who have served you so devotedly, excluded from sharing in such great blessedness?" Seeing him so troubled, the Queen of Heaven replied, "Those of the Cistercian Order are so dear and precious to me that I cherish them in my arms." And opening the mantle with which she seemed to be clothed, [a mantle] of wondrous size, she showed him an innumerable multitude of monks, lay brothers, and nuns.[4]

Earlier in this seventh book, Caesarius tells the story of Bertram of Lombardy, a monk who had an especial devotion to the Virgin and who could not bear to hear anyone casting doubts upon her bodily assumption. So distressed would he become when he heard anything of this nature that he asked his abbot if he might be sent out to one of the monastery's granges so that he would not have to endure any sermons of Saint Jerome in the church or any sermon in the chapter house that might offend him so deeply. The particular sermon of

[4] *Caesarii Heisterbacensis Monachi Dialogus Miraculorum*, ed. Joseph Strange (Cologne: J. M. Heberle, 1851), 2:79 (cap. LIX).

which he was thinking was that which we discussed in chapter one, the very popular sermon on Mary's assumption that circulated under the name of Jerome but was actually composed by Paschasius Radbertus. Paschasius never actually denies the corporeal assumption of the Virgin, but simply says that since we do not know what really happened, we should not speculate on matters that God has preferred to keep secret. There is, after all, no mention of the Virgin's passing in the pages of the New Testament.

To Bertram's request the abbot agreed, and Bertram set off for the nearby grange. But before he could reach it, an angel of the Lord transported him far away and set him down near a little church that happened to be close to the castle of Bertram's own brother (Bertram was of a noble family). Here he experienced a vision of the Mother of God in her glorified body, seated on a throne and surrounded by saints, patriarchs, prophets, virgins, and all manner of holy people. The Mother of God, says Caesarius, greeted Bertram in a familiar way, and said "Bertram, here you'll hear better sermons than the sermons of Jerome!" And that was not all. "I know well, Bertram," she said, "why you have now come forth from your cloister. Know for certain that I am glorified in both substances, that is, in both body and soul, and that I was raised from the dead on the fortieth day." But at that moment, the novice who has been listening to this tale interjects, "This account agrees with the vision of the lady Elisabeth of Schönau," he says, "in which we read that Our Lady revealed her resurrection to her in these very same words."[5]

This is indeed the case, as we saw in the last chapter, and Roger of Forde was clearly familiar with it. Nor is this the only time that Elisabeth appears in Caesarius's work. In the thirtieth vision of his seventh book he tells how some religious had told him that when the nuns of Schönau were chanting the se-

[5] *Dialogus Miraculorum*, 2:46 (cap. XXXVII).

quence *Ave, praeclara maris stella,* "Hail, glorious Star of the Sea," Elisabeth "saw Our Lady, on bended knees, pouring forth prayers for the convent."[6]

We might also note that the Mother of God's patristic knowledge was not confined to pseudo-Jerome. Elisabeth had another vision, not recorded by Caesarius, in which she saw the Virgin Theotokos—she uses the Greek title of "God-bearer"—and, at the instigation of her brother Ekbert (to whom she confided her visions), asked her whether she might tell her, Elisabeth, something about the second- / third-century Greek theologian Origen of Alexandria. He had had a great love for the Virgin, but many of his teachings had been deemed heretical and condemned by the church. Had he been saved or not? But Mary was circumspect. "It is not the Lord's will," she said, "that much should be revealed to you about this."[7] But she then went on to explain that Origen's error did not arise from any malice, but rather "from the excessive fervor with which he sank his thought in the profound depths of the holy Scriptures, which he loved, and in divine secrets, which he wanted to examine too deeply. For this reason, the punishment in which he is now detained is not severe."[8] A special light shines on him, she continued, because of the way he honored her in his writings, "but what will happen to him on the Last Day must not be revealed to you now, for the Lord wishes to keep this among his secrets."[9]

It was not, in fact, rare for Elisabeth to ask such theological questions, though she usually asked them on behalf of her brother Ekbert and his friends. But as Barbara Newman has said in her Preface to Anne Clark's excellent translation of

[6] *Dialogus Miraculorum,* 2:39 (cap. XXX).

[7] *Die Visionen der hl. Elisabeth und die Schriften der Aebte Ekbert und Emecho von Schönau,* ed. Ferdinand W. E. Roth (Brünn: Verlag der Studien aus dem Benedictiner- und Cistercienser-Orden, 1884), 62 (bk. 3.5).

[8] *Die Visionen der hl. Elisabeth,* 62–63.

[9] *Die Visionen der hl. Elisabeth,* 63.

Elisabeth's complete works, "Unlike Elisabeth's medieval audience, modern readers cannot blithely trust her angelic guide and avoid the question of where the answers actually came from."[10] It was rare, however, for Elisabeth to address such questions to the Mother of God herself: they were usually addressed to her angelic guide.

For Elisabeth, Mary as a source of theological information was far less important than Mary as advocate and *mediatrix*, not only for Elisabeth, but for the whole human race. Her prayers restrain her Son from wreaking his vengeance on a sinful world, and, for Elisabeth herself, the Virgin comforts her in the face of terrifying demonic attacks. But as Anne Clark points out in another of her works, Elisabeth's visions of Mary "miss much of the tenderness, even sentimentality, that comes to mark Marian piety in the twelfth century and beyond."[11] There are occasional brief and cursory visions of Mary with the baby Jesus, but overall the Mother of God "remains a figure of regal, even priestly, power who deigns to visit and bless Elisabeth."[12]

This sentimentality, some of it rather cloying, that we find (as we shall see) in some other women visionaries is not shared by the men who appear in the pages of Caesarius or in contemporary biographies. Martinus Cawley has suggested that the visions of the monks are more affected by the ideals of medieval chivalry, while the nuns tend to find "a holy playfulness in dealing with a Child of divine dignity,"[13] and while there is some truth in this, it is by no means the whole truth. There is, in fact, an interesting area of overlap, and the situa-

[10] *Elisabeth of Schönau: The Complete Works*, intro. and trans. Anne L. Clark, preface by Barbara Newman (New York/Mahwah: Paulist Press, 2000), xiv.

[11] Anne L. Clark, *Elisabeth of Schönau: A Twelfth-Century Visionary* (Philadelphia: University of Pennsylvania Press, 1992), 134. This is a very sound study.

[12] Clark, *Elisabeth of Schönau*, 134.

[13] Martinus Cawley, "Our Lady and the Nuns and Monks of XIII-Century Belgium," *Word & Spirit* 10 (1988): 95.

tion becomes more complex once we expand our time frame and our geographical limits. But let us look at two of these male visionaries whose lives have been preserved for us by Goswin of Villers. Both were from the abbey of Villers in what is now Belgium—one, Arnulf, was a lay brother, the other, Abundus, was a monk—and how the Virgin intervened in their lives is not without interest.[14]

Villers itself was founded as a daughter house of Clairvaux in 1146 and came to be one of the largest and most important abbeys in the region. Arnulf was born in Brussels in about 1180 and, after enjoying the world and all its dubious delights, underwent a conversion experience at the age of twenty-two and entered Villers as a lay brother. Here he became known for his dramatic austerities and asceticism—he had much to make up for—as well as his deep devotion to the Mother of God. He died on June 30, 1228. As for Abundus, he was born in about 1189 in Huy (Huy in Dutch, Hoei in Flemish), about seventeen miles west of Liège, received the usual schooling for his time, and, when he was about seventeen, entered Villers as a Cistercian novice. In due course he was professed as a monk, and it was in 1213/14, his seventh year as a Cistercian, that he received the first of the many visions that would mark his life. He died at Villers, surrounded by his brethren, on March 19, 1239. The lives of both were written by Goswin of Villers, a monk and cantor of the abbey, and a fine writer.

In Arnulf's life, the Virgin makes her appearance when she reveals to him the seven joys she experiences in heaven. Arnulf, whose devotion to Mary had been increasing more and more,

[14] For the Latin life of Arnulf, see the *Acta Sanctorum*, June, vol. 7 (Paris: V. Palme, 1867), cols. 558–89, and for that of Abundus, see A. M. Frenken, "De Vita van Abundus van Hoei," *Cîteaux* 10 (1959): 5–33. Complete English translations by Martinus Cawley may be found in *Send Me God: The Lives of Ida the Compassionate of Nivelles, Nun of La Ramée, Arnulf, Lay Brother of Villers, and Abundus, Monk of Villers, by Goswin of Bossut*, intro. / trans. Martinus Cawley, preface by Barbara Newman (Turnhout: Brepols, 2003), 123–98 and 207–46.

had made it a point to meditate each day on the seven earthly joys of the Virgin, but Mary offered him more than this. Among the seven celestial joys are her glory, which is greater than that of all the saints and angels combined, the fact that her will and God's will are now one and the same, and that those who serve her in this world will, "in accordance with the decision of my will," be rewarded in the next.[15]

Mary's appearances in the life of Abundus are considerably more frequent. His first vision of her was similar to that experienced by Elisabeth of Schönau. Abundus sees the Virgin, veiled like a nun, chanting the praises of her divine son with the monks in choir.[16] Sometimes, those who knew of his familiarity with the Virgin would ask him to commend them to her in his prayers, or to ask her whether the soul of a recently deceased relative was in purgatory. But sometimes the Virgin herself would send Abundus on a mission to some sinful person, telling them what they had done and urging them to repent and amend their lives.[17] On another occasion, Abundus had the temerity to ask this most bounteous Lady—*benignissima Domina*[18]—if he might kiss her hand. To this she graciously consented, but then—wonder of wonders!—she drew near to Abundus and kissed him in return, recognizing in him the great love he bore for her.[19]

Then, one Candlemas—February 2, the feast of the Purification—Abundus had a vision more similar to that of many of the women visionaries of his time. He was at Mass when he saw the Virgin with the child Jesus in her arms. She walked around both choirs of monks, the two choirs that faced each other and chanted the Psalms responsively, and presented the baby Jesus to each monk in turn, spending a shorter time with

[15] *Acta Sanctorum*, June VII, 568–69 (II.ii.15); Cawley, *Send Me God*, 162–63.

[16] Cawley, *Send Me God*, 221–22.

[17] Cawley, *Send Me God*, 223–24.

[18] Frenken, "De Vita van Abundus," 21 (§10).

[19] Cawley, *Send Me God*, 224–25.

some and longer with others. So amazed was Abundus at this sight that he forgot to join his brethren when the time came for them to process towards their abbot, and the Mother of God herself had to remind him to do so, tapping him with her hand. She remained visible to Abundus for the whole of the Mass, and disappeared only after the deacon had dismissed the community.[20]

With the story of Abundus's vision on the feast of the Assumption, we are back with Bertram of Lombardy in Caesarius's *Dialogue*. Like Bertram, Abundus could not tolerate any doubts being cast on the reality of the bodily assumption of the Virgin, and, again like Bertram, could not bear to listen to those nasty and heretical insinuations of "Jerome" / Paschasius Radbertus, that suggested that the Blessed Virgin's assumption was (as he saw it) *opinando*, "merely a matter of opinion."[21] He then had a vision of the Virgin herself, who gave Abundus a further display of her patristic erudition. "Although Jerome spoke of my assumption as a matter of opinion," she said, "Augustine, on the other hand, put forth a definitive statement. In one of his sermons he unquestionably asserts the total glorification in me of body and soul."[22] The reference is to the pseudo-Augustinian sermon on the assumption that we discussed earlier, and Mary goes on to reiterate the old argument that since the flesh of the son was the flesh of the mother,[23] it was only right and proper that if the flesh of the one had been raised and glorified, the same should be true of the flesh of the other.

Finally, we might mention the time when Abundus saw the Virgin comforting the monks at harvest time. It was an extremely hot day, and the poor monks were dripping with

[20] Cawley, *Send Me God*, 227–28. For a similar vision, this time with the Virgin censing the monks in choir, see *Send Me God*, 243.

[21] Frenken, "De Vita van Abundus," 24 (§13).

[22] Frenken, "De Vita van Abundus," 25 (§13).

[23] See chap. 4, n. 11, quoting Augustine.

sweat. The Lady fanned the face of each monk with the sleeve of her robe and cleared away the sweat. Then, raising her right hand, she made the sign of the cross and blessed the whole community.[24] Elisabeth of Schönau also saw the Mother of God blessing her with the sign of the cross, and that, says Anne Clark, suggests that for Elisabeth, "there was a very strong association between Mary and priesthood."[25] Abundus appears to have been moving in the same direction.

But let us now turn to the women visionaries themselves. We have spoken of Elisabeth of Schönau, but there were many others, some more important, some less so. Martinus Cawley mentions five who were Cistercian and (in modern terms) Belgian: Alice the Leper, Beatrice of Nazareth, Ida of Nivelles, Ida of Léau, and Lutgard of Aywières.[26] In the biography of Alice the Leper, Mary makes hardly any appearance, but in the lives of the other women, certain themes stand out. Some of these are common, and we have seen them many times before. Mary is, of course, intercessor and advocate, and comforts and encourages the nuns in their difficulties and trials. And, as with Elisabeth of Schönau, she is also the advocate for all humanity, turning away the just anger of her Son at the sinful conduct of men and women. This is especially true of the visions of Lutgard, who emphasizes Mary's role as intercessor for the universal church.

A second important theme is the visions of Jesus as a baby or a young boy, sometimes, though not always, associated with the Eucharist. This is particularly the case with Ida of Nivelles, who, on one occasion, when she was in church for the Christmas Masses, saw the priest elevating the host, and what was in his hands was not a wafer, but "a little boy (*puerulus*), apparently just born, whose beauty was truly beyond the beauty

[24] Cawley, *Send Me God*, 234.

[25] Anne L. Clark, "The Priesthood of the Virgin Mary: Gender Trouble in the Twelfth Century," *Journal of Feminist Studies in Religion* 18 (2002): 18.

[26] Cawley, "Our Lady and the Nuns and Monks," 96–107.

of any other little ones."[27] Ida was stricken with fear at this, for she had never sought to see her Lord in such human form, and thought herself unworthy. But after being reassured inwardly that she was not unworthy, a second vision followed.

At the second Mass she once again saw in the priest's hands the same sweet and lovely little boy and was so terrified that she was unable to join her sisters when they went up to the altar to communicate. Why? Because, understandably, she could not tolerate the thought of eating a living, breathing infant. She therefore stayed in her place, but then, yet again at High Mass, exactly the same thing occurred, but by this time the little boy appeared slightly taller. He was coming down to her from the altar to offer her his embrace and kiss, and actually granted that he might be embraced and kissed by her in return. But finally, so that her sisters would not be scandalized by her apparent refusal to take communion, she begged Jesus

> that he might deign to grant her the possibility of receiving his body without difficulty. The vision therefore came to an end, she went up to the altar with the others, and, wholly at peace, received the author of peace.[28]

Neither Ida nor any of the other visionaries ever forget that Mary is not God, but the mother of God, and that although she might be our necessary advocate and intercessor, the author of grace is God alone. Their visions of the Christ-child tend to lead onwards and upwards, from his humanity to his divinity—indeed, into the midst of the Trinity itself[29]—and for all

[27] Chrysóstomo Henriquez, *Quinque prudentes virgines* (Antwerp: J. Cnobbaert, 1630), 251 (*Vita B. Idae de Nivella*, cap. XXI).

[28] Henriquez, *Quinque prudentes virgines*, 253. For Cawley's translation, see *Send Me God*, 62–64.

[29] See, for example, Henriquez, *Quinque prudentes virgines*, 459 (*Vita B. Idae de Levvis*, cap. VII), where the vision of the Virgin at Mass, with the Christ child in her arms, leads Ida of Léau to see the mystery of the Trinity, *Patremque Filio praesentialiter cohaerentem*.

their fervent devotion to the Virgin, these remarkable women never lapse into Mariolatry.

Despite the temptation to linger longer with these prudent virgins so celebrated by Chrysóstomo Henriquez, we must now leave the boundaries of modern-day Belgium and travel to modern-day Germany, to the Cistercian or sort-of-Cistercian abbey of Helfta, near Eisleben, the birthplace of Martin Luther, where we shall meet Gertrude the Great and Mechtild of Hackeborn. Let us begin with Gertrude.

She was born on January 6, 1256, in Eisleben and entered the monastery school at Helfta at the age of four, as either an oblate or an orphan. Here she was given into the care of Mechtild, the younger sister of the abbess, Gertrude of Hackeborn, and here she received a very thorough education. When she was twenty-five, she experienced the first of a series of visions that would change her life, and that led her to what is technically known as *Brautmystik*, "bridal mysticism" or "nuptial mysticism," in which she saw and experienced herself, physically and spiritually, as the bride of Christ. We may see the same thing in the lives of Beatrice of Nazareth and Hadewijch of Antwerp. Gertrude died at Helfta around 1302 and left behind a number of works, the most important for our purposes being the *Legatus memorialis abundantiae divinae pietatis*, "The Herald of the Memorial of the Abundance of Divine Piety," which usually appears in English, not quite accurately, as *The Herald of Divine Love*. Only the second of its five books was written by Gertrude herself; the other four were composed by other nuns of Helfta. Gertrude was of major significance in the development of devotion to the Sacred Heart of Jesus, which is not here our concern, but she also experienced visions of the Mother of God.

There are three themes in Gertrude's visions of Mary, all of which we have seen before, though not quite in the same way. First, we have more Christmas Day visions of the baby Jesus, but in the first of these it is not Mary who gives the child to Gertrude, but Gertrude herself who takes the initiative. "On the day of your most holy Nativity," she says, "I took you out of the manger, a tender little boy wrapped in swaddling clothes, and pressed you to my breasts."[30] She does not say she suckled the child, though other female visionaries claimed to have done so.[31] The second vision occurred a year later, on the same feast day, but this time, says Gertrude, "I took you from your virginal mother's lap in the form of a most tender and most delicate little babe (*infantulus*) and carried you for a while on my breast."[32] But somewhat later, when it seems she had also been entrusted with the baby Jesus, his blessed mother appeared none too pleased. She had a severe look on her face, and Gertrude feared that she was not happy with the way in which she, Gertrude, had been looking after her son.[33]

Gertrude, in fact, had a complicated relationship with the Mother of God. Although she had no doubts as to the essential nature of Mary's role as intercessor, and although she could praise her in glorious terms, it was not a relationship in which all was sweetness and light. As Sharon Elkins noted in 1997, there were times when Gertrude "felt guilty, anxious, and even angry when she thought about Mary."[34] Gertrude's spirituality was wholly Christocentric, and whereas on the one hand she sometimes thought that the attention given to Mary detracted

[30] *Revelationes Gertrudianae ac Mechtildianae. I, Sanctae Gertrudis Magnae, virginis Ordinis Sancti Benedicti, Legatus divinae pietatis . . .*, ed. Louis Paquelin (Poitiers and Paris: Oudin, 1875), 86 (bk. II.16).

[31] See Caroline W. Bynum, "The Female Body and Religious Practice in the Later Middle Ages," in the same author's *Fragmentation and Redemption: Essays on Gender and the Human Body in Medieval Religion* (New York: Zone Books, 1991), 181–238.

[32] *Revelationes Gertrudianae, I*, 86 (bk. II.16).

[33] See *Revelationes Gertrudianae, I*, 88 (bk. II.16); *Gertrude of Helfta: The Herald of Divine Love*, ed./trans. Margaret Winkworth, intro. Maximilian Marnau, preface by Louis Bouyer (New York and Mahwah: Paulist Press, 1993), 116.

[34] Sharon Elkins, "Gertrude the Great and the Virgin Mary," *Church History* 66 (1997): 721. For a more recent assessment, see Anne L. Clark, "An Uneasy Triangle: Jesus, Mary, and Gertrude of Helfta," *Maria: A Journal of Marian Studies* 1 (2000): 37–56.

from the attention that should be given to her Son, on the other, she was afraid that Mary might be offended by the one-pointed devotion that Gertrude poured out to Christ. Thus, there were times when Gertrude asked Christ to intercede with his mother on her behalf—a curious inversion of the more usual scene when Mary intercedes with Christ.[35]

Yet for all this ambivalence, Gertrude was certain that she was under the special protection of the Virgin. This is the second major theme that we see in her visions. This was revealed to her when, "by a certain spiritual revelation," she learned that she was about to suffer some adversity that would increase her merit, and, not unnaturally, she was afraid. But "the holy Lord took pity on her faint-heartedness and charged his merciful mother, the glorious Empress of Heaven, with being her bountiful helper,"[36] so that whenever the adversity became too great, she might always have recourse to the Mother of Mercy, who would always be there to help her.

The third theme that appears in the visions is when Mary provides Gertrude with instruction. But in this case, the instruction does not concern the superiority of pseudo-Augustine over pseudo-Jerome or the fate of the soul of Origen, as we saw above, but how to pray to the Virgin and how she should be praised. Interested readers may read the details for themselves,[37] but Mary's instructions to Gertrude also contain a touch of Trinitarian theology. Mary appeared to her in the presence of the Trinity, which appeared to her in the form of a three-petaled fleur-de-lys, with one petal pointing upwards and two pointing down. Thus, the Virgin is justly known as "the White Lily of the Trinity"—*candidum lilium Trinitatis*—since she has received into herself all the Trinitarian virtues.

[35] See Elkins, "Gertrude the Great," 720–34 *passim*.

[36] *Revelationes Gertrudianae, I,* 118 (bk. III.1). I have used "helper" for *dispensatrix*—a female dispenser. It is a rare word for describing the Mother of God.

[37] See *The Herald of Divine Love,* 184–86 (bk. III.19).

"The upright petal denotes the omnipotence of God the Father. The two pointing down, the wisdom and benevolence (*benignitas*) of the Son and Holy Spirit, to whom she is found to be most alike." Thus, if we were to address her as the "White Lily of the Trinity and Most Radiant Rose of Heavenly Delight," we would show how her power to help save the human race, her knowledge of exactly how this may be done, and the benevolence that moves it, come directly from the inseparable unity of the three persons of the Trinity.[38]

But we should also note that, although chapter 46 of the third book of the *Legatus* bears the title "Of the Seven Hours of the Blessed Virgin," and although the Virgin is mentioned in every one of them, it is Christ who is providing the instruction, and it is Christ who is the focus of them all. Given Gertrude's undeviating Christocentrism, this will not surprise us.

When the young Gertrude first went to Helfta, she was put in the charge of Mechtild, the younger sister of the abbess. Mechtild was born in 1240/41 of a noble family, and we are now well into the thirteenth century. She seems to have been a devout and pious young woman for whom the religious life came logically and naturally, and, in due course, she followed her elder sister to the abbey of Helfta. Here she gained some renown for her fervor and her devotion, and she was also an accomplished musician and fine calligrapher. She died, still at Helfta, on November 19, 1298, when the great era of the fourteenth-century English mystics—not one of whom was Cistercian—was about to begin.

The book that appears under her name, the *Liber specialis gratiae* or "Book of Special Grace," was not written by Mechtild herself. Her visions and revelations were transcribed and organized by an unknown sister of Helfta, and a considerable portion of the book was actually written by Gertrude the Great. In addition to that, the first of its five books is heavily

[38] *Revelationes Gertrudianae, I,* 163 (bk III.19).

indebted to Elisabeth of Schönau, and much of the rest betrays the unmistakable stamp of another Mechtild, Mechtild of Magdeburg.

She, too, was born of a noble family, and had her first vision at the age of twelve. When she was in her twenties she left home to become a Beguine in Magdeburg. Somewhat later she became a Dominican Tertiary, but her harsh criticism of corruption in the church and laxity in religion aroused fierce opposition. As she grew older she found herself ostracized and, to add to her sorrows, she became blind. Around 1272, however, she was offered support and protection by the community of Helfta and entered the abbey, though whether she took formal vows or just lived at Helfta and took part in the liturgies is unclear. She was in her sixties at the time, blind and infirm, and died at the abbey at an uncertain date. It may have been in 1282 or perhaps some years later. Between 1250 and 1280 she composed, in Middle Low German (she could not write Latin), *Das fließende Licht der Gottheit* (*The Flowing Light of the Godhead*), which is readily available in English translation.[39]

It is hardly surprising, then, that the visions and revelation of Mechtild of Hackeborn bear a marked similarity to those of Elisabeth of Schönau, Gertrude, and the other Mechtild. Those interested in the details may read the work for themselves in the recent and excellent English translation—the first in six hundred years, as the translator says—by Barbara Newman of Northwestern University.[40]

All the main Marian themes appear in Mechtild's book, especially those of Mary as *mediatrix*, intercessor, and advocate, but Mary is much more front and center than in the writings

[39] *Mechthild of Magdeburg: The Flowing Light of the Godhead*, intro. / trans. Frank Tobin, preface by Margot Schmidt (New York and Mahwah: Paulist Press, 1998).

[40] *Mechthild of Hackeborn and the Nuns of Helfta: The Book of Special Grace*, intro. / trans. Barbara Newman, foreword by Richard Kieckhefer (New York and Mahwah: Paulist Press, 2017).

of Gertrude. Nor do we find any of Gertrude's ambivalence. If Gertrude's undeviating Christocentrism makes her nervous about showering too much praise on Christ's mother, Mechtild tends to see Mary as the way to Christ. She, too, has Christ as her focal point, but she sees no conflict between this and her deep devotion to the Mother of God. Like Gertrude, she has much to say about the Sacred Heart of Jesus, though some of her visionary experiences may not always be quite to modern taste. Not everyone will appreciate the thought of sucking the blood from Jesus' heart by means of a fistula, the silver or silver-gilt drinking tube by which communicants received the wine from the chalice in the Middle Ages.[41]

As Caroline Bynum has said, Mechtild's visions "are much more vivid, poetic and affective" than Gertrude's,[42] and they are certainly very much richer in all manner of jewels, gorgeous and glowing vestments, clouds of incense, throngs of angels, and the souls of saints. Mary is present throughout, and Jesus, as we might expect, appears as a baby, a young boy, and, since we are still in the world of *Brautmystic*, of "nuptial mysticism," the spouse of Mechtild's soul. She sees him and his mother seated side by side on glorious thrones,[43] and Christ himself instructs her as to how his mother's virginal heart should be greeted. Hers, he says, was the purest heart, the most humble heart, the most devout and desiring heart, the most fervent in the love of God and neighbor, the most preserving of her son's memory, the most long-suffering, the most faithful,

[41] See *The Book of Special Grace*, 163, 236. For the Cistercians, regulations for the use of the fistula were set forth in the twelfth-century *Ecclesiastica officia*: see *Les Ecclesiastica Officia cisterciens du XII*[ème] *siècle*, ed. Danièle Choisselet and Placide Vernet, La Documentation cistercienne, 22 (Reiningue: Abbaye d'Œlenberg, 1989), 165–67 (53.112–40).

[42] Caroline W. Bynum, "Women Mystics in the Thirteenth Century: The Case of the Nuns of Helfta," in the same author's *Jesus as Mother: Studies in the Spirituality of the High Middle Ages* (Berkeley: University of California Press, 1982), 212.

[43] See, for example, *The Book of Special Grace*, 63 (1.13).

the most solicitous in prayer, and the most zealous in contemplation, "acquiring grace for human beings by her merits."[44]

It is Mary herself who reveals to Mechtild that the opinion of Bernard of Clairvaux (whom Mechtild esteemed[45]) on the matter of Mary's conception was the correct one. Christ, she says, anticipated the hour of my birth by just a little (*aliquantulum*) and sent his grace into my mother's womb in advance. Indeed, "from the very moment that the soul was infused into the body, he filled me with the Holy Spirit, who cleansed me completely from original sin."[46] In other words, we have an immaculate birth, but not an immaculate conception. It is also clear from Mechtild's account of "the admirable Assumption of the blessed Virgin Mary," that Mary's soul first went to meet her son and Lord, and that her body followed later, though in this revelation we are not told when that occurred.[47]

So what are we to say about all these visions? The answer is really very little. There can surely be no doubt that the men and women (it was not just women) who experienced them had really experienced them, but despite all that has been written or surmised on the subject, we still have no idea as to exactly where they came from or how they came about. My own business here is simply to record them and see what they have to say about Mary the Virgin. They certainly contributed greatly to the ever-growing veneration of the Mother of God, and some of them had a profound influence on painting, sculpture, and the like. The dominant feature of the Marian visions is Mary as *mediatrix*, advocate, intercessor, helper, and protector, either of the individual, the monastery, the church, or the whole human race, but Christ, in and with the Holy Trinity, is

[44] *Revelationes Gertrudianae ac Mechtildianae, II, Sanctae Mechtildis, virginis Ordinis Sancti Benedicti, Liber specialis gratiae . . .*, ed. Louis Paquelin (Poitiers and Paris: Oudin, 1877), 11–12; *The Book of Special Grace*, 40–41.

[45] See *The Book of Special Grace*, 102–4 (1.28), "On Saint Bernard the Abbot."

[46] *Revelationes Gertrudianae, II*, 100 (1.29); *The Book of Special Grace*, 104.

[47] See *Revelationes Gertrudianae, II*, 90 (1.26); *The Book of Special Grace*, 97.

always the beginning and the end of all things, the alpha and the omega. And because Christ took his humanity from the earth out of which came humans, animals, and the flowers of the field, says Mechtild in a remarkable vision, so all the hairs of all men and women, the fur of all the animals, and the leaves of the trees and flowers "might shine in the holy Trinity through the humanity of Christ."[48]

We have now reached the fourteenth century, and we shall now make a leap of more than three hundred years to seventeenth-century France and the birth of Armand-Jean de Rancé. It is not that there was nothing going on in Marian theology during that long interval, but it was not going on among the Cistercians. At the end of chapter four we glanced at the ideas of the Oratorian Pierre de Bérulle, the Sulpician Jean-Jacques Olier, and the learned Henri-Marie Boudon, archdeacon of Évreux, and of the other significant Marian writers in this later period, Peter Canisius (d. 1597) and Francisco Suárez (d. 1617) were both Jesuits, and Lawrence of Brindisi (d. 1619) was a Capuchin. They had to deal not only with the bitter controversy over the Immaculate Conception, but also with the anti-Marian sentiments of Luther, Calvin, and the later, more radical, Reformers.[49]

The Dutch theologian and preacher, Peter Canisius, was instructed by Pope Pius V to present a reasoned defense of Marian devotion against the attacks of the Reformers. It was a task conducive to Canisius, who regarded the veneration of the Virgin as the most effective way to Christ, and the result was a massive tome of more than eight hundred pages of densely printed Latin with the title *De Maria Virgine Incomparabili et Dei Genitrice Sacrosancta*, "On the Incomparable Virgin

[48] *Revelationes Gertrudianae, II*, 260 (4.3). In *The Book of Special Grace*, 165, Barbara Newman translates this as "shine in the holy Trinity," but *fulgerent* is in the imperfect subjunctive, "*might* shine." There is a difference.

[49] See Hilda Graef, *Mary: A History of Doctrine and Devotion* (London: Sheed & Ward, 1963–65), 2:1–46.

Mary and Most Holy Mother of God," published at Ingolstadt in 1577. In its five books Canisius deals with Mary's life and all those Marian doctrines questioned or rejected by the Reformers: her immaculate conception (Canisius has no doubts about this), her sinlessness, her perpetual virginity, her divine motherhood, her corporeal assumption, and her veneration in general. The book is extraordinarily learned, replete with quotations from the Fathers, an abundance of medieval and contemporary theologians, and the Reformers themselves, and later theologians had no hesitation in stealing material from its dense and erudite pages. It was, however, a polemical work, an *apologia* for the Roman Catholic tradition against the ideas of Luther and his followers, and not a systematic presentation of Marian doctrine. For that we need to move on to another Jesuit, Francisco Suárez, a Spanish priest, philosopher, and theologian who is generally regarded as one of the greatest scholastic thinkers after Saint Thomas Aquinas.

What Suárez has to say about Mary is contained in a work commonly cited as *De mysteriis vitae Christi*, "On the Mysteries of the Life of Christ," which is actually part of his mammoth commentary on Aquinas's *Summa theologica*.[50] As Sarah Jane Boss has said, "Suárez' treatment of Marian doctrine begins by establishing that she is the Mother of God, and everything else that he says about her follows from this office, from the honor intrinsic to it, and from the Virgin's predestination to it."[51] He deals with Mary's parentage, and (following John Duns Scotus[52]) her pre-redemption and immaculate concep-

[50] Francisco Suárez, *Commentarii et disputationes in Tertiam Partem D. Thomae*, Disputationes I–XXXIII, in *R. P. Francisci Suarez Opera Omnia*, ed. Charles Berton (Paris: L. Vivès, 1860), 19:1–337. For an English translation of Disputationes I, V, and VI, see *The Dignity and Virginity of the Mother of God*, trans. Richard O'Brien (West Baden Springs: West Baden College, 1954).

[51] Sarah Jane Boss, "Francisco Suárez and Modern Mariology," in *Mary: The Complete Resource*, ed. Sarah Jane Boss (London & New York: Continuum, 2007), 257.

[52] See chap. 4.

tion. She received every grace that could be bestowed on a pure and sinless creature and never intentionally turned her mind away from the contemplation of God. He goes on to discuss at some length the nature and scope of her knowledge, and suggests that "from the moment of the Incarnation or at least from the birth of Christ she knew all that belonged to the mystery of the Redemption."[53] This leads him to a full account of Mary's role in the redemptive process, and her role as mediator and advocate. As we might expect, Suárez staunchly defends the doctrine of Mary's corporeal assumption and emphasizes that despite her greatness in heaven and the way in which she is exalted above all the angels, Mary can only intercede with God on our behalf. It is only he who can bring about our salvation. Suárez's systematic and balanced presentation of Marian doctrine might not have persuaded many Protestants, but it certainly laid the foundation for the development of modern Roman Catholic Mariology.

Both Peter Canisius and Suárez were Jesuits, and, reacting against the Marian excesses of the later Middle Ages, justly attacked by the Reformers, presented balanced and sober accounts of Marian doctrine. The same cannot be said of the Capuchin Lawrence of Brindisi, who returned to the Franciscan fervor of an earlier age and who, in his *Mariale*,[54] offers a portrait of Mary that no Protestant could possibly countenance and of which no self-respecting theologian could possibly approve.

The author, born in Brindisi in 1559, was educated in Venice, became a Capuchin in Verona, undertook further studies at the University of Padua, and enjoyed a distinguished career both in his own order and in the service of the Holy See. He

[53] Graef, *Mary*, 2:23.

[54] *S. Laurentii a Brundusio Opera Omnia*, volume I (Mariale) (Padua: Ex Officina Typographica Seminarii, 1928); English translation by Vernon Wagner, *Collected Sermons and Homilies of St. Lawrence of Brindisi*, Volume I: *Mariale* (Delhi: Media House, 2007).

died in 1619 and was buried in the Poor Clares' Convent of the Annunciation in Villafranca del Bierzo in Spain. But if the work of Canisius and Suárez was an attempt at presenting a balanced and orderly account of Marian theology, the *Mariale* of Lawrence was meat and drink to those who wished to elevate the Virgin to the stature of a goddess, the *asherah* so heartily condemned by the Hebrew prophets.

Saint Lawrence—he was canonized in 1881—compares Mary to her divine Son, and is prepared to say that she is like him in nature, grace, virtue, dignity, and glory.[55] He is even prepared to say that Mary has reached the sanctity of Christ. When she was in the world, she was "a miracle of virtue and holiness, clearly superhuman, superangelic, truly divine."[56] One of his favorite expressions for Mary is *sponsa Dei*, "spouse of God," but in his descriptions of their marital relationship, Lawrence introduces ideas that can only make a theologian blanch. If I may quote Hilda Graef,

> Even the greatest and sincerest lovers of the blessed Virgin will probably agree that [his] description of God as an infatuated husband tamed by Mary is nothing less than blasphemous, however much allowance we may make for the enthusiasm of the preacher and the fact that he is, of course, speaking metaphorically.[57]

For Lawrence of Brindisi, Mary has become, effectively, part of the Trinity, most like God in the divine attributes of power, wisdom, and goodness, and although it is possible to interpret his more outlandish statements in a vaguely orthodox way, his grossly exaggerated expressions simply confirmed the contemporary Protestant view that Roman Catholics were Mariolaters who placed the mother of Jesus on just the same level

[55] See Graef, *Mary*, 2:27.

[56] Laurentius, *Opera Omnia*, 1:13 (I.7): *Sed fuit etiam miraculum virtutis et sanctitatis plane superhumanae, superangelicae, vere divinae, Maria in mundo.*

[57] Graef, *Mary*, 2:28.

as God. This was not untrue. We saw at the end of chapter four how the people of the French countryside, in the late seventeenth century, would often tell Henri-Marie Boudon "that the holy Virgin was on the same level as God himself, or even higher."[58]

It is a relief, now, to turn to Armand-Jean de Rancé, abbot of la Trappe, who was no mystic, no visionary, and no Mariolater, but who, like Baldwin of Forde before him, had his feet firmly set on the ground, and had a greater devotion to the Mother of God than many have hitherto suggested.

[58] See chap. 4, n. 40.

Part Three

Armand-Jean de Rancé

Chapter Thirteen

The Virgin at La Trappe

Armand-Jean le Bouthillier de Rancé was born in Paris on January 9, 1626.[1] He was one of a number of surviving children, having two brothers and five sisters. The family was well to do and enjoyed close relationships with powerful figures at the royal court and in the church. His elder brother, Denis-François, had always been somewhat sickly, and when he died in 1637 at the age of seventeen, Armand-Jean found himself facing a career not in the military (as his family had first intended), but in the church. Since Denis-François had possessed a number of valuable benefices, these now came to Armand-Jean, and at the age of eleven he found himself prior or commendatory abbot of five religious houses, one of them being the dilapidated Cistercian abbey of la Trappe in the wilds of Normandy.

A commendatory abbot, we might add, was an abbot who was not elected by his own community, but appointed by the pope or local ruler. Such abbots were normally secular prelates who were given the abbeys as a reward for services rendered, and, for the most part, they were no more than absentee landlords whose chief concern was making as much profit as

[1] What follows is essentially a brief summary (with some additions) of the material in David N. Bell, *Understanding Rancé: The Spirituality of the Abbot of La Trappe in Context*, CS 205 (Kalamazoo, MI: Cistercian Publications, 2005), xv–xxv. For a much more detailed account, see Alban J. Krailsheimer, *Armand-Jean de Rancé, Abbot of la Trappe: His Influence in the Cloister and the World* (Oxford: Oxford University Press, 1974).

possible from the abbeys they had been given. In this they were generally remarkably successful, and, with but a few exceptions, the commendatory system was an unmitigated disaster for French monasticism.[2]

The young Rancé was educated at home by tutors until it was time for him to enter the Collège d'Harcourt of the University of Paris. All the evidence indicates that he was an intelligent and dedicated student, and he took his MA in 1646. Two years later he was ordained to the diaconate by Paul de Gondi, the future Cardinal de Retz, and in 1651 he was ordained as a priest by his uncle, the archbishop of Tours. By this time he was the head of his family, his father having died in 1650, and one of the properties he had inherited was a country estate at Véretz, just about a hundred and twenty miles southwest of Paris. He loved the place and spent as much time there as possible. By 1654 he was a doctor of theology of the Sorbonne, and a year later his uncle sent him as a delegate to the General Assembly of the Clergy of France. Once there, he did all that was required of him, but found the proceedings too long and too boring. Before the Assembly had concluded, Rancé—now just about thirty—had quietly slipped away to his beloved Véretz.

By this time he had made his way in society, and had fallen in love with Marie d'Avaugour, duchesse de Montbazon, a statuesque and wholly immoral beauty at least fourteen years his senior.[3] She was the wife of Hercule de Rohan, duc de Montbazon—he was in his sixties when they married—and she bore him one son and two daughters. She was a woman who possessed that indefinable something that made her irresistibly attractive to men, and she was not miserly with her favors. Cardinal de Retz, who was not unacquainted with such things, said that "she loved only her own pleasure and, above

[2] See further Bell, *Understanding Rancé*, 53–55.

[3] For a more detailed account of Madame de Montbazon, see Bell, *Understanding Rancé*, 176–90.

and beyond her pleasure, her own interests. I have never seen anyone who preserved in vice so little respect for virtue."[4]

When and how she and Rancé first met are unknown, but there is no doubt that he adored her, and the efforts of a number of well-meaning admirers of Rancé to show that their relationship was entirely platonic may be regarded as no more than wishful thinking. He still loved her in April 1657 when she contracted *la rougeole*, which might have been measles or scarlet fever (both of which were far more dangerous in her day than in ours[5]), and died after just a few days. At the time of her unexpected death, Rancé was at Véretz and had planned to go to Paris to meet her. This he did, but exactly what happened then is not entirely clear.

One of the most widespread tales in circulation at the time was that after Rancé had arrived in Paris, he hurried to the residence of his beloved and rushed into her chamber, only to be confronted with a hideous sight. There lay the dead body of Madame de Montbazon, but her head had been cut off to make her body—she was a tall woman—fit a coffin that had been made too short.

The unpleasant story of the short coffin is undoubtedly false, but the tale itself may not be without foundation. The duchess, as we have said, had died suddenly and unexpectedly, and there was almost certainly an autopsy. In Rancé's time, the removal of the head was a common part of the procedure, and autopsies might be carried out not in a hospital, but in a private dwelling.[6] It is therefore possible that, by some ghastly mischance, Rancé did indeed stumble across the corpse of his deceased mistress, and that her head had indeed been removed during the post-mortem.[7] Whatever the facts of the case, there

[4] Cardinal de Retz, *Mémoires*, ed. Maurice Allem (Paris: Pléade, 1956), 157.

[5] See David N. Bell, "Daniel de Larroque, Armand-Jean de Rancé, and the Head of Madame de Montbazon," *Cîteaux* 53 (2002): 315–17.

[6] See Bell, "Daniel de Larroque," 312–14.

[7] For a full and detailed discussion of the story of Madame de Montbazon's head, see Bell, "Daniel de Larroque," 305–31.

is no doubt that the death of the duchess proved a turning point in Rancé's life, and it played a significant role in his leaving the world for the silence of la Trappe.

He sold Véretz and, save for la Trappe, divested himself of the other benefices he had inherited from his brother. He had decided to enter the abbey as its regular, not commendatory, abbot, and spent the months from September 1662 to January 1663 at la Trappe, overseeing some very necessary rebuilding and refurbishing of what had become a dilapidated monastery populated by half a dozen monks living under no rule and little roof. It seems, however, that the time he spent there provided him with the final confirmation he needed that God was leading him to the Cistercian path—and not just the Cistercian path, but the Cistercian path of the Strict Observance.[8]

On June 13, 1663, he took his vows as a Cistercian novice at the abbey of Perseigne, just about thirty miles from la Trappe, and after a grueling year's novitiate—a year was standard at the time—he entered la Trappe as its regular abbot on July 14, 1664. He would govern the house for just over three decades, from July 1664 to May 1695, when ill health forced him to resign.

His time as abbot was not easy. Some of the difficulties he faced were made for him, some he made for himself, and beyond the cloister walls, his abbacy was marked by controversy. There was, inevitably, an on-going and unresolvable dispute with the superiors of the Common Observance, who were, by definition, opposed to his reforms. At the heart of the Strict Observance lay the strict observance of the Rule of Saint Benedict, a rule that, in Rancé's opinion, was being generally ignored and that needed to be re-established as the basis and foundation of monastic life. In Rancé's eyes, the Common Observance had introduced far too many dispensations and mitigations

[8] It is not quite accurate to use the terms "Strict" and "Common" Observance at this time, but it is certainly convenient: see further Bell, *Understanding Rancé*, 60–70.

into the Rule, especially in the matter of diet (the Strict Observance was and is strictly vegetarian, the Common Observance was and is not), and he had no time for any of them. His own approach to the Rule was actually nuanced and subtle, and what he was calling for was not a return to the letter of the Rule, but a return to its true spirit.[9] The Common Observance, not unnaturally, saw this not as a call to return to the ideals of their founder, Saint Benedict, but as an attack on their whole way of life, and there was really no hope of any reconciliation. Indeed, the Order today is still divided into two groups, one referring to themselves as the Cistercians of the Strict Observance and the other as the Order of Cîteaux.

There were other conflicts too. One was with a former friend, Guillaume Le Roy, commendatory abbot of Haute-Fontaine, who, in earlier and happier days, had spent time with Rancé at Véretz and had been welcomed at la Trappe in June 1671. The dispute centered on what were technically referred to as "humiliations," one of the techniques used at la Trappe for training a monk. "A vigilant and loving superior," wrote Rancé, "will take care to train a monk by reproaches, sharp reproofs, stinging words, public embarrassment, hard work, and degrading occupations,"[10] and even if a monk tries to do well, the superior will always find something to criticize. This could easily be misunderstood as involving the deliberate invention of non-existent faults—the technical term here was "fictions"—in which case the superior would be lying, which is a serious sin. This was exactly how humiliations were understood by Guillaume Le Roy, and it led to a long drawn-out and wordy conflict between him and Rancé that began in about 1671 and lasted for almost a decade. Neither side came out

[9] See David N. Bell, "Rancé and the Rule: His Approach to the Rule of Saint Benedict, with a Translation of His Conference for the Feast of the Saint," *Cistercian Studies Quarterly* 54 (2019): 181–210.

[10] Armand-Jean de Rancé, *De la sainteté et des devoirs de la vie monastique* (Paris: F. Muguet, 1683), 1:314, quoted in Bell, *Understanding Rancé*, 125.

particularly well, and the spirit of Christian charity was noticeable by its absence.

About another decade was taken up in an even nastier quarrel with Dom Innocent Le Masson, General of the Carthusians. This lasted from 1683 to 1692 (officially), and the question at issue was whether the Carthusians could or could not justly be accused of laxity. Rancé had suggested, fairly delicately, that they could, and this infuriated Le Masson, who, in 1683, published a long and extremely critical refutation of Rancé's comments that included some highly critical comments on Rancé himself.[11] It was an intemperate attack, and in 1689 Rancé, who, it must be admitted, did not take kindly to criticism, replied just as intemperately with a long letter pointing out in no uncertain terms how, why, and where Dom Innocent was wrong.[12] The quarrel degenerated from bad to worse, and although it was officially ended by royal command in 1689 (the king imposed silence on both parties), it was still sizzling under the surface seven years later.

Finally, again for about a decade, there was the controversy with the learned Maurist Dom Jean Mabillon on the question of monastic studies. This lasted from 1684 to 1693, and the question was simple: what should a monk read, and what books should a monastic library contain? Putting the matter as briefly as possible, Rancé wholly supported reading and study for the purposes of transformation (basically *lectio divina*), but had no time for reading and study simply for the purposes of information. Erudition, he said, and by erudition he meant learning for the sake of learning, "is the reef on which humility founders, and vanity, which is the most common result of study, has often inflicted a thousand mortal wounds on the hearts of scholars who, despite all their enlightenment, were not even aware of what was going wrong."[13]

[11] See Bell, *Understanding Rancé*, 146.

[12] See Bell, *Understanding Rancé*, 146–47.

[13] *Abbé de Rancé: Correspondance*, ed. Alban J. Krailsheimer (Brecht and Paris: Cîteaux-Le Cerf, 1993), 2:434 (letter dated October 5, 1690).

Mabillon, on the other hand, held the view that the labor of the mind could be used for the greater glory of God, and that there could be a true spirituality of scholasticism. It could be seen, for example, in both Aquinas and Bonaventure, and, for Mabillon and his confrères, it was the Maurist tradition. It follows, then, that there was no right or wrong in the dispute between Mabillon and Rancé—the two were arguing from different premises—but it must be said that throughout the long and (as usual) verbose dispute, Mabillon always retained a gentlemanly courtesy that one does not always find in Rancé.[14] He was a man who made enemies easily, and it was not always their fault.

These were the principal disputes—there were others of lesser consequence—that occupied much of Rancé's time as abbot. It cannot be said that they display him at his best. But his continual labors and ardent asceticism took their toll. By 1694 he was suffering acutely from gastric problems and severe rheumatism or rheumatoid arthritis, and the incessant pain gave him no rest either by day or by night. Both his legs were swollen and inflamed, as was his right hand, so much so that he could no longer sign his letters. Finally, when he was unable to walk without assistance, he had no choice but to enter the infirmary at la Trappe, and in May of the following year he resigned as abbot. He lived on to see three successors. The first was Dom Zozime Foisil, who died unexpectedly in March 1696. The second was Dom Armand-François Gervaise, an erratic and turbulent monk who deserves a biography to himself and who was forced to resign in 1698. And the third was Dom Jacques de La Cour, who became abbot in April 1699 and who was with Rancé when he died on Wednesday, October 27, 1700, between one and two o'clock in the afternoon.[15] He was seventy-four, and lucid until his very last moment.

[14] See further Bell, *Understanding Rancé*, 111–14.

[15] See Charles-Félix-Hyacinthe, comte de Charencey, *Histoire de l'abbaye de la Grande-Trappe* (Mortagne: Georges Meaux, 1896–1911), 1:327–52.

Rancé was always a controversial figure, and has generally evoked feelings of either love or loathing—there is no gray area—but it is not my business here to present an *apologia* for the abbot of la Trappe. My task is far simpler: to examine the place occupied in his life and thought by the Mother of God and to present an annotated translation of his five Marian sermons, one for the feast of Mary's Nativity, one for the feast of the Annunciation, and three for the feast of the Assumption.

In 2003 Sister Anna Maria Caneva, a Cistercian nun of the Strict Observance, wrote that "it has repeatedly been said that Rancé scarcely mentions Mary,"[16] and although the word "repeatedly" is something of an exaggeration, there is truth in what she said. She goes on to say that, in her view, this assessment is unjust, and refers to the idea to be found in Bérullian spirituality that Mariology cannot be separated from Christology (that is eminently clear from what we have already said in this present book) and that Rancé erected a new statue of the Virgin above the high altar in the abbey church at la Trappe, and she rightly refers to Pierre Le Nain's account of his abbot's devotion to the Mother of God as it appears in the second (1719) edition of his *Vie de Dom Armand-Jean Le Bouthillier de Rancé*.[17] All these observations are quite correct, but all require further elaboration.

In 1974, the late Alban Krailsheimer, whose admirable study of Rancé remains indispensable, observed that "in his works and in his letters his references to the Virgin and saints are sparse, perhaps surprisingly so."[18] There are, he says, occasional references to the saints, but

> what is particularly striking is his reticence about the Virgin. Even when writing to nuns, or on one of her feasts, Rancé

[16] Anna Maria Caneva, "Communion with God and the Brothers: Reading Rancé," *Cistercian Studies Quarterly* 38 (2003): 334.

[17] Caneva, "Communion with God," 334–35.

[18] Krailsheimer, *Armand-Jean de Rancé*, 75.

> almost never mentions her. One of his biographers[19] goes out of his way to stress Rancé's deep reverence for Mary and his insistence that his monks should always mention her name with special respect, but this is in the context of an allegation that worship of the Virgin and saints was neglected at la Trappe (a familiar charge against supposed Jansenist sympathizers).[20]

Krailsheimer refers further to an unpublished manuscript of some seven hundred pages preserved in the *Bibliothèque nationale de France* that contains selections from Rancé's writings arranged alphabetically under various headings,[21] and notes that there is but a single entry under *Vierge*, "the Virgin." On the other hand, Krailsheimer (like Caneva) also points out that it was Rancé who, in his enlargement and refurbishing of the abbey church, "replaced the usual tabernacle with a pyx suspended from the arm of a statue of the Virgin placed above the altar. This unusual (but not unique) arrangement is as eloquent in its symbolism as any number of pious references in writing."[22] Krailsheimer's conclusion, therefore, is that Rancé's apparent neglect of the Mother of God was not indifference but reticence, a reticence that (he suggests) was another instance of the abbot's "general dislike for expressing emotion that he none the less felt deeply and of his reluctance to introduce variety into a single-minded concentration on God and penitence."[23] These are just points, but, as with the comments of Sister Caneva, all of them require further exploration.

There are, in fact, three areas that must be examined more carefully before we can come to any just conclusion as to Rancé's true attitude to the Mother of God: first, the evidence

[19] Krailsheimer is referring to Jacques Marsollier (see below), but he would have done better to refer to Pierre Le Nain.

[20] Krailsheimer, *Armand-Jean de Rancé*, 75.

[21] Paris, BnF, MS 19,324: see Krailsheimer, *Armand-Jean de Rancé*, 75–76.

[22] Krailsheimer, *Armand-Jean de Rancé*, 76.

[23] Krailsheimer, *Armand-Jean de Rancé*, 76.

from his biographers; second, the evidence from the statues of the Virgin (there was more than one), with their inscriptions, erected at la Trappe under Rancé's administration; and third, the abbot's own writings on the Mother of God, for Krailsheimer misleads us when he states that even on one of her feasts "Rancé almost never mentions her." Let us begin with the biography by Pierre Le Nain.[24] Born in Paris in 1640, he was the younger brother of the renowned ecclesiastical historian Louis-Sébastien Le Nain de Tillemont. He was ordained as a priest in the congregation of Saint-Victor in 1667, but just over a year later, on November 21, 1668, he transferred to la Trappe, where Rancé had been regular abbot for some four years. He made his profession twelve months later and from then on devoted himself to the maintenance and progress of the Reform. In due course he was appointed sub-prior of la Trappe, and was a friend and colleague of Rancé for thirty-three years. He survived his abbot by thirteen years, and died on December 14, 1713.

His biography of Rancé is essential reading, though the form in which we have it now is not the form in which Le Nain wrote it. The first edition was published in 1715, three years after his death, and the second edition, which is so different as to be almost a different book, four years after that in 1719. Rancé's friend Jacques-Bénigne Bossuet, bishop of Meaux, almost certainly had a hand in reworking parts of the first edition, but who provided the extensive additions and rewritings of the 1719 version remains unclear. Whoever it was appears to have had access to original writings or records of Rancé himself.

What Le Nain has to say about Rancé's devotion to the Mother of God is of first importance, but there is a vast difference between the brief report that appears in the first edition of his biography and the much expanded version that appears in the second. Here is Le Nain's account as it appeared in 1715:

[24] See Bell, *Understanding Rancé*, 7–8.

> After Jesus Christ, nothing touched [Rancé] more than his holy Mother. He had always honored her with a special veneration, but being then more free and therefore better placed to offer her his prayers, he would do so with a tender and wholly remarkable devotion. We would often hear him say that there was nothing he valued more in his heart or that touched him more than that which concerned her honor.[25]

The version that appeared in 1719 is far longer, and to appreciate it we need to remember that, at la Trappe, the Little Office of the Virgin was said regularly and was familiar to every monk. Indeed, according to the 1671 *Description de l'abbaye de la Trappe* by André Félibien des Avaux (who was well acquainted with both Rancé and the abbey), it was said before Matins, and between the Office of the Virgin and Matins there were thirty minutes of meditation:

> In summer they sleep for eight hours and in winter for seven. They get up at two o'clock in the morning to go to Matins, which normally lasts up to four and a half hours, for besides the main Office they always begin with [the Office of] the Virgin, and between [this and the main Office] there is half an hour's meditation.[26]

The traditional hymn for the Office at Prime, Terce, Sext, None, and Compline begins *Memento, salutis auctor, quod nostri quondam corporis, ex illibata Virgine, nascendo, formam sumpseris. Maria, mater gratiae, mater misericordiae, tu nos ab hoste protege, et hora mortis suscipe,* "Remember, author of [our] salvation, that, being born of a pure Virgin, you once took on the form

[25] Pierre Le Nain, *La vie du Révérend Père Dom Armand Jean Le Boutillier de Rancé, Abbé et Réformateur de la Maison-Dieu Nôtre-Dame de la Trappe, de l'Étroite Observance de l'Ordre de Cîteaux* ([Rouen]: [s.n.], 1715), 3:118.

[26] David N. Bell, *Everyday Life at La Trappe under Armand-Jean de Rancé: A Translation, with Introduction and Notes, of André Félibien des Avaux's* Description de l'Abbaye de La Trappe *(1689)*, CS 274 (Collegeville, MN: Cistercian Publications, 2018), 76.

of our [human] body. Mary, Mother of Grace, Mother of Mercy, protect us from the Enemy and receive us at the hour of death." Three lines from this hymn appear in Le Nain's (revised) text—*Memento salutis auctor* (with the incorrect *salutaris* for *salutis*), *ex illibata Virgine*, and *Maria, mater gratiae*—but the theme of the hymn runs through the entire passage. Mother of Grace and Mother of Mercy are titles familiar to us from the earlier chapters of this present book, as are the other titles that appear in Le Nain's lengthy and vitally important account. Here, then, is a complete translation:[27]

> After [Rancé's] devotion to the most holy sacrament of the altar, which should occupy the first place in the heart of every true believer, [there comes next] a devout love for the most holy Virgin Mother of God. The Reverend Father's veneration for this Queen of Heaven and Earth was so great that it could not possibly have been any greater. He himself never pronounced the majestic name of Mary without bowing his head, and when, one day, he noticed that one of his monks failed to do so, he reproved him so strongly that he made all the other brothers shake in their shoes. He finished correcting the monk with these words: "What's this? Do you mean to pronounce this holy name as if it were just an ordinary name? Ah! If you had seen but a single ray of the light that surrounds this Queen of the Angels, you would have been seized as much with dread as with deference, and I doubt that your soul would have been able to tolerate that radiance without being separated from your body!" As he said these things, his face seemed to blaze with fire, which made one think that he was then receiving some special favor from this Mother of Pure Love, who has so much tenderness for those who love and serve her.
>
> When the brothers who came to see him in his room withdrew from his presence, he would bid them farewell in this way: "I commend you to Our Lord and his holy Mother."

[27] A very much abbreviated translation appears in Caneva's "Communion with God," 335, but it is essential to have the whole text.

This true son of the great Saint Bernard would imitate this holy Father in leading all his dear children to a true devotion for the Patroness of their Order. "I never tire," he said to them one day, "of speaking to you of how I am obliged to commend you to the most holy Virgin. This is something I do at every opportunity. Indeed, it is impossible to draw your attention too often to this duty, since one can truthfully say that, in fact, our very salvation depends upon it, and I have always considered as being worthy of reproof the ideas of those who say that this is not a precept and that one can be saved without invoking the holy Virgin. Truly, since we know that the entire world continues in being solely by the merit of the incarnation and the birth of [God's] Son—that which is the foundation of human salvation and which alone opens for us the gate of heaven—I cannot see how anyone could be so rash or so presumptuous as to claim that they can enter [heaven] without revering her whom [God] used to give us entrance. How can we acknowledge to the full what we owe to the goodness of a God who willed to become incarnate to save the world from shipwreck unless we also revere her whom he used to form that holy humanity in which and through which he sanctified the world? And if our redemption is bought with his blood, how can we fail to recognize the intimate relationship between this blood and the blood of her by whom he was formed? How, I say, can we fail to recognize [a relationship] that is so intimate that, according to the Fathers, the flesh of the Savior is the same as the flesh of Mary: "*Caro Christi, caro Mariae*"?[28] It follows from this that any indifference one may have for the Mother must also apply to the Son.

I cannot understand how anyone can have a care for their salvation if they do not have recourse to this divine Mother,

[28] "Flesh of Christ, flesh of Mary." Rancé is paraphrasing Augustine, *Sermo* 362.xiii.13; PL 39:1619: *sicut vera caro Mariae, vera caro Christi, quae inde susumpta est*. See chap. 4, n. 11. As we have seen earlier, the idea played an important role in the development of the doctrine of Mary's bodily assumption.

either to obtain the graces we need, or to be happily guided from this vale of tears to the haven of our salvation, or to be rescued from the disorderliness and vices in which we have the misfortune to be immersed. This, indeed, would be to neglect the most powerful assistance and the most effective means we have, next to the Son, of receiving such favors.

The church, who, as our good mother, has always applied herself to seeking out the most profitable ways of ensuring the salvation of her children, could not have found a more appropriate means than this. Indeed, she has judged it so effective that, to lead [her children] to persuade the very Son [of God] to grant them the help they need, she believes that all we need do is have him before our eyes [and remember] that he has willed to take birth in the womb of this chaste mother. It is this that she puts in our mouth and that we say to him every day: *Memento salutaris auctor*. Remember, you who are the author and principle of our salvation, that, for love of us, you willed to take birth in the womb of a Virgin Mother, wholly pure and ever virgin: *Ex illibata virgine*. If the church says no more to him, it is because she judges that this is enough to have him understand all that we await from him. And then, immediately afterward, she addresses the Queen of the Angels to teach us that it is through her and by her intervention that we may expect the graces from her whom she calls their Mother: *Maria, mater gratiae* [Mary, Mother of Grace]. For after the merits of her Son, it is primarily on her mediation that we should rely in the matter of our salvation.

For this reason, my dear brothers, we cannot be too diligent or too assiduous in addressing her. You will tell me, perhaps, that every day you chant hymns and canticles in her praise. My reply to you is that this is a good thing, but you should not stop there. You will certainly not fulfill the obligations you owe to her as monks, and as monks of the Order of Cîteaux [in particular], if you do not add to the prayers and suffrages we say publicly and in common some private practices by which you honor her as you call on her: the recitation of the rosary, for example (for those who have some spare time), or litanies, or some other prayers. [You should also] make aspirations and elevations of the heart[29] to her as to our Protectress, saying to her from the depths of your heart: *In te sunt oculi nostri; ne pereamus Virgo benedicta* ["To you our eyes are turned; do not let us perish, O blessed Virgin!"[30]]. I tell you, my brothers, as far as I am concerned, I count it a day lost and very badly spent if I do not find a few moments to call on her for aid, commending to her my salvation. I encourage you, too, to do the same, and if you fail to do so it will only be by deviating from my express wishes. For as I have just said to you, devotion to the holy Virgin is one of the most powerful aids for your sanctification that God has placed in your hands."

Such were the tender and devout sentiments of the holy abbot of la Trappe for the immaculate Mother of God, the Patroness of his monastery.[31]

Such is the account in the second edition of Le Nain's Life of his beloved abbot, and it is by far the longest account of Rancé's devotion to the Mother of God to appear in any of the biographies. Nevertheless, the very much briefer discussion that appears in the work of Jacques Marsollier is also important for showing us that the accusation that the veneration of the Virgin was neglected at la Trappe was by no means new. Marsollier was archdeacon of Uzès and a professional historian,[32] but although he wrote well, he also wrote too hastily,

[29] *Aspirations* and *élévations de cœur* are technical terms of seventeenth-century French spirituality. An aspiration is a brief, memorized, ejaculatory prayer repeated as often as it comes to mind. An elevation is similar, though not linked to a particular prayer. The mind and the affections turn to God (or, in this case, to the Mother of God), and, for a few moments, the soul soars above the things of this world in a burst of pure love.

[30] This echoes the prayer in the *Breviarium Romanum: Domine Deus, ad te sunt oculi nostri, ne pereamus*, which, in turn, is part of the response *Congregatae sunt gentes*. Rancé redirects it to Mary.

[31] Pierre Le Nain, *La vie de Dom Armand-Jean Le Bouthillier de Rancé, Abbé & Réformateur de l'Abbaye de la Maison-Dieu-Notre-Dame de la Trappe* (Paris: L. de Hotelfort, 1719), 2:486–88.

[32] See Bell, *Understanding Rancé*, 6–7.

and his biography of Rancé is not without error. Nevertheless, he is correct when he tells us that there were three libellous accusations levied against Rancé and his monastery:

> The first was that the Virgin was not honored at la Trappe, the second was that hardly any Masses were said there, and the third was that there was no liking there either for the king or for the government, that [the abbey] harbored suspect persons, and that cabals against the State were hatched there.[33]

All three accusations, says Marsollier, have been explained and shown to be manifestly false. How? Because the practices that Rancé established at la Trappe required that "six Masses were said every day: one of the Office of the Day, one of the Virgin, one for the dead, a fourth for the king, one for the benefactors, and a sixth for the persecutors and enemies of the monastery."[34] And to this regimen the abbot added a further requirement that every day, before Vespers, there should be fifteen minutes of prayers for the king. This, says Marsollier, was done at the monastery "avec le plus d'exactitude,"[35] and as far as he was concerned, the evidence of these six Masses and the royal prayers did away with all three of the calumnies we mentioned above. In any case, as Professor Krailsheimer has reminded us, allegations of neglect in venerating the Virgin and the saints were familiar charges against supposed Jansenist sympathizers,[36] and although Rancé was not himself a Jansenist, the austere way of life at la Trappe and his own

[33] Jacques Marsollier, *La vie de Dom Armand-Jean Le Bouthillier de Rancé, Abbé régulier et Réformateur du Monastère de la Trappe, de l'Étroite Observance de Cisteaux. Nouvelle Édition* (Paris: H. L. Guerin & L. F. Delatour, 1758), 2:127–28.

[34] Marsollier, *Vie de Rancé*, 2:127.

[35] Marsollier, *Vie de Rancé*, 2:127.

[36] Krailsheimer, *Armand-Jean de Rancé*, 75.

friendship with a number of prominent Jansenists made him deeply suspect.[37]

Rancé's devotion to the Mother of God was shared by at least one of his monks, Dom Jacques Minguet. He had been for many years abbot of the Strict Observance monastery of Châtillon-en-Lorraine, and he entered la Trappe at the advanced age of seventy-seven "to end his days in the penitential way of life observed there and especially in the practice of obedience, in which he acquitted himself with such fidelity and religious devotion that one can say that no one surpassed him in the subjection and submission of his spirit."[38] According to André Félibien, Dom Minguet had a profound love for his Lord and Savior,

> but in loving the Son in this way, he lacked nothing in honoring his holy Mother with a remarkable devotion. Apart from the usual fasts, he also fasted every Saturday, the day devoted to the worship of the Holy Virgin, and since he knew that the Queen of the Angels is the refuge of sinners, the consolation of the afflicted, and the succor of the faithful, he addressed to her unceasingly his desire that, through her intercession, he might share in the merits of the blood of Jesus Christ poured out on the Cross.[39]

Let us now turn to the second of the areas we mentioned above: the evidence for Rancé's attitude to the Mother of God

[37] On Rancé and Jansenism, see the references in the index to Bell, *Understanding Rancé*, 361.

[38] *Relation de la vie et de la mort de quelques religieux de l'abbaye de la Trappe. Nouvelle édition* (Paris: G. Despez, 1755), 1:145–46. The *Relations* might not be much to the taste of the modern-day palate, but they are essential reading if one is to understand the true nature and spirit of la Trappe under Rancé.

[39] Bell, *Everyday Life at La Trappe*, 118–19. Dom Minguet's devotion may have been influenced by the fact that in the monastic church at Châtillon there was an ancient stone statue of the Virgin, who, it was believed, had protected the abbey from a number of calamities. It was also a place of Marian pilgrimage.

as it appears from the statues of the Virgin, with their appropriate inscriptions, that were erected during his abbacy. There were, in fact, three, as André-Jean-Marie Hamon informs us. Père Hamon (1795–1874) was the parish priest of Saint-Sulpice in Paris, and a man as devoted to his flock (three times he refused to be made bishop) as to his spiritual and ecclesiastical writing. In the fifth volume of his *Notre-Dame de France ou Histoire du culte de la Sainte Vierge en France* he tells us that the Virgin was always honored at la Trappe with a special devotion, and, to remind the brothers of her importance, Rancé erected three statues of the Mother of God. The first, placed above the altar in the church,

> was of a beauty so pure and perfect that one found it worthy of classical antiquity. The abbot had acquired it for a very high price, being of the opinion that, for the sake of the Mother of God, one could depart from the rule that prescribed poverty everywhere, even in the church. In one hand she held the infant Jesus; in the other, a hanging chain bearing the holy Eucharist, as had been the case at Cîteaux for many centuries. At her feet, an angel with arms outspread contemplated the holy sacrament; another [angel], with bowed head and arms crossed [on the breast], adored it in profound recollection. . . . A second statue of the Virgin could be seen in the lay-brothers' choir, and a third over the entrance to the abbey, with these words of Saint Bernard: *Ipsa tenente non corruis, protegente non metuis, propitia pervenis*—that is to say, "Upheld by Mary, one does not fall; protected by her, one does not fear; with her favor, one arrives at one's goal."[40]

[40] M. le curé de Saint-Sulpice [= André-Jean-Marie Hamon], *Notre-Dame de France ou Histoire du culte de la Sainte Vierge en France, depuis l'origine du christianisme jusqu'à nos jours. Cinquième volume* (Paris: H. Plon, 1865), 5:147–48. The quotation is taken from Bernard's second homily *in laudibus Virginis Matris,* which actually reads *Ipsa tenente non corruis, ipsa protegente non metuis, ipsa duce non fatigaris, ipsa propitia pervenis*, "Upheld by her, one does not fall; protected by her, one does not fear; guided by her, one does not tire; with her

The first of the three statues was clearly the most important, and was erected in 1682 as part of a major refurbishing of the monastic church. According to Pierre Le Nain,

> In place of the statue of the holy Virgin that was there, [the abbot] put up a new one, accompanied by two angels and certain other decorations. He thought that the one that had been there at the beginning of the Reform did not reflect the feelings of religious life and devotion for [the Mother of God] that were there in the monastery, and that in this matter it was God's will that one should *not* retain the simplicity and poverty which [otherwise] one sought to practise in all things. In his opinion, an image that was more spirited and life-like would have greater impact and be better suited to arouse devotion. He saw this as being essential, all the more so in that one would leave to posterity a monument to the double devotion that was always manifest in this house, for [devotion] to the Son [of God] and his Mother were never separated. His thought here was that nothing was more worthy of the Mother than to give her Son to his servants, nor anything more worthy of the Son than to be given to them by the hand of his Mother. This is what is depicted in the different postures of the two angels at the foot of the statue of the holy Virgin who holds the hanging chain with the vessel that contains the most holy sacrament of the altar.[41]

---

favor, one arrives at one's goal" (*In laudibus Virginis Matris, hom.* 2.17; SBOp 4:35). That Rancé believed this to be so cannot be doubted.

[41] Le Nain, *Vie de Rancé* (1715 ed.), 2:72–73. The idea that devotion to the Son cannot be separated from devotion to his Mother, and vice versa, was standard teaching among the Cistercians from Bernard onwards. According to Marsollier, *Vie de Rancé*, 2:85, "[Rancé's] sense of pious devotion (*piété*) for the Mother of God did not allow him to content himself with what had been placed there at the beginning of the [Strict Observance] Reform. He even believed that he should leave to posterity a most remarkable monument of his devotion to the Holy Virgin, whom the Order of Cîteaux had always regarded, after God, as its special protectress."

André Félibien provides us with rather more detail:

> On [the high altar] is the statue of the Virgin standing upright holding her Son on her left arm, and in her right hand is a little pavilion under which is suspended the Holy Sacrament in accordance with the ancient custom of the church. Under this statue on the pedestal that supports it is written [in Greek] THEOTOKÔ, that is to say, "To the Mother of God."[42]
>
> However holy and august are the ceremonies of the church, there are always those who seek only to find there something to criticize. You therefore come across those who want to find fault with this sort of suspension [of the Holy Sacrament] and have it pass for a novelty, and even as something injurious to the honor of the Virgin, to have her image serve to carry the holy ciborium. But such people are ignorant of the fact that this is in accordance with the ancient practice of the Order of Saint Benedict, for in the past the Holy Sacrament was supported in just the same way by the statue of the Virgin on the high altar at Cîteaux. It is only recently that this usage has been changed in the monasteries of this Order with tabernacles being placed on altars—a practice that was introduced [only] a short time ago.[43] You might even say that it would be a sort of impiety not to wish that the statue of the Virgin should serve to support the Holy Sacrament since faith obliges us to believe that the sacred body of Jesus Christ is there present in its reality, and that the greatest honor that the Holy Mother could receive would

[42] THEOTOKÔ was written in Greek capitals. For another description of the statue and the suspended ciborium, see Louis Dubois, *Histoire de l'abbé de Rancé et de sa réforme* (Paris: A. Bray, 1866), 1:619–20.

[43] The custom of placing the tabernacle on an altar, though not at first the high altar, dates, effectively, from the early sixteenth century, when Matteo Giberti (1495–1543), bishop of Verona, instructed the priests of his diocese to place the receptacle on an altar. In 1614 Pope Pius V required the same thing in all churches in the diocese of Rome. Félibien is quite correct, therefore, in maintaining that the custom was introduced into Cistercian churches in what, for him, was the recent past.

be to carry it still: she whose whole glory and happiness was to carry [that body] in her womb and suckle it at her breasts.

Also, Monsieur l'Abbé [de Rancé] himself, as if anticipating this offence that would be so injurious not only to the Mother but also to the Son, composed these two couplets in which he displays the honor the Virgin receives by still bearing today the glorious body of her Son, and that she alone is worthy of such a holy task.

> *Si quaeras natum cur matris dextera gestat.*
> *Sola fuit tanto munere digna parens.*
> *Non poterat fungi majori munere mater,*
> *Nec poterat major dextera ferre Deum.*

[If you ask why the Mother carries the Son on her right arm,
It is because this Mother alone was worthy of such a great honor;
No other mother could have rendered a greater service,
No arm was more worthy to carry God.][44]

Of the second and third statues of the Virgin—those in the lay-brothers' choir and over the entrance to the abbey—we have no description, although (as we have seen) the *curé* of Saint-Sulpice tells us that the third of the statues was adorned with a quotation from Saint Bernard, and according to Louis Dubois, "the abbé de Rancé had already signaled his devotion to the august Mother of God by placing, as at Cîteaux, her image on the lintel of the gateway [to the abbey], so that this would be the first thing on which one's eyes would light, and that everyone would understand that Mary was especially honored in this place that bore her name."[45]

Let us therefore turn to the third area we must consider: Rancé's own writings on the Mother of God. Professor Krailsheimer, as we have seen, tells us that the abbot almost never mentions her, even on one of her feasts, but that is not

[44] Bell, *Everyday Life at La Trappe*, 73–74. The couplets are elegiac couplets, a hexameter followed by a pentameter. Mary supports the physical body of the baby Jesus with her left arm, and his sacramental body with her right.

[45] Dubois, *Histoire*, 1:619.

quite the case. Apart from the five homilies we have already mentioned, there are also a series of "Reflections on the Feast of the Purification" in Rancé's *Conduite chrétienne adressée à son altesse royale Madame de Guise*.[46] Madame de Guise was Elisabeth d'Orléans (1646–1696), who, having married Louis-Joseph de Lorraine, later the duc de Guise, thereby became the duchesse de Guise. Her life was unhappy, for she had but one child, who died in infancy, and her husband died from smallpox at the age of twenty-one. She was very pious and very proud, and it is doubtful that anyone with less than Rancé's charisma and authority could have been her spiritual director. But there seems to have been a real friendship between them. Madame de Guise died from cancer in 1696, and *Conduite chrétienne* was published the following year.[47] What does Rancé have to say to this haughty aristocrat? The answer is simple: Her Royal Highness must practise humility, and the perfect example of perfect humility is Mary.

Madame de Guise is about to make an eight-day retreat. The first day is a day of preparation and an examination of her conscience before God, and then, on the second day, "you can consider the profound humility of the holy Virgin," how she concealed all the graces she had received from the world and appeared in its eyes as just an ordinary woman, a woman of the people.[48] Mary, in fact, "knew no other glory than to imitate her Son,"[49] and her Son, says Rancé elsewhere, exemplified in his incarnation the uttermost perfection of humility. What could be more humbling than for the second Person of the Trinity to take on the limitations of mortality, the Infinite to become finite? "None could carry humility and obedience

[46] Armand-Jean de Rancé, *Conduite chrétienne adressée à son altesse royale Madame de Guise* (Paris: F. & P. Delaulne, 1697), 191–201.

[47] Further on Madame de Guise, see David N. Bell, "'A Holy Familiarity': Prayer and Praying According to Armand-Jean de Rancé," *Cistercian Studies Quarterly* 51 (2016): 355–57.

[48] Rancé, *Conduite chrétienne*, 192.

[49] Rancé, *Conduite chrétienne*, 193.

further than he, who humbled himself and subjected himself even to death: *semetipsum exinanivit, factus obediens usque ad mortem* ["he emptied himself, becoming obedient even unto death"].[50] On the third day, Rancé counsels the duchess to consider further "this great humility of the holy Virgin."[51] Did it bring her any worldly recompense? It did not. On the contrary, it brought only tribulations, for as Saint Simeon said to her, "Your soul will be pierced by a sword."[52] Indeed, affliction will be the lot of all those souls that love Christ.

On the fourth and fifth days of her retreat, Madame de Guise is instructed to consider more deeply the meaning of Simeon's prophecy. She must note that although God warns the holy Virgin that she must prepare herself for the cross and all the pains and contradictions that attend it, he also consoles her by revealing to her the true nature of the child she bears: that he will be a light to lighten the Gentiles, and the glory of his people Israel:[53] "It is in this way that he sustains the souls who serve him when he allows them to fall into temptation, and he never fails to sweeten the bitterness by secret dispositions[54] that are the pure effects of his mercy."[55] The last three days of the duchess's retreat are not specifically related to Mary, but the essence of the exercise is simple: if the duchess wishes to belong to God and serve him, then she must "prefer humiliation to glory, lowliness to greatness, and tribulations to human joys and comforts."[56]

[50] §15 of the conference for Mary's Nativity (chap. 14 below), quoting Phil 2:7-8.

[51] Rancé, *Conduite chrétienne*, 193.

[52] Luke 2:35.

[53] Rancé, *Conduite chrétienne*, 196, quoting Luke 2:32.

[54] A *disposition*—another technical term in French spirituality—can be a predisposition (i.e., a natural aptitude) or a state of mind that may be cultivated and developed by the individual or (as here) infused into the soul by God.

[55] Rancé, *Conduite chrétienne*, 196–97.

[56] Rancé, *Conduite chrétienne*, 197.

As we might expect, this emphasis on humility is a key theme that runs through all Rancé's writings on the Mother of God, but it is not the only theme. A second—that of separation or withdrawal from the world—derives from the story of Mary's sojourn in the Jerusalem Temple. Rancé is here following the story of the Virgin's early years as it appears in the *Protevangelium* of James, and it forms the background for Rancé's teaching in his conference for the feast of the Annunciation.

What, then, can we say about Armand-Jean de Rancé's attitude to the Mother of God? It is clear that, for him, Mary is the model of humility, of withdrawal from the world, of purity of heart, of mortification, of prayer and contemplation, and of obedience to God. In her he sees the epitome of monastic perfection. His approach, however, is moral rather than theological. That is to say, although, as we shall see, he clearly accepts the doctrine of the Immaculate Conception, he does not discuss either its theology or its theological problems. Again—and this time with Bernard—he has no doubt of Mary's role as *mediatrix* and her co-operation with her Son in the work of salvation, but nowhere does he elaborate on the matter. This is not surprising. There was no place for theologizing at la Trappe, and its abbot regarded high-flying theological speculation as no more than an exercise in "curiosity,"[57] and the distrust and condemnation of "curiosity" lay at the heart of Rancé's dispute with Mabillon on the question of monastic studies.[58] Rancé's regulations are quite clear on this point: in the conferences "we banish everything to do with scholastic

[57] See Rancé's forceful condemnation of *curiosité* in his *Conduite chrétienne*, 303–4, and, generally, Richard Newhauser, "The Sin of Curiosity and the Cistercians," in *Erudition at God's Service: Studies in Medieval Cistercian History, XI*, ed. John R. Sommerfeldt, CS 98 (Kalamazoo, MI: Cistercian Publications, 1987), 71–95.

[58] See Bell, *Understanding Rancé*, 111–14 and 277–78.

theology and disputed questions, and everything else that can dry up the heart."[59]

There can surely be no doubt of Rancé's devotion to Mary, and Sister Caneva was quite right in pointing out that devotion to the Son and the Mother cannot be separated. Rancé, as we have seen, entirely agreed. He could not enter his monastery without being welcomed by the Virgin, and he could not enter the monastic church without being in her presence. Neither could his monks or lay brothers. On the other hand, he was no Louis-Marie Grignion de Montfort (1673–1716), whose *Glories of Mary, Secrets of the Rosary,* and *True Devotion to Mary* enjoyed huge popularity. Indeed, as Henri-Jean Martin has said, "the Virgin was the center of worship during the Counter Reformation,"[60] and books extolling her virtues, her mediation, and her miracles were legion in seventeenth-century France. Many of them, to be sure, were "abysmal in their puerility"[61] (Rancé would have had no time for such), but they reached a very wide and eager audience. The prolific Rancé wrote no such books, and there is no reason that he should have done. His concern was with the holiness and duties of the monastic state, with penance and penitence, with humility and humiliations, with dying to the world in order to live to God. For all of these the Virgin was a model, the true *exemple d'humilité,* whose mediation was essential if he and his monks were to achieve the goal they sought.

When Rancé rose at 2 a.m., he and his monks chanted the Office of the Virgin, and before they retired at night they sang the *Salve Regina*. The Mother of God, with her divine Son, was always there, and I see no reason to think that Pierre Le Nain

[59] Armand-Jean de Rancé, *Règlemens de l'abbaye de Nôtre-Dame de la Trappe en forme de Constitutions: Avec des reflexions, et la Carte de Visite à N. D. des Clairets* (Paris: F. Delaulne, 1718), 58 (VII).

[60] Henri-Jean Martin, trans. David Gerard, *Print, Power, and People in 17th-Century France* (Metuchen / London: The Scarecrow Press, 1993), 99. See generally 99–100.

[61] Martin, *Print, Power, and People,* 99.

was lying when he said that there was nothing that touched the heart of Rancé more than Mary, that he always honored her with a special devotion, and that "we would often hear him say that there was nothing he valued more in his heart or that touched him more than that which concerned her honor."[62] Let us see, then, what Rancé has to say about Mary in his conference for the feast of her Nativity.

[62] See n. 25 above.

Chapter Fourteen

Armand-Jean de Rancé: The Conference for the Feast of the Nativity of the Virgin

Introduction

The sermon or homily for the Nativity of Mary is not, strictly speaking, a sermon or homily, but a conference, and the same is true of the other four sermons or homilies on the annunciation and the assumption. The nature and purposes of the conferences are set out in detail in Rancé's Regulations.[1] They were generally held on Sundays, though if some feast day of obligation fell on a Wednesday or Thursday, on those days as well. They were not held in the church but normally in the chapter room. What they were, were instructive talks for Rancé's monks, but it is obvious that conferences, sermons, and homilies were first cousins, if not siblings.

The conference for the feast of Mary's Nativity was delivered by Rancé "at the request of certain novices" on September 8—the day of the feast—of an unknown year, and it offers an excellent summary of Rancé's attitude to Mary. The abbot takes as his text Song of Songs 7:1, "How beautiful are all your steps,

[1] Armand-Jean de Rancé, *Règlemens de l'abbaye de Nôtre-Dame de la Trappe en forme de Constitutions: Avec des reflexions, et la Carte de Visite à N. D. des Clairets* (Paris: F. Delaulne, 1718), 52–59 (VIII).

Daughter of the Prince!"[2] and opens by telling the novices who have requested the conference that they could not have chosen a better day to consecrate themselves to God. For "just as this day of blessings shows us the first steps taken by this Virgin when she entered the world, so, at the same time, she puts before our eyes a rare example and a model of consummate perfection" (§1).

The essential structure of the conference could not be simpler. Although the soul of the Virgin was replete with all virtues, there were four that stand out: her love of withdrawal from the world, her purity of heart, her humility, and her obedience. If, then, a monk wishes to be as perfect as possible in his chosen vocation, let him imitate the Virgin in these four areas. As Saint Ambrose says, she is a mirror for the faithful (§3). Thus, in the first half of the conference, Rancé shows how these four virtues were exemplified in Mary, and in the second half, he shows how they should be exemplified in the lives of monks. What could be more obvious for those who wish to lead an angelic life—*une vie toute angélique* (§1)—than to imitate the Queen of the Angels? Yet Rancé never forgets that to imitate Mary is to imitate Christ, for the imitation of Christ is the central feature of the Christian religion. Only he can reconcile heaven and earth, and only he can appease God's just anger at our sinful condition (§5).

Rancé's account of Mary's withdrawal from the world (§§7–9) follows the story of her early years as it appears in the *Protevangelium* of James. In the Temple she gave herself utterly to God, and "he prepared her for that degree of holiness and state of blessedness to which she had to come in order for her to bring his plans to fruition" (§9). Her purity (§§10–11) follows from this, for while she was withdrawn from the world in the Temple, God became the beginning and end of all that she did

[2] *Gressus* in Latin actually means feet, but Rancé's exegesis demands the idea of steps or footsteps (*démarches*).

and thought, and, as Rancé says, "he was in her head, her heart, her eyes, her mouth, and her hands" (§10).

This leads to a discussion of the Virgin's humility (§§12–14), for humility is the basis of all perfection: "Jesus Christ founded and grounded every spiritual structure on this virtue" (§12), and, as we have seen in every writer discussed in these pages, it is Mary's humility that is recognized by God as her greatness. She might have thought to herself how much she had renounced worldly things, or how, day and night, she had meditated on God's law, or the degree to which she put her own will into his hands, but she did not. She said but one thing: "He has regarded the humility of his handmaid"[3] (§14).

If humility is the basis of all perfection, "obedience is born of humility and flows from it" (§15). And there is but one example of a humility and an obedience that exceeds that of the Virgin, and that is the humility and obedience of Christ himself. Did he not empty himself, taking on the form of a servant for our sake? Did he not obey his divine Father, even if it meant dying a slow and hideous death on the cross?

Then, at §16, Rancé begins to apply these four virtues to the monks listening to him. He goes on to explain that withdrawal from the world is not just physical separation, but a true change of heart (§17), and he spends some time in contrasting the way of life of worldly people with the way of life of a religious (§18). They are completely opposite! But when you read the gospels, it becomes clear that this separation from the ways of the world—not necessarily separation from the world itself, but from *the ways* of the world—is something that is enjoined on all Christians, not just monks and nuns.

He begins his discussion of purity, the second characteristic of the Virgin, at §22, emphasizing that it is much more than simply abstaining from lewd actions, desires, and thoughts: what we are speaking of here is total purity of heart (§23). But

[3] Luke 1:48.

at the basis of purity of heart is the eradication of self-will, which is why God and, through God, Saint Benedict (whom he calls "the interpreter of God's wishes" [§25]) has given us so many holy rules, and laid down so many regulations covering the tiniest details of our way of life. The reason is simple: to produce "the perfect mortification of self-will" (§25).

Then, at §26, Rancé begins his account of how every monk should imitate the humility of the Virgin. One of the main ways lies in being patient and forbearing when injured by others: "if, in doing good, you endure with patience the ill-treatment you receive, it is this that makes you pleasing to God" (§26). But this is not just to be regarded as advice, says Rancé; it is a command, a precept, and he quotes 1 Peter 2:20-21 to prove his case. If Christ has suffered, so should we if we are to follow in his steps and imitate him. And then, once again, in §28, he contrasts the way of life of those within the cloister with the way of life of those in the world.

The fourth and last virtue displayed by the Mother of God is obedience (§§29–31), and Rancé begins by quoting Saint Bernard: "all humility boils down to obedience, and the subjection of our own will to that of God"[4] (§29). It follows, then, that those who are truly obedient will what they know God wills, and hold in horror what they know he does not will. True peace, therefore, comes from submitting one's entire will to the will of God and becoming his willing instrument.

And so, in conclusion, the abbot tells his brothers to imitate the Virgin, to take her as their model, for in so doing they will be imitating Christ. All these virtues and practices are set forth in the gospels, and if we follow them with all our desire and all our intentions, this will constrain her, at the side of her Son, "to grant you her potent intercession that is always heeded, and from this infinite goodness she will acquire for you not only the grace of bringing to completion the sacrifice you have

[4] See Bernard, *De diversis, sermo* 26.2; SBOp 6 / 1:194.

begun, but also [the grace] of persevering in your commitment" (§33).

Rancé's sources for the conference, apart from the Vulgate and the liturgy, are Ambrose of Milan, Bernard, and the Rule of Saint Benedict. He rarely translates his Latin quotations (though I have done so below), and we must assume that the monks of la Trappe could understand what he was saying. How long it would take to deliver the conference depends, of course, on the speed at which it was delivered. We may assume, however, that Monsieur de la Trappe did not gabble and that his stately French would be delivered in a stately fashion. Before his conversion and his withdrawal to la Trappe, he was regarded by many, including himself, as a very fine preacher.[5] Having read aloud one page of the 1720 edition in as stately a voice as I could manage, and multiplied that by the total number of pages, I would estimate that the delivery of the entire conference would occupy almost an hour. This was fairly standard for sermons at the time.[6] Here, then, is Rancé's own account of why and how Mary should be our model. It has been translated from Rancé's *Instructions ou Conférences sur les Epîtres et Évangiles des Dimanches et Principales Festes de l'Année, et sur les Vêtures & Professions Religieuses. Tome quatrième* (Paris: F. Delaulne, 1720), 4:300–330, reproduced (with some typographical errors) in *Collection intégrale et universelle des Orateurs Chrétiens. Deuxième série*, vol. 90 of the entire series (= vol. 23 of the second series), ed. Jacques-Paul Migne (Paris: J.-P. Migne, 1866), 593–604.

[5] See David N. Bell, *Understanding Rancé: The Spirituality of the Abbot of La Trappe in Context*, CS 205 (Kalamazoo, MI: Cistercian Publications, 2005), 31–32.

[6] See David N. Bell, *A Saint in the Sun: Praising Saint Bernard in the France of Louis XIV*, CS 271 (Collegeville, MN: Cistercian Publications, 2017), 53–54.

Instruction or Conference for the Feast Day of the Nativity of the Holy Virgin, at the request of certain novices.

[Mary, Model of Perfection][7]

Quam pulchri sunt gressus tui, Filia Principis! (Song 7:1)
"How beautiful are your steps, Daughter of the Prince!"[8]

1. My brothers, you could not find a better time, nor one more appropriate, to renew the desires you have conceived to consecrate the rest of your days to God than the feast we celebrate today. It is the feast of the Nativity of the Queen of the Angels, and you, therefore, have great cause to expect and hope that she will look favorably on the resolution you have made to embrace a life that is wholly angelic. And just as this day of blessings shows us the first steps taken by this Virgin when she entered the world, so, at the same time, she puts before our eyes a rare example and a model of consummate perfection.

2. *Quam pulchri sunt gressus tui in calceamentis, Filia Principis*! ["How beautiful are your feet in shoes, Daughter of the Prince!"[9]]. In these words the Holy Spirit bears witness to the guidance that [the Virgin] gave us in her life on earth, for he assures us that all her steps are always accompanied by a wholly singular beauty, purity, and integrity. We can say, in fact, that no step she took, nor any one of her acts, nor any thought she conceived, nor any of her desires was unworthy of the holiness of him who, as part of his eternal plan, had destined her to become his mother, and in his wisdom, he chose for this great task a creature who, throughout the whole of her life, did nothing that was not holy or beyond reproach.

[7] This subtitle appears in the Migne edition only (593).

[8] See n. 2 above.

[9] Song 7:1.

3. Judge from this, my brothers, whether you could come upon a happier set of circumstances, for she sets forth before you this unique work, this masterpiece of the hand of the Almighty, that so splendidly encompasses the state of mind, the virtues, and the divine qualities that should form and fashion the whole of the [monastic] state and profession you wish to embrace. Saint Ambrose assures us that the way of life of this holy Virgin (which was ever pure and ever perfect) is like a mirror held before the eyes of the faithful, [a mirror] in which they should see and adopt all the rules and maxims for their own conduct and way of life. They should note there what they should avoid, what they should imitate, what they must choose, and what they must practise. They will see there a wondrous chastity that ought to be the principal ornament of their [monastic] state—that is to say, this ultimate perfection, without which there is no such thing as perfect chastity: *Sit vobis tanquam in imagine descripta virginitas vitaque beatae Mariae, de qua velut in speculo refulget species castitatis et forma virtutis* ["Let the virginity and life of blessed Mary be set forth for you as in a likeness, in which is reflected, as in a mirror, the nature of chastity and form of virtue"[10]].

4. It is from this spring, so abundant and so fruitful, that you should take the instructions, the truths, the illuminations without which a truly religious way of life is impossible: *Hinc sumatis licet exempla bene vivendi* ["From this one may take the pattern of a good life"[11]]. In a word, it is the flaming torch that should enlighten you, the clear light by means of which you should guide your steps, the touchstone that should lead you to recognize and distinguish what there is of good and bad in your actions. And this insight, more than any other, should bring you into that holy state of mind without which you

[10] Ambrose of Milan, *De virginibus ad Marcellinam sororem*, II.6; PL 16:208C, reading *vita Mariae* for *vitaque beatae Mariae* and *refulgeat* for *refulget*.

[11] Ambrose, *De virginibus ad Marcellinam*, II.6; PL 16:208C, omitting *bene* in *bene vivendi*.

would not know how to conduct yourself before God any more than before people, and which you must have in order to make yourselves worthy of the promise you wish to make: *Ubi tanquam in exemplari magisteria expressa probitatis; quid corrigere, quid effugere, quid tenere debeatis ostendit* ["Where, as in an example, are shown the clear rules for an upright life: what needs to be corrected, what avoided, and to what you should hold fast"[12]].

5. These are some of the examples that God sets out for us to imitate. These are some of the instructions he gives us to follow. And since there is nothing more needful for all Christians than to bind themselves to the imitation of Christ (for their salvation is linked to the faithful way in which they manifest the perfections of this man-God, and there is not one of them who should not take every care and make every effort to strive to acquire this likeness [to Christ] if they wish to have a part in his kingdom), so he shows himself to them in a variety of ways to lead them to this goal: now in the person of his apostles, now in that of his martyrs, sometimes as his virgins, his chaste spouses, and sometimes in [the person] of his holy monks. But today, he uses the person of his holy Mother, for she has a greater capacity to arouse our devotion, and make a more vivid and profound impression upon us, by the way in which we should recognize in her the one who produced in her womb and gave to the world him who alone was capable of reconciling earth and heaven, and of appeasing God's anger that the world, for so many centuries, had so justly and unhappily brought upon itself.

6. My brothers, if you truly want to make the best use of this great example, you must choose from this unfathomable abyss of graces, this ocean of all manner of good things, blessings, and riches, whatever is most appropriate and essential for your

[12] Ambrose, *De virginibus ad Marcellinam*, II.6; PL 16:208C, reading *effingere* for *effugere* and *ostendunt* for *ostendit*.

[monastic] state, whatever is most suitable for you, and whatever can contribute most in transforming you into perfect monks, for it will be of little service to us if we examine this immense subject with no more than a general and hasty glance. Therefore, to help you apply them to yourselves justly and usefully, I will tell you that, among all these innumerable virtues with which it has pleased God to adorn and fill the soul of this holy Virgin, as the heavens [are filled] with an infinite multitude of twinkling stars, I have noted four principal points that you should consider as the basis, the essence, and the truth of the profession to which you are convinced he has called you. I will tell you what they are: the love of withdrawal [from the world], purity of heart, humility, and obedience. These are the graces that shine out so brilliantly in the whole way of life of the Mother of God, these are the holy states of mind with which she was favored for her own sanctification, as well as for the salvation of all those who, moved by sincere devotion, will examine [the details of] her life.

7. This great soul fled from worldly people from her tender youth,[13] and even though God, through an unparalleled protection, had preserved her from all corruption,[14] she does not leave fear behind, nor [cease from] taking whatever precautions she thinks necessary: she separates herself from the world and chooses to withdraw from it. [Her purpose is to establish herself] more securely in a state in which, either because she found there greater strength to resist the temptations that could attack her innocence, or, by living unknown [to the world] and being neither impeded nor diverted by human company, she would have better means and facilities for profiting from the talents that had been entrusted to her, for making progress in this divine love with which she felt herself ablaze, and for

[13] As was mentioned in the introduction, Rancé is here following Mary's story as it appears in the *Protevangelium* of James.

[14] *De toute iniquité*: the reference is to the doctrine of the Immaculate Conception.

enjoying the presence of her God in peace. [It is] like a tree that one transplants into the bottom of a valley by a running stream, so that by receiving constant refreshment it can remain forever green and produce fruits of a beauty and excellence impossible in a less happy location: *sicut lignum quod plantatum est secus decursus aquarum* ["like a tree planted by running waters"[15]].

8. Do not think that the Virgin was idle in her strict retreat, that she had no occupation and did nothing. She did there what Jesus Christ himself did in the course of his own hidden life. She applied herself to those tasks suitable to her state, she did not scorn (if I may make use of the words of Scripture) to work with wool and flax and to make use of her hands, which were so wise, so nimble, and so skillful: *quaesivit lanam et linum, et operata est consilio manuum suarum* ["she sought wool and flax, and worked them by the skill of her hands"[16]]. But above all, she filled her days with holy occupations: she prayed, she spoke with her Creator with all the more freedom and constancy as, for love of him, she imposed upon herself a profound silence with regard to his creation. The temple that was there before her eyes ceaselessly recalled to her mind what wonders God had worked there, it enkindled her faith, and it made her pious devotion more eager and more ardent. She constantly offered him thanks for having delivered her from all dangerous dealings [with the world], and her heart, pierced with this knowledge, could not bear to bring before him anything that might offend him.

9. She bemoaned in his presence the [moral] blindness of human beings and the depths of their degeneracy. She appeased his anger. She held back his arm when he was ready to punish them for their sins and avenge himself upon them for the infinite number of offences they were committing against his supreme Majesty. In short, by her unceasing efforts,

[15] Ps 1:3.
[16] Prov 31:13.

she raised herself to a higher [level of] virtue, and since she had only God in mind, and since she was dead to all else, he alone filled her heart. Thus, since she reserved for him a fervor ever renewed, her love could only be increased and inflamed, and, unknown to her, he prepared her for that degree of holiness and state of blessedness to which she had to come in order for her to bring his plans to fruition. [And this he did] in such a way that [a way of life] considered by those with no knowledge of the ways of God as contemptible and useless was actually a noble occupation, whose only measure and limits were those that it pleased God to set for her.

10. As to her purity, is there any opinion we should not entertain concerning it? The earth is the source of corruption, the world is the origin of impurity, and those who are attached to the earth do, speak, and think only those things that are earthly and corruptible: *qui est de terra, de terra est, et de terra loquitur* ["whoever is of the earth, of the earth he is, and of the earth he speaks"[17]]. But this Virgin, wholly pure and completely separated [from the world], had God alone[18] as the goal, the beginning, and the end of all her actions, words, and thoughts. He filled all the space in her heart she had refused to created things, and since there was nothing there that might contend with him for the position he ought to occupy there,

[17] John 3:31.

[18] *Dieu seul.* It is just possible that this is a passing allusion to the ideas of Henri-Marie Boudon (1624–1702), archdeacon of Évreux. His motto was *Dieu seul*, and among his many publications was a volume with the title *Dieu Seul: le saint esclavage de l'admirable Mère de Dieu*, 2nd ed. (Paris: E. Michallet, 1674). We mentioned the book in chap. four. He had a profound devotion to the Mother of God and was a staunch supporter of the doctrine of the Immaculate Conception, thereby arousing the ire of the Jansenists. More than twenty of his works are listed in the 1752 catalogue of the library of la Trappe, including *Le saint esclavage*, and Rancé was almost certainly familiar with his ideas. See Pierre Pourrat, trans. Donald Attwater, *Christian Spirituality, Volume IV: Later Developments, Part II, from Jansenism to Modern Times* (Westminster: The Newman Press, 1955), 115–18.

he gave himself to her in ways that cannot be described. He was in her head, her heart, her eyes, her mouth, and her hands. God was wholly present in everything she did, and, since he possessed her in a most intimate way, we could say of her, with far more justice than Saint Paul said of himself, *vivo ego; jam non ego, vivit vero in me Christus* ["I live; now not I, but Christ lives in me"[19]]. In her there was no thought or any action that he did not fashion and that was not his work, and she had never had any cause to say or cry out with this holy apostle, *infelix homo, quis me liberabit de corpore mortis hujus*? ["Unhappy man [that I am]! Who will deliver me from the body of this death?"[20]].

11. Saint Ambrose says that she was as chaste in her [inward] spirit as in her [outward] senses, and after telling us of her interior and principal virtues (of which all the others are the effects and consequences), he passes on to those gifts that may be discerned outwardly and to her outer characteristics. He assures us that everything that could be seen in her filled [those who saw it] with edification, and not only was there nothing ignoble in her, neither in her glance, nor in her words, nor in the tone of her voice, but her appearance and her countenance were a living image of the holiness and beauty of her soul: *ita ut ipsa corporis species, simulacrum fuerit mentis, figura probitatis* ["so that her physical form may have been the image of her soul, the representation of all that is proper"[21]].

12. I do not know how we could ignore the depths of her humility—this is the third characteristic to which we have drawn to your attention[22]—for it is the foundation of all her perfection. Jesus Christ founded and grounded every spiritual structure on this virtue, as though on a rock, on stone, [a foundation] that ought to impart to them immovable constancy

[19] Gal 2:20.

[20] Rom 7:24.

[21] Ambrose, *De virginibus ad Marcellinam*, II.7; PL 16:209B.

[22] The first two are withdrawal from the world and purity of heart.

and unwavering steadfastness. And just as no creature has ever exhibited a virtue equal to that of this soul so dear to God, so, too, there has never been any humility that was not inferior to hers. And although this may seem an obvious argument, the saints have not failed to prove it by the evidence they have taken from the main events of her life.

13. But for me, there is not one of these [events] that touches me more than what she said to holy Elizabeth at the time of her visit to her.[23] When she was speaking to her of the grace that God had bestowed on her in choosing her to be the mother of his son, she did not seek the reason for this in her virtue, but in her lowliness. At no time did she think, at no time did she say, "God has taken into account the fact that I have renounced all the things of earth so as to bind myself uniquely to his service. God has taken into consideration the fact that I have cut myself off from all dealings with men and women so as to have [dealings] with him alone, that I have meditated on his law day and night,[24] that I have known no other glory but his, that in all things I have put my will into his hands, and that here below I have sought happiness only in what was pleasing to him."

14. In place of all these thoughts, that undoubtedly would have come to a soul less great and less exalted than hers—less humble, we would say—she said only these words: *quia respexit humilitatem ancillae suae* ["because he has regarded the humility of his handmaid"[25]]: he has cast his eyes on the abasement and lowliness of his handmaid. Given the profound humility that filled her entire being, she could have had no other point of view—if, that is, the omnipotence of God had not seen fit to do the greatest thing it had ever done in a vile and contemptible creature, for such was the regard and opinion she had of herself. Has there ever been a humility equal to that which, at

[23] See Luke 1:39-56.

[24] See Ps 1:2.

[25] Luke 1:48.

one and the same time, hid what she [truly] was, and that which brought forth from her mouth a confession so astonishing and so contrary to the feelings she could have had [of herself], given all the gifts, graces, and advantages she had received from God through the operation of his Holy Spirit?

15. The fourth of the qualities of which we have spoken to you is obedience. It is impossible not to believe that the holy Virgin possessed it in the highest degree, since her humility had been brought to perfection, and obedience is born of humility and flows from it as the stream flows from the spring. It is pride that makes the human heart incapable of subjecting or submitting itself. [It is pride] that hardens it and renders it unyielding. But since [pride] had never entered this great soul, and since God, by a special privilege, had preserved her from its malice, she had as much of a tendency and inclination to obey as others have to oppose and resist: so much so that we can be certain that her obedience was total, and that in her it lacked none of the conditions she could [possibly] have possessed. She was sincere, faithful, prompt, exact, and persevering, and if it were possible to enter into the details of her life, you would see everywhere the perfection of obedience. In this way, the mother, in anticipation and by the secret inspiration of the Holy Spirit, was conformed to the example that her Son would give her, for none could carry humility and obedience further than he, who humbled himself and subjected himself even to death: *semetipsum exinanivit, factus obediens usque ad mortem* ["he emptied himself, becoming obedient even unto death"[26]].

16. You see, my brothers, what great instruction God is giving you today, not just to you who are still free to leave [the monastery],[27] but to all who are listening to me. Yet it is not enough just to hear [this teaching]: if you wish to profit from it you must put it into practice, lest God be angered by the way

[26] Phil 2:7-8.

[27] I.e., the novices who requested the conference.

you have scorned his word, and [lest] his truth, instead of giving you life, as was his intention, should bring about your death.

17. You must follow the example of the Virgin, therefore, and separate yourselves from the world, and your withdrawal must be a faithful re-enactment of her own. In other words, your flight [from earthly things] must be total, and you must efface the world for ever from your heart. Do not believe, my brothers, that leaving the world [involves no more] than forsaking a town to live in the desert, or stripping yourself of your self-indulgent habits to take on those of the poor, or changing your outward form and figure, your occupations, food, relationships, practices, and a variety of other things to which you have been accustomed in the course of your life. The thing that deceives most people in our [monastic] profession is that, having made all these changes, they think that they have fulfilled their duties, but they delude themselves. For if the heart is not changed, they have done nothing but deceive and seduce themselves. I say "seduce themselves" because they cling to this difference [in their human condition] and are satisfied with it, and while they believe that they are doing everything that their [monastic] profession demands of them, they remain on the surface and never enter the depths of the true nature of their [monastic] state. It is this empty conviction that has brought about the devastation of cloisters, that has rendered monks negligent, and that has led them to reduce all their obligations to a few merely outward practices.

18. You will never fall into this misfortune, my brothers, if you know—as undoubtedly you do know—how worldly people conduct themselves, and then take pains to do exactly the opposite. They love pleasure; you must love pain.[28] They love joy; you must love sorrow. They seek honor and glory; you must seek humiliation and dishonor, or, at least, to suffer

[28] *Peine*, which means pain, punishment, sorrow, affliction, difficulties, or trouble, or all these together. *Peine* is the characteristic of the penitential life.

silently[29] when God permits [such suffering] to strike you. They love good cheer; you must love penance and penitence.[30] They love talking to people and dealing with them; you must love recollection[31] and silence. They love showing off and appearing in public; you must love a secret life, withdrawn [from the world]. They love amusements and laughter; you must love sorrow and tears. They are eager to avenge injuries; you must be long-suffering and endure them. They love litigation and business transactions; you must keep peace with the whole world.[32] They love repose, and wish to live uselessly and idly; you must live with vigils and manual labor.[33] They gratify their senses with everything that delights them; you must refuse to your [senses] whatever they demand of you. They value riches; you must esteem poverty. They do not know what it is to offer prayers to God—they see it as an unpleasant form of subjection, and do not know how to deal with it—but you must find in this exercise your consolation and your repose. The thought of death terrifies them, and they only ever think of it despite themselves; you must be on familiar terms with it and regard it as a blessed event. Their whole concern is with living; yours should be in preparing yourselves for dying.

[29] Lit. "in peace or quiet" (*en paix*), i.e., the suffering is accepted willingly as a gift from God.

[30] "Penance and penitence" is the same word in French: *pénitence*.

[31] *Recueillement* or recollection is an important technical term in seventeenth-century French spirituality. It is the deliberate withdrawal of the mind and intellect from outward, earthly, temporal things in order to focus them on the *eternalia* and the inward presence of God in the soul. For Saint Teresa of Àvila, who had much to say on the Prayer of Recollection, it is the highest form of active prayer. See further Bell, *A Saint in the Sun*, 545–46.

[32] See further David N. Bell, *Everyday Life at La Trappe under Armand-Jean de Rancé: A Translation, with Introduction and Notes, of André Félibien des Avaux's* Description de l'Abbaye de La Trappe *(1689)*, CS 274 (Collegeville, MN: Cistercian Publications, 2018), 91–94.

[33] For Rancé's views on the importance of manual labor and vigils, see chapters XIX and XX of his *De la sainteté et des devoirs de la vie monastique* (Paris: F. Muguet, 1683), 2:257–336. For a brief summary, see Bell, *Understanding Rancé*, 218–21.

19. In a word, you must walk by ways that are the complete opposite of the paths they tread: if, that is, you wish to follow the example of the Virgin, and fulfill that precept of first importance that requires you to separate yourselves from the rules of conduct of worldly people: *alienum se facere ab actibus saeculi* ["to separate yourself from the ways of the world"[34]]. Without this, as I have said to you many times before and say to you now again, it is impossible to live a truly religious life—and when I say a religious life, I do not mean to speak only of the life of monks, but the life of all Christians.

20. Christians say whatever pleases them to hide a truth that seems hard for them, [a truth] that fights against all their natural inclinations and that goes against all the stirrings that flesh and blood inspire in them: [namely], that they should act in a manner becoming [to Christians], or that they are actually unworthy of the faith they profess, or that they are obliged to imitate Jesus Christ in their capacity as his disciples (since a Christian is nothing other than a disciple of Jesus Christ), or [that they should] torment themselves, and cry out, and smash themselves to pieces. They know, in fact, only how to avoid what I tell you is the truth! Yet in his own life, Jesus Christ conducted himself in exactly the way I have just described. This is what he practiced, this is what he taught, this is what he preached to the whole of Israel—that is, to his whole church—and those who wish to be [true] Christians must follow him in these [rules of conduct]. They must embrace them despite themselves, and they must base their lives on these principles and holy rules. And if they maintain that they are exempt from them, or that it can be of no benefit to them to live according to the instructions of their Master, then they must renounce their claim to be one of his disciples and acknowledge, to their shame and misfortune, that they do not possess that faith that they profess outwardly and in public.

[34] RSB 4.20, which reads *saeculi actibus se facere alienum.*

21. But if you, my brothers, have the faithfulness that they do not have, and if you enter into these duties with that devotion and exactness that is required of you by the will of God and your own [monastic] state, you will be given their crowns and fill the places they have so unfortunately relinquished.

22. The second characteristic [of the Virgin] of which we have spoken, my brothers, is purity. Nothing should commend itself to you more, and we will be imposing nothing on you when we say to you that you ought to regard it as the basis and beauty of your [monastic] state. But do not think that this purity consists only in abstaining from lewd actions, desires, and thoughts. It goes much further than that and extends to the whole of one's life. A monk must know that he is indissolubly bound to preserve himself from anything that may tarnish to the slightest degree the chastity of his soul and body, and to live in such a way that there is nothing in his conduct that could warrant reproach.

23. To those of you who think otherwise, I ask what use it is if a monk guards himself from major impurities, yet has a heart polluted with other vices that, because they have less obvious ugliness and deformity, do not trouble him at all, yet [in the end] bring death upon him and separate him from God forever? This is what inevitably must happen if, for example, he gives way to impatience, murmuring, laziness, insensitivity, mistrust, rash judgments, gluttony, dissipation, vanity, the love of glory, or the curiosity that comes from learning.[35] [And the same thing will happen] if he does not show his superior that total obedience that is his due, or if he refuses his brothers all the edification and charity that is demanded of him. Such are the deviations from the Rule[36] into which those monks fall who live in cloisters, but who do not observe a strict [claustral] discipline.

[35] *Curiosité des sciences*: see chap. 13, n. 57.

[36] *Dérèglemens*. One could also translate the word as "irregularities."

24. I wish they would ask me what advantage there can be in this chastity, if it is to be limited by the strict bounds they claim to give it.[37] I wish they would think of what the Holy Spirit teaches them: that a monk is the temple of God, that this temple is holy, and that [God] will destroy all those who have the audacity and rashness to profane it: *si quis autem templum Dei violaverit, disperdet illum Deus, templum enim Dei sanctum est, quod estis vos* ["if anyone violates the temple of God, God will destroy him, for the temple of God, which you are, is holy"[38]]. The soul of a monk is therefore consecrated to the worship of God by a special consecration, and this [soul] must respond to the grandeur of its commitment and make itself worthy of it. This is why [God] has given us so many holy rules, and why he wishes us to live in such complete subjection and dependence.

25. Why otherwise would Saint Benedict, who should be regarded as the interpreter of [God's] wishes, have laid out the tiniest details of his disciples' behavior and actions? Why would he have demanded that they be continually in the presence of death and the judgments of God? Why did he forbid them everything that cannot draw them closer to these things, and prohibit so rigorously anything that might distance them from them? What is the reason for this strict silence, this rigorous solitude, this unshaken stability,[39] this harsh deprivation of all joy, amusements, diversions, and all else that delights human beings? What is the reason for this perfect mortification of self-will, this rigorous custody of all the senses, if not that, by

[37] I.e., if they limit it to the *impuretés grossières* "major impurities" mentioned at the beginning of §23.

[38] 1 Cor 3:17.

[39] *Stabilité* in the technical Benedictine monastic sense. It is "primarily a question of perseverance in the way of obedience within the structure of cenobitic life, and only secondarily of material permanence in a place" (Claude J. Peifer, *Monastic Spirituality* [New York: Sheed and Ward, 1966], 297).

taking such great care and using all these precautions, they might preserve (if I may use the words of Scripture) their garments without stain and in their first beauty: *beatus qui vigilat et custodit vestimenta sua* ["blessed is he who is vigilant and takes care of his garments"[40]]? And that God should never look down on them from the heights of heaven and not see them in a state of purity worthy of the excellence of their vocation?

26. The third characteristic [of the Virgin] is humility, and it is inseparable from the other two since, as we have told you,[41] it is their foundation. But so that you should know exactly what it should be and how you ought to practice it, I will say to you that you will possess it as you should if—as Saint Benedict commands you—you consider yourselves inferior to the rest of humankind, and remain patient and at peace in the face of any affront that may be done to you. See how far your humility should extend! These [two commands] are like the two main branches of a wholly divine tree, and from them, as a necessary consequence, one sees the birth and burgeoning of an infinity of shoots. But most monks cannot adjust themselves to this, and they find an abundance of reasons to excuse themselves from such a demanding obligation. But how can we stomach the idea that men consecrated to mortification and suffering should find this yoke too severe? This yoke, I say, that the Holy Spirit imposes on all those who have the glory of bearing the name of Jesus Christ, and to which, on pain of eternal damnation, they must submit themselves? This is what his apostle [Peter] teaches us when he tells us that what is pleasing to God is when we suffer the abuses and wrongs done to us, or the injustices that happen to us, with a view to pleasing him. For what glory can you have before God if you suffer for [only] those sins or faults that you yourself have committed? But if, in doing good, you endure with patience the ill-treatment you receive, it is this that makes you pleasing to

[40] Rev 16:15.

[41] See §12 above.

God: *quae enim est gloria, si peccantes et colaphisati suffertis? sed si bene facientes patienter sustinetis, haec est gratia apud Deum* ["for what glory is it if, in sinning and being beaten for it, you bear it? But if you do well and then (being ill-treated) bear it patiently, this is worthy of thanks before God"[42]].

27. We might almost have regarded this instruction [merely] as advice, and have been persuaded that we were free to take it or leave it, if the apostle had not made it clear and had not declared to us that it is, in fact, a precept. He states clearly that it is this to which you have been called, since Jesus Christ has suffered for love of us, leaving you an example that you might follow in his steps: *in hoc enim vocati estis, quia et Christus passus est pro nobis, vobis relinquens exemplum, ut sequamini vestigia ejus* ["For to this you are called, because Christ also suffered for us, leaving you an example that you should follow his steps"[43]]. After such words as these, so explicit and down to earth, it is impossible to doubt that this is an obligation, and we cannot but be aware that it is absolutely essential to listen to the voice of God and submit ourselves to it. But in case anyone should want to create some difficulty about such a clear statement, the apostle dismisses and destroys [any such difficulty] by adding that it is an example left us by Jesus Christ himself, that we might follow him: *vobis exemplum relinquens, ut sequamini vestigia ejus* ["leaving you an example that you should follow his steps"[44]].

28. We can only grieve, my brothers (and I say this to you in passing), when we consider the fate of those who live in the world, and that multitude of persons of all sorts and conditions who walk, without being aware of it, in paths that lead them only to death. For where do we see anyone who is not ready to render—I do not say only violence for violence, but even

[42] 1 Pet 2:20.
[43] 1 Pet 2:21.
[44] 1 Pet 2:21.

violence for justice, when [justice] injures them or conflicts with their own interests? There is nothing they would not do to get the better of someone who causes them some inconvenience, whether or not they have right on their side. Yet God commands us to suffer injustice. His will is that we should be at peace and in charity with those who ill treat us. His elect are formed by fulfilling his wishes. This is how they assure their election and open for themselves the gate to his kingdom. And it follows that those who take the opposite paths shut that gate against themselves forever.

29. The last characteristic for which the holy Virgin sets us such a great example is obedience. There is nothing of which I have spoken to you more often or with greater emphasis, my brothers, because I am convinced of what Saint Bernard says, [namely,] that those who put their trust in any practice of devotion, religion, or wisdom other than humility [alone] are foolish and out of their minds: *Insipiens est enim et insanus quicunque in aliis vitae meritis, quicunque in alia religione, seu sapientia, nisi in sola humilitate confidit* ["For it is foolish and absurd to put one's confidence in the merits of others, or in some other religious attitude or wisdom, rather than in humility alone"[45]]. But in the opinion of the same saint, all humility boils down to obedience, and the subjection of our own will to that of God.[46] It follows, therefore, that those who are truly obedient will what they know God wills, and hold in horror what they know he does not will. Therefore, says the same saint, they must embrace whatever they learn of the will of God in the holy Scriptures, or whatever [God] instills in their heart by the operation of his Spirit, such as the exercise of charity, humility, chastity, obedience, and all the other virtues [mentioned] in all the holy instructions contained in the Rule of which you[47] wish to make profession. It must carry you there with zeal and

[45] Bernard, *De diversis, sermo* 26.1; SBOp 6/1:194.

[46] See Bernard, *De diversis, sermo* 26.2; SBOp 6/1:194.

[47] I.e., the novices who asked for the conference.

ardor, [carry you] to all those things that you know for certain ought to please him. And, from the opposite point of view, you should detest all those things that you know are the object of his hatred, such as the vices, dissoluteness, unfaithfulness, and transgressions of those particular points and truths that our [monastic] profession teaches us.[48] These are some of the obvious ways in which you will not err in your obedience.

30. There are, however, those dubious and doubtful encounters by which you can easily be misled, for on these sorts of occasions there is nothing more usual than to follow the course of one's own will, while deluding and deceiving oneself that one is doing [the will] of God. The only way we can avoid this danger, which is much greater than you think, is to suspend our own judgment, decide nothing [according to our own will], and always be ready to embrace the will of God as soon as it is made known to us. Thus he to whom God's Providence has subjected us and who holds his place for us has told us this: *Si voluntatem suam suspensam tenuerit, donec Praelatum suum interroget, et ab eo quaerat Dei voluntatem* ["If he places his own will in abeyance until he consults his Superior and seeks from him the will of God"[49]].

31. It will then follow, my brothers, that you will enjoy unchanging repose and uninterrupted tranquility, and, in accordance with the words of the Prophet [David], you will show that those who submit themselves perfectly to God's law[50] will be free from trouble, will not fall into error, and will live in profound peace: *Pax multa diligentibus legem tuam, et non est illis scandalum* ["Great peace have they who love your law, and for them there is no stumbling block"[51]].

[48] These last three sentences follow Bernard, *De diversis, sermo* 26.3; SBOp 6/1:195–96.

[49] Bernard, *De diversis, sermo* 26.3; SBOp 6/1:196, reading *Domini voluntatem* for Rancé's *Dei voluntatem*.

[50] Lit. "God's order (*ordre*)."

[51] Ps 118:165.

32. Such, my brothers, are the basic predispositions of the profession you wish to follow. It is these that form the yoke to which you wish to submit yourselves. Jesus Christ, as I have told you, teaches them to us by his word and his example, he justifies them by the lives of his apostles and martyrs, and he sanctifies them by the example of her whom he has placed at the head of his saints and angels. She possessed them with such excellence and distinction that we can apply to her, in preference to all others, these words: "O daughter of the King of Kings, how beautiful and glorious are your footsteps!" *Quam pulchri sunt gressus tui, filia Principis* ["How beautiful are your steps, daughter of the Prince!"[52]].

33. If you wish to have a part in this glory, this beauty, and [if you wish] her to communicate with you, then speak to this holy Virgin not only with prayers and songs of praise, but also in your actions and works. What I mean to say here is [that you should speak to her] by imitating her in this withdrawal from the world, this purity, this humility, this obedience that have so justly drawn to her so many everlasting blessings: *Ecce enim ex hoc beatam me dicent omnes generationes* ["For behold from henceforth, all generations shall call me blessed"[53]]. And never doubt that on this blessed day she says to you from the heights of heaven these words of the apostle [Paul]: *Imitatores mei estote, sicut et ego Christi* ["Be imitators of me, as I am of Christ"[54]]. Use all your efforts, then, to conform yourselves to Jesus Christ by means of all these virtues and practices set forth in the gospels,[55] and, as I have done, find all your happiness and all your consolation in pleasing him. It is these desires of yours and these intentions, if they are sincere and ardent, that will constrain her, at his side, to grant you her potent intercession that is always heeded, and from this infinite goodness she

[52] Song 7:1. Rancé returns to the verse with which he began his conference.

[53] Luke 1:48.

[54] 1 Cor 4:16; 11:1.

[55] *Ces pratiques évangéliques.*

will acquire for you not only the grace of bringing to completion the sacrifice you have begun, but also [the grace] of persevering in your commitment when you take it upon yourselves with this holy and meticulous fidelity. For without this, your whole religious life will be no more than an emptiness, a phantom, a sham, which will never bring you the rewards and crowns for which you hope.

Chapter Fifteen

Armand-Jean de Rancé: The Conference for the Feast of the Annunciation

Introduction

Rancé's conference for the feast of the Annunciation was also delivered at the request of a novice, though who that novice was we have no idea. There is no clue in the conference. Nor do we have any idea as to its date, save that it would have been delivered on March 25, which has been the date of the feast from the earliest times. Sometimes, as in his conference on the Nativity of the Virgin, Rancé addresses the novice directly, sometimes he addresses all the brothers, sometimes he addresses all Christians, and what he has to say is rarely comfortable. The content of both conferences, in fact, is noticeably similar.

He takes as his text a brief passage from the Cistercian liturgy for the feast of the Annunciation—"May we conceive [Christ in ourselves] through purity of heart" (§1)—and tells us that if we wish to do this, then all we need do is to imitate the way of life of the Virgin: "She teaches you the path you should tread and the way you should take to achieve such great happiness" (§3). And what is this path? It is the path of separation or withdrawal from the world, something we saw in the conference on the Virgin's Nativity, and on which Rancé elaborates at length in his *De la sainteté et des devoirs de la vie monastique*.[1] And whither did the Virgin withdraw? To the temple in Jerusalem, but her withdrawal, says Rancé, involved much more than a simple change of place. It is the whole world that must be left behind, he tells the novice, "not only by separating yourself from it physically, as you have done up to now, but by withdrawing your heart. You must abandon forever its ideas and precepts, and renounce forever all that it can offer you" (§6). This is a principle that Rancé reiterates again and again: God will not come to us until we give ourselves entirely to him. And once he has come to us, he will stay with us only if we place him at the forefront of all our thoughts and desires, and seek no comfort save that which comes from him (§8).

So what is the temple into which we must withdraw and, like Mary, hide ourselves from the world? Not, obviously, that in Jerusalem, nor even the abbey of la Trappe, even though it has borne the name of the "House of God," *Domus Dei de Trappa*, for almost six hundred years (§11). No. The temple of which Rancé is speaking is the temple of our own heart, as Saint Paul tells us in 1 Corinthians 3:16, *Templum Dei estis vos*, "You are the temple of God." That is where Christ dwells, and that is where we will find him, provided we seek him alone, and are not diverted or distracted for a single instant from the service he demands of us and which we are obliged to render to him (§12).

And what do we do in this spiritual temple? We do what the Virgin did in the temple in Jerusalem. We pay heed to every movement of the Spirit, and our only ambition is to submit our will to his (§14). In this way we prepare ourselves to receive Jesus Christ into our hearts as Mary received him into her womb. This, too, is something Rancé emphasizes again and again elsewhere, and in so doing he is simply echoing the Lord's Prayer—"Your will be done"—and both Jesus himself and his mother. "Not as I will, but as you will," says Christ in

[1] Armand-Jean de Rancé, *De la sainteté et des devoirs de la vie monastique* (Paris: F. Muguet, 1683), 2:3–161.

the Garden of Gethsemane; "Be it done with me according to your word," says the young Mary when Gabriel appears to her.

This, however, brings up an interesting point. If God is truly omnipotent, will not his will be done anyway? If he is truly all powerful, will not everyone do his will, whether they like it or not? They will, says Rancé elsewhere (not in this conference), but there is a difference between doing God's will willingly and unwillingly. Here is what he says:

> Jesus Christ says that his food is to do the will of his Father.[2] Our emptiness and aridity come from our not feeding on this food. This food never fails us, since we can never avoid doing the will of God. But it is not enough just to do his will: we must also wish to do it. Despite themselves, the demons do his will, but they certainly do not want to. Everything obeys God naturally. The whole of nature is obliged to carry out his orders, and it is this that gives movement to all beings. Demons and sinners are the only ones who obey him despite themselves.[3]

Our business, then, is not only to do God's will, but to will to do God's will, and to will no other. And since that can be achieved only if we wholly eradicate self-will and self-love, that, says Rancé, is an awesome challenge that applies not only to monks and nuns, but to all Christians. "Do not think," he tells the novice who requested the conference, "that this obligation to conceive Jesus Christ in one's heart is only for monks and solitaries. It involves all those who have the happiness of belonging to him and bearing his name: those who are of the world and those who no longer belong to it. There is no Christian who is not charged with this duty" (§16). We have seen

[2] John 4:34.

[3] Jacques Marsollier, *La vie de Dom Armand-Jean de Bouthillier de Rancé, abbé régulier et réformateur du Monastère de la Trappe* (Paris: Jean de Nully, 1703), page 82 of the separately paginated appendix to the second volume.

exactly the same sentiment in the conference in the Nativity of the Mother of God.

If, then, every one of us is bound by the obligation to conceive Jesus Christ in our soul, how exactly is this to be achieved? The means, says the abbot, are no less clear than the obligation. They are *les privations & les renoncemens*, "privations and renunciations," for does not Christ himself tell us that whoever does not renounce his father, his mother, and his own soul—in short, all things—for the love of him cannot be his disciple (§17)?[4]

But Rancé is subtle here, and distinguishes external from internal renunciation. That is to say, we may live in the world—sometimes we have no choice in the matter—but we must not love it. We may have riches and businesses and responsibilities and houses, but we must not attach ourselves to them nor seek to find our happiness in them (§18). In other words, as Saint John says, we may be in the world, but not of the world.[5] Then, in §§19–20, Rancé laments that this is so often not the case. People in general are addicted to the good things of this world, they love what Christ orders them to hate, but "if their whole life is lived in opposition to his wishes, then nothing in what they do will be of any benefit to them" (§20).

But if we are all obliged to renounce the world and conceive Christ in our hearts, what difference is there between those outside the cloister and those within? How do those who have taken religious vows differ from those who have not? The answer is simple: more is demanded of them. Their separation from the world is more complete, their renunciation more absolute, their way of life more perfect (§21). Rancé leaves us in no doubt here. "I say to each and every one of you," he says, "that God demands great things of those who, by the inspiration of his Holy Spirit, have bound themselves to such a contract as the one that you have made" (§22). But now, once

[4] Luke 14:26.

[5] John 15:19; 17:14-16.

again, Rancé addresses the novice who had requested the conference. If God demands much of you, he says, God will provide you with the means to achieve it. God may command you to leave the world, but at the same time he will give you all the means, support, and help you need to uphold you in the obligations of your monastic estate (§23).

What you are embarking upon, continues the abbot, is a life wholly dedicated to God, and he then summarizes the course of the monastic day (§24). And, he adds, the monastic habit you now wear will be a great advantage to you in this matter. How? Because it will continually remind you that you no longer belong to the world, it will help you to fight against its alluring temptations, it will alert you if you find yourself falling into danger (§25). In short, "it will show you the poverty, humility, abasement, and penitence in which you have promised God that you will pass your days" (§26). After all, says Rancé, quoting Saint Bernard, "What have you to do with the world who have renounced the world?" (§26).

And so, finally, Rancé returns to the subject with which he began his conference, namely, the imitation of the Virgin:

> Imitate this Queen of the Angels in your divorce from the world and in all the circumstances that go with it. Make this separation as complete as you can so that when Jesus Christ sees that you have made proper preparation he may come to be in you, taking there a new birth, and, by bestowing upon you new graces and blessings, move you swiftly along in his service. (§27)

Rancé makes no great show of learning in this conference, and his sources are limited. Apart from quoting John of Damascus, whom he cites by name, and Bernard of Clairvaux, whom he does not,[6] he quotes directly (in Latin) from Genesis

[6] Rancé gives no source for his citation of "S. Jean de Damas" on page 190, and for his quotation from Bernard simply writes "*Bern.*" in the margin of

(once), Psalms (once), Luke and John (both twice), 1 Corinthians (once), and Hebrews (twice). As we have seen, his text is taken from the Cistercian liturgy, and, as we saw in his conference for the Nativity of the Virgin, he was obviously familiar with the *Protevangelium* of James. But the conferences were never intended to be displays of intellectual pyrotechnics,[7] and their subjects were to be taken from "Saint John Climacus, Cassian, the lives of the holy Fathers of the Desert, Saint Basil, Saint Bernard, and other holy Fathers of the church."[8]

The translation that follows is taken from the *Instructions ou Conférences sur les Epîtres et Évangiles des Dimanches et Principales Festes de l'Année, et sur les Vêtures & Professions Religieuses. Tome quatrième* (Paris: F. Delaulne, 1720), 4:188–208, reproduced (with a few typographical errors) as *Conférence LXXVIII* in the *Collection intégrale et universelle des Orateurs Chrétiens. Deuxième série*, vol. 90 of the entire series (= vol. 23 of the second series), edited by the indefatigable and invaluable Jacques-Paul Migne (Paris: J.-P. Migne, 1866), 552–60.

---

page 207. See further nn. 14 and 36 below, where both passages are identified.

[7] See David N. Bell, *Understanding Rancé: The Spirituality of the Abbot of La Trappe in Context*, CS 205 (Kalamazoo, MI: Cistercian Publications, 2005), 217.

[8] David N. Bell, *Everyday Life at La Trappe under Armand-Jean de Rancé: A Translation, with Introduction and Notes, of André Félibien des Avaux's* Description de l'Abbaye de La Trappe *(1689)*, CS 274 (Collegeville, MN: Cistercian Publications, 2018), 145.

Instruction or Conference given on the Feast Day of the Annunciation of the Virgin at the Request of a Novice

[The dispositions we need to carry [within us] in order to give birth to Jesus Christ in our hearts][9]

Eumdem pura mente concipiamus. Coll. Eccl.[10]

"We form Jesus Christ in ourselves by the purity of our heart."[11]

1. I cannot give you any advice, my brother, that will be more useful to you or of greater benefit than to say to you that you should use every effort to try to deserve that these words, which the church puts in our mouth this day and which we have just spoken, may be fulfilled in you: *Ut eumdem pura mente concipiamus, et fervido imitemur affectu* ["That we might conceive him through purity of heart and imitate him through the fervor of our love"[12]]. I would tell you that Jesus Christ takes form in your heart as he took form in the womb of his mother, and that he comes into being in you, as he came into being in her, by the grace and work of his Holy Spirit.

[9] The Migne edition alone provides the subtitle (552).

[10] This is part of the collect / *oratio* for March 24 *pro commemoratione S. Gabrielis, Archangeli: Deus, qui per Archangelum tuum Gabrielem, Salvatorem mundi sacratissime Virgini concipiendum nuntiasti; da ut eumdem et pura mente concipiamus, et fervido imitemur affectu, per eumdem Christum Dominum nostrum. Amen* ["Oh God, who, by your archangel Gabriel, announced to the most holy Virgin that she was about to conceive the Savior of the World, grant that we too might conceive him through purity of heart (lit. "mind") and imitate him through the fervor of our love, through the same Christ Our Lord. Amen"]. See *Missale Cisterciense*, auctoritate et praelo R[mi] D. D[ni] Benedicti Wuyts editum (Westmalle: Fratres Abbatiae Westmallensis Ordinis Cisterciensis in Religio, 1877), 365.

[11] This is Rancé's slightly expanded translation.

[12] See n. 10 above.

2. I will be so bold as to say to you, my brother, that this coming to be that I am now talking about is no less miraculous and no less worthy of our admiration than the other: perhaps even more so, for there can surely be nothing more extraordinary than to see a God eager to give himself, to come to be, in a soul stained by sin, [a soul] that, in a display of unequaled ingratitude, has made a pact with his enemies to rise up against him and go to war with him. This is not how the Holy of Holies wished to enter the womb of a Virgin, whom we may call the Holy of Holies, whom he preserved from all iniquity,[13] whom he filled with graces and blessings, and who never framed a thought, action, or emotion that could be displeasing to him.

3. If you ask me what you should do to acquire this honor of which I am speaking to you, I would say to you, my brother, that by following the way of life of the holy Virgin, you have all that you need. She teaches you the path you should tread and the way you should take to achieve such great happiness. God, who had destined the holy Virgin for this great work of human redemption, inspired her to do two things: one was to separate herself from the world, and the other, according to John of Damascus,[14] was to withdraw and hide herself in his temple, as in a harbor and haven, and live there in sacred quiet and holy tranquility. Indeed, nothing was less suited to the holiness with which she was filled than to live among people,

[13] Unlike Bernard, for whom he had such great admiration, Rancé accepted the doctrine of the Immaculate Conception.

[14] See John of Damascus, *The Fountain of Wisdom*, Part III ("An Exact Exposition of the Orthodox Faith"), IV.xiv. A copy of *Sancti Ioannis Damasceni Opera*, edited by Jacques de Billy and published by Guillaume Chaudière at Paris in 1577, was in the la Trappe library (see David N. Bell, *The Library of the Abbey of La Trappe from the Twelfth Century to the French Revolution, with an Annotated Edition of the 1752 Catalogue* (Turnhout: Brepols / *Cîteaux – Commentarii cistercienses*, 2014), 446 [J.23]). It had probably formed part of Rancé's collection before he entered the abbey. For the section dealing with the Virgin, see fol. 316v of Jacques de Billy's edition. The basis for John's account is the *Protevangelium* of James.

for she took no part in their interests, their occupations, or their pleasures. For how would it have appeared if she had dwelt among them, witnessing their excesses and unruly behavior, and yet preserving, so to speak, the purity of her own vision by the wickedness in which she would have seen them living?

4. She therefore made the better choice of withdrawing, and, in the secrecy of her retreat, of revealing to God the evils of his people that were known to her and, by her prayers and sighs, mitigating that righteous indignation they would have brought down upon themselves by their infidelities and sins, and also to possess then and there, without distraction or discontinuity, in continual contemplation,[15] the One she should enjoy for all eternity.

5. For her dwelling, she chose and entered the temple as a place of blessing. [And why?] Perhaps so that the presence of this great building, especially consecrated to the worship and service of God, would have served to enliven her pious devotion. Or perhaps so that, recalling to herself the memory of so many wonderful things that his omnipotence had brought about, it would quicken her faith and give more life to her religious sensibilities. Or perhaps so that by subjugating her freedom and placing herself under the guidance and direction of his priests and ministers, she would add to the holiness of her life and activities the merit of obedience by imitating Jesus Christ in a holy anticipation[16] that desired that all that she did

[15] *Par une contemplation continuelle*: this does not refer to the heights of mystical contemplation such as we find described by, for example, Richard of Saint-Victor. That was something Rancé discouraged (see Bell, *Understanding Rancé,* 228–30). For Rancé, "to contemplate" usually means no more than to reflect on, muse on, think about, ruminate, or ponder. It is much the same as Bernard's "consideration" (*consideratio*).

[16] I.e., in anticipation of her obedience when, after being told by the archangel Gabriel that she would have a child by the Holy Spirit, Mary said "Behold the handmaid of the Lord; be it done with me according to your word" (Luke 1:38).

and all her mortal life would bear the characteristic mark of blessing.

6. Here, my brother, here is what should be the rule of your own life! Here is the model you must follow! I tell you, you must leave the world behind, not only by separating yourself from it physically, as you have done up to now, but by withdrawing your heart. You must abandon forever its ideas and precepts. You must renounce forever all that it can offer, as having nothing whatever in common with the profession you wish to undertake, nor with the obligation you have to prepare yourself for the graces you hope to receive as a consequence from the goodness of Jesus Christ.

7. For how else should you hold yourself ready for him to visit you from the heights of heaven, to work and complete in you the mystery of your salvation, by granting you the joy of his presence? Should you not take every care to place yourself in a state to receive him, to rid yourself of that which you know he cannot approve, to banish from your heart everything you cannot keep there without displeasing him, to make sure, in a word, that he finds there no enemies and no competitors, to place your heart entirely in his hands so that he encounters nothing there to limit his authority, nor hinder in any way the absolute power he should exercise there?

8. What if the work to prepare his ways[17] and open all doors to him is so demanding? And when you have received him, what should you not do to keep him, and never give him reason to regret the grace he has bestowed upon you? There is but one way in which you can avoid this misfortune, and that is to neglect nothing that can show him the marks of your thankfulness and gratitude. [How?] By placing him at the forefront of all your thoughts and all your desires, by desiring no comfort save that which will come from him, and by rejecting

[17] See Luke 1:76.

all other [forms of consolation] as false joys, joys that have nothing trustworthy about them and whose only purpose is to deceive you.

9. If you wish to acknowledge the mercies he has shown you as much as you should, then, I tell you, you must strive unceasingly to please him by your continual progress, piling zeal on zeal without respite, fervor on fervor, faith on faith, hope on hope, charity on charity, obedience on obedience, humility on humility, piety on piety, thus progressing from virtue to virtue and from grace to grace. Thus, through your faithfulness, he may know that there is nothing [you desire] in your heart so much as to use his gifts in a holy manner, and that in this way you bind him to yourself by your continued outpourings and contacts [with him].

10. Yet it will not be enough, my brother, to have broken away from the world in the way I have just described to you, to have separated yourself from it, and to have banished from your home, so to speak, all created things so that the Creator may take complete possession. To keep him there and prevent yourself from losing him, you must withdraw into his temple, you must hide yourself there as in a holy refuge so as to be protected from all the tempests that may endanger the course of your voyage.

11. The temple of which I speak is not a physical building, a mass of stone you can see before you. It is not even this dwelling, this monastery, which by a special Providence has borne the name of *House of God* for almost six hundred years: *Domus Dei de Trappa*. It is not for no good reason that we may apply to it these words of the prophet [David], "Blessed are those who dwell in your house," *Beati qui habitant in domo tua, Domine*,[18] for [those who dwell here] are blessed now, and will be in the future, provided they keep the holy rules established

[18] Ps 83:5.

there. I call these [rules] holy because we take them from our Fathers, who were themselves holy men and saints,[19] and we do nothing but serve God according to the instructions they have left us, and walk in his presence in strait and narrow ways. It is a benefit and joy that has no equal.

12. And so, my brother, you are at a loss to know just what this temple is that I have been telling you about. I will leave you in doubt no longer. I tell you that it is you, you yourself, who are this temple! *Templum Dei estis vos* ["You are the temple of God"[20]], says the Holy Spirit through the mouth of the Apostle. You must therefore enter within yourself. There you must find Jesus Christ, who dwells there. You must always bear him in mind, and he must be the sole object of all your desires and all your aims. You must deny yourself everything to enjoy him. You must strip yourself of everything to possess him alone. You must take the greatest care to guard all the approaches to your soul to ensure that nothing enters there that may divert or distract you for a single instant from the service he demands of you and which you are obliged to render to him.

13. In short, the way in which you continually apply yourself to pondering what Jesus Christ does in you at every moment, and what he brings about [in you] by perpetually infusing his Spirit, must stir you up and inflame you, and produce in you a wholly new vigor. As a result of this, far from being worn out by the difficulties you may encounter in the life you have embraced, you will, on the contrary, count them as nothing! You will say with the holy patriarch [Jacob] that the pains you endure are nothing when compared to the good things you enjoy and what you feel of the mercies that God has bestowed

[19] This works better in French: "I call these rules *saintes*, because we take them from our Fathers, who were *Saints*."

[20] 1 Cor 3:16.

upon you: *Videbantur dies pauci, prae amoris magnitudine* ["The days seemed but few because of the greatness of his love"[21]].

14. And in order for you, in this spiritual temple, to do exactly what the holy Virgin did in the physical temple and, like her, to be faithfully obedient, pay heed to every movement of the Spirit that will fill you. Do everything that Jesus Christ seems to ask of you promptly and with pleasure. Let your only ambition be to submit your will to his. Observe the tiniest thing he inspires you to do, and let these [inspirations] be your unvarying rules that you will count yourself happy to obey without question. You see here how you can imitate the holy Virgin and how, following her example, you can prepare yourself to receive Jesus Christ in the depths of your heart as she received him in her womb. And if there is anything that can gain for you that grace from God that is essential for you if you are to complete the sacrifice that you have begun and that you are renewing today by what you have asked me to do, it is to constrain him to take up his abode in you, to remain in you, to establish his dwelling in you in accordance with his own words: *Ad eum veniemus, et mansionem apud eum faciemus* ["We will come to him and make our abode with him"[22]].

15. For as he bears with him both fire and light,[23] he will enlighten you, he will make it clear to you that nothing will profit you more than to persevere in the path you have chosen, and he will fill you with a holy ardor that will consume and dispel the temptations that normally appear, rising like clouds on the path of those who go to him by ways more strict and narrow.

16. But do not think, my brother, that this obligation to conceive Jesus Christ in our heart is only for monks and solitaries.

[21] Gen 29:20. This refers to Jacob's serving Laban for fourteen years so that he might marry Laban's two daughters.

[22] John 14:23.

[23] See Heb 12:29 (fire); John 1:9 and 8:12 (light).

It involves all those who have the happiness of belonging to him and bearing his name: those who are of the world and those who no longer belong to it. There is no Christian who is not charged with this duty, and those who have not at one time received him into their hearts and in whom he will not have dwelt as in his temple—these, I say, will have nothing in common with him in eternity and no part in his kingdom.

17. If the obligation to conceive Jesus Christ cannot be questioned, the means by which we can deserve such a great honor are no less fixed and settled. These means are privations and renunciations, and Jesus Christ, who took care not to fail to give us all the advice and instruction we need on this point of such great importance, set out for us no others. He tells us in so many places that whoever does not renounce his father, his mother, and his own soul—in short, all things—for the love of him cannot be his disciple: *Si quis venit ad me, et non odit patrem suum et matrem, etc., non potest meus esse discipulus* ["If anyone comes to me and does not hate his father and mother, etc., they cannot be my disciple"[24]].

18. It follows, then, that those who live entangled with the world must separate themselves from it. They must leave it. And although this separation may not be external, but only internal, it should nevertheless be real and effective. This pronouncement may appear hard—*Durus est hic sermo* ["This saying is hard"[25]]—but it cannot be changed, and God has never known, nor will ever know, any way to make it easier. He allows them, or even orders them, to live in the world, but he forbids them to love it. He permits them to make use of its goods and riches, but he does not want them to be attached to them. He certainly wants them to have [business] establishments and responsibilities, but he does not want them to find their happiness in these things, nor that they depend on them

[24] Luke 14:26.

[25] John 6:61.

for their comfort and repose. He wants them to have houses, but he does not want them to treat them as fixed and permanent dwellings. In short, his will is that they should live here below as if in a foreign country, a place of banishment and exile, that they should sigh unceasingly for their true homeland, and that they should have engraved at the very bottom of their hearts these words of the apostle: *Non habemus hic manentem civitatem, sed futuram inquirimus* ["We have here no lasting city, but we seek one that is to come"[26]].

19. It is a surprising thing, my brothers,[27] that the patriarchs of the old law could not take it upon themselves to build houses. They dwelt in tents and tabernacles—*in casulis habitando* ["they lived in humble dwellings"[28]]—because they were living in hope of entering a land that God had destined for them, even though they would not be able to possess it for four hundred years after the promise he had made them. Such was the result of the greatness of their religious belief and their faith. But in our days, my brothers, people act in a way quite contrary to that of these great saints. They build magnificent palaces and fill them with goods and wealth without measure or limit. They decorate and beautify them. They fill them with furniture and rich trappings, as if they would have them forever, and they have lost every notion and every memory of the kingdom promised by Jesus Christ: that kingdom, I say, that possesses infinite beauty and value, that lasts eternally, and whose enjoyment is not postponed for many centuries. For since we may die at any moment, there is not one person who may not receive from his hand this new world for which he has told us to hope.

[26] Heb 13:14.

[27] Rancé now addresses the brothers in the plural; hitherto he has been speaking to the novice who requested the conference.

[28] Heb 11:9. *Casula* is the diminutive of *casa*, "house," and would normally be translated by "hut" or "small cottage." The Greek original is *skēnē*, "a tent." The point is that Abraham, Isaac, and Jacob did not build for themselves permanent dwellings.

20. But what we see, and what we cannot think of or speak of without sorrow, is how much people are attached to transitory things, and since these earthly affections possess their hearts, contrary to God's orders, some of them can neither be persuaded nor understand that they must renounce earth to gain heaven, nor that they must sacrifice time to deserve eternity. Others, who claim to be more submissive and religious, cling to the good things of the world for a whole variety of reasons and, being obliged to renounce them, do so with so many reservations, so many qualifications—we would say with so much covetousness—that if they have not been touched or persuaded by the word of Jesus Christ, and if they want to love what he orders them to hate, and if their whole life is lived in opposition to his wishes, then nothing in what they do will be of any benefit to them. This is not the way to conceive Jesus Christ in one's heart and fulfill this great precept that it is absolutely essential to observe. I make an exception, as always, of that small number of people, that cherished few, to whom Jesus Christ addresses these words: *Nolite timere pusillus grex, quia complacuit Patri vestro dare vobis regnum* ["Fear not, little flock, for it has pleased your Father to give you a kingdom"[29]]. He calls them a small number (though the actual number may be large) in contrast to that innumerable multitude whom he has rejected and who are not of this company.

21. This obligation [to conceive Jesus Christ in our heart] is therefore common both to people living in the world and to monks, but to a different extent and a different degree. The former can fulfill the obligation, even though they may do so in ways shared by all.[30] But the latter, whose estate and calling are more lofty, can satisfy [this demand] only in ways that are more excellent and more perfect. And you must believe that God will not receive from their hands—or rather from their

[29] Luke 12:32.

[30] *Avec des dispositions communes*. The contrast is between those who live in the world but are not of it, and those who leave it altogether.

hearts—any offering that is not perfect. He wants them to renounce absolutely everything, and that this [renunciation] be as all-embracing in its breadth as in the interior dispositions[31] that should accompany it.

22. I say to each and every one of you, my brothers—and I never lose an opportunity to bring it to your attention—that God demands great things of those who, by the inspiration of his Holy Spirit, have bound themselves to such a contract as the one that you have made. Take care that you do not dishonor the dignity of your [monastic] profession by mean or lukewarm intentions. Respond [appropriately] to the fact that God has chosen you, and in everything you do show that you are aware of the notable way in which he has treated you.

23. My brother,[32] do not be afraid of this truth that I declare to you, do not be shocked by the extent of your duties. If God demands much, he provides you with effective means [to achieve it]. He has no wish to expose your faithfulness to tests beyond your strength. He commands you to leave the world, but at the same time he gives you all the means, support, and help that you need to uphold you in the obligations of your [new] estate. He surrounds you, as it were, with bulwarks and barriers so that you will not be so weak or so unfortunate as to return your heart, any more than your body, to the condition from which his mercy alone has drawn you.

24. I tell you, my brother, as if you had pronounced your vows, and without describing to you the different graces that come with your profession, I will tell you that all that someone who has consecrated himself [to God] has to do is to cast an eye on his [monastic] state: this on its own will suffice to show him what he has promised to God and what he owes him, and I cannot think of any better or more effective way to make him

[31] *Les qualitez intérieures.*

[32] Rancé now returns to the singular and once more addresses the novice who has just been clothed.

understand and feel that the world is now nothing to him and that he should think about it no more. His days are spent in exercises that pertain to God alone, or in activities that only concern his [monastic] profession. He rises from bed and begins his day by chanting God's praises, and this is followed by a period of holy reading.[33] Then comes a further chant in his praise, then manual labor, then meditation, then prayers, and then it is time for the meal that, if we are to describe it correctly, is a matter of austerity and penance.[34] In short, all [his days] are spent in these types of activity, unceasingly and with no spare time. There is no place here for the world, save in those prayers when we commend to God its needs and necessities, and this is enough to show a strict and faithful monk the extent to which he should be separated from the world.

25.[35] No less insistent is the lesson taught you by the habit you now wear: not only because it will not allow you to forget that you no longer belong to the world, but because it cannot give rise to any temptation that will lead you to think about things you have abandoned and that should be forever effaced from your memory. It will alert you to the danger in which you find yourself, and the obligation you have to fight against [such temptations] and resist them.

26. If thoughts of license and laxity come to you, your habit will remind you of the subjection in which you should live. And if there should arise a desire for glory or reputation or good living or pleasure—in other words, some transitory good, whatever it may be—this habit of yours will speak to you and show you the poverty, humility, abasement, and penitence in which you have promised God that you will pass your days.

[33] *Une lecture sainte*, i.e., *lectio divina*. See further David N. Bell, "Armand-Jean de Rancé on Reading: What, Why, and How?" *Cistercian Studies Quarterly* 50 (2015): 161–93.

[34] See Bell, *Everyday Life at La Trappe*, 133–37.

[35] This paragraph is devoted to the importance and symbolism of the novice's new habit.

If there should awake in you a desire to have communication and dealings with people, the form and simplicity of your habit will remind you that you no longer have anything to do with them and that they no longer have anything to do with you, and that you cannot take part in their amusements and affairs without shame. All those who come in contact with you and who belong to that world that you have renounced by a public profession will have no other thought but that your outer piety and religious devotion is a true reflection of your inner feelings, morality, and truth.[36] *Quid tibi cum saeculo, qui saeculum deserueras?* ["What have you to do with the world who have renounced the world?"[37]]

27. Finally, my brother, imitate this great example that the church puts before you today. Let the principal themes appear in your own conduct. Imitate this Queen of the Angels in your divorce from the world and in all the circumstances that go with it. Make this separation as complete as you can so that when Jesus Christ sees that you have made proper preparation he may come to be in you, taking there a new birth, and, by bestowing upon you new graces and blessings, move you swiftly along in his service. And then, surmounting every obstacle you may meet on your way, you may complete by a joyous commitment this great work you have begun.

[36] This is a paraphrase of what, literally, reads "you have the appearance and exterior of a piety and religion of which you have nothing less than the feelings, morality, and truth."

[37] Bernard, *Ep*. 2.11 to Fulk, later archdeacon of Langres; SBOp 7:21. Rancé has *deserueras* for the SBOp *spreveras*, a variant not recorded in the *apparatus criticus* in SBOp.

Chapter Sixteen

Armand-Jean de Rancé: The First Conference for the Feast of the Assumption

Introduction

Rancé delivered three conferences for the feast of the Assumption, all of them shorter than his conferences for Mary's Nativity and the Annunciation. At the present day, the gospel for the feast is Luke 1:41-50, which contains Elizabeth's words to Mary at the time of the Visitation and the first part of the *Magnificat*. This reading, however, dates only from after 1950, when Pope Pius XII made the formal dogmatic definition of the assumption on November 1 of that year and promulgated a new Office and Mass for the feast. Before that, the gospel was Luke 10:38-41, which tells the story of Jesus visiting the home of Mary and Martha. That, therefore, is the gospel that forms the basis for Rancé's first conference.

Medieval commentators were, of course, well aware that there are two quite different Marys here—Mary of Bethany and Mary the mother of Jesus—and were careful to explain what was going on. This is how Guillaume Durand / William Durandus, one of the most important authorities on medieval liturgy, explained it in the thirteenth century. It seems at first glance, he says, that the gospel has no relevance to the feast, but this is not the case. How does the gospel begin? It begins by saying that Jesus "entered a certain little castle"—*intravit*

Iesus in quoddam castellum—which we would normally translate as "Jesus entered a certain town." But here we need the word *castellum*, "little castle," for who is this *castellum* but the Virgin Mary? And why is she called a *castellum*? "Because she is terrible against demons and has armed herself well against the devil and against vices."[1] And why a "little castle" rather than just "a castle," a *castellum* rather than a *castrum*? Because the diminutive form of the word signifies her humility and her unique status.

Furthermore, in rearing her child, fleeing with him to Egypt, and visiting Elizabeth and serving her, she symbolized Martha and the active life, while in her contemplative life she symbolized Mary Magdalene. "For this reason, we read later in the gospel, 'Mary kept all these words, pondering them in her heart,'" which is the text of Rancé's conference. Thus, says Durandus, "these two sisters symbolize the active life and the contemplative life, which were plain to be seen in the blessed Virgin Mary, and through them, in a sublime, honorable, and delightful way, she received Christ into herself."[2] This is precisely the way in which Rancé explains the gospel for the feast.

There is no discussion in the conference of exactly when the assumption took place, that is, whether Mary was assumed into heaven body and soul at the very moment of her physical death, or whether her body died a normal physical death and was then resurrected and assumed into heaven sometime later. By Rancé's time, the universal view of the Orthodox East was that Mary died a natural death and that her body was resurrected—like that of her son—three days later. The general, but not universal, view of the Roman Catholic West was that both the body and soul of the Virgin were taken into heaven at the moment of her physical passing. When Pius XII defined the doctrine infallibly in 1950, he deliberately left the question

[1] Gulielmus Durandus, *Rationale divinorum officiorum* (Naples: Joseph Dura, 1859), 691 (VII.xxiv.7).

[2] Durandus, *Rationale*, 691 (VII.xxiv.8).

open. I suspect that Rancé would have viewed the matter as being one of those examples of "curiosity," those arid and useless discussions that have nothing to do with true spirituality. As we saw in Chapter Thirteen, he banished from the conferences "everything to do with scholastic theology and disputed questions, and everything else that can dry up the heart."[3] When the Mother of God was assumed into heaven is irrelevant. What is important is that she is there now, ready to offer us her mediation and intercession.

Following Durandus and a host of others, Rancé sees Mary the Virgin as uniting in her one person the virtues of Mary of Bethany and Martha, the contemplative and the active lives (§§2–3). The symbolism goes back to the earliest days of patristic exegesis, but in Rancé's case we have to be careful. As we pointed out in the last chapter,[4] contemplation, for Rancé, does not refer to the heights of mystical rapture such as we find described by, for example, Richard of Saint-Victor or Bernard himself in the fourth degree of love in his *De diligendo Deo*. If, with Guigo II, the twelfth-century prior of La Grande Chartreuse, we wish to tread a path that leads from reading to meditation, from meditation to prayer, and from prayer to contemplation, when our flesh is no longer opposed to our spirit and when we become, as it were, wholly spiritual (*quasi totus spiritualis*),[5] we may find that in Rancé. But those who aspire to the highest reaches of the mystical path, seeking to enter that spiritual marriage that the great Teresa of Àvila likened to rain falling in a river, when there is nothing there but water, and it is no longer possible to separate the water of the river from that which fell from the heavens,[6] will read his works in vain.

[3] See chap. 13, n. 59.

[4] Chap. 15, n. 15.

[5] *Guigues II le Chartreux, Lettre sur la vie contemplative (L'Échelle des moines), Douze méditations*, ed. Edmund Colledge and James Walsh, SCh 163 (Paris: Cerf, 1970), 86–97.

[6] Teresa of Àvila, *The Interior Castle*, VII, 2, 4.

For Rancé, "to contemplate" (*contempler*) usually means no more than to reflect on, muse on, think about, ruminate, or ponder, and it is much the same as what Saint Bernard meant by "consideration" (*consideratio*). Nor does Rancé make much difference between contemplation and meditation. Both involve the mind at work—they are not ecstatic states infused into the soul by God—though they may produce, as they produced in Mary, "indescribable consolations and sweetnesses" (§2).

"Consolations"—the same spelling in French and English—was one of the technical terms of seventeenth-century French spirituality. Consolations are "God's warm, peaceful, joyful, encouraging visitations that effect tears of love, repentant sorrow, a desire for heavenly things, prompter service of God, and affectively intensify faith, hope and love."[7] Consolations may be transitory, such as the tears that lead to a greater love of God, but they may also produce a permanent change of state, such as the continual experience of an indescribable inner joy that can never be lost even in the midst of the greatest adversity.

Mary, then, combined both contemplation and action by being able to have God in mind while she attended to her normal, everyday duties. God, we might say, was ever in her head and her heart, even as her hands went about their work in the world, and "the love she had for the life of withdrawal never prevented her from performing all those external works that God's order required of her with a care and diligence that was wholly edifying" (§3).

And so, says Rancé to his monks, "it is virtually impossible that this image should not recall you to your duties and your monastic calling, and that you should not see in the way of life of this Queen of Mortals and Angels what you yourselves should imitate in yours" (§5). Once again, we are back with

[7] *A Dictionary of Christian Spirituality*, ed. Gordon S. Wakefield (London: SCM Press, 1983), 94.

Mary as our model—he says just the same thing in §1, at the very beginning of his conference—and we, just like her, must meditate on God's law while at the same time "putting into practice those holy truths that this entails" (§4).

Then, in §5 and §6, Rancé cites a number of passages from the Rule of Saint Benedict where the saint explains just what it means to hold God in mind while undertaking all those outward activities that the Rule enjoins. Ideally, a monk's life should be a *commerce perpétuel*, an "unending interaction," with God (§8), and his occupation should be that of Mary, who, it will be remembered, sat at the feet of Jesus and listened to his words while Martha bustled about the room, busy with much serving.

But now, in §9, Rancé turns his attention to Martha, from contemplation to action. And what does he say? "All you need do is open your eyes to see what God requires of those who undertake the commitment you have undertaken" (§9). He then summarizes a number of requirements of the Rule and emphasizes that when the brothers are busy carrying them out, they are not doing it for themselves, for their own benefit. Indeed not. Like Martha, they are doing what they need to do for the sake of Jesus Christ.

But then Rancé introduces a new element. He brings in the raising of Lazarus from John's gospel and concentrates on the words in John 11:35: "and Jesus wept." And what Jesus did, so must we. "You must place Lazarus with his sisters," he tells his monks, "and your [inner] meditation and all your outward activities must be accompanied by tears" (§10). He says the same thing elsewhere[8] and emphasizes that monks are not weeping just for their own sins, but also for the sins of others. Remember, he says, there is no such thing as a small sin—a sin is a sin is a sin—and even if we ourselves were as innocent as

[8] See David N. Bell, *Understanding Rancé: The Spirituality of the Abbot of La Trappe in Context*, CS 205 (Kalamazoo, MI: Cistercian Publications, 2005), 88–89.

John the Baptist, we should still be weeping for the sins of those in the world who continually violate God's law. You must do what you can, he tells his monks, "to wash away the horror of their sins and ingratitude with the water of your tears" (§11).

Do we see this in the blessed Virgin? Indeed we do. She must have shed tears over the desolation of Jerusalem. She must have wept over the treachery of her nation that resulted in the death of her son. And did not Saint Simeon foretell that her soul would be pierced by a sword? There must have been countless occasions, says Rancé, when her eyes flooded with tears (§12).

Rancé then draws together the threads of his conference and summarizes his message. Everything a monk needs to do is set forth in the story of the Virgin's own life: meditating on God's law, putting that law into practice, and grieving over everything "that takes away from the limitless veneration and profound obedience that are owed to him" (§13). This will not be easy, but in §14 he offers words of encouragement. When problems or difficulties or temptations arise, as arise they will, drive them away with Christ's own words to Martha: "*Quid turbaris erga plurima*?" "Why are you troubled about so many things?" If the demands of your way of life seem too much for you, say these same words. If you find yourself unwilling to do what you are instructed to do, once again, say these very same words. And do not hesitate to turn to her who is eager to help and on whose mediation we may depend, for she is "the universal Mother of all the faithful," and the special Protector (*Protectrice*) of the Order of Cîteaux (§15).

Rancé's sources for this conference are primarily Scripture, especially the gospel of Luke,[9] and the Rule of Saint Benedict. In §11, however, when he is speaking of the enormity of every sin and the need to weep for them, he cites as his authorities

[9] The other books cited are Exodus, Proverbs, Matthew, and John, though there are allusions to others.

Saint Catherine of Genoa, Arsenius the Great, Bernard of Clairvaux, and Ephrem Syrus. Arsenius, Ephrem, and Bernard appear frequently in the pages of Rancé's *De la sainteté*, and Rancé was intimately familiar with their writings. His source for Catherine was her Dialogue on Purgatory (*Trattato del Purgatorio*), and his source for Arsenius was the *Vitae Patrum* compiled by the Jesuit Heribert Rosweyde and first published in 1615. His source for Ephrem was the Latin translation of his works by Gerhard Jan Voss printed at Cologne in 1675, and his source for Bernard was the edition of his *opera omnia* by either Horstius or Mabillon, depending on the date of the conference. All are listed in the 1752 catalogue of the library of la Trappe.[10]

The translation that follows is based on the text in Armand-Jean de Rancé, *Instructions ou Conférences sur les Epîtres et Évangiles des Dimanches et Principales Festes de l'Année, et sur les Vêtures & Professions Religieuses. Tome quatrième* (Paris: F. Delaulne, 1720), 4:209–24, reproduced (with a few typographical errors) as *Conférence LXXIX* in the *Collection intégrale et universelle des Orateurs Chrétiens. Deuxième série*, vol. 90 of the entire series (= vol. 23 of the second series), edited by Jacques-Paul Migne (Paris: J.-P. Migne, 1866), 560–65.

[10] See David N. Bell, *The Library of the Abbey of La Trappe from the Twelfth Century to the French Revolution, with an Annotated Edition of the 1752 Catalogue* (Turnhout: Brepols / *Cîteaux – Commentarii cistercienses*, 2014), 322–23 (B.71–84), 392 (E.3), 475 (M.35), and 544 (R.82).

Instruction or Conference Composed for the Feast Day of the Assumption of the Holy Virgin

[Following the example of Mary, we must meditate on God's law and keep it][11]

Maria autem conservabat omnia verba haec, conferens in corde suo ["Mary kept all these words, pondering them in her heart"]. Luke 2:19

"Mary guarded all these words, meditating on them in the depths of her heart."[12]

1. God, my brothers, watches sleeplessly over those who serve him, and puts before our eyes at every moment the true nature of our monastic state. He fears that if we lose the memory of this, we should fall into unfaithfulness and error, and end up by doing nothing less than stripping from our [monastic] profession, all holy as it is, those advantages that are so necessary for our sanctification. Today, in the person of the holy Virgin, he shows us what we should be and what we should do, and in her we may see a model of the sort of life that should be led here on earth by those who are consecrated to withdrawal from it and destined for heaven.

2. This Virgin, so cherished and favored by God above all other creatures, was raised to an eminent perfection and, so far as was possible, to consummate holiness. And she also united in her own person those two states that form part of or, rather, that comprise the life of those who belong to God and who are uniquely engaged in his service, namely, contemplation and action.[13] She possessed to the highest degree the holy

[11] The Migne edition alone adds the subtitle.

[12] This is Rancé's translation of the text. It is somewhat free, but that is not unusual.

[13] Contemplation and action in Rancé are discussed in the introduction to this conference.

virtues and qualities of both these states. She worshiped God. She contemplated him. She listened to him in perfect peace and tranquility. She received and preserved the illumination and understanding that he was pleased to grant her for the sanctification of her way of life: *Maria autem conservabat omnia verba haec, conferens in corde suo* ["Mary kept all these words, pondering them in her heart"].[14] In wholly divine meditation, she enjoyed indescribable consolations and sweetnesses,[15] and, when necessary, she acted for his glory with all the zeal, fervor, and purity of a soul completely penetrated and completely filled with his love.

3. This is just what the church sets before us today[16] in the gospel, where it speaks of how attentively Mary of Bethany regarded Jesus Christ and listened to the life-giving words that issued from his sacred lips, *sedens secus pedes Domini audiebat verbum illius* ["also sitting at the Lord's feet, she was listening to his word"[17]], and how concerned was holy Martha, her sister, to have everything she thought necessary ready to receive this divine guest: *Martha autem satagabat circa frequens ministerium* ["but Martha was busy with much serving"[18]]. The church, I say, has been moved in a special way by the Spirit of God to teach us how admirably the Virgin possessed both these dispositions by applying to her this [passage from the] gospel on this feast day of her Assumption, which is the day of her glory and her triumph, thus making it clear to us that what was separated in these two sisters has been reunited in her one person. We see that she was no less great, and no less worthy of admiration, in action than in contemplation, that she had received from God this twofold talent, and that, by the effect of an extraordinary grace, neither one of these gifts ever

[14] This is the text of Rancé's sermon, cited at the beginning.
[15] For "consolations," see the introduction to this translation.
[16] August 15, but we have no idea of the year.
[17] Luke 10:39.
[18] Luke 10:40.

presented any obstacle to the other, as is always the case in less perfect souls. She preserved a profound recollection[19] in all those external activities in which she found herself engaged. Her heart, impervious as it was to anything contrary to her duties, was never weakened or diverted from them. And the love she had for the life of withdrawal [from the world] never prevented her from performing all those external works that God's order required of her with a care and diligence that was wholly edifying.

4. It is virtually impossible, my brothers, that this image should not recall you to your duties and your monastic calling, and that you should not see in the way of life of this Queen of Mortals and Angels what you yourselves should imitate in yours. I mean by this the obligation you have to pass your days in meditating on God's law and in putting into practice those holy truths that this entails. This is why you are monks! This is why the hand of God has taken you from the midst of the world and withdrawn you from its dissipation! Yes, my brothers, your monastic profession is completely summed up in this double duty. God demands both from you in equal measure, and he has given you all these rules and regulations, all these different practices, as ways and means to help you achieve this end.

5. My brothers, if you are not as convinced of this truth as you should be, it would be easy to prove it by citing a thousand passages from your Rule. And the intention of Saint Benedict, who gave you this Rule, is so clear and evident on this point that you cannot possibly be left in any doubt. As to the obligation to keep God in mind and to hold yourselves before him at all times, is there anything [in the Rule] that is more obvious? Is it not for this reason that Saint Benedict commands you to begin every activity you undertake by addressing yourself to God and asking him with fervent prayers that he bring it to a

[19] For the nature of *recueillement* or recollection, see chap. 14, n. 31.

conclusion: *imprimis, ut quidquid agendum inchoas bonum, ab eo perfici instantissima oratione deposcas* ["First of all, whenever you begin any good work that has to be done, beg, with the most fervent prayers, that it be brought to perfection by him"[20]]?

6. Is it not for this reason that he wants you to long for God's eternity with every beat of your heart, *omni concupiscentia spirituali vitam aeternam desiderare* ["to long for eternal life with all spiritual desire"[21]]? It is difficult to love him with such ardor if he is not continually before our eyes. Is it not with the same intention that he tells you that you should never lose sight of the judgments of God, and that the two faces of eternity—I mean its rewards and punishments—should be the usual subjects of your meditation?[22] Is it not in the same vein that he says that your prayer should be pure and accompanied by that spirit of compunction that is the effect of the operation and presence of the Spirit of God,[23] who, according to the Apostle, prays within us with cries and unspeakable groanings, *postulat pro nobis gemitibus inenarrabilibus* ["he asks for us with unspeakable groanings"[24]]? And again, is it not for this reason that he instituted this lengthy chanting of the Psalms, which, according to the instructions he gave on the matter, should be so much an expression of the heart that the mouth utters nothing but what the heart feels and thinks, *sic stemus ad psalendum ut mens nostra concordat voci nostra* ["let us stand to chant the psalms in such a way that our mind and our voice are in one accord"[25]]?

7. It is in this wholly divine activity that you tell God of your needs, lay bare to him your miseries, solicit his mercies, and reveal to him the greatness of your love and your gratitude for

[20] RSB, Prol. 4.
[21] RSB 4.46.
[22] RSB 4.44–47 and 7.62–66.
[23] See RSB 20.4.
[24] Rom 8:26.
[25] RSB 19.6.

all the graces he has bestowed on you. And this can be even more effective if, in obedience to the precept given you by this great servant of God, you add to it the reading of divine Scripture and the books of the holy Fathers that are always in your hands,[26] for by these means God does but one thing: speak to you and instruct you.

8. Can we not say, then, that your life is no more than an unending interaction[27] with God, and that your occupation is that of Mary, *quae etiam sedens secus pedes Domini audiebat verbum illius* ["who, sitting at the Lord's feet, was listening to his word"[28]]? [Can we not say] that you are seated or, rather, are prostrate at the feet of Jesus Christ by the way in which you continually worship him, by the lowliness of your monastic profession, and by the profound peace that accompanies this, and that you too spend your days in listening to him? I do not know, my brothers, whether you have experienced this happiness, or whether what I have just said to you has made any impression on you. What I do know is that there is nothing here below to compare with the place that Jesus Christ has given you in his house, provided you are sufficiently faithful to recognize and value the grace you have received from him.

9. Let us now turn [from contemplation] to action, which is the obligation you have to express your [inner] piety outwardly in a tangible way. All you need do is open your eyes to see what God requires of those who undertake the commitment you have undertaken. Your life is completely filled with religious and penitential exercises, and there is not a single moment that does not have its own specific purpose. You keep vigil, you work, you fast, you serve your brothers. Indeed, you

[26] See RSB 48 *passim*. For a detailed discussion of what was read and how it was read, see David N. Bell, "Armand-Jean de Rancé on Reading: What, Why, and How?" *Cistercian Studies Quarterly* 50 (2015): 161–93.

[27] *Commerce perpétuel.*

[28] Luke 10:39.

are doing just what Martha was doing: *Martha autem satagabat circa frequens ministerium* ["but Martha was busy with much serving"[29]]. You are preparing something for Jesus Christ to eat. You are preparing a meal for him that he needs. For are you not feeding Jesus Christ when, by living your own life according to the Rule,[30] you edify your brothers? When your own zeal warms those who are apathetic? When your austerity challenges their laxity and arouses in them the spirit of penitence? When the energy with which they see you serving God dissipates the lassitude that possesses their souls? When you respond to their needs with charitable works, you are providing them with spiritual food, food that is more precious and more excellent than any other since it cannot go rotten: *operamini non cibum qui perit, sed qui permanent in vitam aeternam* ["do not labor for the food that perishes, but for that which endures to everlasting life"[31]]. Jesus Christ receives this food in them, for truly, what they are is the members and parts of that body of which he is the head, and he has stated unequivocally that what charity[32] has us do for the least of those who belong to him, he counts as being done to himself: *quandiu fecistis uni ex his fratribus meis minimis, mihi fecistis* ["as long as you did it to one of these, the least of my brothers, you did it to me"[33]].

10. Such, my brothers, are the principal obligations of your monastic state, but if you want a complete account, lacking in nothing, then Lazarus must play his part.[34] You must place him with his sisters, and your [inner] meditation and all your

[29] Luke 10:40.

[30] Lit. "by the regularity of your way of life" (*la regularité de votre conduite*).

[31] John 6:27.

[32] Generally speaking, *amour* (*amor* in Latin) is the generic term for love, and may refer to all forms of love, good or bad alike. *Charité* (*caritas* in Latin) always refers to love that is properly directed, namely, to God and our neighbor. It is the highest form of love. We discussed this in chap. 8.

[33] Matt 25:40.

[34] Rancé now introduces Lazarus from chapter 11 of the gospel of John.

outward activities must be accompanied by tears.[35] It is so natural to your monastic profession to live in lamentation that if this be not the case, that profession is imperfect and lacks its most essential feature. You know—I have told you hundreds of times—you *know* that God has destined you not only to weep for your own sins, but to weep still more for the faults, mistakes, and uncounted excesses of those who sin with unshed tears, neither repenting nor feeling the least remorse, whose only pleasure seems to lie in doing evil, and of whom it is written, *laetantur cum male fecerint, et exultant in rebus pessimis*: they rejoice when they have done evil, and they exult in the most sinful things.[36]

11. There is no sin, however small it may seem to you, which, when measured by the truth of God and seen in all its ugliness and deformity, does not demand torrents of tears. "But it's so small," you tell me, and I admit, that's how we see it. Yet God is offended! Is it a trifling matter to displease an Infinite Majesty? The saints, who judged the things they did in their true light, were of an entirely different opinion. Saint Catherine of Genoa thought as we do.[37] Saint Arsenius, Saint Bernard, Saint Ephrem,[38] and so many others thought exactly the same thing. But even supposing, my brothers, that you were as innocent as Saint John the Baptist and that your way of life was beyond reproach, in the world God's law is violated, and there

[35] See John 11:35: "and Jesus wept." Rancé has much to say on the need for tears in his *De la sainteté et des devoirs de la vie monastique* (Paris: F. Muguet, 1683).

[36] Prov 2:14, which reads literally, "they rejoice when they have done evil, and exult in the worst things." It is rare for Rancé to translate his Latin quotations.

[37] Rancé is referring to the discussions of sin in the *Dialogue on Purgatory* (*Trattato del Purgatorio*) of Catherine of Genoa (1447–1510). A copy of *La vie et les Œuvres de S*[te]*. Catherine de Gênes* by Jean Desmarets de Saint-Sorlin (1575–1676) was to be found in the library of la Trappe: see Bell, *The Library of the Abbey of La Trappe*, 475 (M.35). Catherine was beatified in 1675, but not actually canonized until 1737, many years after Rancé's death.

[38] See n. 10 above.

are those who listen to what the devil tells them to the detriment of what they owe to Jesus Christ. That is enough to make you to weep for their misfortune, to do what you can to appease the wrath of a God so justly angered, and to wash away the horror of their sins and ingratitude with the water of your tears.

12. This attitude is no less present in the holy Virgin than the other two.[39] There can be no doubt that all her prayers, all her activities, and all that she did in her life were accompanied by lamentations, for this all-blessed Mother was too determined to imitate in all things the charity[40] of her Son. It was impossible, therefore, that she should have seen him shed tears over the desolation of Jerusalem[41] and yet hold back her own. It is impossible that she would not have been deeply moved by the treachery of her nation and the ingratitude of those of her race, by the unjust way in which her son had been treated, and by the punishment that she knew had been prepared for them. And if, in a deeply spiritual way,[42] we look at all that she did, even the very least of her actions, and see that *conservabat omnia verba haec in corde suo* ["she kept all these words in her heart"[43]], it is impossible that she should not have shown in an outward way the marks of her overwhelming sorrow, and that the sword of bitter affliction with which her soul would be pierced (in the words of Saint Simeon[44]) would not have drawn from her eyes floods of tears on countless occasions.

[39] I.e., contemplation and action.

[40] See n. 32 above.

[41] See Luke 19:41.

[42] *Avec une Religion extrême*, which cannot be translated literally. In Rancé's France *religion* was a word of wide meaning. It could mean religion in general, the Christian religion in particular, religious devotion, religious sentiment, religious faith, or the religious way of life, i.e., monasticism. Sometimes it is better translated by "piety," "spirituality," or "godliness."

[43] This is from the text of Rancé's sermon, cited at the beginning.

[44] See Luke 2:35: "and a sword shall pierce your own soul."

13. You see, my brothers, how Jesus Christ prevents you from forgetting who you are. You have here an exact depiction of the principal duties of your profession. You have the whole thing set out before you in the Virgin's own life. You learn there to meditate unceasingly on God's law. You learn to put that law into practice. You learn to eat your bread with bitter herbs, *cum lactucis agrestibus*,[45] and to grieve in the presence of God for all that happens in the world that takes away from the limitless veneration and profound obedience that are owed to him.

14. In short, my brothers, if you wish to profit from this great mystery, and show Jesus Christ how thankful you are for the graces he grants you on this blessed day, ally yourselves with his intentions, and regard the holiness of the Virgin, brought to complete perfection as it is, not only as the object of your veneration and adoration, but still more as the Rule of your life, and do not think yourselves rash in wishing to imitate the mother when you have an incontestable instruction to imitate the Son.[46] But if you want to make this undertaking easier, you must arm yourselves by being strictly vigilant, you must place yourselves under a severe discipline,[47] you must allow nothing to enter your heart that might distract you from so holy a task, and you must banish from it everything that might tarnish its purity. And as soon as you perceive something arising in your heart that does not conform to this intention you have formed,

[45] Exod 12:8. The Latin actually means "with wild lettuce." Rancé has *laituës amères*, "bitter lettuce," but bitter herbs (as in the Hebrew) is what he means.

[46] See 1 Cor 11:1; 1 Pet 2:21.

[47] A "discipline," in both French and English, is a term for a whip or scourge, and "taking the discipline" was another term for self-flagellation. It was occasionally done at la Trappe—see David N. Bell, *Everyday Life at La Trappe under Armand-Jean de Rancé: A Translation, with Introduction and Notes, of André Félibien des Avaux's* Description de l'Abbaye de La Trappe *(1689)*, CS 274 (Collegeville, MN: Cistercian Publications, 2018), 119, n. 175—but that is not what is meant here. The "severe discipline" is the discipline of living the monastic life strictly in accord with the Rule of Saint Benedict.

say these words that Jesus Christ said to Martha: *Quid turbaris erga plurima* ["Why are you troubled about so many things?"[48]]. If a proud or sensual thought should arise, say *Quid turbaris erga plurima?* You are troubled with the care of many things. If your solitude bores you and leads you to seek diversions inappropriate to your calling, say *Quid turbaris erga plurima?* If the manual labor is a burden to you and you find yourself caught unawares by thoughts of ease and idleness, say *Quid turbaris erga plurima?* If you find the austerity you practise distasteful, and if you find yourself longing for an easier and less demanding life, say *Quid turbaris erga plurima?* If you feel your charity attacked, and there arises in you some disaffection for your brothers, say *Quid turbaris erga plurima?* If the books that speak to you of your monastic calling start to bore you, and you find yourself tempted to read a whole variety of others, say *Quid turbaris erga plurima?* If you are told to do certain things and, in so doing, feel in yourself an enthusiasm and eagerness opposed to that state of recollection[49] in which you ought to spend your days, say *Quid turbaris erga plurima?*

15. Finally, declare total war on all your passions, however small, however insignificant they may be. Remember, my brothers, that this instruction of Jesus Christ, *porro unum est necessarium*, "one thing alone is necessary for you,"[50] applies to you more than anyone else. But above all, turn to her whose triumph you celebrate today, so as to obtain from God all the faithfulness you need. You have the right to ask it of him, and to hope that he grant it through her mediation, not only because she is the universal mother of all the faithful,[51] but because she is especially the Protector of this holy Order of which you are part, and that it is under her banner and patronage that you have the glory and happiness to serve Jesus Christ.

[48] Luke 10:41.

[49] See n. 19 above.

[50] Luke 10:42.

[51] *La Mère commune de tous les fidèles.*

Chapter Seventeen

Armand-Jean de Rancé: The Second Conference for the Feast of the Assumption

Introduction

This is the second of Rancé's conferences for the feast of the Assumption, and it was yet another conference delivered at the request of certain novices who had come to la Trappe to join the Reform. This time there were six of them, but the conference provides no clue as to who they were. Rancé's text for the conference is John 12:24, "Unless a grain of wheat falls into the ground and dies, it remains but a single grain. But if it dies, it brings forth much fruit." The association of this verse with the assumption of Mary lies in the general principle of dying and rising, though the Mother of God only puts in a single appearance in the conference, and that at the very end. The question that runs through the whole conference is straightforward: what does it mean to die to God, to one's neighbor, and to oneself? And the answer is equally straightforward, though immensely difficult to achieve: the total eradication of self-will and self-love.

For Rancé, his contemporaries, and the whole Western patristic tradition, self-will and self-love are the same thing. This had been established by Augustine, who, in the West, occupied a position of authority similar to that of a fourth member of the Trinity. Love is a directed form of will. It is not something you fall into, but something you cultivate and develop. It is not a romantic attachment, but, as Augustine says in his *De Trinitate, valentior est voluntas*, love is a stronger, more intense, more vigorous form of will.[1]

Rancé begins his conference with the simple and unarguable statement that everybody wants peace and tranquility. This is true, and Rancé quotes Augustine to prove his case (§3). No Westerner would disagree with him. But since he is speaking to monks, he is speaking here of the peace that the world cannot give, a peace that is "the fruit of a pure conscience," and that comes from subduing and calming of the passions (§1). Any soul that wishes to acquire this true peace must eradicate its passions and covetous desires and acquire righteousness (Rancé is again quoting Saint Augustine [§5]). What he must do, in fact, is destroy himself, so that by dying to himself, righteousness might spring up within him, and, as Augustine says once again, "peace is the consequence and natural effect of righteousness" (§6).

But what exactly does it mean to destroy oneself? "Let me explain," says Rancé at the beginning of §8. There are three aspects to it: "the first with regard to God, the second with regard to your neighbor, and the third with regard to yourselves" (§8). So let us begin at the beginning.

Destroying oneself with regard to God means the total and complete renunciation of our self-will. God's will takes the place of the human will that we have abandoned, and "we are then so dead to any urges of our own that the only thing we do is obey and submit" (§9). And since God is now all in all to us, we are truly righteous, and since peace is the natural consequence of righteousness, we are also truly at peace.

Destroying oneself with regard to one's neighbor has two aspects, and we must remember here that Rancé is speaking

[1] Augustine, *De Trinitate*, XV.xxi.41; PL 42:1089. See also *De civitate Dei*, XIV.vii.2; PL 41:410, and Étienne Gilson, trans. L. E. M. Lynch, *The Christian Philosophy of Saint Augustine* (New York: Random House, 1967), 134–35.

to monks, not lay people. The first is total and complete obedience to one's superiors in the monastery. You must treat what they say as if it comes from the mouth of God himself, and—once again—it is their will that must take precedence over your will. Your own self-will must be annihilated, and then, since you are now acting righteously with regard to your superiors, you will find yourself at peace. As to your brothers, you destroy yourself with regard to them when you serve them with love and respect, always putting what they need or require before your own desires. Yet again, we are speaking here of the renunciation of self-will, for there is nothing—no desire, no personal inclination, no preference—that you will not give up for the love of the brethren (§11).

Destroying oneself with regard to oneself is just what we might expect it to be. It is cleansing ourselves from the cesspit of self-love, which, as we saw above, is exactly the same as self-will. The carnal self must give way to the spiritual self; "it must submit and surrender to it" (§12). Then, since we are no longer divided against ourself, we may be said to be righteous, and if we are righteous we shall be at peace. In other words, all the three aspects of self-destruction, with regard to God, neighbor, and ourselves, come down to precisely the same thing: the renunciation and abolition of self-will. This, says Rancé, is the meaning of the text on which he bases his conference. The grain of wheat must die if it is to bring forth fruit. And what is that fruit? It is that righteousness that brings true peace (§13).

And now, says the abbot, addressing not the novices who requested the conference but the monks who have taken their vows, if you do not find this peace, do not blame either the monastery or God. Blame yourselves! "You yourselves are the cause of your own evils!" (§14). There is still too much self-will left in you, and if you say that your conscience is clear, it is simply because you are not asking it the right questions. "You may hope as much as you like for greater tranquility and greater peace, but you will never have either unless you return to the very nature of your monastic calling: to that poverty, deprivation, and self-annihilation (*anéantissement*) which is its essence, its reality, and its foundation" (§16).

So what of you novices, asks the abbot. You have not yet taken your vows and may think that you are free as air, and that, in consequence, all these difficult demands do not apply to you. You couldn't be more wrong! You are not as free as you think! Who led you here, to the austerity and regulated life of la Trappe? God, in the person of the Holy Spirit. This calling, says Rancé, is "a special grace" (§17), and you therefore owe to God everything he demands of your professed brothers. You must do all that you can to make God's plans for you succeed, which means that you are bound to "exactly the same works, the same exercises, the same disciplined activities of the religious life and piety that comprise the whole state to which you feel yourselves destined" (§17). In other words, yet again, you must eradicate self-will, and in somewhat startling words, Rancé tells them that they have to give themselves the death-stroke! "You have to commit that murder so strongly commended by the very mouth of Jesus Christ himself" (§19), for did he not say that whoever shall lose his life for him shall find it?[2]

And now, finally, in §19, the Virgin makes her appearance. You cannot choose a better day, says Rancé, to commit yourselves to this task than this feast of her glorious Assumption. In her you will see that virtue essential to your calling, namely, humility. True humility is the same as the self-destruction of which, again and again, he has been speaking, and the Virgin's humility was so great that (as Saint Bernard said) God deemed her worthy to bear the Savior of the world. That virtue raised her higher than the angels, placed her on a throne, and "it is from this throne, so exalted and luminous, that she is aware of all our needs and continually intercedes before God on our

[2] Matt 10:39.

behalf" (§20). It is she, says Rancé, once again quoting Bernard, "who obtains for us the forgiveness of our sins, the healing of our ills, the alleviation of our sufferings, and constancy in our afflictions" (§20).

So let us call on her *avec une entière confiance*, "with complete confidence," for she is the refuge of sinners and "never fails to listen to all those who return to Jesus Christ with pure and sincere intentions, and to mediate on their behalf before him when they implore her help" (§21). Rancé may have introduced the Virgin only at the very end of his conference, but there is no doubt of his devotion to her and his dependence on her mediation and intercession.

Rancé's sources for the conference are, as usual, limited. As we have seen, the conferences were not the place for theological pyrotechnics, which, in any case, Rancé would have regarded as a waste of time. Apart from the liturgy, he cites eight books of the Bible—Psalms, Isaiah, Matthew, John, Galatians, Ephesians, 1 Timothy, and James—together with two standard authorities: Augustine at the beginning and Bernard at the end. In the case of Augustine, his sources are *The City of God* and the *Enarrations on the Psalms*; in the case of Bernard, not surprisingly, he quotes his fourth sermon on the Assumption.

The conference is translated from the text in Armand-Jean de Rancé, *Instructions ou Conférences sur les Epîtres et Évangiles des Dimanches et Principales Festes de l'Année, et sur les Vêtures & Professions Religieuses. Tome quatrième* (Paris: F. Delaulne, 1720), 4:225–42, reproduced (with a few typographical errors) as *Conférence LXXX* in the *Collection intégrale et universelle des Orateurs Chrétiens. Deuxième série*, vol. 90 of the entire series (= vol. 23 of the second series), edited by Jacques-Paul Migne (Paris: J.-P. Migne, 1866), 565–72.

Second Instruction or Conference Composed for the Feast Day of the Assumption of the Virgin at the Clothing of Six Novices

[Following the example of Mary, we must die to the world and its desires and practise humility][3]

Nisi granum frumenti cadens in terram mortuum fuerit, ipsum solum manet ["Unless a grain of wheat, falling into the ground, dies, it remains alone"]. John 12:24.

"If the grain of wheat, falling onto the ground, does not die and rot, it remains barren and can produce nothing."[4]

1. I have no doubt, my brothers, that your intention in making the request you have just made is to find a way to spend your days in peace and tranquility. I do not mean that false and delusive peace that one finds in laxity and easy living, but in that which is found only in the order established by God and that comes from his hand. This is the peace that the world does not know, and that it cannot give to those who love and serve it, *pacem quam mundus dare non potest* ["the peace that the world cannot give"[5]]. The peace of which I am speaking is the fruit of a pure conscience, the effect of the subduing and calming of the passions, and today this peace is all too rare, not only in the world, but even in the majority of monasteries, where it should be at their source and center. But there is no

[3] The Migne edition alone gives the subtitle.

[4] This is Rancé's paraphrase of the Johannine text.

[5] This is part of the *oratio pro pace*, the Collect for Peace, in the Roman Missal (and also, in English, in the Anglican Book of Common Prayer): *Deus, a quo sancta desideria, recta consilia et iusta sunt opera: da servis tuis illam, quam mundus dare non potest, pacem*, "God, from whom come all holy desires, all right counsels, and all righteous works, give to your servants that peace that the world cannot give" (*Corpus orationum*, 160A, no. 1088a, and 160E, no. 3783). It is based on John 14:27, which reads, in Greek, "Peace I leave with you. My peace I give to you. Not as the world gives do I give to you."

need for me to tell you this, for if you were not so convinced of it as you obviously are, you would have settled down in cloisters more conveniently located and closer to home, and would not have made so great a journey or left your own part of the country to seek a retreat in regions so far distant.[6]

2. To help you achieve what you have proposed, my brothers, and to make it easier for you to enjoy that holy peace for which you yearn, you must enter fully into that state of mind set forth in these words of the gospel: *Nisi granum frumenti cadens in terram mortuum fuerit, ipsum solum manet* ["Unless a grain of wheat, falling into the ground, dies, it remains alone"[7]]. Just as the grain of wheat rots and corrupts before it produces anything and justifies the farmer's expectations, so must you die to yourselves, to your desires, to your covetousness, and to all your passions, so that you may give yourselves up entirely to the quest for truth and righteousness, which is, as it were, the mother of that peace you so earnestly desire.

3. For what Saint Augustine says on this subject, my brothers, cannot be questioned: everyone wants peace, everyone desires it, everyone seeks it, and even those who by what they do seem to be most opposed to it have it in view as their goal.[8] A warrior, for example, or some hothead or firebrand, incites brawls and altercations only to bring about peace. His desire to be master everywhere and rule everyone in peace makes him disturb peace itself! It is true, then, to say with the same

[6] Let us remember that, at this time, la Trappe was situated in the remote and forested wilds of Normandy, and even in 1817 William Fellowes, whose *Visit to the Monastery of la Trappe in 1817* was published a year later, had difficulty in finding a guide who knew the way to it. All the roads that lead to it now date from the later nineteenth century. See David N. Bell, *Everyday Life at La Trappe under Armand-Jean de Rancé: A Translation, with Introduction and Notes, of André Félibien des Avaux's* Description de l'Abbaye de La Trappe *(1689)*, CS 274 (Collegeville, MN: Cistercian Publications, 2018), 46, n. 4.

[7] John 12:24, the text of the sermon.

[8] For this and what follows, Rancé is dependent on book 19, chap. 12, of Augustine's *City of God: De civitate Dei*, XIX.xii.1–3; PL 41:637–40.

teacher that although everyone desires peace and seeks it, there are very few who take upon themselves the effective means and sure ways of acquiring it.

4. The reason for this, my brothers, as the same saint tells us, is that they do not go to the trouble of acquiring righteousness,[9] *nolunt operari justitiam* ["they do not wish to labor for righteousness"[10]]. They make no attempt to acquire this virtue that is so holy and so necessary, even though you cannot have peace without it: righteousness and peace are two sisters who never part company, who walk hand in hand, and who are united by bonds that render them inseparable: *justitia et pax osculata sunt* ["righteousness and peace have kissed"[11]]. Thus, so long as a soul is subject to its passions and follows its covetous desires, it is disordered and uncontrolled, and since it is not then righteous, it cannot have peace. *Fac justitiam et habebis pacem, duae amicae sunt; si amicam pacis non amaveris, non te amabit ipsa pax, nec veniet ad te* ["Act righteously and you shall have peace, for the two are friends. If you do not love the friend of peace, peace itself will not love you and will not come to you"[12]].

5. Now according to Saint Augustine, peace is simply the tranquility produced by good order—*pax tranquillitas ordinis* ["peace is the tranquility of order"[13]]—but good order and the passions are not on good terms. Our passions are thrown into confusion by everything they encounter and give rise to revolt and rebellion, and this must necessarily do away with any repose or peace. This is what is meant when it says in Scripture

[9] *La justice* in French, *justitia* in Latin, can mean justice, righteousness, uprightness, probity, integrity, fairness, or goodness in general. Here I have translated it consistently as righteousness.

[10] Augustine, *Enarratio in Ps.* 84.12; PL 37:1078.

[11] Ps 84:11.

[12] Augustine, *Enarratio in Ps.* 84.12; PL 37:1078.

[13] Augustine, *De civitate Dei*, XIX.xiii.1; PL 41:640: *Pax omnium rerum, tranquillitas ordinis.* I.e., the peace of mind that comes from having everything in its proper place.

that there is no peace for the impious, that is to say, for those ruled by their passions, *Non est pax impiis* ["There is no peace for the impious"[14]]. But this does not refer only to those who abandon themselves to what the world calls impiety or godlessness, but more generally to all those who remove themselves from the hand of God and the order established by him. They show no indications of piety in their way of life, for by refusing God what they owe to him and denying him the obedience they are obliged to give him, they commit the greatest of all unrighteous acts. They cannot therefore find peace, because peace is the consequence and natural effect of righteousness.

6. And so, my brothers, if you want to succeed in what you intend and enjoy the peace and tranquility you have come to seek in this solitude, be faithful in keeping yourselves in the order established by God. Do his will. Kill off everything in you that conflicts with what you have resolved and intend. In other words, mortify your lusts, your vices, all those bad habits you have picked up from associating with the world, all those passions that, until now, have done nothing more than stir up in you storms and tempests. Bury yourself alive in subjection and humility and, as the grain of wheat is sown in the bosom of the earth, bring about your own destruction so that God may cause true righteousness to spring up in you. Then, from this, you will see born in you that peace you seek as the stream flows from the spring or, rather, as the fruit comes forth from the flower or from the bud that encloses it, in accordance with these words of the prophet [Isaiah], *Erit opus justitiae pax* ["The work of righteousness shall be peace"[15]].

7. To explain more clearly what I mean, my brothers, I would say that this destruction of which I speak is so necessary and that our heart's peace is so essentially bound to it that you

[14] Isa 48:22. This is usually translated as "there is no peace for the wicked," but here we need to keep the pious / impious distinction.

[15] Isa 32:17.

cannot have peace without it. Even to hope for it or promise it to yourself would be rash. But this destruction has three aspects and works in three different ways: the first with regard to God, the second with regard to your neighbor, and the third with regard to yourselves.

8. Now you are obviously eager to know just what I mean by this, so to satisfy such a reasonable and just desire, I would say, first, that we destroy ourselves with regard to God when we renounce our own self-will so completely and so entirely that God's will takes the place of what we have abandoned, and that his will does everything in us and brings everything about. Our dependence on God is then so perfect that nothing can resist his will: it is not just his orders that are carried out, but even his slightest desires. We are then so dead to any urges of our own that the only thing we do is obey and submit. And since, in this holy state, you now give to God all that you owe him, it is true to say that in this regard you are truly righteous, *operatur justitiam* ["he works righteousness"[16]], and, as a result, you will therefore be at peace.

9. Second, your destruction with regard to your neighbor has two aspects: the first in reference to your superiors [in the monastery], the second in reference to your brothers. With regard to your superiors, you are destroyed when you regard them as being given to you by God to guide you and therefore accept their orders as his own. You respect them for the position they hold, and you obey them so strictly and so faithfully that they never find in you any opposition or defiance. You listen to them as if it were God speaking to you through their mouths. You see things only through their eyes, and the trust you have in them is so great that just a single one of their words calms the temptations that can creep up on you, and destroys all the problems, doubts, and difficulties that can arise from the envy of the demons or your own frailty. In short, when you

[16] Ps 14:2.

rely on them rather than on your own ideas, reasons, and insights, you are doing what God wants you to do, and since you are now what you should be with regard to your superiors because of your righteous attitude, it follows that you will find yourselves at peace.

10. As to your brothers, you destroy yourself with regard to them when you treat them with that respect and charity[17] that the Rule you intend to embrace prescribes for you, and when you show them how much you esteem them every time you meet them. [You destroy yourself] when you offer them any sort of service, as the need or the occasion may demand, or when you always prefer what you know they desire to your own personal inclinations, or when you are always ready to put yourselves to one side in order to edify them, help them, or please them.[18] [You destroy yourself] when there is nothing of which you will not happily deprive yourself for the love[19] you have for your brothers, being convinced that there is not one of them who is not superior to you in his piety and in the religious way he lives his life.

11. Third, you destroy yourself with regard to yourself when you attack the root of all the different desires and natural inclinations that are formed in you—that is to say, when you labor to overthrow that self-love that is like a cesspit from which come all our disorders and evils, and when you belittle yourself in your own eyes and, following the example of the prophet [David], come to the knowledge and realization of your own nothingness: *Ad nihilum reductus sum* ["I am brought to nothing"[20]]. [You destroy yourself] when your carnal self is

[17] *Charité.* As we said in chap. 8, charity always and without exception refers to the highest and most perfect form of love, a love that comes from God and is directed towards God.

[18] See RSB 71.1-5.

[19] Here Rancé uses the word *amour*, not *charité*, but with no distinction in meaning.

[20] Ps 72:22.

so overthrown and weakened that since it now has no strength to rise up against your spiritual self, it must submit and surrender to it. The flesh can no longer rebel against the spirit,[21] for by living a life of righteousness you have removed from it all its resources. Thus, since there is now no longer any discord or division within you, you must of necessity find yourself at peace.

12. You see, my brothers, what it means to destroy yourselves. You see how similar it is to the grain of wheat that can yield nothing if it does not rot away. You see the one and only way in which the peace you so desire can be given to you. It is the fruit of righteousness, as we have already said: *Opus justitiae pax* ["The work of righteousness is peace"[22]], and this righteousness assumes a destruction as complete and as absolute as we have just explained to you.

13. This being so, my brothers, and I am speaking now to those of you who have taken your vows,[23] if it should ever happen that this peace, which is so necessary for you and which you so much desire, passes you by, and you find yourselves disoriented and confused, or if your souls do not come to enjoy this sacred repose that we experience in these solitudes where we are led by the Spirit of God, or if the heaven of your heart finds itself troubled by tempests, do not blame either your monastic calling or the God who has committed you to it. Instead, enter into the depths of your own conscience and examine carefully all that is hidden there. Uncover all its secrets, and you will find that the reason you have no peace is that you have no righteousness. And why not? Because instead of annihilating yourselves, separating yourselves from yourselves, and destroying yourselves as you should, you are opposed to your duties, opposed to the order established by God,

[21] See Gal 5:17.

[22] Isa 32:17.

[23] Lit. "who are committed" (*qui sont engagez*).

opposed to the obligations you have undertaken, and altogether full of yourselves, that is to say, full of your own desires and your own self-will. You can certainly conceal this opposition and hide from yourselves what you truly are, but you cannot deny the fact that you yourselves are the cause of your own evils! The passions, desires, and attachments you retain, which are contrary to the life of self-denial and renunciation you ought to live, deservedly disappoint your hopes and produce in you at one and the same time no more than false consolations[24] and real miseries.

14. But you tell me that your conscience gives you no qualms! I hear you. But that is not because it does not have good reason to do so! It says nothing, because you are not asking it the right questions and not being sufficiently demanding! I know perfectly well that you are not guilty of gross abuses or real scandals, but there are faults that, though more subtle and understated, are no less dangerous and no less deadly. If we do not take account of them, it is only because they do not have that shocking seriousness that would naturally call attention to itself and that we could only regard with horror.

15. I will not go into this at length, but let me ask you, for example, whether you have done everything demanded of you by your Rule with regard to your brothers, whether you have shown them all the charity that the Rule requires, or whether you have been a source of inspiration for them. Has there been anything remarkable in your own conduct that could serve as instruction and example for your brothers? Have you suffered in patience the faults and weaknesses you have seen in them, whether of body or spirit? In short, have you been faithful in doing everything demanded of you by the laws of a holy society? Examine everything you ought to have done in detail, and I will be very surprised if you do not put

[24] The nature of "consolations" was discussed in the last chapter.

your finger on the cause of the unhappiness you are experiencing. The greatest problem is that we often abandon God before we have come to know him, and because we fail to realize our mistake and have no qualms about leaving him, we die in our sin and don't even realize we are guilty until the very moment that we are punished. You may hope as much as you like for greater tranquility and greater peace, but you will never have either unless you return to the very nature of your monastic calling: to that poverty, deprivation, and self-annihilation that is its essence, its reality, and its foundation.

16. As for you, my brothers,[25] you who are still free and not yet stripped of the garments of the old self,[26] you will say to yourselves that all these various practices I have just explained do not apply to you. I agree, provided you are thinking of them in terms of a vow you have not yet made. But if you consider them in light of the obligation you have to make yourselves fit to do what God has called you to do, you are not as free as you think! Tell me, I beg you, who led you here? You will undoubtedly reply that it was God's inspiration, the urging of his Holy Spirit that drove you from the world and thrust you into this retreat. But if this is so, what reason can you possibly have to think that you owe God nothing for following these impulses? This calling is a special grace. It is a talent[27] and a deposit[28] that has been entrusted to you. You must make proper use of it and turn it to good account,[29] that is to say, you must do all that you can to make God's plans succeed, and to this end you must make use of all the means he puts into your hands, whether he wants you to complete the work

[25] Rancé now once again addresses the six novices who requested the conference.

[26] See Eph 4:22.

[27] Rancé is referring to the parable of the talents in Matt 25:14-30.

[28] See 1 Tim 6:20: *O Timothee, depositum custodi,* "guard what is deposited with you."

[29] I.e., you must make a spiritual profit, as in the parable of the talents.

you have begun, or whether he has bound you to it only for a certain limited time. But those means are exactly the same works, the same exercises, the same disciplined activities of the religious life and piety that comprise the whole state to which you feel yourselves destined. And unless you do all that you can to acquit yourselves faithfully in these things, you will have failed to respond to what he wants of you, you will have abandoned one of the main things you owe him, and he will have reason to complain and say of you that although you have truly heard his voice, you have not condescended to do the work you need to do to discover his intentions and ascertain his will.

17. In summary, my brothers, you will find that the only things that can establish you in that interior repose and peace for which you have already made so many advances and taken so many steps are that stripping off and destruction of which we have spoken at such length, though there is still more to say. All the rebellions and civil wars that surge up deep in our souls have their roots, as the apostle [James] says, in the unruliness of our desires and covetousness: *Unde bella et lites in vobis? Nonne ex concupiscentiis vestris quae militant in membris vestris?* ["whence come these wars and altercations within you, if not from your desires, which are at war in your members?"[30]]. Thus you cannot hope for peace unless you destroy these formidable foes. In other words, you yourselves have to give yourselves the death-stroke! You have to commit that murder so strongly commended by the very mouth of Jesus Christ himself, that murder that, rather than making you guilty, makes you innocent and righteous: *qui perdiderit animam suam propter me, inveniet eam* "[whoever shall lose his life for me shall find it"[31]].

[30] Jas 4:1.
[31] Matt 10:39.

18. My brothers, you cannot find a time better suited to the commitment you are about to make than this day on which we celebrate the glorious assumption of the holy Virgin,[32] and it can only be joy for her to see you enter upon a state that demands a virtue that was, as it were, essential to her. I mean humility, that virtue that was always so dear to her and is nothing other than the self-destruction I have proposed to you—that virtue, I say, that she brought to such an eminent degree of excellence and perfection that, as Saint Bernard thought and said, she was worthy of having the eternal Word descend into her womb and cast upon her glances of infinite blessing: *digna plane quam respiceret Deus* ["wholly worthy that God should look upon her"[33]].

19. This is the virtue that raises her today to such a high degree of glory that there is nothing above her save him who cannot be below anyone. It is from this throne, so exalted and luminous, that she is aware of all our needs and continually intercedes before God on our behalf. Indeed, it is true to say that all the graces that earth receives from heaven are the result of this potent mediation, which is like a channel through which pass all those indications and effects that God gives us of his protection and goodness. It is she, says Bernard again, who obtains for us the forgiveness of our sins, the healing of our ills, the alleviation of our sufferings, and constancy in our afflictions: *reis veniam, medelam languidis, contritis corde robur* ["forgiveness for the guilty, healing for those ailing, strength for those whose hearts are contrite"[34]]. In other words, all the

[32] The holy Virgin finally makes her appearance in what, in Rancé's French, is the penultimate paragraph of the conference, though what he now has to say leaves us in no doubt as to her importance.

[33] Bernard, *In Assumptione beatae Mariae, sermo* 4.7; SBOp 5:249. For *respiceret Deus* Bernard has *respiceret Dominus*, and the verb *respicere* echoes the Vulgate text of Luke 1:48: "He has regarded (*respexit*) the humility of his handmaiden."

[34] Bernard, *In Assumptione, sermo* 4.9; SBOp 5:250, though what Bernard actually says is *reis veniam, medelam aegris, pusillis corde robur, afflictis consola-*

good things that happen to us are the fruits and effects of her supplications and prayers.

20. And so, my brothers, call on her with complete confidence, and hope for everything from her whom God has made the refuge of all sinners. If she never fails to listen to all those who return to Jesus Christ with pure and sincere intentions, and to mediate on their behalf before him when they implore her help, you yourselves have even greater reason to look for her favor and find her ready to offer you her hand, you who have made your commitment in an Order, in a house, and in a monastery that professes to serve Jesus Christ under her protection, under her name, and under her patronage.

---

tionem, periclitantibus adiutorium et liberationem: "forgiveness for the guilty, healing for the sick, strength for the faint-hearted, consolation for the afflicted, help and deliverance for those in danger."

Chapter Eighteen

Armand-Jean de Rancé: The Third Conference for the Feast of the Assumption

Introduction

This is the last of Rancé's three conferences for the feast of the Assumption, though neither the assumption nor Mary is ever specifically mentioned. It takes up the thread of the other two, namely, the overcoming of the carnal self and the eradication of self-will, but has more to say on the practical means by which this is achieved. It was delivered on the feast of the Assumption, August 15, at the solemn profession of a monk, but we have no idea of which monk (there is no clue in the conference), nor of the year in which it was delivered.

Rancé takes as his text 1 Corinthians 15:31, "I die daily," and tells the monk who is about to make his profession that nothing summarizes better the step he is about to take (§1). Furthermore, he says, the duties that your monastic profession will demand of you are designed and intended to be the most effective way of bringing about this self-destruction, and he echoes Saint Bernard in saying that while worldly people do all that they can to prolong their days on earth, monks do all that they can to end them (§2).

These demands and duties are designed to destroy both body and spirit. As for the body, they are all hard and difficult, and every one of them is intended to weaken the strength and vigor of that body (§3). The monastic life, says Rancé, should be a crucifixion, a true martyrdom, and he quotes Saint Bernard and Saint Teresa of Àvila to prove his point (§§4–5). Given, then, that a monk's business is to die, not to live, meditation on death should be his principal occupation. And far from plunging him into despondency or despair, this should give him joy, just as a prisoner anticipates with pleasure the moment he will be given news that he has been freed (§6). Those who are attached to the world, whose delight is in transitory things, and who have nothing to expect from the future, naturally fear death. But for true religious, who scorn worldly things and have their eyes fixed on those that are eternal, "how could they possibly look with any trepidation on the moment that is guaranteed to bring them delight?" (§7).

Rancé then presents a lengthy list of things that a monk might find difficult and with which he may need help: laziness, sloth, apathy, gloom, despondency, memories of the world he has left behind, and so on. The best remedy for all of these, he says, is to say, from the depths of his heart, "I die daily," and if a monk has death in mind rather than life, he will realize how valuable these trials and temptations truly are (§8).

At §9 Rancé turns his attention to the human spirit. This, too, must be destroyed, but it is clear from this paragraph that the destruction of the spirit is no more and no less than the destruction of self-will. This is the same theme that runs through all three conferences on the Assumption, and the destruction of self-will and self-love is the purpose of monastic life. That is what the Rule of Saint Benedict was designed to do, and the most important requirement of that Rule is that monks be absolutely and unquestionably obedient to their superiors. As the Rule itself says, "they may not have either their own bodies or their wills at their own disposal" (§10). This is one of the *leitmotifs* of Rancé's spirituality.

What a monk has to do, in fact, is to make a complete sacrifice of himself, a whole burnt offering, on the altar of God. "He lays on the altar of penitence his soul, his spirit, his will, his reason, all that he is, there to be consumed by the fire of his obedience and his love for God" (§11). And if you think I am going too far in saying this, says Rancé, then I would remind you that the words are not mine, but those of Jesus Christ himself. Did he not say that whoever does not renounce his father, his mother, all his property, all that he has, even his own soul, is not worthy of him?[1] (§12).

The monastic state demands absolute and complete detachment from the world and from oneself, and if anyone thinks other than this, they are wrong, wrong, wrong. And if anyone commits themselves to it without being prepared to say with Saint Paul, "I die daily," all they will find is loss and condemnation (§13). Is this a hard path? Yes indeed! "But only for those who lack faith and whose own heart is hard" (§14). And does not Saint Paul also say that "there is no comparison between the sufferings of this present life and the glory of that to come" (§14)? Is it really worthwhile to devote oneself to a few transitory moments of so-called freedom and dubious pleasure here below and find in exchange only eternal damnation?

Therefore, says Rancé, once again addressing the brother who is about to be professed, if anyone tells you that the Rule is flexible, that it may be mitigated or changed, do not believe them. You must take the Rule for what it is, word for word,[2] and if you do, two things will happen. The first is the realization that in making this commitment, you lose all the rights you may once have had over your own person (§16). And the

[1] See Luke 14:26-27, but Rancé changes the uncompromising *odit*, "hates," of the Vulgate text for the less strident *renoncer*, "renounces." In so doing, we might add, he is closer to the Greek original, for at the basis of the Greek verb *misein* is the idea of preferring one thing to another, and what Christ is saying here is that those who are determined to follow him must be prepared to put him first and their families second. It's not about hating our parents, it's about getting our priorities straight. And what is true for all Christians is, *ipso facto*, yet more true for monks and nuns.

[2] In fact, as we mentioned in chap. 13, Rance's approach to the Rule is much more subtle than appears in this bald statement: see David N. Bell, "Rancé and the Rule: His Approach to the Rule of Saint Benedict, with a Translation of His Conference for the Feast of the Saint," *Cistercian Studies Quarterly* 54 (2019): 181–210.

second is the realization "that the rewards that our Rule can obtain for us from God's goodness are uniquely linked to the way in which, strictly and faithfully, we do all that is demanded of us" (§16).

In short, Rancé tells the newly professed monk, if you are truly detached from yourself and the world, "this death, so to speak, that is so complete and absolute, will put you beyond every temptation that could possibly trouble your repose and prevent you from enjoying the fruits of your withdrawal from the world" (§17). You must die daily! And if you think this path is hard, it is! Indeed, it is beyond all reason! But it is the path that leads to everlasting bliss.

And so, says Rancé, in his final paragraph, if you who are about to take your vows find all this too hard and too difficult, if you do not believe that God will offer you his grace to help you overcome all these difficulties, then go no further and go somewhere else! But if you are truly determined to put yourself in the hands of Jesus Christ and offer yourself wholly to him alone, then the step you are about to take can only be a blessing for you, and "the happy death I have proposed to you will be the beginning of a life that will have no end" (§18).

Such, in summary, is Rancé's teaching in the third of his conferences for the Assumption. There is no mention of Mary, no mention of the feast, no mention of the assumption. But the principal theme is clear, and it is a theme common to virtually all spiritual traditions: the overcoming of egocentricity and the sense of self. Whether we regard it as a consequence of the sin of Adam and Eve, or whether we regard it as some quirk of evolution, there is no doubt that we are self-centered human beings, and we find the broad and easy path of comfort and pleasure far easier to tread than the narrow way of asceticism and austerity. Most of us need a certain amount of self-love, if only to keep us alive—"love your neighbor, *as yourself,*" we are told—but the path set out by Rancé was not intended to lead to life but to death. Or, more accurately, it was intended to lead to eternal life at the cost of life in this world. Rancé, we might add, did not invent this; he took it straight from Saint Bernard. "Monks," said the saint (and Rancé quotes him), "have not been instructed in the school of Hippocrates and Galen, who teach the preservation of life, but in that of Jesus Christ, who tells us to lose it."[3] "As we have said so many times," says Rancé,

> monks do not come to monasteries to live, but to die, and they should be neither surprised nor frightened to see frequent deaths. What they seek is the salvation of their souls, not the preservation of their life and health.[4]

This was certainly the case at la Trappe, where, in the early days, the mortality was so high as to cause adverse comment and considerable criticism. This was partly because of the unhealthiness of the site, and partly of a diet severely deficient in protein.[5] But as Rancé said, "I regard our monastery as my tomb,"[6] and that is all there is to it.

The translation that follows is based on the text in Armand-Jean de Rancé, *Instructions ou Conférences sur les Epîtres et Évangiles des Dimanches et Principales Festes de l'Année, et sur les Vêtures & Professions Religieuses. Tome quatrième* (Paris: F. Delaulne, 1720), 4:243–58, reproduced (with a few typographical errors) as *Conférence LXXXI* in the *Collection intégrale et universelle des Orateurs Chrétiens. Deuxième série*, vol. 90 of the entire series (= vol. 23 of the second series), edited by Jacques-Paul Migne (Paris: J.-P. Migne, 1866), 572–77.

[3] Bernard, *In Cantica, sermo* 30.4–5; SBOp 1:216–17.

[4] Armand-Jean de Rancé, *De la sainteté et des devoirs de la vie monastique* (Paris: F. Muguet, 1683), 2:459–60.

[5] See David N. Bell, *Everyday Life at La Trappe under Armand-Jean de Rancé: A Translation, with Introduction and Notes, of André Félibien des Avaux's* Description de l'Abbaye de La Trappe *(1689)*, CS 274 (Collegeville, MN: Cistercian Publications, 2018), 98, n. 131, with further references there.

[6] See David N. Bell, *Understanding Rancé: The Spirituality of the Abbot of La Trappe in Context*, CS 205 (Kalamazoo, MI: Cistercian Publications, 2005), 107.

Third Instruction or Conference Composed for the Feast Day of the Assumption of the Virgin at the Profession of a Monk

[On the spirit of mortification][7]

Quotidie morior ["I die daily"]. 1 Corinthians 15:31.

"I die every day."

1. My brother,[8] there is nothing I can say that will be more useful to you at this present time, when you are just about to give yourself up to God, than these two words of the Apostle, and I encourage you to keep them in your mind's eye at all times: *quotidie morior*, "I die every day." There is nothing that summarizes better, or expresses more clearly, the nature of the step you are about to take. For it is true to say that as soon as you have made your vows, everything you do at every moment of your life will be nothing other than the fulfillment of these words, *quotidie morior* ["I die daily"], though this will not be perfectly accomplished until the moment that God himself completes your sacrifice by completely destroying the victim. I mean by that the moment that it pleases him to bring your life to an end, for you will then cease to live on earth, or, rather, you will die on earth in order to live the life of the angels in heaven.

2. Until then, however, the only words that should be uttered by the lips of your heart are *quotidie morior*, "I die every day," and if you faithfully carry out all the duties that your monastic profession demands of you, you will find that there is nothing better suited to leading and guiding us to true self-destruction, whether it be of the body or of the spirit. You see here the difference between worldly people and monks. The

[7] The Migne edition alone provides the subtitle.

[8] "My brother" is in the singular: Rancé is addressing the brother who is about to be professed.

former die every day without wishing for this destruction or even thinking about it, whereas the latter, on the contrary, think of it and desire it. The former do all that they can to prolong their days on earth; the latter do all that they can to end them.[9]

3. First of all, my brothers,[10] let us consider our natural, physical life.[11] All the outward activities that form the body[12] of your monastic state are hard and painful. There is not one of them that does not attack and, little by little, weaken the strength and vigor of your body, [not one of them] that does not lead to death, even though you may not notice it. And since there is no let up in these activities, and since they follow on, one from the other, there is not a single day on which you should not say with the apostle, *quotidie morior* ["I die daily"].

4. My brother,[13] you must be convinced that the withdrawal [from the world], the solitude, the fasts, the abstinence, the austerity in food, the manual labor, the hard beds, the long vigils, the silence, the continual vigilance, the spiritual diligence, the renunciation of all pleasure, and so many other practices or attitudes that are part of your monastic profession are, to put it bluntly, the instruments of your martyrdom. And just as those who confess the name of Jesus Christ and whom his Providence has destined to uphold his faith look with pleasure on the instruments of torture they are more than ready to endure, so you, too, must find your joy and consolation in all these activities demanded by the Rule [of Saint Benedict] and all these different practices that prepare you for that death for which you are destined.

[9] See further n. 14 below.

[10] Rancé now addresses all the brothers.

[11] *La vie naturelle.*

[12] The first eight paragraphs of the conference concern the physical bodies of the monks and the bodily austerities and mortifications of everyday life at la Trappe. At §9, Rancé turns to the spirit; this section involves primarily the total destruction of self-will, the annihilation (*anéantissement*) of self, which has been his theme for all three of his conferences for the assumption.

[13] We are back with the brother about to be professed.

5. What can be more natural or more necessary for someone committed to such an undertaking as the one you are about to embrace than to ponder deeply what is required of him? How can he pass his time more usefully and, indeed, more enjoyably than in doing what can help him achieve his goal? In the view of the saints, our monastic profession is a contract with death. Some call it a crucifixion, others say that the first step a monk should take is to free himself from any fear of death. Saint Bernard says that the religious profession is a true martyrdom and calls it a school in which we learn to die.[14] And in the last century,[15] Saint Teresa [of Àvila], who cannot be accused of those excesses one may want to attribute to earlier times, says to all her daughters that they will never succeed in their plans if they do not resolve to swallow down all at once both death and the loss of their health.[16] What else can we learn from all this, my brother, except that meditation on death should be a monk's principal occupation, and that he turns aside from his goal and true purpose every time he fails to keep this in mind?

6. Now do not think that this attitude fills his heart with bitterness or makes him despondent. It should, in fact, have quite the opposite effect. This is a captive joyfully looking forward to the moment he will be given his freedom. This is a

[14] This is a brief summary of the well-known discussion in Bernard's thirtieth sermon on the Song of Songs, where he contrasts the school of Hippocrates and his followers, who teach us how to preserve our lives in this world, with the school of Jesus Christ and his disciples, who teach us how to lose it: see n. 3 above.

[15] Teresa lived from 1515 to 1582.

[16] Rancé does not give his source for this citation of Teresa, but it is from book 11, chap. 4, of her *Camino de perfección*: "Si no nos determinamos a tragar de una vez la muerte y la falta de salud, nunca haremos nada," "Unless we are determined to swallow down death and loss of health at one and the same time, we will never get anywhere." The complete works of the saint, in French translation, were to be found in the la Trappe library: see David N. Bell, *The Library of the Abbey of La Trappe from the Twelfth Century to the French Revolution, with an Annotated Edition of the 1752 Catalogue* (Turnhout: Brepols / *Cîteaux – Commentarii cistercienses*, 2014), 574 (T.29–35).

criminal anticipating with pleasure the moment when he will be given the news of the pardon for which he has hoped. This is a pilot who, in the course of navigating his ship, finds comfort every time the day dawns when he will bring his vessel safe to port.

7. My brothers, I say this to all of you: death is hard only for those who are attached to the world, who love its diversions and sensual pleasures because the rewards they offer come here and now. And since they have nothing to expect from the future, the blow that takes their own life takes everything they have, and, as a result, the only thing left for them to share is grief and sorrow. But for true monks, such as you should be, who have only scorn for the things here below and who live uniquely in faith and desire for those things that are eternal, how could they possibly look with any trepidation on the moment that is guaranteed to bring them delight? For far from doing them any harm, we may say that they should find in death the very summit of their joy and consolation.

8. If, for example, someone should find himself unexpectedly tempted by laziness or sloth,[17] and this produces a distaste for the manual labor and exercises of his monastic profession, what remedy can there be that is more effective or more ready to hand than to say from the depths of his heart, *quotidie morior* ["I die daily"]? "There is no day on which I do not die, and I am perfectly ready to see the end and reward of all my labors." If he should find himself oppressed by boredom, apathy, or gloom, he should not fail to say to himself, *quotidie morior*, "I have no more than a day to live, and God is about to grant me the happiness and joy of his saints." If the world comes back to haunt him, and if he is pestered by thoughts of the things he has left behind, let him cry aloud, *quotidie morior*, "I am at the end of my days, and God is about to set me in a new world, a world of such beauty and richness, of which this one is not

[17] *Paresse*: laziness, indolence, idleness, lethargy, sloth.

even a shadow or image." In short, you must believe that thinking and meditating on death is of infinite value, and it never fails to bring about blessings and salvation to those who are careful to keep up the practice.

9. Now, my brothers, let us turn our attention to the spirit.[18] There is no state that is more destructive to the spirit, and, immortal though it may be, that gives it, so to speak, a more effective death stroke than the profession you have embraced. "What?" you say, "How can this be?" [I shall explain.] There is nothing that gives more life to the spirit or nourishes it more, nothing that is more natural to it or characteristic of it, than to will or not to will, to act independently, to follow its own instincts, and to judge everything by its own light and its own judgment. But your monastic calling puts an end to all these things: it deprives the spirit of them and completely removes from it that freedom with which it was born. Thus, by forbidding all its principal activities, it assuredly attacks and destroys its very life, and since the spirit continues to die, it is not only with regard to the life of the body, but even more with regard to the life of the spirit that we have reason to say, "I die every day," *quotidie morior*.

10. But lest you think that I am simply offering my own opinion here or retailing my own ideas, remember this: it is not I but your Rule that is speaking to you, and it is your Rule that teaches you that you are required by your vows to strip yourselves so completely [of self-will] that from the very moment you pronounce those vows, you lose all the rights and all the freedom you may once have had to do what you want and act as you like. [From that moment], you must be so utterly and absolutely dependent on your superiors that you are no longer permitted to do anything regarding your body or your will except by their orders, their intentions, and their guidance: *Quibus nec corpora sua, nec voluntates licet habere in propria po-*

[18] See n. 12 above.

testate ["they may not have either their own bodies or their wills at their own disposal"[19]].

11. The step you are about to take is not just a partial sacrifice in which you may keep back part of the sacrificial victim. No. It is a whole burnt offering that requires the destruction of the entire victim. Nothing may remain that is not immolated and consumed by the fire. What this means is that the person who is consecrated offers and abandons himself without any reservation or any conditions, that he lays on the altar of penitence his soul, his spirit, his will, his reason, all that he is, there to be consumed by the fire of his obedience and his love for God.

12. You will find that I have not gone too far in anything I have just said to you if you know what it is to be a Christian, and if you have ever understood the full force of those words, uttered by the mouth of Jesus Christ himself, when he said that whoever does not renounce[20] his father, his mother, all his property, all that he has, even his own soul, and does not take up his cross to follow him, is not worthy of him,[21] that is to say, would not enter his kingdom. We have no choice but to accept this statement, and it excludes all those who refuse to subject themselves to it. We can soften its sense as much as we like, we can explain it in such a way as to weaken its strength and rigorous demands, but we cannot stop Jesus Christ from demanding that all those who wish to be numbered among his disciples (that is to say, all who desire to be saved) must be ready, every single time his service requires it, to carry out to the letter everything contained in these words. For if he had not intended to speak to us of such harsh obligations, so troubling and contrary to all our natural inclinations, he would not have expressed himself in such a challenging and extraordinary way.

[19] RSB 33.4.

[20] See n. 1 above.

[21] See Luke 14:26-27.

13. I am therefore going to state a simple truth. Whoever has any other ideas as to the perfect detachment that the monastic state demands is wrong. And whoever commits himself to it without intending and resolving to live in it and die in it every day of his life, in such a way that he can say with the apostle *quotidie morior*, then far from finding there his sanctification, as he had hoped, he will find there only his loss and condemnation. That is why there is nothing that needs to be made clearer to those about to take the step you are about to take, because these days there is nothing on which we can deceive ourselves more easily. Far from seeing in the religious life all its renunciations, privations, austerities, crosses, and inward and outward mortifications, we find instead secret ways to live an easy and undemanding life, thus depriving ourselves, by the most deplorable of all evils, of all the goods and advantages that the religious life can bring about.

14. But why, someone will say, why must I spend my whole life in crosses and mortifications? That's really hard! It is hard, that's true! But only for those who lack faith and whose own heart is hard. For does not the apostle teach us that there is no comparison between the sufferings of this present life and the glory of that to come, which will be our reward?[22] And that if we die to this life, which is totally animal and earthly, it is only to live a life that is totally spiritual and holy?[23] Or, in a word, to live henceforth in the bosom of God,[24] in the company of Jesus Christ and his angels?

15. What more need I say to have us separate ourselves from the ideas and way of life of those of whom I have just spoken, those who, rather than advancing from virtue to virtue like the saints, do just the opposite, going from iniquity to iniquity, from disorder to disorder, like the wicked. Do we not realize

[22] Rom 8:18.
[23] See 1 Cor 2:14-15.
[24] See John 1:18.

that when we manage to find a few moments of false and uncertain freedom today, before the night has passed our souls will be told, as was the miser in the gospel, *Stulte, hac nocte animam tuam repetunt a te* ["Fool, this night do they demand your soul from you"[25]]? And yet we squander so many of the good things and benefits that God has put in our hands to gain his eternity, and we deprive ourselves of it forever.

16. In summary, my brother,[26] pay no heed whatever to those who may speak to you of a flexibility your Rule does not possess and who, by their far-fetched explanations, will do their best to hide from you what it actually demands. To take it for what it truly is, take it word for word; if you do, you will see two things with your own eyes, whatever anyone may say to you to the contrary. The first is that the stripping off and renunciation required of you cannot be any greater than that specified by these words [of the Rule]: *quippe qui ex illo die nec proprii corporis potestatem se habiturum sciat* ["that from that day, he may know that not even his own body is at his disposal"[27]]. In other words, from the moment a religious makes his commitment, he loses all the rights he may once have had over his own person. The second is that the rewards that our Rule can obtain for us from God's goodness are uniquely linked to the way in which, strictly and faithfully, we do all that is demanded of us, *quae cum fuerint a nobis die noctuque incessabiliter adimpleta, et in die judicii reconsignata, illa merces nobis a Domino recompensabitur quam ipse promisit* ["when we have carried them out unceasingly by night and day, then, when we have returned them on Judgment Day, we shall be rewarded with the wages from the Lord that he himself has promised us"[28]].

[25] Luke 12:20.

[26] Rancé again addresses the brother about to be professed.

[27] RSB 58.25.

[28] RSB 4.76.

17. When it is clear to your conscience that there is nothing to be found in your conduct to cause you reproach, and that your life is not subject to the scruples and remorse of those who walk in wide and broad ways,[29] this will bring you comfort. But more than that, this detachment, this total separation of yourself from yourself, this death, so to speak, that is so complete and absolute, will put you beyond the reach of every temptation that could possibly trouble your repose and prevent you from enjoying the fruits of your withdrawal. For what could possibly harm a person who has no ties to anything, who regards each day as his last, and who is so utterly in the hands of God that he obeys him alone and those whom God has commanded him to obey, and who, in all sincerity, can combat everything troublesome or vexatious that might happen to him with these words of the Apostle, *quotidie morior*? But this subjection, someone will say to you, is really unpleasant. That is true, but it will not last long, *quotidie morior*. This command is irksome, [they say,] it is against all reason. But what can it do for me? Why should I want to follow my own inclinations for the little time I have left? *Quotidie morior*! It's true that this is a sharp reproof, but what does that matter? It passes in an instant, and I have but a single day to live: *quotidie morior*. Alas, [they say,] these restrictions [on what we do] cannot be borne! But how are we to judge them, since they are about to end and be followed by everlasting freedom? And should we not bear in mind what the Apostle says, that this moment of suffering in this present life, so brief and passing, brings about in us an eternal weight of sublime and incomparable glory? *Id enim quod in praesenti est, momentaneum et leve tribulationis nostrae, supra modum in sublimitate aeternum gloriae pondus operatur in nobis* ["For what is at present light and passing in our tribulation brings about in us, in a way that exceeds all measure, an eternal weight of glory"[30]].

[29] I.e., the wide and broad ways that lead to destruction: see Matt 7:13-14.
[30] 2 Cor 4:17.

18. But when all is said and done, my brother, if what I have said to you frightens you, if this mortification that is so demanding exceeds your resolve, and if you do not have enough trust in God's protection to hope that his grace will help you deal with what undoubtedly seems to be beyond your strength, then I would advise you to go no further. If you do, your commitment, instead of giving you the happiness you have hoped for, will have just the opposite effect, and the step you take will bring about no more than an everlasting regret for having taken it. But if you find yourself in the right frame of mind, as I am convinced is the case, and absolutely determined to put yourself entirely in the hands of Jesus Christ, holding and keeping nothing back either with regard to your body, your spirit, your heart, or your senses, and if you are convinced that the true happiness of a monk is uniquely attached to his subjection and total dependence [on God], I can say to you, and indeed assure you, that the step you are about to take will be a source of blessing for you and that this happy death I have proposed to you will be the beginning of a life that will have no end.

Chapter Nineteen

Drawing the Threads Together: The Cistercians and Mary

In the year 418, Saint Augustine wrote a long letter to a young student named Dioscorus, a young student, we might add, somewhat over-full of questions, and told him that if he was seeking the way to truth, then Christ has already prepared it for him. There are three steps on that path, says Augustine, and of these three the first is humility, the second is humility, and the third is humility. "And as often as you ask me the question, that is what I would say." It is not that there are no other precepts that might be given, but unless humility precedes, accompanies, and follows every good action, pride will snatch its goodness out of our hands.[1]

This is the song of every Cistercian writer from Bernard to Armand-Jean de Rancé, and it follows naturally from the fact that in the Latin text of the *Magnificat*, Mary tells us that God regarded her for her humility, *humilitas*, not for her greatness. Indeed, this is one of the few themes in Marian theology that has a solid biblical foundation, for many of the others, essential as they are—Mary's mediation, intercession, advocacy, and so on—are theological constructs sometimes developed from apocryphal sources of doubtful authenticity. We saw in the first chapter that all our information on Mary's birth and death

[1] Augustine, *Epistola* 118.iii.22; PL 33:442.

comes from non-biblical sources, and we have also seen that the immensely popular *Protevangelium* of James had a profound impact on the development of Marian doctrine. Ogier of Locedio was particularly credulous when it came to non-biblical sources.

It is only to be expected, then, that of all the virtues the Virgin possessed—and writer after writer tells us that she possessed all of them—her humility should take pride of place. Bernard leaves us in no doubt on this score in the first of his homilies in praise of the Virgin Mother, and Rancé, in his conference for Mary's Nativity, states that humility is the basis of all perfection and that "Jesus Christ founded and grounded every spiritual structure on this virtue."[2] Aelred exhorts his monks to imitate Mary's wonderful humility, and, following Bernard, says that nowhere is this humility more apparent than in Mary's offering herself for ritual purification when she clearly had no need to be purified at all![3]

Ogier of Locedio and Baldwin of Forde both wax eloquent on the theme, and Baldwin, again following Bernard, distinguishes two sorts of humility, one that derives from a command and one that is the result of our own decision. The former is an obligation; the latter, which is the greater good, comes from our own free will, and that, of course, was the humility of the Virgin. John of Forde, yet again following Bernard, states that humility is the mother of all the virtues, and that Mary possessed this humility in three forms: first, humility with regard to herself, second, with regard to her neighbor, and third, with regard to God. "The first lies in the truest knowledge of oneself; the second in compassion and respect for one's neighbor; the third in the most humble contemplation of God."[4] Mary's contemplation of God is a matter to which we shall return in due course.

[2] Chap. 14, §12.

[3] See chap. 5, n. 25, and chap. 9, n. 20.

[4] Chap. 11, n. 30.

Yet great though it is, Mary's humility cannot equal that of her divine son, who emptied himself, taking the form of a servant, for our salvation—Philippians 2:7 is regularly cited—but Guerric of Igny elaborates on this point by distinguishing no fewer than seven types of humility exhibited by Christ.[5] Guerric then goes on to explain that we should imitate Christ in all these forms of his humility, for the Christian way is no more and no less than the imitation of Christ, and Rancé says the same thing in his conference for the feast of Mary's Nativity.

Mary's role is essential here, for not only does her own perfect humility reflect that of her son, but had there been no Mary, there would have been no Jesus. Not one of the Cistercian writers discussed in these pages can be accused of Mariolatry, for all of them are agreed that although the Virgin is our necessary mediatrix, advocate, and intercessor, the grace of forgiveness and the promise of salvation come from God alone.

But Mary and her son are so united, in the womb, in life, and afterwards in heaven, that to praise the one is to praise the other. Gertrude the Great might have been concerned that the praise she would give to the Virgin detracted from the praise she should give to her son, but neither Bernard nor anyone else would have agreed with her. What does Bernard say? "It cannot be doubted that whatever praises we offer to the mother apply to the son, and, conversely, when we honor the son, we do not take away from the glory of the mother."[6] Ogier uses precisely this text to defend his own fulsome praises of the Mother of God.[7]

But despite this, and despite the fact that we are told, time and time again, that Mary and Jesus are crowned and enthroned side by side in Paradise, we do not go to Mary through Jesus—that indeed would be grave heresy—but to Jesus through Mary. In his long sermon on the Nativity of Mary—the

[5] See chap. 6, n. 53.

[6] Bernard, *In laudibus Virginis Matris, hom.* 4.1; SBOp 4:46.

[7] See chap. 10, n. 46.

sermon on the Aqueduct—Bernard urges us to seek grace and to seek it through Mary, and adds shortly afterwards that God's will is "that we should have everything through Mary."[8] In the course of time, "To Jesus through Mary" would become the watchword of Pierre de Bérulle and the so-called French School, and would find its zenith in the rather extravagant writings of Bérulle's follower, the priest and preacher Louis-Marie Grignion de Montfort, who died in 1716. As we saw in chapter four, for Bérulle, human beings go through Mary to Christ, and through Christ to the Trinity, an idea clearly stated some five hundred years earlier by Amadeus of Lausanne: "Through the Mother we are reconciled to the Son and through the Virgin to God, wholly snatched back from death and given over to life."[9] Mechtild of Hackeborn had just the same idea.

Mary is above all our *mediatrix* and advocate, which has been the teaching of the church from very early times. The germ of the idea appears in the *Book of Mary's Repose*, though the actual title, both in Latin and Greek, probably dates from about the seventh century. The concept, however, is certainly earlier and is intimately associated with the old and common patristic theme of the Eve-Mary parallel: all that went wrong with Eve has been rectified by Mary. This leads, as we have seen, to the idea of Mary as *co-redemptrix,* cooperating with her son in the work of redemption, and despite the obvious theological difficulties associated with this doctrine, it proved to be universally popular in both East and West until the Reformation.

Occasionally, we find things going a little too far when Mary, interceding and mediating on behalf of sinners, not only expects to be heard but *demands* to be heard. Germanus, the eighth-century patriarch of Constantinople, whom we met in chapter two, tells us that Mary's maternal power with God is so great that she can obtain forgiveness for even the very greatest sinners. Why? Because God will not fail to hear and obey his pure

[8] Chap. 5, n. 31.

[9] Chap. 8, n. 51.

and sinless mother.[10] But lest this be thought a Greek extravagance, does not Aelred of Rievaulx say the same thing, if rather more delicately? As the *mediatrix* between us and the Father, he says, Mary "demands with a sort of right (*iure quodammodo*) the salvation of sinners, for which reason she herself deserves to become their mother."[11]

In Scripture, says Guerric of Igny, it is Eve who is called "the mother of all the living"—*mater cunctorum viventium*[12]—but the truth of the matter is that, because of her sin, she should be called the mother of the dying, for all she produced was death. It is Mary who deserves to be called the mother of the living, "for she herself, like the church of which she is the type, is the mother of all who are reborn to life."[13] This matter of the motherhood of Mary is of first importance, and we must now say something about it. It is a rich doctrine.

Mary's motherhood is twofold: physical and spiritual. Of her physical motherhood, there is little to say. She was a pure vessel who, by grace, conceived and gave birth to the incarnate second person of the Trinity, the Savior of the world. By the fourth century it was generally assumed that she conceived as a virgin, gave birth as a virgin, and retained her virginity for the rest of her days. This is clearly expressed in the *Protevangelium* of James, and despite occasional protests by theologians such as Jovinian and Helvidius, whom we met in chapter two, it was hardly ever questioned until the time of the Reformation. What was questioned was at what stage she was made a pure vessel for the incarnation of the Son of God, and that is a matter to which we shall return in a moment.

Mary's spiritual motherhood is a more subtle matter. We have just heard Guerric of Igny saying that Mary may be called "the mother of all who are reborn to life," and that she is the

[10] See chap. 2, n. 20.
[11] Chap. 9, n. 56.
[12] Gen 3:20.
[13] Chap. 6, n. 32.

type (*forma*) of the church, and Aelred of Rievaulx and John of Forde say much the same thing.[14] The principle is based, of course, on the old Eve-Mary parallel, but Guerric goes further than this.

At the heart of his spirituality is the idea that Christ must be formed in us, and that Christ has not just two bodies—the human and the divine—but three: the human, the spiritual, and the divine. So far as I am aware this perspective is unique to Guerric. The matter is discussed in some detail in chapter six, but what Guerric says, in essence, is that the spiritual form of Christ is "the form of the life he led in the body for the formation of those who were to believe in him."[15] In other words, it is not Christ in the womb or Christ in glory, but Christ in action, doing what he did all the days of his earthly life and leaving us an example that we might follow in his steps. By imitating Christ, we re-conform ourselves to Christ and thus bring about the birth of the spiritual Christ in our own souls.

So what is the role of Mary in this process? It is vital. First, because she brought forth that being in whom, as Saint John says, was life, and that life was the light of all human beings.[16] Second, and here we are in the Augustinian realm, just as in the first Adam all died,[17] so in the Second Adam all are re-born and made alive. And third, if Mary had not given birth to the first form of Christ, the physical form, we would have had no one to imitate and, by conforming our lives to his, bring about the birth of the second form of Christ, the spiritual form, in our own souls. By conforming ourselves to Mary's son, therefore, we ourselves become, as it were, little Marys, giving birth to the spiritual Christ, as Guerric says: "*O matres beatae,*" he says to his monks, "O blessed mothers of such a glorious offspring, watch over yourselves until Christ be formed in you.

[14] See chap. 9, n. 11, and chap. 11, nn. 40–42.

[15] Chap. 6, n. 25.

[16] John 1:4.

[17] This was explained in chap. 2.

Take care that no violent blow from outside should injure this delicate fetus, that you do not introduce into your womb—that is, your soul—anything that might extinguish the spirit you have conceived."[18]

Guerric's Marian theology, which is linked inextricably with his Christology, is impressive. Indeed, if I may be permitted a personal note, I had not realized how remarkable a theologian Guerric was until, having read carefully what he had to say about Mary, I was lured into an equally careful reading of the rest of his sermons. Nor had I realized how much he was esteemed among the Cistercians, for when John of Forde is defending his somewhat suspect idea that not only was Mary a channel for the incarnation, but that she also made a positive contribution to the purity and innocence of Jesus, he cites as his authorities Anselm of Canterbury, an unimpeachable source whom no one could dispute, and "that most learned man from Igny," namely, Guerric.[19]

But even now we have not finished, for Guerric also calls Mary the type or *forma* of the church. The logic is straightforward. First, Mary is the channel of grace who, full of grace, brought forth the author of grace, Christ himself. Second, although God can do what he wills where he wills, the church is the usual channel of grace, so Cyprian of Carthage could say that "outside the church there is no salvation."[20] Third, the body to which Mary gave birth was not only, from a physical point of view, the incarnate body of God, but also, from a mystical point of view, the church itself, which is the mystical body of Christ. But since all those who have been baptized and thereby spiritually reborn in the waters of regeneration are the members of the body of Christ, it follows that just as Jesus of Nazareth, whose father was God, was the son of Mary, so we, too, are children of our mother the church, and, according to

[18] Chap. 6, n. 47.

[19] Chap. 11, n. 47.

[20] Cyprian, *Epistola* 72.21; PL 3:1123B: *salus extra Ecclesiam non est*.

Saint Augustine, "those who have not wished to have the church as their mother will not have God as their Father."[21]

The most explicit explanation of this view is not to be found in Guerric, but in the writings of Isaac of Stella. The heart of Isaac's argument lies in the fact that the baby that Mary brought forth is unquestionably the head of the church, but, without all of us, not the church itself. This is the very heart of Isaac's Christology: we are concerned not just with Christ, but with Christ *totus et integer*, "whole and complete," head and body. What does this mean?

It means that Christ has three births. The first is his eternal generation from God the Father, the second is his physical birth from Mary, and the third is his sacramental birth in the church. Mary, that is to say, gives birth to the head of the church, and we, the children of the church by our baptism, make up his body. Only then is Christ truly and completely the God-man, "whole and complete."

If, then, Christ is to be whole and complete, head and body, he must have two virgin mothers, Mary and the church, and Isaac says so:

> Mary and the church are one mother and many, one virgin and many. Each is mother and each is virgin. Each conceives without lust through the same Spirit, and each, without sin, brings forth an offspring for God the Father. The former, in the absence of all sin, gave birth to a head for the body; the latter, by the remission of all sins, brought forth a body for the head. Each is a mother of Christ, but neither one, without the other, gives birth to the whole Christ.[22]

Thus, says Isaac, whatever may be said of Mary in particular may be said of the church in general, and whatever may be said of the church in general may be said of Mary in particular.

[21] Augustine, *De Symbolo ad Catechumenos, sermo alius* xiii.13; PL 40:668.

[22] Chap. 8, n. 27.

And in saying this, Isaac merges Christology, Mariology, ecclesiology, and sacramental theology, and makes it clear that the only way in which we human beings can be re-conformed to the whole Christ—*totus et integer*—is through Mary and the church together. There is, however, a difference. The virgin mother church should be pure and immaculate, but is not. The Virgin Mother of God, on the other hand, is certainly pure and immaculate, but when did she become so?

Those who ever suggested that Mary might have sinned—John Chrysostom in the fourth century, for example, or Philip of Harvengt in the twelfth—were in a decided minority, and all the Cistercians discussed in these pages were united in their belief in her purity and sinlessness. With the exception of Rancé and, possibly, Ogier of Locedio, none of them believed that Mary had been conceived without original sin, but all of them believed that she had been cleansed of it by the time of her birth. It was hard to contradict the overwhelming authority of Augustine and Bernard—if Mary had been conceived in the usual way, she must have inherited original sin—but no one was prepared to say that when she conceived Jesus she was not wholly pure.

The controversy over the doctrine of the Immaculate Conception was long, wordy, and acrimonious, but by Rancé's time, the theological wind was clearly blowing in the direction of its acceptance. In 1693 Pope Innocent XII extended the feast to the whole church, together with an Office and an Octave, though it was not until 1708, eight years after Rancé's death, that Clement IX not only prescribed the feast for the universal church, but made it a holy day of obligation for all Christians.[23] There is no doubt that Rancé accepted the doctrine. As to Ogier, we are dependent on a single passage in his homilies on the Lord's Supper, which certainly seems to imply the idea.[24] But if this is so, it is a later development in Ogier's thought, and

[23] See chap. 4, n. 19.

[24] See chap. 10, n. 45.

nowhere does he say anything more about it. Nowhere in any of the Cistercians do we find anything like the discussions of William of Ware, John Duns Scotus, or Peter Auriol, with his distinction of Mary's inheriting original sin *de jure*, but not *de facto*.[25] And as we saw in chapter seven, the late Ferruccio Gastaldelli's suggestion that Geoffrey of Auxerre was an avant-garde theologian who maintained and defended the doctrine of the Immaculate Conception cannot be sustained.

So if Mary was cleansed from original sin before her birth, when exactly did the cleansing occur? The majority view appears to have been that it took place at the very moment of the Annunciation—Guerric and Stephen of Sawley are eminently clear on this point, and Aelred may have agreed with them, though that is not certain[26]—but Mechtild of Hackeborn had it from the lips of Mary herself that "from the very moment that the soul was infused into the body, he filled me with the Holy Spirit, who cleansed me completely from original sin."[27] Exactly when Mary's soul was infused into her body, Mechtild does not say, and we do not find (nor would we expect to find) the Aristotelian discussions of *animatio*, "animation," that we find in Albert the Great, Thomas Aquinas, and Bonaventure, all of whom agreed that the cleansing could not possibly have taken place before animation.[28] Bernard himself leaves the question open: Mary was sanctified in her mother's womb, and that is all there is to it. He would not be so rash, he says, as to inquire into the details.[29]

Bernard's view of Mary's bodily assumption is much the same. That is a question about which Hilda Graef has said, "he seems deliberately to have left it in the dark."[30] Nowhere in

[25] See chap. 4, n. 9.

[26] See chap. 6, n. 16; chap. 10, n. 23; and chap. 9, nn. 24–25.

[27] Chap. 12, n. 46.

[28] This is discussed in chap. 3.

[29] Chap. 3, n. 19.

[30] Hilda Graef, *Mary: A History of Doctrine and Devotion*, 2 vols. (London: Sheed & Ward, 1963–1965), 1:236.

any of his four sermons for the feast does he actually state that Mary's body is in heaven together with her soul, though by Bernard's time the letter of pseudo-Augustine that affirmed the bodily assumption, supported by popular piety, was rapidly proving far more popular than the letter of pseudo-Jerome (actually written by Paschasius Radbertus) that advocated caution in the matter.[31]

Of Bernard's followers, Guerric, like his master, never actually states explicitly that Mary is present in heaven in her body, though he certainly implies it, but Geoffrey of Auxerre, Amadeus of Lausanne, Stephen of Sawley, and Ogier of Locedio are in no doubt whatever: Mary is in heaven bodily, seated on a throne of glory at the right hand of her Son. Aelred and Isaac of Stella are not quite sure how she got there—both quote the same verse from 2 Corinthians, "whether with the body or without the body I do not know, God knows"—but while Isaac is content to limit himself to what the fathers have said,[32] Aelred is more daring and is prepared to put forth his own opinion, though hedged about with cautions. "I dare not state it as a fact," he says,

> but this is what I think: that because of his measureless love for his mother, Christ did not only place her soul in heaven, but also raised up her body, so that she could be in his presence with both body and soul and may even now have received that bodily immortality for which everyone hopes on the Day of Judgment.[33]

Roger of Forde, on the other hand, was advised by his teacher, Baldwin, to keep silent on the question on the grounds that it was still too contentious, and that is what he did.[34] Armand-Jean de Rancé never discusses the question at all.

[31] See chap. 1.
[32] See chap. 8, n. 7.
[33] Chap. 9, n. 36.
[34] See chap. 11, n. 57.

The visionaries, of course, had an advantage. They knew what had happened from the lips of Mary herself, and Elisabeth of Schönau, Bertram of Lombardy, Abundus of Villers, and Mechtild of Hackeborn all bear witness to the bodily assumption of the Mother of God. And we also have it from Mary herself that the affirmative letter of pseudo-Augustine is to be preferred over the hesitant letter of pseudo-Jerome.

None of these writers was quite sure when the assumption took place, whether at the moment of Mary's physical death or some days later, usually three, after she had been buried and resurrected. The general opinion was certainly the latter, but the matter was still undecided in 1950, when Pope Pius XII deliberately left the question open.

If, then, Mary is now in Paradise, crowned and enthroned beside her son as Queen of Heaven, what is the relationship between them? Bernard, Guerric, John of Forde, and, especially, Aelred of Rievaulx all have something to say on this. For Bernard, Mary penetrated the depths of the Divine Wisdom in a way we cannot possibly conceive and thus was immersed in, enveloped by, clothed with, and surrounded by the inaccessible light of God, "as far as is possible for any created being without being personally united with it."[35]

Guerric seems to go further, though we are now in realms far beyond the limits of normal human understanding. Christ does not set up a separate throne for his mother, but she is herself his throne. Since she shared her humanity with him, he will now share his divinity with her. As his mother, she used to demand from her little son the kiss of his lips, but he will now kiss her with the whole of him, not lip to lip but spirit to spirit in an everlasting kiss, because, says Christ, "I shall not see myself as being sufficiently glorified until you are glorified with me."[36]

[35] Chap. 5, n. 44.

[36] Chap. 6, n. 21.

Aelred, too, tells us that once in heaven, Christ "conjoined (*coniunxit*) the soul of that holy Virgin with his divinity,"[37] and explains what he means in the following way. Mary's *intellectus* / intellect, the highest part of the human rational soul, "was illumined by divinity itself, whose dwelling-place it was, and, so to speak, deified (*deificata*) in God,"[38] and so came to participate in divine eternity, in truth, and in charity. In this way, Mary, in her intellect, was wholly conformed to the image and likeness of God, which meant that she lived in the continual remembrance of God, something she possessed "more fully and more perfectly than any other created being, just as she loved him more abundantly."[39] John of Forde, who had certainly read Aelred, says much the same thing, though much more briefly. It cannot be doubted, he says, that by continual contemplation Mary had achieved such a high degree of spiritual penetration that she would have seen Christ in glory and have been transformed into the same image.[40]

Mary, in fact, represents in herself both the active and contemplative lives, both Martha and Mary of Bethany, and Aelred says so.[41] So do many others, for before Pius XII had made the formal dogmatic definition of the assumption in 1950 and promulgated a new Mass and Office, the gospel reading for the feast was Luke 10:38-41, which tells the story of Jesus visiting the home of Mary and Martha. It is this gospel, therefore, that forms the basis for Rancé's first conference for the feast of the Assumption, though as we saw in chapter fifteen, what Rancé understands by contemplation is far more down to earth than the usages we find in Aelred or, indeed, in almost any other of the Cistercians we have considered in these pages. For him, "to contemplate" (*contempler*) usually means no more than to

[37] Chap. 9, n. 41.
[38] Chap. 9, n. 43.
[39] Chap. 9, n. 52.
[40] Chap. 11, n. 36. We may compare Ogier of Locedio: see chap. 10, n. 67.
[41] See chap. 9, n. 15.

reflect upon, think about, ruminate, or ponder—it is not a rapturous state infused into the soul by God—and it is much the same as what Saint Bernard meant by "consideration" (*consideratio*). Nor does Rancé make much difference between contemplation and meditation. Both involve the mind at work, though they may produce, as they produced in Mary, "indescribable consolations and sweetnesses."[42]

But now, since we have come back down to earth with Rancé, let us stay there, and say something of the role of Mary in our everyday lives. In these pages we have witnessed many titles given to the Virgin. Some reflect her glory and greatness, some reflect her humanity and tenderness. On the one hand, she is the Mother of God, the Theotokos, "God-Bearer," Our Lady, Ever Virgin, Second Eve, Queen of Heaven, Queen of the World, Queen of Virgins, Mistress and Empress of the Angels. On the other, she is our *mediatrix*, our advocate and intercessor, the *co-redemptrix* with her son in the work of salvation, the Star of the Sea, the passageway to heaven, the very Mother and Queen of Mercy.

Of all these titles, that of Star of the Sea was (and is) one of the most popular, and it cannot be denied that, even if it comes from a misreading of a manuscript, those who wish to pray to the Mother of God will probably find it more pleasing to call on "Mary, Star of the Sea" than on "Mary, Drop of Seawater."[43] Bernard's splendid peroration in praise of Mary as the guiding star is justly celebrated—we summarized it briefly in chapter two[44]—and Aelred of Rievaulx follows closely in Bernard's footsteps. What he has to say on Mary as the Star of the Sea is obviously indebted to this passage. She is the shining star who can guide us through the storms and vicissitudes of this life, help us to overcome its trials and tribulations, and offer us help and support in times of difficulty, distress, or doubt: "With

[42] See chap. 16, §2.

[43] See chap. 2.

[44] See chap. 2, nn. 34–35.

your eyes on this star, you will not be afraid; following this star you will not be led astray; following it to the end, you will rejoice in eternity."[45]

Amadeus of Lausanne is a little more unusual. He begins in good solid Bernardine fashion by telling us that Mary is the Star of the Sea who guards all those who sail upon the dangerous oceans of the world and would have foundered had it not been for Mary's aid. But then, suddenly, Virgil makes an appearance. If Mary had not protected us, he says, we would have been engulfed by the sinful abyss of Scylla or lured to our death by the temptations of the Sirens. Both Scylla and the Sirens come from Virgil's *Aeneid*.[46] But protect us she does, and all penitent sinners who look to her can be sure that she will hear them.

There can be no doubt that Mary's most important roles are as our *mediatrix* and our model, and the two roles are clearly connected. First of all, how is Mary our model? According to Aelred, if in Christ we may see the seven virtues of humility, obedience, righteousness, forbearance, mercy, purity, and charity, then, "as an outstanding example of all these virtues, we have the most blessed Virgin Mary."[47] She also received the seven gifts of the Holy Spirit as they appear in Isaiah 11:2—Amadeus of Lausanne and John of Forde say the same thing[48]—and, as we saw above, in her we may witness, at one and the same time, the virtues of both Martha and Mary, the active and the contemplative lives.

For Armand-Jean de Rancé, Mary embodies the four virtues of a love of withdrawal from the world, purity of heart, humility, and obedience. She is therefore a model for all Christians, but especially for Rancé's monks. In her too we may see a supreme example of the eradication of self-love and self-will—

[45] Chap. 9, n. 63.

[46] Virgil, *Aeneid*, III.432 and V.864. See chap. 8, n. 50.

[47] Chap. 9, n. 13.

[48] See chap. 8, n. 41, and chap. 11, n. 38.

the key to the spiritual life—which also applies to all Christians, though God demands more of those who dwell in cloisters. We must renounce everything for love of him, and what this means is a life of poverty, humility, abasement, and penitence, in imitation of the Virgin.

To imitate the Virgin, then, is to imitate Christ, and that is no small task. Will we err and fall by the wayside? Of course we will! And that is why all the writers who appear in these pages emphasize the need for Mary's advocacy, intercession, and mediation. They are all perfectly well aware that forgiveness comes only from God, but Mary (as we saw above) has the ear of God, and we may assume that she will be granted that for which she asks. She is our mediator and intercessor, says Rancé, and she "never fails to listen to all those who return to Jesus Christ with pure and sincere intentions, and to mediate on their behalf before him when they implore her help."[49] If you find yourself tempted, says Bernard, look to Mary. If you find yourself being wrecked on the rocks of tribulation, call on Mary. If the vessel of your soul is beaten about by the winds of the passions, look to Mary. If you find yourself foundering in the gulfs of melancholy or despair, think on Mary.[50]

The influence and impact of Bernard is to be seen in every one of the Cistercian writers considered in this book. Some, clearly, were more deeply influenced than others, but there is not one who was not influenced at all. Bernard, as Father Chrysogonus Waddell has said, may have been "hopelessly unoriginal"[51] with regard to what he said about Mary, but his unoriginal ideas had a major impact. Why? I suggested in chapter five that there were two main reasons. The first is the beauty and balance of Bernard's language, for although he can wax florid on occasion, his language never approaches that somewhat suffocating hot-house hyper-floridity that we can

[49] Chap. 17, §21.

[50] See chap. 2, n. 34.

[51] Chap. 5, n. 22.

find in Amadeus of Lausanne or Ogier. The second reason, quite simply, was Bernard's fame. He was known throughout Europe, and his writings enjoyed a huge circulation, not just among Cistercians. For John of Forde (for example) to say something in a commentary that only ever had the most restricted circulation is one thing;[52] for Bernard, whose writings were virtually ubiquitous and whose name was known everywhere, to say it was quite another. Others who followed in his footsteps made their own contributions, not least in the realm of popular devotion to the Virgin—Aelred's threefold meditation at the end of his *De institutione inclusarum* and Stephen of Sawley's fifteen joys of Mary are a case in point—but Bernard remained their foundation, and, indeed, his four homilies in praise of the Virgin Mother and his splendid sermon on the Aqueduct still retain their power.

Rancé's five conferences for the feasts of the Virgin will never have the same appeal. Despite his own deep devotion to the Virgin and the esteem, the highest esteem, in which she was held at la Trappe, this devotion and this esteem are not really reflected in his conferences. What he says about the need to eradicate self-will so that we can truly say, with Mary, "be it done with me according to your word," cannot be faulted. It is, as we have said, a central idea in all spiritual traditions. But people nowadays do not generally like to be told to die daily, and the demand for absolute and unquestioning obedience tends to fall on unreceptive ears. And whereas in the monastery, the business of a monk or nun is not to live, but to die, the business of those of us in this world who are neither monk nor nun is more nuanced. We are indeed to die to the world, to separate ourselves from it, but not necessarily by retreating within the walls of the cloister, and not by eagerly embracing an early death. The key, as Rancé makes clear, is the Johannine idea of being in the world but not of it. A physical

[52] John's commentary on the Song of Songs survives in a single manuscript and was never widely circulated.

separation from the world is not the calling for all, but a spiritual separation, or indeed a mental separation, is demanded by the Gospel.

If we can keep our eyes firmly fixed on God, then what Augustine said long ago remains ever true: *Dilige, et quod vis fac*, "Love, and do what you will."[53] But what does Augustine mean here? He does not mean "Do whatever you want." No. What he means is, first, love God, and if we truly love him we will never wish to do what he does not want us to do. It is just the same with true human love. And second, if we never wish to do what God does not wish us to do, we are striving to make our will his will, to make ourselves willing collaborators with him in his divine work, and that, for Rancé and so many others, is the end of the spiritual path. *Fiat voluntas tua*, "your will be done."

At the heart of this is humility—we are back where we began this final chapter—for humility is no more and no less than the honest recognition of our position. On the one hand, we are made to the image of God, an image that can never be lost, and therein lies our glory. On the other, we are images who have lost the likeness through sin and, more often, through sheer stupidity, and therein lies our misery. Our business, then, and not one of the writers we have mentioned in these pages would disagree, is to recover the lost likeness. That this is a difficult task is not in question; it is very difficult indeed, and we need all the help we can get. And whence does that help come? Rancé, in his first conference for the feast of the Assumption, echoes the thoughts of all those Cistercians, and so many others, who have gone before him:

> Turn to her whose triumph you celebrate today, so as to obtain from God all the faithfulness you need. You have the right to ask it of him, and to hope that he grant it through her mediation, not only because she is the universal mother

[53] Augustine, *In evangelium Joannis ad Parthos, tract.* VII.8; PL 35:2033.

> of all the faithful, but because she is especially the Protector of this holy Order of which you are part, and that it is under her banner and patronage that you have the glory and happiness to serve Jesus Christ.[54]

By the early afternoon of October 27, 1700, the time of Rancé's death, the tiny spring that had burst forth seventeen centuries earlier in Galilee, when an *almah*, a young Jewish girl of child-bearing age, conceived a remarkable child in a remarkable way, had become an ocean, an ocean that covered the entire Christian East and the whole of the Roman Catholic West. There was not one of Rancé's monks and not one of his Catholic contemporaries who would have doubted that Mary could do all that everyone believed she could, for the ocean that flowed from that little spring had accumulated materials from theology, philosophy, apocryphal scriptures, mythology, courtly literature, Arthurian romance, veneration, popular piety, popular devotion, visionary experiences and revelations, and multitudinous miracle stories. What could she not do?

In the twelfth century, Caesarius of Heisterbach, whom we met in chapter eleven, had been expostulating on the glories of the blessed Virgin to one his novices and asked him whether now he would like to learn of the great benefits the world had received and still receives through her. *"Nihil plus sitio,"* says the novice, "I thirst for nothing more." So, says Caesarius,

> She is the preserver of the world, the comforter of those in tribulation, the faithful defender of her servants. By her, sinners are enlightened, those in despair returned to confession, apostates from God miraculously reconciled to God by her, the righteous consoled with revelations. Her name and remembrance[55] heal the sick, put demons to flight, unlock chains, cast out fear, subdue temptations. By her the fainthearted are strengthened, the lethargic aroused, exiles merci-

[54] Chap. 16, §15.
[55] Isa 26:8.

> fully recalled. She loves those who love her, or, rather, she anticipates and honors them with love, and because she is just, she punishes and brings low those who scorn her. She attends the dying and guides the souls of the dead to eternal life.[56]

The views of Caesarius remained, generally speaking, the views of Roman Catholic Europe in the seventeenth century and also the views of the High Church tradition in England. But as we have seen, there is no doubt that the exuberance of Marian devotion could sometimes get a little out of hand, and in subsequent centuries it became necessary for the Roman Catholic Church to present a somewhat more balanced view of the question as to exactly what Mary was and is, what she could and can do, and exactly what part she should play in the life of the church. Hence the apostolic exhortation *Marialis Cultus*, promulgated by Pope Paul VI on February 2, 1974, and the encyclical *Redemptoris Mater*, issued by Pope John Paul II on March 25, 1987. Both of these are documents of the first importance, but far outside the scope of this present study. As I said in the introduction to this little volume, what happened in Marian devotion and theology after the death of Armand-Jean de Rancé, both in the church generally and among the Cistercians in particular, is a discussion I am happy to leave in hands more able than mine.

[56] *Caesarii Heisterbacensis Monachi Dialogus Miraculorum*, ed. Joseph Strange (Cologne: J. M. Heberle, 1851), 2:2–3 (lib. VII.1).

Select Bibliography

Main Primary Sources

Abundus of Villers (d. 1239)

A. M. Frenken, "De Vita van Abundus van Hoei." *Cîteaux* 10 (1959): 5–33.

Aelred of Rievaulx (d. 1167)

Sermons in Corpus Christianorum, Continuatio Mediaevalis 2A, 2B, and 2C. Other works in Corpus Christianorum, Continuatio Mediaevalis 1, 2D, 3, and 3A.

Amadeus of Lausanne (d. 1159)

Amadée de Lausanne: Huit homélies mariales. Ed. Jean Deshusses; trans. Antoine Dumas; intro. and notes by Georges Bavaud. SCh 72. Paris: Cerf, 1960.

Arnulf of Villers (d. 1228)

Acta Sanctorum. June. Paris: V. Palme, 1867. 7:558–89.

Baldwin of Forde (d. 1190)

Sermons in Corpus Christianorum, Continuatio Mediaevalis 99.

Bernard of Clairvaux (d. 1153)

Works in Sancti Bernardi Opera. Edited by Jean Leclercq, C. Hugh Talbot, and Henri M. Rochais. 8 vols. Rome: Editiones Cistercienses, 1957–1977.

Caesarius of Heisterbach (d. ca. 1240)

Caesarii Heisterbacensis Monachi Dialogus Miraculorum. Ed. Joseph Strange. Cologne: J. M. Heberle, 1851.

Cistercians, Early Documents

Waddell, Chrysogonus. *Narrative and Legislative Texts from Early Cîteaux: Latin Text in Dual Edition with English Translation and Notes*. Studia et Documenta, IX. Brecht: Cîteaux – Commentarii cistercienses, 1999.

Elisabeth of Schönau (d. 1164)

Die Visionen der hl. Elisabeth und die Schriften der Aebte Ekbert und Emecho von Schönau. Ed. Ferdinand W. E. Roth. Brünn: Verlag der Studien aus dem Benedictiner- und Cistercienser-Orden, 1884.

Geoffrey of Auxerre (d. ca. 1200)

Canal, José María. "El Marial inédito de Gaufredo de Auxerre (m. c. 1178)." *Ephemerides Mariologicae* 19 (1969): 217–77. (Marian sermons)

Gastaldelli, Ferruccio. *Commentary on the Song of Songs*. In *Goffredo di Auxerre, Expositio in Cantica Canticorum*, edited by Ferruccio Gastaldelli. Temi e Testi 20. 2 vols. Rome: Edizioni di Storia e Letteratura, 1974.

Gastaldelli, Ferruccio. "Il sermone 'De muliere amicta sole' di Goffredo d'Auxerre e un confronto con san Bernardo." In *Maria, l'Apocalisse e il Medioevo: Atti del III Convegno Mariologico della Fondazione Ezio Franceschini, Parma 10–11 maggio 2002*, edited by Clelia M. Piastra and Francesco Santi. Florence: Galluzzo, 2006. 59–79.

Gastaldelli, Ferruccio. "Une mariologia d'avanguardia nel secolo XII: Immacolata concezione e Assunzione corporea di Maria secondo Goffredo d'Auxerre." In *Figure poetiche e figure teologiche nella mariologia dei secoli XI e XII*, edited by Clelia M. Piastra and Francesco Santi. Florence: Galluzzo, 2004. 71–107.

Gertrude the Great (d. 1302)

Revelationes Gertrudianae ac Mechtildianae. I, Sanctae Gertrudis Magnae, virginis Ordinis Sancti Benedicti, Legatus divinae pietatis . . . . Edited by Louis Paquelin. Poitiers and Paris: Oudin, 1875.

Gilbert of Hoyland (d. 1172)

Sermons on the Song of Songs in PL 184:11–252.

Guerric of Igny (d. 1157)

Guerric d'Igny. *Sermons.* Ed. John Morson and Hilary Costello; trans. Placide Deseille. 2 vols. SCh 166, 202. Paris: Cerf, 1970, 1973.

Ida of Nivelles (d. 1231)

Henriquez, Chrysóstomo. *Quinque prudentes virgins.* Antwerp: J. Cnobbaert, 1630. 199–297.

Isaac of Stella (d. ca. 1169)

Sermons in SCh 130, 207, and 339.

John of Forde (d. 1214)

Sermons on the Song of Songs in Corpus Christianorum, Continuatio Mediaevalis 17 and 18.

Mechtild of Hackeborn (d. 1298)

Revelationes Gertrudianae ac Mechtildianae. II, Sanctae Mechtildis, virginis Ordinis Sancti Benedicti, Liber specialis gratiae . . . . Ed. Louis Paquelin. Poitiers and Paris: Oudin, 1877.

Ogier of Locedio (d. 1214)

Beati Oglerii de Tridino, abbatis monasterii Locediensis ordinis Cisterciensium in diocesi Vercellensi, Opera quae supersunt . . . . Ed. Giovanni-Battista Adriani. Turin: Ex Officina Regia, 1873.

Rancé, Armand-Jean de (d. 1700)

Marian conferences in Armand-Jean de Rancé, *Instructions ou Conférences sur les Epîtres et Évangiles des Dimanches et Principales Festes de l'Année, et sur les Vêtures & Professions Religieuses.* Tome quatrième. Paris: F. Delaulne, 1720. Reprinted in the *Collection intégrale et universelle des Orateurs Chrétiens.* Deuxième série, vol. 90 of the entire series (= vol. 23 of the second series). Ed. Jacques-Paul Migne. Paris: J.-P. Migne, 1866.

Conduite chrétienne adressée à son altesse royale Madame de Guise. Paris: F. & P. Delaulne, 1697.

De la sainteté et des devoirs de la vie monastique. Paris: F. Muguet, 1683.

Règlemens de l'abbaye de Nôtre-Dame de la Trappe en forme de Constitutions. Avec des reflexions, et la Carte de Visite à N. D. des Clairets. Paris: F. Delaulne, 1718.

Roger of Forde (fl. ca. 1182)

Rigg, Arthur G. "Roger of Ford's Poem on the Virgin: A Critical Edition." *Cîteaux* 40 (1989): 200–14.

Talbot, Charles H. "The Verses of Roger of Ford on Our Lady." *Collectanea O.C.R.* 6 (1939): 44–54.

Stephen of Sawley (d. 1252)

Wilmart, André. "Les méditations d'Étienne de Salley sur les Joies de la Vierge Marie." In André Wilmart, *Auteurs spirituels et textes dévots du Moyen Âge latin: Études d'histoire littéraire.* Paris: Études augustiniennes, 1971. 317–60.

William of Saint-Thierry (d. 1148)

Works in Corpus Christianorum, Continuatio Mediaevalis (Turnhout: Brepols) and SCh (Paris: Cerf). In a number of cases, the SCh editions are superior to those in CCCM.

Select Secondary Sources

Barré, Henri. "Le '*Planctus Mariae*' attribué à saint Bernard." *Revue d'ascétique et de mystique* 28 (1952): 243–66.

Bell, David N. *Everyday Life at La Trappe under Armand-Jean de Rancé: A Translation, with Introduction and Notes, of André Félibien des Avaux's* Description de l'Abbaye de La Trappe *(1689)*. CS 274. Collegeville, MN: Cistercian Publications, 2018.

Bell, David N. *A Saint in the Sun. Praising Saint Bernard in the France of Louis XIV*. CS 271. Collegeville, MN: Cistercian Publications, 2017.

Bell, David N. *Understanding Rancé: The Spirituality of the Abbot of La Trappe in Context.* CS 205. Kalamazoo, MI: Cistercian Publications, 2005.

Bell, David N. "The *Vita Antiqua* of William of Saint-Thierry." *Cistercian Studies [Quarterly]* 11 (1976): 246–55.

Boss, Sarah Jane. "Francisco Suárez and Modern Mariology." In *Mary: The Complete Resource*, edited by Sarah Jane Boss. London & New York: Continuum, 2007. 256–78.

Boss, Sarah Jane, ed. *Mary: The Complete Resource*. London & New York: Continuum, 2007.

Burton, Pierre-André, ed. *Bibliotheca Aelrediana Secunda: Une bibliographie cumulative (1962–1996)*. Louvain-la-Neuve: FIDEM, 1997.

Burton, Pierre-André. "Bibliotheca aelrediana secunda: Supplementa." In *A Companion to Aelred*, edited by Marsha L. Dutton. 294–324.

Caneva, Anna Maria. "Communion with God and the Brothers: Reading Rancé." *Cistercian Studies Quarterly* 38 (2003): 309–36.

Cawley, Martinus. "Our Lady and the Nuns and Monks of XIII-Century Belgium." *Word & Spirit* 10 (1988): 94–128.

Clark, Anne L. *Elisabeth of Schönau: A Twelfth-Century Visionary*. Philadelphia: University of Pennsylvania Press, 1992.

Clark, Anne L. "The Priesthood of the Virgin Mary: Gender Trouble in the Twelfth Century." *Journal of Feminist Studies in Religion* 18 (2002): 5–24.

Clark, Anne L. "An Uneasy Triangle: Jesus, Mary, and Gertrude of Helfta." *Maria: A Journal of Marian Studies* 1 (2000): 37–56.

Dean, Ruth J. "Elizabeth, Abbess of Schönau, and Roger of Ford." *Modern Philology* 41 (1944): 209–20.

Denzinger, Heinrich. Ed. Peter Hünemann. *Enchiridion symbolorum definitionum et declarationum de rebus fidei et morum: Compendium of Creeds, Definitions and Declarations on Matters of Faith and Morals. Latin – English*. 43rd ed. San Francisco: Ignatius Press, 2012.

Dietz, Elias. "When Exile Is Home: The Biography of Isaac of Stella." *Cistercian Studies Quarterly* 41 (2006): 141–65.

Dubois, Louis. *Histoire de l'abbé de Rancé et de sa réforme*. 2 vols. Paris: A. Bray, 1866.

Dutton, Marsha L. "The Cistercian Source: Aelred, Bonaventure, and Ignatius." In *Goad and Nail: Studies in Medieval Cistercian History, X*, edited by E. Rozanne Elder. CS 84. Kalamazoo, MI: Cistercian Publications, 1985. 151–78.

Dutton, Marsha L., ed. *A Companion to Aelred of Rievaulx (1110–1167)*. Leiden: Brill, 2017.

Elder, E. Rozanne. "Shadows on the Marian Wall: The Cistercians and the Development of Marian Doctrine." In *Truth As Gift: Studies in Honor of John R. Sommerfeldt*, edited by Marsha L. Dutton, Daniel M. La Corte, and Paul Lockey. CS 204. Kalamazoo, MI: Cistercian Publications, 2004. 537–74.

Elkins, Sharon. "Gertrude the Great and the Virgin Mary." *Church History* 66 (1997): 720–34.

Elliott, James K. *The Apocryphal New Testament: A Collection of Apocryphal Christian Literature in an English Translation*. Oxford: Oxford University Press, 2005.

Foster, Paul. "The Protevangelium of James." *The Expository Times* 118 (2007): 573–82.

Gambero, Luigi. *Mary and the Fathers of the Church: The Blessed Virgin Mary in Patristic Thought*. Trans. Thomas Buffer. San Francisco: Ignatius Press, 1999.

Gambero, Luigi. *Mary in the Middle Ages: The Blessed Virgin Mary in the Thought of Medieval Latin Theologians*. Trans. Thomas Buffer. San Francisco: Ignatius Press, 2005.

Gastaldelli, Ferruccio. "The Marian Reflections of Geoffrey of Auxerre." *Cistercian Studies Quarterly* 52 (2017): 161–86.

Graef, Hilda. *Mary: A History of Doctrine and Devotion*. 2 vols. London: Sheed & Ward, 1963–1965. A combined edition, containing both parts, was published in 1985.

Härdelin, Alf. "St. Aelred of Rievaulx on the Imitation of Mary." In *Mary and the Churches: Papers of the Chichester Congress, 1986, of the Ecumenical Society of the Blessed Virgin Mary*, edited by Alberic Stacpoole. Dublin: Columba Press, 1987. 30–41.

Holdsworth, Christopher J. "John of Ford and English Cistercian Writing 1167–1214." *Transactions of the Royal Historical Society* 11 (1961): 117–36.

Hoste, Anselme. *Bibliotheca Aelrediana: A Survey of the Old Manuscripts, Old Catalogues, Editions and Studies concerning St. Aelred of Rievaulx.* Steenbrugge: In Abbatia Sancti Petri, 1962.

Izbicki, Thomas M. "The Immaculate Conception and Ecclesiastical Politics from the Council of Basel to the Council of Trent: The Dominicans and Their Foes." *Archiv für Reformationsgeschichte* 96 (2005): 145–70.

Krahmer, Shawn Madison. "Aelred of Rievaulx and the Feminine in the Marian Sermons for the Feasts of the Assumption and Purification." *Cistercian Studies Quarterly* 35 (2000): 459–78.

Krailsheimer, Alban J. *Armand-Jean de Rancé, Abbot of la Trappe. His Influence in the Cloister and the World*. Oxford: Oxford University Press, 1974.

La Corte, Daniel M. "The Abbatial Concerns of Aelred of Rievaulx Based on his Sermons on Mary." *Cistercian Studies Quarterly* 30 (1995): 267–74.

Le Nain, Pierre. *La vie de Dom Armand-Jean Le Bouthillier de Rancé, Abbé & Réformateur de l'Abbaye de la Maison-Dieu-Notre-Dame de la Trappe*. Paris: L. de Hotelfort, 1719.

Le Nain, Pierre. *La vie du Révérend Père Dom Armand Jean Le Bouthillier de Rancé, Abbé et Réformateur de la Maison-Dieu Nôtre-Dame de la Trappe, de l'Étroite Observance de l'Ordre de Cîteaux*. [Rouen]: [s.n.], 1715.

Longère, Paul, ed. *La Vierge dans la tradition cistercienne, communications présentées à la 54e session de la Société française d'études mariales, Abbaye Notre-Dame d'Orval [15–17 septembre] 1998.* Études Mariales. Bulletin de la Société Française d'Études Mariales. Paris: Éditions Médiaspaul, 1999.

Marsollier, Jacques. *La vie de Dom Armand-Jean de Bouthillier de Rancé, abbé régulier et réformateur du Monastère de la Trappe.* Paris: Jean de Nully, 1703.

Marx, C. W. "The *Quis dabit* of Oglerius de Tridino, Monk and Abbot of Locedio." *Journal of Medieval Latin* 4 (1994): 118–29.

Mayeski, Marie Anne. "'At the Feet of His Dearest Mother': Aelred's Teaching on Mary in the Sermons of the First Clairvaux Collection." In *A Companion to Aelred*, edited by Marsha L. Dutton. 149–66.

Mills, Matthew J. "Behold Your Mother. The Virgin Mary in English Monasticism, c. 1050–c. 1200." D.Phil. dissertation, Regent's Park College, Oxford, 2016. Freely available online at https://ora.ox.ac.uk/objects/uuid:c72df193-cdbe-4fc1-b59f-714015846599/download_file?safe_filename=Mills%2BDPhil%252C%2BDissemination%2BCopy.pdf&file_format=application%2Fpdf&type_of_work=Thesis.

Mills, Matthew J. "Stephen of Sawley's Meditations on Our Lady's Joys and the Medieval History of the Rosary." *Cistercian Studies Quarterly* 50 (2015): 423–39.

Morson, John. *Christ the Way: The Christology of Guerric of Igny*. CS 25. Kalamazoo, MI: Cistercian Publications, 1978.

Newhauser, Richard. "The Sin of Curiosity and the Cistercians." In *Erudition at God's Service: Studies in Medieval Cistercian History, XI*, edited by John R. Sommerfeldt. CS 98. Kalamazoo, MI: Cistercian Publications, 1987. 71–95.

O'Connor, Edward D. *The Doctrine of the Immaculate Conception: History and Significance*. Notre Dame: University of Notre Dame Press, 1958.

Pelikan, Jaroslav. *Mary Through the Centuries: Her Place in the History of Culture*. Rev. ed. New Haven: Yale University Press, 1998.

Pezzini, Domenico. "The Sermons of Aelred of Rievaulx." In *A Companion to Aelred*, edited by Marsha L. Dutton. 71–97.

Reynolds, Brian K. *Gateway to Heaven: Marian Doctrine and Devotion, Image and Typology in the Patristic and Medieval Periods*. Volume 1: *Doctrine and Devotion*. Hyde Park, NY: New City Press, 2012.

Rubin, Miri. *Mother of God: A History of the Virgin Mary*. New Haven: Yale University Press, 2010.

Sharp, Tristan. "A Treatise with Too Many Authors? The *Speculum novitii* Attributed to Stephen of Sawley." *Cîteaux* 65 (2014): 277–97.

Shoemaker, Stephen J. *The Ancient Traditions of the Virgin Mary's Dormition and Assumption*. Oxford Early Christian Studies. Oxford: Oxford University Press, 2006.

Shoemaker, Stephen J. *Mary in Early Christian Faith and Devotion.* New Haven: Yale University Press, 2016.

Stolz, Travis D. "Isaac of Stella, the Cistercians and the Thomas Becket Controversy: A Bibliographical and Contextual Study." Ph.D. dissertation, Marquette University, 2010. Readily available online at http://epublications.marquette.edu/dissertations_mu/87.

Warner, Marina. *Alone of All Her Sex: The Myth and the Cult of the Virgin Mary*. London: Weidenfeld and Nicolson Ltd., 1976. Many subsequent reprints.

Index of Persons

Index of Principal Marian Themes